Practical Palm Pre webOS Projects

Frank W. Zammetti

Apress®

Practical Palm Pre webOS Projects

President and Publisher: Paul Manning
Lead Editor: Frank Pohlmann
Technical Reviewer: Greg Hrebek
Editorial Board: Clay Andres, Steve Anglin, Mark Beckner, Ewan Buckingham, Gary Cornell, Jonathan Gennick, Jonathan Hassell, Michelle Lowman, Matthew Moodie, Jeffrey Pepper, Duncan Parkes, Frank Pohlmann, Douglas Pundick, Ben Renow-Clarke, Dominic Shakeshaft, Matt Wade, Tom Welsh
Coordinating Editor: Fran Parnell
Copy Editor: Kim Wimpsett
Compositor: Bob Cooper
Indexer: Ann Rogers and Ron Strauss
Artist: April Milne
Cover Designer: Anna Ishchenko

Distributed to the book trade worldwide by Springer-Verlag New York, Inc., 233 Spring Street, 6th Floor, New York, NY 10013. Phone 1-800-SPRINGER, fax 201-348-4505, e-mail orders-ny@springer-sbm.com, or visit http://www.springeronline.com.

For information on translations, please e-mail info@apress.com, or visit http://www.apress.com.

Apress and friends of ED books may be purchased in bulk for academic, corporate, or promotional use. eBook versions and licenses are also available for most titles. For more information, reference our Special Bulk Sales–eBook Licensing web page at http://www.apress.com/info/bulksales.

The source code for this book is available to readers at http://www.apress.com. You will need to answer questions pertaining to this book in order to successfully download the code.

This book is dedicated to all the unsung heroes of the world, those who the absence of which would degrade all our lives to the point where the sweet release of death would seem preferable to continuing this mortal existence. Ironically, the absence of those I refer to would all but guarantee this outcome!

I of course refer here to the constants of the physical world:

G, the gravitational constant, whose vigilance secures us to this very world;

c, the speed of light, who dictates the universal structure of the space-time continuum in which we live;

h, Planck's constant, the existence of which defines the size of quanta used to describe light and other entities upon which we depend;

e, the electric constant, which gives rise to the properties of the electromagnetic fields our technology depends upon;

and finally, the Boltzmann constant, without which the relationship of energy at the particle level to the temperature at the bulk level would be unknown to us.

I thank you all, and your unnamed brethren, on behalf of all who inhabit this universe!

Contents at a Glance

Contents

Foreword

The Web will win. That statement may seem provocative perhaps, but for many the Web has already won and just needs to finish growing up and become the full-featured platform it is destined to be. The Web is the platform of choice for millions of developers, and the emergence of the mobile Web is only going to attract more developers as they discover the uniquely new applications that can be built for it.

For me, it was clear with the introduction of Gmail in 2004 and Google Maps in 2005 that soon anyone would be able to build desktop-class applications using web technologies. Now, Ajax applications have become mainstream, and much of what was possible only with native applications running on a desktop computer can now be done with web applications. And better than native applications, web applications are built to be connected; are built to work with fresh, dynamic data that's frequently updated; and are developed with much less time and effort.

Although all platforms support the Web, only Palm's webOS embraces the Web to its core, allowing web applications access to the underlying operating system and hardware that native applications have enjoyed for years. Only webOS provides web applications with a full life cycle: webOS applications can run in the foreground and background and are supported by an elegant notification system. And webOS accomplishes this using a rich and beautiful UI built with the convergence of the Web and mobile devices in mind.

All other platforms segregate web applications in the web browser, separating them from the rest of the device and not giving them the power, outside of their sandbox, that the proprietary native applications enjoy. This separation implies that web applications are inferior, but the web platform is evolving and will soon stand near equal to conventional platforms. HTML 5 standards for local storage, web workers, canvas, geolocation services, and more are narrowing that gap, and efforts by Mozilla, Google, and others are driving the Web forward in other areas like 3D and graphics. The engines that the web platform run on have grown exponentially too. The new JavaScript engines of V8, TraceMonkey, and Nitro deliver leading-edge VMs that can lead with performance and advanced memory management.

It's a great time to be a developer. Web development is fast and iterative; you can build something bit by bit and see it come to life. With webOS, you can bring that experience to mobile devices. It doesn't matter whether you're a professional, trying to craft the ultimate, high-performance service, or a hobbyist, looking to explore some ideas and build something for yourself. Wherever you are on the spectrum, you can apply your skills to webOS, learning what you need from this book.

Frank W. Zammetti has written a terrific book. He gives you some hard reference material to learn webOS and the Mojo framework, from concepts to detailed methods and interfaces, and for those of you who just want practical examples and to jump into coding, he's got some projects that are both practical and fun.

Most of all, it's about developers being developers and having fun with software. So dive in, have fun, and write some apps!

Mitch Allen, CTO of Software at Palm, Inc.
Sunnyvale, California
November 2009

About the Author

■ **Frank W. Zammetti** is a genius of unspeakable evil, and I want to be your class president (go Google that phrase now!). He has written a number of books for Apress about web development, has been the keyboardist for a failed progressive-metal band, has jumped out of a perfectly good airplane, and believes the moon landing was in fact real but cannot believe for even a second that *Two and a Half Men* is still on the air!

I'm here all week folks. ☺

Frank is a lead developer for a major financial company in the United States who he has been with for 13 years. He is the creator of a number of open source projects and a contributor to many more. Frank has done some public-speaking engagements for various groups and technology conferences. He has written a number of articles for various publications and has started his own small business developing mobile/cloud-based software products for various platforms.

Frank likes walks in the park, sunset dinners, and flowers blooming in the meadow in April.

He is an avid human being who enjoys existing and considers it his greatest accomplishment. Frank is husband to a great dame named Traci, his best girl, his Gal Friday even. He is father to two eaters of his food and spenders of his money named Andrew and Ashley who he hopes are one day rich so they can afford the very best retirement home for him.

About the Technical Reviewer

 **Greg Hrebek** is a developer, consultant, and technical reviewer in cutting-edge technologies. His consulting company Syntactix LLC specializes in system development for all phases of the development life cycle. Currently it offers a shipment-tracking application called Pack 'n' Track for webOS and have many more innovative applications on the way. He can be found online at http://www.gosyntactix.com.

Acknowledgments

I've written six books for Apress thus far, and in each and every case I could not have done it without the help of a lot of great folks, and this book is no exception! I'd like to thank Fran Parnell, who was an especially pleasant project manager to work for; Frank Pohlmann, who served as a fantastic editor and who actually brought the initial idea for the book together; and Kim Wimpsett, who kept me honest as the copy editor this time around. If I somehow missed anyone, please accept my apologies and heartfelt thanks! I've had a great time working with all of you, and this book very much continues my very positive experience writing for Apress (even after we compressed the schedule!).

I'd also like to thank a couple of folks at Palm who were a huge help as well, starting with Mitch Allen who was invaluable in making this book happen in so many ways I can't count them all! Chuq Von Rospach also provided assistance a couple of times, even if he doesn't know he did, via forum posts. Lisa Brewster and Judy Vander Sluis helped expedite the applications from the book getting into the App Catalog. Dion Almaer and Ben Galbraith lent some assistance as well near the end. Thanks to all of you, and keep up the great work!

Introduction

When I was but a wee lass, my school—the first on Long Island, New York, I remember being told—got this thing called a *computer*. I vaguely remember hearing about such a contraption in sci-fi shows like *Star Trek*, but I didn't really know what it was. At that time, one of the teachers who had taken the lead there, a great guy by the name of Mr. Mincio, asked the five best students in the school, of which I was one at the time (I didn't keep that up for much longer, but I digress), to join the fledgling "computer club." Four of us said yes.

I'm very glad I did because that decision has charted the course for much of my life. Interestingly, three weeks later, I was the only student who stuck around. Everyone else wanted out.

Later that year, my parents bought me my first computer for Christmas: a Timex Sinclair 1000. That was, by any standard of almost any day, decidedly not a great piece of hardware. That didn't matter to me, though; I couldn't be happier with it, and I learned more than I can recount with it.

Those early days of my career in computers were immensely exciting. Everything was new, every now seemingly mundane programming trick learned was a wonder, and every seemingly clever hack figured out was of Aristotelian proportion. There was great joy to be had in simply learning, in experimenting, and in figuring out what these wondrous machines could do!

Shortly thereafter, I graduated to a much better computer: an Atari 800XL. There I started to play with the Assembly language and really began understanding the machine through game programming. A year or so later I finally had saved up for the machine that really brought it altogether, a Commodore 64. Things were never the same for me after that (and, oh, do I have some stories I could tell you from those days!).

The theme of fun, excitement, and figuring out what a new platform is capable of is something I've rarely had the joy of experiencing since that period in my life, which is a real downer! Fortunately, Palm has remedied that with its creation of webOS!

It may sound corny, or a little self-serving given that I've written a book on the subject, but I can say with all honesty that the experience I've had with webOS thus far mimics that excitement—that feeling of being on a journey of discovery. I don't know what OS the smartphones of the future will run and I don't know if it'll be a Palm OS or not (I'm sure Google and Apple will have something to say about that), but I firmly believe that we'll see the immense influence that webOS had on that OS.

You are in for a journey, that's for sure! I believe you'll find webOS to be a very fun environment to play in, and I hope you'll have at least some small measure of the excitement I've had with it.

Who This Book Is For

This book is for programmers. More precisely, it's for programmers who favor the "learn by example" approach.

I don't know about you, but I've ready plenty of books and articles where all they present are fragments of applications and small, contrived bits of code to illustrate a given point. Now, without question, that is sometimes precisely what you want. Oftentimes, however, what you really want is a whole application that is explained in its entirety so you can see how all the pieces fit together as you explore it little by little. This is precisely what this book seeks to do.

This book presupposes some knowledge on your part, though. Palm's webOS utilizes a web technology development model, meaning you're working with HTML, CSS, and JavaScript. It would obviously take a book probably four times the size of this one to teach you all that, so it is assumed that you've got a decent foundation in those topics and in web development in general.

What you *don't* need, however, is experience developing for mobile platforms of any sort. One benefit to the model Palm has chosen with webOS is that it truly is just web development, and it doesn't matter whether you've never developed for a smartphone before.

An Overview of This Book

I've broken the book down into two parts. The first part is comprised of the first two chapters, and the second part consists of the final five chapters. The first part introduces the basics of webOS, introduces the Palm Pre, and introduces the tools required to work with them. The second part consists of five individual, real webOS applications.

More precisely, here is what you'll find inside:

- Chapter 1 gives a brief history of the smartphone, the Internet (because it's core to webOS), how they've converged, and what the result has been. This chapter goes into the basics of webOS, introduces the Palm Pre and its hardware, describes its user interface design, and introduces the Mojo JavaScript framework that is the basis of all webOS applications. It describes the tools you'll need and how to set them up and ends with your average, prototypical "Hello World" application.

- Chapter 2 goes into quite a bit of detail about Mojo and the widgets available for use in webOS applications and discusses the on-device services that give you access to the features of the phone.

- Chapter 3 presents the first application, Code Cabinet. This is a utility for programmers where they can store snippets of code, categorize them, and search for them. Here you'll get an introduction to things like widgets, Mojo, and the on-device database facilities.

- Chapter 4 presents the Local Business Search application, which allows the user to look for businesses in the area around them. Here you'll see a few neat UI tricks including the "dark" UI theme. You'll get to play with the GPS capabilities of the Pre, and you'll see how to use remote web services in your webOS applications.

- Chapter 5 explores a game, Engineer. This gives you some exposure to the <canvas> tag and how to use it as well as the accelerometer services available in your applications. You'll learn about events and some more widget goodness.

- Chapter 6 introduces the Twitter Monitor application. This runs in the background and monitors your friends on Twitter and alerts you when specified keywords appear in their tweets. You'll learn about background applications, multistage applications, and more about interacting with remote services.

- Chapter 7 is where you'll find the Time Tracker application, the largest of them all that brings a lot of what you will have learned up until then together. This is a cloud-based application that uses a server-side component running in the Google App Engine (and yes, we'll be exploring that code too!). The application allows you to track the time booked against projects and see summaries of their status. You'll be introduced to a bunch of new widgets and new Mojo API functions, and generally you'll get a really good look at a lot of webOS concepts altogether.

There's a lot of ground to cover, but it's going to be a heck of a ride, I promise!

Obtaining Source Code

If you're anything like me, you'll agree that work sucks. What I mean is, effort that isn't actually necessary tends to not be something I enjoy. Or, to put it more succinctly, I'm lazy!

However, I generally try to get as much code printed in my books as possible so that they pass the Bathroom Test™; that is, you can read them during your…how shall I say it…private time and basically be able to follow everything along.

That being said, this isn't the mid-1980s where you'd happily open up your copy of *RUN* (an old Commodore 64-focused magazine) and type in the 20 pages of machine language code for the parachuting game the magazine published. No, we're better than that now (read: lazier), and typing in all the code yourself would be a monumental waste of your valuable time. Therefore, all the source code for this book is available for download on the Apress web site (`http://www.apress.com`). Simply go to Apress.com, click the Source Code link, and then find this book in the list. Click it, and you'll find a download link lurking somewhere on the next page.

Obtaining Updates

As my wife will no doubt tell you at the slightest provocation, I am far from perfect, regardless of what I may say. As all good authors[1] no doubt try to do, I've done my best to make sure everything here is accurate, correct, and true. Plus, there has been a technical reviewer checking it out; there has been my editor checking it out; and there has been a copy editor, production editor, and so on, down the line.

All that being said, mistakes are likely to have crept in quite by accident. Especially given that webOS is still quite new, as well as that it was just barely released when I started writing this book and there were changes along the way, it's even more likely that there are some errors.

Thankfully, Apress maintains an errata list for its books like any good publisher does, and you can access that on its web site just by searching for this book. You can submit errata for anything you find, and I for one will thank you in advance for doing so because it only helps anyone who reads this book.

Contacting the Author

I'm quite an easy guy to get a hold of; I'm not exactly one of those people who try to hide themselves on the Internet.

If you take that to mean I have an ego the size of Mt. Kilimanjaro, you're about right!

If you'd like to contact me for any reason, even identity theft (take it, it ain't worth much!), then feel perfectly free to do so at `fzammetti@etherient.com`. I also maintain a blog at `www.zammetti.com`, and I'm on Twitter under `fzammetti`. You can even catch me on IM if you want: on AOL I'm `fzammetti`, on Yahoo! I'm `fzammetti`, and on MSN I'm `fzammetti@hotmail.com`.

Or you can go buy a giant surplus doomsday laser weapon and etch a message on the face of the moon to me. Go ahead; I don't think anyone will mind.[2]

---

[1] How's that for the power of positive thinking?

[2] Zapping Paris with said laser weapon is *not* recommended, however!

PART 1
■ ■ ■
Laying the Foundation

The important thing is not to stop questioning.

—Albert Einstein

The dumbest people I know are those who know it all.

—Malcolm Forbes

Human beings, who are almost unique in having the ability to learn from the experiences of others, are also remarkable for their apparent disinclination to do so.

—Douglas Adams

A computer lets you make more mistakes faster than any invention in human history...with the possible exceptions of handguns and tequila.

—Mitch Ratliffe

Creativity is the sudden cessation of stupidity.

—Albert Einstein

Never trust a computer you can't throw out a window.

—Steve Wozniak

CHAPTER 1

■ ■ ■

The New Kid(s) on the Block

The Palm Pre, webOS, and Mojo

The last roughly 25 years has brought us some technological advances that we all but take for granted these days but that in a very real way transformed the world in which we live, not to mention *how* we live. The rise of the cell phone, the Internet, and PDAs[1] are three nearly parallel paths that altered our way of life forever. The point at which they meet represents a true paradigm shift in human history.

In this chapter, we'll briefly look at where we've been, technologically-speaking; where we are now; and where we're going, namely, to the Promised Land on the back of Palm's webOS. We'll learn how to get started developing for devices running it and what those devices, the Palm Pre in particular, have to offer. We'll see our first bit of code, we'll get it up and running (don't worry if you don't have a Pre; you can still play along, courtesy of the webOS emulator), and we'll create the foundation upon which the rest of this book will build.

Captain Kirk's Communicator Never Looked So Quaint

Let me tell you a story. It's a story from antiquity that, if you're younger than about 30, you just may not believe because it sounds too far-fetched! It's a story of a backward time, a technological dark ages some would say, and the dawn of a new age of mankind that came on its heels. It's the story of a time when you were all alone in the world, in a manner of speaking—an island unto yourself.

It hardly seems possible, I know! But trust me, everything you're about to read is the truth, the whole truth, and nothin' but the truth. So, pull up a rock to lean on, start up a fire, get the s'mores ready, and join me 'round the campfire!

You see, the time I'm referring to is a time before tweeting and blogging and geocache games. This was a time where if you wanted to remember something you just heard, you'd had better hope you had paper and pencil handy!

It was also a time before cell phones, a time when you couldn't simply tap a button on your Bluetooth headset or say a person's name and be connected to them. No, you used to have to look for these now almost mythical boxes that were oftentimes made all out of glass (to make them seem more like some magical place I suppose) in which you could find a rather large black box with a keypad, a silver part on the bottom, and something you could hold in your hand up to your ear. In other words, it

---

[1] PDAs haven't been around for 25 years, of course. They've been around only since 1993 when Apple introduced its Newton MessagePad device, which is what most consider the first true PDA. Still, the 25-year span I refer to here encompasses the mass acceptance of cell phones, the Internet, and PDAs as a whole.

was a booth with a phone in it! Figure 1-1 shows two of these creatures called *phone booths*, which is a rare site indeed nowadays.

Figure 1-1. A long time ago in a galaxy far, far away (The Doctor[2] would be proud!)

Into this phone went quarters[3] or any other loose changes you could find on the ground around the booth! You put the money in—twenty-five cents to make a local phone call (at least in the United States), or more to make calls to further-off places (which at the time might have been only the next town over). You dialed the number and hoped the line wasn't busy (especially if your car had broken down), and you hoped the person was home because there was no call waiting, no answering machines, and no voicemail.

---

[2] This is of course a reference to The Doctor, the lead character of the seemingly perpetual British sci-fi television show *Dr. Who*. The Doctor has a space/time ship called the TARDIS (Time and Relative Dimension in Space) whose outward appearance is that of a British phone booth.
[3] Or, if you were of the hacker brethren, there were tricks to avoid needing coins or any other money at all. But you didn't hear that from me, and don't come knocking on my door looking for a how-to, either!

And if you were calling from a jail cell looking for someone to bail you out who happened to not be home, well, too bad. You'd better make friends with the toughest-looking guy in the cell with you quickly!

All of this hinged on actually finding a phone booth because there were no cell phones. In fact, there were barely even cordless phones at home, no Skype application on your Wi-Fi-connected Sony PlayStation Portable (PSP), no Google Voice, and no text messaging. Yes, your very life might, in some extreme cases, come right down to your luck in breaking down, being attacked, or having a medical emergency within reach of a public phone.

It's a marvel we even survived as a species!

Eventually, though, a revolutionary device called the *cell phone* hit the scene and more or less started to do away with public phones. Cell phones at first were large and bulky and didn't have any capabilities beyond making simple phone calls. They were also extremely expensive, so few people had them, and those who did oftentimes had them hardwired to their cars! In Figure 1-2, you can see for yourself if you're too young to remember what early cell phones looked like. And by the way, if you can't tell from the picture, that thing is larger than the average person's head (and I suspect put out enough radiation to roast a small chicken, but I digress).

Figure 1-2. An old cell phone (that was so big it doubled as a sledgehammer!)

As relatively simplistic as early cell phones were, people quickly saw the usefulness in them, and technology, doing what technology always does, began to evolve and build upon the concept rapidly. Cell phones got smaller, more powerful, and more useful to more people. They got cheaper too, to the point where even kids can now afford them! They began to do a lot more than just make and receive calls, but I'm getting ahead of myself a bit.

I Feel So Alone, an Island Among Many

Roughly in parallel[4] to the development of cell phones was the introduction of this thing called the Internet. At first it wasn't very popular; in fact, it was barely known to most people. As a matter of fact, it wasn't even what most people thought of as "being online" for about a decade.

What you generally had before the Internet came into the public conscious, and then for a long time only if you were lucky, was a modem connected to your slow, underpowered, probably 8-bit computer that you could use to connect to other slow, underpowered, 8-bit computers. At first it was just one computer at a time—via something called a bulletin board system (BBS) that you interacted with. You'd connect to it, log in, read messages that had been posted, post some of your own in response, perhaps download or upload some files, and then disconnect. The next user would then connect (they had to

---

[4] The Internet has, in one form or another, existed since the late1960s. However, what we all know (and love, I presume) as the Internet has really only existed for roughly the past 20 years or so.

wait for you to finish because you were tying up the only phone line connecting the BBS to the outside world), and the whole process would start again for them. Oh, and did I mention that, by and large, BBSs were nothing but text or, if you were lucky, some ASCII art?[5] Figure 1-3 shows what one of these BBSs looked like (and this is actually a somewhat more advanced BBS!).

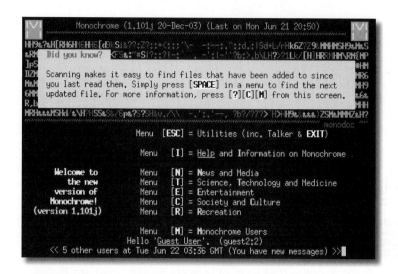

Figure 1-3. An early BBS (and an eye exam chart in some optometry offices!)

Doesn't that just about sound like prehistoric times[6] compared to what we have now?

Of course, eventually the situation improved (*improved* being a very relative term): we found ways to network a bunch of BBSs together and ways to have more than one phone line at a time set up so more than one user could connect at a time and even interact with each other to some limited extent. After a while, rather large, private, commercial networks such as Delphi, QuantumLink, and, probably the most famous of them all, CompuServe, emerged. These things were revelations compared to what came before, as you can see for yourself in Figure 1-4.

---

[5] ASCII art is a way of drawing pictures with just the ASCII character set. Some rather elaborate graphics have been pulled off by accomplished ASCII artists.

[6] If you were "on the BBS scene" for a while, you'll recognize that there were, in fact, some pretty advanced BBSs with color graphics and even some rudimentary multimedia capabilities. These advances were, by and large, on the tail end of the BBS era, though; certainly this was never the majority.

Figure 1-4. *CompuServe, an incredible leap forward (no, seriously!)*

Eventually, these sorts of private networks gave way to the Internet itself; in fact, some of those private networks and the companies that ran them were the early Internet service providers (ISPs)[7] that people used to get on the Internet. The Internet of course has existed for decades, but here I'm referring to the Internet of the past roughly 15 to 20 years, which is in most important regards vastly different and clearly superior to what it started as. The Internet began to blossom in a hurry in this time frame, primarily the World Wide Web portion of it.

A Computer in the Palm (Ahem) of Your Hand

At about the same time as cell phones began to really evolve and the Internet came into vogue in a big way, another technology hit the scene: PDAs. A PDA was (and still is, since you can still buy them) a trimmed-down computer, oftentimes one with specialized, built-in software that you frequently could not change or add to.

Leading the way in the creation of the PDA was a company called Palm. I'm not sure historically if Palm invented the PDA concept itself, but it was pretty much inarguably the leader of that market for a lot of years. Its devices were the most popular for a long time, and for a while the name Palm was absolutely synonymous with PDA. In fact, I remember when people didn't use the term *PDA*; they used the term *Palm* in its place, which was always a bit frustrating to me as a Windows CE[8] user!

Palm's PDAs did quite a bit. You could write notes to yourself, and they had calculators, contact lists, appointment managers, games, and all sorts of personal productivity tools and utilities. Most models allowed you to install new software on them to add all sorts of capabilities. They were quite small computers in the palm of your hand (gee, I wonder where they got the name from?). They weren't terribly powerful in terms of computing power, but they more than got the job done. Figure 1-5 shows one of the earlier models from Palm, the PalmPilot.

---

[7] Delphi was in fact the first ISP I personally used. All text, no real instructions...which made finding the *you-know-what* sites hard to find and hardly worth it (wink, wink)!

[8] Windows CE is Microsoft's portable version of Windows for mobile devices. Nowadays it's called Windows Mobile, which arguably makes more sense anyway!

Figure 1-5. *An early PalmPilot PDA*

One of the things a Palm couldn't do, for a while at least, was get you onto the Internet. Later models could do so via Wi-Fi, but for a long time this wasn't the case. Before too long, the Internet had all but supplanted the private networks like CompuServe, but you were still tethered to a desktop computer to access it; your PDA, be it from Palm or not, couldn't really help there. Likewise, while cell phones were improving leaps and bounds, they were still about making and receiving phone calls and not much more for a long time. (Although most had very simple PDA-like capabilities, a true PDA was far beyond them.)

The Times, They Are a-Changin'

But then, the inevitable started to happen: the parallel development paths of cell phones, the Internet, and PDAs began to converge. Their merging, which we are in the midst of right now, is the paradigm shift I hinted at earlier.

Cell phones eventually began to have more and more of the capabilities of PDAs, and after a while, there was no longer a need to carry both, which was the case for a good long time. Cell phones also began to provide a connection to the Internet. At first this connectivity was a somewhat painful experience: Wireless Access Protocol (WAP) browsers provided a very much watered-down view of the World Wide Web, the part of the Internet that most people actually think of when you use the term Internet.[9] In fact, the web pages had to be specially coded using WAP standards to be viewable.[10]

Eventually, though, at the point in history we find ourselves at today, we have high-speed, so-called third-generation (3G) wireless connections to the Internet. They are always on (well, unless we explicitly turn them off, of course) and allow for information to constantly be updated on the mobile device.

The three technologies melded together in a pretty predictable way actually, and the inevitable march of technology really started to take hold. In the past maybe five years, give or take a little, we've reach the logical apex of this convergence: the dawn of the age of the *smartphone*.

---

[9] There's also things like newsgroups, FTP, and even Gopher. Although Gopher is pretty much dead these days, you can still find some Gopher servers out there.
[10] Some phones could reformat non-WAP pages, but I never personally saw one that made that less than a painful experience!

Smartphones are cell phones that have all the capabilities of any good PDA while also providing more or less a full, rich, persistent connection to the Internet from virtually anywhere. The technology contained in these types of devices is far beyond anything that came before them, and they are, in many cases, not much different from having a full-blown computer right in your hands (albeit with different means of human-machine interaction, as we'll see).

Some of the pioneers in the world of smartphones were Research in Motion, creator of the popular Blackberry, and Microsoft, to name two of the bigger ones. One of the names *not* on that list, though, and the name most would have expected to see, is Palm. I don't think it's at all unfair to say that Palm got passed by pretty quickly by its competitors. It certainly had some horses in the race in the form of its Treo line of devices, but to be blunt about it, it didn't have the same level of success as other vendors did.

Those vendors, such as Microsoft, produce the Windows Mobile operating system that device manufacturers such as HTC used in devices like the Mogul, as shown in Figure 1-6.

Figure 1-6. The HTC Mogul, my favorite cell phone (until I got my Pre, that is!)

These devices could do nearly everything anyone on the go could want. They take the best from cell phones and PDAs and connect it all to the Internet. But Palm, the early pioneer in PDAs (and even in some ways in terms of connectivity, since some of the models could connect to the Internet before many other vendors' offerings could) was left out in the cold a bit. It did have a successful offering in the Treo line of smartphones, but the word *successful* is of course relative. It's hard to deny that for a period of a few years the name Palm didn't carry the same weight as other names, not the least of which is Apple.

Apple Raises

That heading is of course a gambling reference because what happened next was arguably the most important historic event in the smartphone space to date. In 2007 the world saw Apple jump into the game with the introduction of its iPhone device, shown in Figure 1-7. The iPhone changed the game because it really leapfrogged what people thought a smartphone could do. When you use an iPhone, because of things like multitouch gestures and fluid animations built into the operating system and because of the sheer processing power and memory the device contains, you truly do get the feeling someone took a full desktop computer and just shrunk it down! More so than any previous device, the iPhone in many ways reinvented what a smartphone could do.

The other big game changer that Apple introduced, something some might quite reasonably argue was in some ways the bigger deal, was the App Store. This is a virtual store that you can browse from your iPhone to purchase software for your device. This was a big deal because it made the iPhone even *more* like a desktop machine by allowing easy access for users to an incredibly huge number (60,000 or so at the time of this writing) of applications, all at the ready and easily accessible.

Figure 1-7. *The iPhone (for some, a phone; for others, a religious event)*

The iPhone is also a very much "connected" device: it provides *full* Internet access from anywhere. The iPhone contains a portable version of Apple's own Safari web browser, the web browser found on Mac OS (and even Windows nowadays), which is quite a good browser. Having Safari on a mobile device does away with the need for developers to do any special tricks: it will load, render, and work with any web site out there and will do so, more or less, just like on a desktop. This includes all the fancy JavaScript and Ajax tricks we're all used to today. There's no need for WAP anymore, and there's no need to have multiple versions of your site for different clients.

The iPhone also does email, Twitter, Facebook, MySpace, and all that social stuff the cool kids are into these days. No longer do you have to wait to get home to update your Facebook status or tweet about the great deal on jelly donuts you just got at Dunkin' Donuts. You can do it right then and there!

Of Course, There's Got to Be a Downside

Nothing is perfect of course, and that includes the iPhone. One of the things that most people would consider a bit of a negative is that programming apps for the iPhone requires a fairly competent developer. Development for the iPhone is (generally) done in Objective C. It also requires a Mac because that's the only operating system the iPhone SDK and developer tools currently support. So, there is a bit of a barrier to entry there.[11]

---

[11] Some people would say this barrier is a very good thing because the App Store is loaded with what most people consider garbage applications, and if the barrier were a little higher, maybe that wouldn't be the case. I'm of the opinion that the more software there is available for a given platform, the better, even if it means I have to cut through some muck to find the gold.

Early on, Apple promised that developers could use standard web technologies to develop iPhone apps, and although this is technically true, most iPhone apps are not currently written that way. The promise has gone a bit unfulfilled.

Perhaps more important is that over the past decade, application development in general has shifted from targeting a specific hardware and/or operating system, away from running applications locally, to running them "in the cloud," so to speak. Web application development has become the biggest driver in application development. To be sure, plenty of development is still done in C, C++, and even Assembly, and the applications run on one specific piece of hardware, but web development has become huge and has fundamentally changed the nature of application development overall.

However, here's the iPhone, still expecting developers to develop applications "the old-fashioned way." Does no one have an answer? Does no one have another approach that might better align with the way applications are by and large developed today?

Hmm, what do you say we go stroke Palm's ego a little bit, shall we?

Back with a Vengeance: Palm Calls

As I mentioned earlier, Palm was unquestionably an early pioneer in the PDA space. Its devices were extremely well regarded for a very long time and for good reason: they were easy to use, reliable, and, with add-on software, quite powerful. They were especially good in terms of user interface, being very logical and well thought out.

However, Palm didn't quite keep up with the competition as well as it might have, to the point where some felt its business itself might be in jeopardy. Palm needed something to change its fortunes, and as luck would have it, the rise of the smartphone (and a brilliant idea on Palm's part) provided just the opportunity.

The folks at Palm had the same thought that others have at some point, which is "As powerful and connected as modern smartphones are, why would developers want to program in a way that is largely contrary to that? Wouldn't they want to use the same technologies and techniques they are using everywhere else, namely, web technologies?" The answer I suspect for most of us these days is a resounding "Yes, please!" Palm, to its credit, didn't just have a good idea—it acted upon it!

That's precisely what Palm is doing these days, and it is because of this that the name Palm once again is carrying the same weight and the same sense of success that it once did. The iPhone is, as of this writing at least, still the king of smartphones, but Palm has unleashed two weapons that very well may change that, possibly even by the time you're reading these words!

Notice I said they unleashed *two* weapons, not just one. Palm has done something very smart indeed and in many ways something truly revolutionary. Let's look at each prong of the attack in turn, starting with what is arguably the less important (but more obvious) one: the Palm Pre.

Say Hello to My Little Friend: The Palm Pre

The Palm Pre is a smartphone of the highest order, meant to compete head-on with Apple's iPhone and the other competitors vying for smartphone supremacy. At the time of this writing, the Pre is available on Sprint's cell network only; however, there are already rumors of it coming to other carriers in short order, and my suspicion is that as you read this it is available elsewhere already.

The Palm Pre, which you can gaze longingly at in Figure 1-8, is a technological powerhouse by any standards you choose to measure it by.

Figure 1-8. *The Palm Pre, in the flesh (so to speak)*

The Palm Pre sports a 3.1-inch 320×480 LCD display capable of 16.7 million colors. This is a multitouch-capable LCD, meaning you can pluck two fingers down on it, and the device can register both touches simultaneously. The device can be rotated, and the screen display will autorotate into landscape or portrait mode as applicable.

The Pre has a built-in QWERTY keyboard, GPS, Bluetooth, Wi-Fi, and a 3.2-megapixel digital camera (with flash). It of course is a full-blown cell phone too, with all the trimmings that entails (voice, texting, and so on). Within this beast you'll find a Texas Instruments OMAP3430 ARM-based CPU running at 600MHz and 8GB flash memory for storage and 256MB RAM to run your applications within.

In other words, this thing (which most likely is the result of recovered alien technology from the Roswell crash in 1947!) is more powerful than the average desktop was in just the year 2000 and is many hundreds (maybe even thousands...I haven't done the math) more powerful than the computers that landed men on the moon in 1969, all of this in something the size, roughly, of a deck of playing cards!

If this doesn't amaze the heck out of you, then you are either *far* younger than me and take all this stuff for granted or need to reread those specifications once more! Hardware-wise, the Pre is without question a powerful computing device that more than earns the term *smartphone* and compares very favorably to any device currently available (currently being August 2009 when I wrote this).

From Hardware to Software: webOS

The one thing I didn't mention in the previous section is actually the second prong to the Palm assault and is almost certainly the more important element. The Pre, for all its hardware magnificence, probably wouldn't have been enough to get Palm back on the top of the mountain because the iPhone, in most people's opinion, is a fantastic device that is the king of the hill. Palm needed something more—something that would really distinguish it from Apple and everyone else.

A smartphone without a great operating system (OS) is just an impressive piece of technology. What makes it truly useful and desirable, and what makes the iPhone so well regarded, is the OS. This is from where Palm's second and more important development came from, in the form of webOS.

webOS is what sets the Pre apart from its competitors and what many people feel is a revolutionary achievement. One of the first things that sets it apart is that webOS is in no way, shape, or form tied to the Pre. webOS can run on other devices just fine, which is the opposite of what Apple has done with the iPhone. In typical Apple fashion, whether you personally like it or not, the company controls it all—the hardware, the software...it's all under Apple's control with the iPhone.

Palm, on the other hand, has taken a more Microsoft-like approach in that it has created an OS that can be used on a multitude of devices (and as you read this there likely are devices other than the Pre out there). Unlike Microsoft, however, Palm has also created the first device to use webOS, the Pre.

What sets webOS apart from the rest? The foremost thing is that developing an application for webOS is writing a web application and nothing more. You write HTML, you write CSS, and you write JavaScript. webOS provides a rich set of application programming interfaces (APIs) and services that allow you to interact with the device from your JavaScript code. Let me say that again so you don't miss it: developing an application for webOS and any device running it such as the Palm Pre is not *like* writing a web application; *it is* writing a web application, and you use all the same technologies and techniques (including Ajax) that you use to write any other web-based application these days.

■ **Note** However, there is one important difference: there is no request-response cycle like with a typical web app. A webOS application is more like so-called sovereign web apps, in other words, those that can be loaded off the local file system and run in an entirely self-contained manner.

This is a revolutionary concept. It's not entirely original per se because other systems work this way too, but Palm is really the first mainstream company to offer this and is the only one in the smartphone space.

Why is it revolutionary and so important? Simply stated, it's because it makes the barrier to entry far lower than competing platforms and allows developers to reuse the knowledge they've built up over the last 10 to 15 years or so.

Another revolutionary aspect to webOS is that it is built from the ground up for "life in the clouds," that is, data storage and even program execution out in the cloud—the Internet, in other words. Things like alerts from remote sources, data updates, and remote synchronization are all considered core parts of the user experience and as such are dealt with in a fundamental way by the OS. These aren't just tacked-on afterthoughts as it seems sometimes with other platforms.

All of this means that webOS gives you the power of native applications while doing so by building upon the strengths of the web development model at the same time as providing a richer experience that is focused squarely on the concerns of modern mobile users.

If you're interested in more technical details, you'll be interested to know that webOS is a Linux derivative based on the 2.6 kernel. It uses the standard driver architecture managed by udev, and it utilizes its own proprietary boot loader (there is, as I'm sure you can guess, a good mix of Palm-provided components as well as open source goodness mixed into webOS). Two file system partitions are present: a private ext3-based partition for internal use and a FAT32-based "media" partition for your own storage, which can be mounted via USB as an external storage device to make transferring files back and forth painless. Media files are handled via gstreamer, and this support includes support for numerous codec for both audio and video. Playback can be file or stream based.

■ **Note** Most of the time you couldn't care less if webOS was based on Linux or AmigaOS from back in the day, but in at least one case it'll matter: debugging in the emulator. You'll be logging into the operating system and watching files with Linux standard command-line tools. I don't know about you, but the fact that I can SSH into my cell phone is kind of freaky and really cool! I'll talk about this a bit more later.

You can see the overall structure of webOS in Figure 1-9. It's not a complex model by any stretch, but this should help you visualize where the code you'll be writing lives. In a nutshell, the diagram shows that your application, at the highest level, is interacting primarily with something called the Mojo framework, which we'll be looking at quite a bit. Through Mojo you'll be accessing on-device services. The UI System Manager component, a part of webOS itself essentially, serves to in a sense coordinate all these parts to provide the user experience. Finally, underneath it all is that Linux-based "core," or webOS.

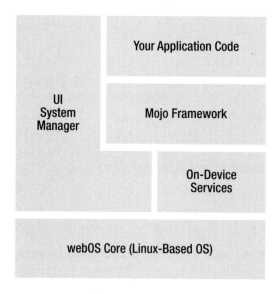

Figure 1-9. The structure of webOS at a high level

Most of this book will be focused on learning about the Mojo framework by way of writing applications. In short, Mojo is your doorway into webOS and the Palm Pre.

The term *application environment* is one you'll hear in Palm circles; it refers to the portions of webOS that are exposed to your application, namely, Mojo and the Palm Services, which are on-device servers (pretty much just like the servers you connect with on the Internet) that provide more "low-level" types of functions to your application. For example, loading an MP3 into the audio player, launching a web page in a browser, and sending an e-mail generated by your application are all examples of things that the services allow you to do.

The application environment also includes the user interface, which is what we're going to talk about next, as luck would have it!

The User Interface Is Where It's At

One of the key aspects of webOS is the user interface (UI), since this is essentially what represents the bulk of the user experience. webOS provides a rich set of metaphors for the user to interact with and does so in a simple, logical way. The user interface of webOS takes into account the primary constraint of its users: they are mobile! They don't have full keyboards to type on, and they don't have massive, honkin' monitors in front of their faces. They often don't even have comfy chairs to plop down in.

The UI of many smartphones, and certainly cell phones before them, don't take this into account enough. The iPhone really paved the way for proper UI design in this space in terms of how you interact with the device. Relatively simple (and in some ways obvious) things such as providing large targets on a touch screen to tap and using gestures instead of dedicated hardware buttons are types of things that make the experience much better for mobile device users.

Oh, and did I mention that webOS looks really beautiful? Well, it does, and Figure 1-10 should, I think, convince you.

Figure 1-10. The Palm Pre's UI in all its glory

As you can see, this is a long way from the black-and-white, low-resolution PalmPilots of the past. In fact, the UI of the Pre and webOS more specifically compares very well to any modern smartphone out there.

Multitasking and Activities

One of the primary factors that many people (including me) put webOS above even the vaunted iPhone is multitasking. It's not an original idea to be sure, and it isn't unique even today in smartphones, but few operating systems do it as well. The iPhone, for example, is limited to one application running at a time.[12] With a webOS device like the Pre, though, that limitation is not present, and in fact you are highly *encouraged* to keep applications running in the background with webOS because then they can participate in cloud-based services, such as updating information, and so on.

With webOS, Palm introduces a specialized meaning for the term *activity*. The idea is that a given activity might encompass a number of different applications or multiple independent views of one application. For example, perhaps you are composing an e-mail to a friend and in the middle of that you need to go look up information on a web site. So, you launch the web browser, go to the web site you need, and copy the information from it you want to send. You then bring the e-mail application back to the forefront, which is right back where you left it in the middle of composing your message. You can

---

[12] There are in fact some exceptions to this. For example, you can play music in the background on the iPhone. Those exceptions are very few and very far between, though.

paste the information and continue on your way. All of this could be seen as being part of the same activity, that of composing an e-mail that contains some information from an outside source. The multitasking nature of webOS makes this sort of activity a reality, and it is the *card view* that is your interface into this multitasking world.

The Card View

The user interface at a fundamental level supports this notion of multitasking; it's not just an afterthought. The primary way it does this is by introducing the card view. Figure 1-10 shows this view. Simply stated, all running applications are fanned out across the screen, as you would a deck of cards (hint, hint!), and you can flip between them at the touch of your finger.[13] You can swipe left and right across the screen to scroll through your open cards. You can rearrange them by holding down on one and then "shuffling" the deck by moving the application's card where you want and lifting your finger. All of this is done with animations and transitions throughout so the experience is smooth and interesting and also fulfills usability guidelines that say animation in a UI helps provide visual cues to the user that allows them to be more effective.

An application may have multiple cards open at a time. An example of this is if you open two bookmarks in the web browser at the same time; each will be its own card, almost like having two instances of the web browser open. Many applications will be housed within a single card, and it is the needs of the application as well as the design that the developer followed that determines this.

This card view is the primary means of navigating between applications in webOS and is a simple, elegant, and yet powerful UI metaphor that is unique to the webOS experience.

Navigation and Gestures

You'll notice there that I mentioned taps, swipes, and dragging. These are examples of gestures, and there are many present in webOS:

- *Tapping* is the most common, and this is simply putting your finger down and quickly lifting it up. This is synonymous with clicking a mouse button on your desktop PC and serves to act upon the object tapped. For instance, tapping a button performs whatever action is tied to that button.

- Quickly *flicking* your finger up from the gesture area (the area below the screen on the Pre specifically designed for gesturing) will minimize (turn it into a card) the current application and return you to the card view. This gesture does double duty by bringing up the Launcher if you're already in card view (the Launcher will be discussed shortly).

- A quick *swipe* from right to left in the gesture area is the back gesture, which serves a similar function to the back button in a browser. With a webOS application, each time a new screen (termed a *view* in webOS parlance) is shown, you can go back to the previous one with this gesture (if the top-level view is currently showing in the application, then this gesture will also return you to the card view).

- When in card view, you can close an application by "throwing it off the top of the screen," that is, *flicking* the card upward.

---

[13] It should be noted that webOS does not require a touch screen, but it is optimized for it, I'd say. Likewise, a device running webOS doesn't need to have a keyboard as the Pre does.

- *Scrolling*, say a list of items, is achieved by flicking up or down on the list. You can stop the scrolling by tapping anywhere on the screen. This scrolling obeys the laws of physics, so you'll see it slow down over time and eventually stop on its own (in other words, it has momentum and is affected by virtual gravity!).

There are more gestures than this, but these are the basics and likely the ones you'll find yourself using most frequently to navigate a webOS application. The point of course is that all this can be done with your fingers and is very intuitive: to activate a button, for example, you tap it, just as you would in the real world.

The Launcher

The Launcher is another important part of webOS. Figure 1-11 shows the Launcher, and simply stated, it is where all your applications' icons live and where you…wait for it…*launch* them from! There is also a Quick Launch bar underneath that is always present when an application isn't maximized where you can launch favorite applications from or bring up the full-blown Launcher.

Figure 1-11. *The webOS Launcher, home to all your apps*

Once you launch an application, it takes over the screen and becomes the application in the foreground, in other words, a maximized application as you're used to on a desktop computer.

Somewhat similar to the Launcher is the Quick Launch bar, which is present when in card view. This is a small bar of icons across the bottom of the screen. You can place the icons for your four favorite applications here, and one icon is always present to bring up the Launcher. This bar can also be dragged up onto the screen, where it becomes the wave bar, which is a nifty, if a little bit superfluous, bit of eye candy.

The Status Bar

The *status bar*, another element of the webOS UI, is always present at the top and is where you see things such as battery status, connection status, and the current time. You'll also notice a drop-down menu in the upper-left corner. This is called the *application menu*, and it is tied to the current foreground application. A given application may or may or may not make use of such an application menu (you'll see examples of both in this book), but it gives a nice, consistent interaction point to all applications that want it.

■ **Note** An application can request to be full-screen, which gives it use of the status bar area as well. I think in general you don't want an app going full-screen, from a usability perspective, but you can if you need or want to do that. Also, the application menu can change within an application based on the current view within that application, fully under the control of the application itself.

Alerting the User to Background Activity: The Dashboard

Since webOS is fundamentally a multitasking environment that allows you (and even encourages you) to leave applications running in the background, these background tasks need a way to interact with the user when necessary. On other phones, these sorts of interactions are entirely obtrusive and disruptive to whatever you're trying to do at the time. webOS takes a different approach.

When a background application wants to convey some information to the user, it can do so in a couple of ways. The first is in fact a disruptive way called a *pop-up*. This isn't any different from any other pop-up you're already familiar with: it is a modeless (which means it blocks all other UI interactions until dealt with) dialog box where the user has to take some action to proceed. Things such as answering an incoming call are implemented as pop-ups and are reasonable that way. Other things, such as your stock prices being updated 500 times a day, would be a really bad idea to do with a pop-up! Figure 1-12 shows an example of a pop-up.

Figure 1-12. A pop-up dialog (playing the part of a waiter apparently!)

For things such as those stock prices, a banner is provided. A *banner* is the combination of an icon and some simple text that appears along the bottom of the screen, just below the application area (in an area called the *notification bar*). This is not part of the current application, but the current application's area will shrink slightly at the bottom to create the space for the banner. This text can scroll across the banner area if you want to display longer messages. Figure 1-13 shows an example of a banner.

Figure 1-13. *A banner notification indicating the battery is being charged*

A banner can, like a slug slowly moving across your porch (albeit a *useful* slug in this case!), crawl across the screen in a little scroller and then leave a remnant of itself in the form of an icon in the corner. At this point, there is some functionality available to the user by virtue of tapping on the notification bar where the icons sit. This brings up the *dashboard*, as shown in Figure 1-14.

Figure 1-14. *The dashboard showing a new event (which you could now tap to open)*

Within the dashboard you can find any notification messages that were previously displayed as banner messages that have not explicitly been cleared. More than this, though, the panels in which these messages sit are actually full-fledged views that the application they are tied to can use to display extended information. This can include widgets and controls for the application too; for example, in the case of the music application, it shows information about the current track, as well as some controls to jump to the previous and next tracks and pause the current track.

All of the UI elements described here—from gestures to the card view, status bar, Launcher, dashboard, and various types of notifications, all within the context of a fundamentally multitasking environment—make webOS a phenomenal place to do your work on the go. At the same time, it's a joy

19

to use and look at, owing to small touches such as the water-like "ripple" effect when you tap something to the zooming transitions you see when you bring an application to the foreground. webOS, and by extension the Palm Pre device, stand up exceedingly well to any other device on the market today, which is likely for some time to come (and indeed, that is *precisely* Palm's goal with webOS).

Local Storage Facilities

Palm's webOS provides a couple of different mechanisms for storing data locally:

- Cookies, the ubiquitous way of storing data in a browser, are available to you. Cookies are great for small pieces of information that don't necessarily have to be stored in a durable persistent store. Cookies can be cleared by the user at any time, so they are not generally regarded as durable. However, it should be noted that currently cookies are cleared only when an application is deleted, and the version of the SDK available at the time of this writing actually bungles that and leaves the cookies in place even when the application is deleted! The point remains valid, though: cookies should not be considered a durable form of data storage except for data that it is acceptable to lose (in other words, user settings would probably be fine; contact information probably would not be).

- HTML5 storage is an embedded version of the SQLite database engine that provides a more or less full-featured relational database management system (RDBMS). Here you can create databases and tables and store your data relationally.

- Mojo Depot (which is in fact a wrapper API around the HTML storage mechanism) provides a somewhat more high-level interface to storing data where you work with objects. You'll create JavaScript objects and store them without concern for the underlying table structures involved. This is similar to popular object-based storage systems such as Hibernate in the Java world.

Which storage mechanism you choose will largely be a matter purely of choice; however, things that should persist over a long period of time should probably go in HTML5 or Mojo Depot data storage since they are more durable than cookies. In the end, though, use your brain, and you'll probably be fine with whatever you decide! You'll have an opportunity to see all three in action in the projects to come, so you'll be able to make an informed decision for sure.

■ **Note** One of my eagle-eyed technical reviewers pointed out that the Depot mechanism requires the entire contents of a given depot to be loaded at once and processed by the application. Therefore, Depot is not really well-suited to large data sets. The HTML5 storage mechanism is the better choice in those cases since you can query it like any SQL-based database and load only the data you need into memory at any given time.

Guiding Principles of webOS UI Design

Palm has put forth some principles that a "good" webOS application should follow. These guidelines are meant to achieve a pleasant user experience—one that is simple yet powerful for the user and that is simply enjoyable to use. These principles include the following:

- The webOS operating system is designed to be fast and simple to use, and therefore applications on the platform should strive for the same thing. Actions that the user performs in an application should respond as quickly as possible and should be easy to learn for beginning users as well as efficient for more experienced users.

- You should try to design your application in terms of physical metaphors. This means that there should be objects in the application, be it a button or an item in a list, with which the user can interact. For example, a common metaphor in webOS applications is that you can delete an item from a list by swiping the item right to left. webOS provides a lot of the other aspects of this guideline automatically, such as physics-based list scrolling (in other words, they have momentum and slow down over time) and transitions between views. However, to the extent you have to deal with these things yourself, you should strive for the same thing as webOS itself provides.

- Make sure data is always as current as possible. This means that your application should do things like automatically pulling data from remote sources or being able to received pushed data updates. Your application may also have to manage its own local cache of data so that updates can be replicated to the cloud using synchronization. Another aspect of this is being able to use an application when the device is offline. Although this obviously negates the ability to have 100 percent up-to-date information, your applications should be able to handle these sorts of situations (within technical limitations, of course).

- Common functions in an application should be very easy and quick to access. For example, the most common operations should usually be found right there on the screen with nice, big tap targets, while less frequently used functions can be "hidden" in an application menu.

- Remember, users are interested in getting work done without disruption, and you should therefore do as little as possible to block them. This means minimizing the use of pop-up dialog boxes and using the notification facilities webOS exposes correctly so that they get the information they need (as a banner for example) while not breaking their mental train of thought.

- Be consistent when you design your applications. This means making sure things within the application are consistent (in other words, a red button always means a negative choice), but it also means making your apps work similarly to other webOS applications. Of course, a certain amount of creative license is involved, but for example, being able to flick an item in a list right to left as previously described should be the preferred way you allow items to be deleted. That way, users will know how to use your application automatically based on their prior experiences. Just as importantly, this will keep them from becoming frustrated and hating your application for being unnecessarily different from all the others they already know how to use!

- Going along with the theme of consistency is making sure the user can perform actions repeatedly and can also back out of actions easily. Also, place interface elements consistently so that the user isn't left hunting for something that, for some reason unbeknownst to them, moved on them. In a nutshell: consistency, consistency, consistency!

One thing to realize is that Palm hasn't reinvented the wheel: the principles spelled out here are all generally accepted practices in the world of usability, that is, human-device interaction science.

Following these sorts of principles even outside the world of webOS will allow you to create applications that users *want* to use.

How Palm Got Its Mojo Back

When you write an application for webOS, you'll be talking to what's called the *Mojo framework*. With most other smartphones, you are coding directly to an API provided by the operating system and sometimes even going directly at the hardware itself, most commonly via C or C++. (Java is another common option, although it's in many ways more similar to webOS, but it's also not as prevalent.) A webOS application, however, is different in that it is essentially running within a runtime *on top* of webOS, namely, a web browser. (More specifically, Palm calls this runtime the UI System Manager, and it is built on top of WebKit, the engine that powers Safari and other web browsers.) Now, you won't by looking at it know you're running within a web browser because the operating system effectively *is* the web browser and hides this from you (in the sense that you won't see typical web browser "chrome" elements like buttons and toolbars and such), but that's basically what is happening. That's how you get to code a webOS application using standard web technologies like HTML, CSS, and JavaScript.

Mojo is in fact a JavaScript library that acts as an intermediary between you and webOS. It's an API that allows your application access to the underlying facilities of the device from JavaScript and gives you a simple, unified way to use the capabilities of the device and the operating system.

The Mojo framework is conceptually split into three parts: the APIs, services, and widgets:

- The APIs are JavaScript classes and functions you make use of from your code. These come in JavaScript "packages," which are really just classes…which are really just functions (oh, what a vicious circle!). It's a common organizational structure that allows for grouping areas of common functionality together in a logical manner.

- Services, something we'll get into in more detail later, are essentially local (meaning running on the Pre) servers that you can access using Ajax-like techniques that provide somewhat lower-level access to features of the Pre (things like playing audio and launching a true web browser, for example). At first you may think that this approach means that using services would be slow; after all, using Internet-based services introduces latencies into your application, even if they are barely noticeable. The difference here is that the servers are running on the local device, alongside your application, so there's no network latency involved. Also, since this is done fundamentally at the OS level, efficiencies can be built in to make the whole thing as efficient as any other local cross-namespace method invocation would be on any other platform.

- Widgets are of course the UI elements that you'll use to build your applications. You can certainly create an entire webOS application using nothing but plain CSS, HTML, and JavaScript, but using the widgets lets your UI make use of all the power webOS offers.

Mojo, being a proper framework, provides more than just APIs for you to call it; it also provides a prototypical architecture for your application to follow. Much of a webOS application is based around the notion of conventions; that is, as long as you follow certain guidelines and structural recommendations, there will be less code to write because Mojo will know how to execute your application intrinsically. It removes a lot of plumbing-type code from your responsibility, which is a very good thing for us generally lazy developers!

A structure of a webOS application is based on the well-known Model-View-Controller (MVC) pattern (shown in Figure 1-15), which provides separation between various concerns in your application, namely, the parts responsible for displaying information, the parts responsible for implementing the underlying logic of the application, and the parts dealing with the data the application works on (as well as the data itself). This structure maps to the default locations where you'll put various parts of the code that make up your application, and by following this pattern, Mojo knows where to find the parts of your application it needs by default and knows how to make use of those parts.

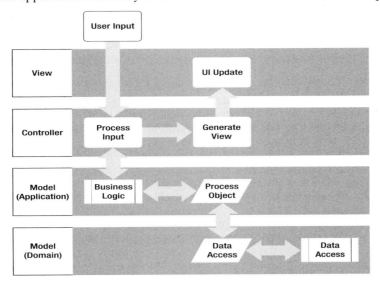

Figure 1-15. The MVC architecture, generalized for UI interactions

Mojo Standard Directory Structure

Figure 1-16 shows the basic structure your application will follow. This is the basic directory structure that most webOS applications will generally take (as with all "rules," they can be broken at times, but those times are few and far between if you're doing things "right" within the context of webOS).

Figure 1-16. Basic directory structure of a webOS application

At the root of the directory structure you will find a number of files:

- index.html, which is the HTML for your stage (we'll get to what that is shortly). This is required.

- sources.json, which lists the JavaScript files that make up your application. This is required but will nearly always be present.

- appinfo.json, which is some meta-information that describes your application to Mojo (one of the things you can do is specify the name of the stages' HTML file, so index.html won't always be correct). This is required.

- An icon that represents your application.

We'll get into each of these in some detail as we proceed, but for now, that's a decent enough overview.

In the root directory, you'll also find an app directory, and this is where the code of your application lives.

As a web application, you may have images, scripts, and style sheets, and by convention you'll find them in directories named images, javascripts, and stylesheets, right off the root. This is *not* a required structure per se. Your application won't fail to work if you do something different with regard to these resource files, but it's a convention you should probably stick to since it makes sense and makes understanding your application's structure easier and consistent with most others.

In the app directory you'll find some subdirectories including assistants, models, and views. The assistants directory contains JavaScript files that control scenes (which we'll also get to shortly), and the views directory contains HTML files corresponding to a given scene. The models directory is frequently not needed but is located where application data models can reside (in my experience it is more common to not have anything here).

As I alluded to earlier, the parts of an application fall into some basic categories that are built into the directory structure, these being views and assistants primarily. Before we can really talk about these things, though, we need to cover two basic concepts: stages and scenes.

Note This application structure is highly recommended, but most of it is not required. What *is* required is an app directory with the contents as described here and an appinfo.json file and an index.html file, both in the root (the index.html file might be named differently, as specified in appinfo.json). Certainly any added content above and beyond the recommended structure is fine and is dependent on your needs.

Stages

A *stage* is a container for your application, much like the tab of a tabbed web browser can be considered a container for a web site. A stage is conceptually represented by a card, and an application can have more than one stage, or *card*, opened, if necessary, although one is frequently sufficient (in my work with webOS I've seen very few examples that have more than one).

A stage is also an HTML document that serves as the foundation that the scenes of your application are shown on. The HTML document representing a stage tends to be pretty sparse, as you'll see throughout this book, and most of the time it really has no content that the user sees. The stage can usually be pretty bare because it's the scenes where most of the action tends to take place. You'll see later that, for a typical application, there is a single HTML document that is initially loaded and effectively serves as the stage for the application. This document, in the absence of any scenes, also serves as the view of the stage. You could in fact construct an entire webOS application with nothing but this single-stage HTML document serving as its view, but that's a bit atypical because scenes are what you'll usually use to present a view of an application.

Scenes (Views and Assistants)

A *scene* is a view into your application. Like a stage, it is built from an HTML document (more precisely, it's an HTML fragment), but tied to that document is something called a *scene assistant*. This is simply a

JavaScript object that aids the controller for the scene. Mojo will spawn a controller for the scene automatically, but most of the functionality behind the scene is provided by the assistant you program (hence it assists the controller).

Remember MVC? Well, the HTML document for the scene is your view, while the scene assistant is your controller (for all practical purposes it is, even though it's not truly the controller). The model might be some data stored in a local database or a remote system that provides data, or you may not even have a model at all in some cases.

The HTML document that makes up a scene's view is in fact a fragment of HTML, meaning it's not a complete document with a `<head>` and `<body>` and all that. For example, this is a perfectly valid scene HTML document:

```
Here is a button:
<br>
<div id="myButton" x-mojo-element="Button"></div>
```

I don't want to get ahead of myself here, but it would be uncool of me to point this out now: did you notice that x-mojo-element attribute? Obviously, that isn't a standard HTML attribute of a `<div>` tag. This is actually a marker that allows Mojo to parse your scene's HTML and convert that `<div>` into a button widget. This is most often how you'll create widgets, and as you can see, it nicely keeps your view separated from the other layers in good MVC fashion.

Now, back to scenes! An application must[14] have at least one scene, and most applications will tend to have quite a few more. You can conceptually think of a scene as different pages of a web site that the user navigates between. Or if you prefer, think of the stage as the desktop in a typical Windows or Mac computer and scenes as windows that appear over it. The only difference is that for that analogy to work, windows on your desktop would have to be only maximized, and moving to another means leaving the one you're currently looking at.

The Scene Stack

When the user navigates from one scene to another, the previous scenes are not necessarily lost. Each time a new scene is shown, it is pushed onto a scene stack. The previous scenes sit below the current one on the stack. If a given scene is closed, it is popped off the stack, and the scene below it, if any, is again shown. This again is very much like navigating a web site when you use the back button of your browser.

Your application's code is indirectly responsible for the stack in the sense that your code will be pushing scenes onto the stack to show them, and sometimes it will pop the current one off to show the previous one, although a scene can also be popped by the user if they use the back gesture. webOS really manages the stack, though; you don't have to create it or anything like that yourself. You simply tell webOS that you want to display a new scene, and the stack is maintained automatically.

Application Life Cycle

I'm about to make a statement that I think is destined to go down in history in the annals of obvious statements as king of the hill: a webOS application begins by being installed on your device! This is part of the life cycle of an application, of course; in fact, you could argue it's the single most important step in the process! An application gets installed by going to Palm's App Catalog, as shown in Figure 1-17, which is the online store where you can browse, download, and purchase webOS applications. When you select an application, it will be automatically installed and added to your Launcher for you. It's that easy!

---

[14] This is what the documentation says, but in fact I've seen and have put together applications that only have a stage and nothing more. You do tend to see some warning messages in your log files from it (we'll get to log files in a bit!), but the application will still work.

Figure 1-17. *The Palm App Catalog*

Once an application is installed, Mojo and webOS also provide your application with a well-known runtime life cycle, or series of events that occur at prescribed times when your application is executed. The first step is that Mojo will read the `appinfo.json` file. This provides the operating system with vital information about your application.

Next, the AppController will be executed and will delegate to your provided app assistant. This is a JavaScript class you provide that can handle things such as arguments passed to the application at launch and initial stage setup. You usually will not need an app assistant (they come into play most frequently with background, or *headless*, applications), and thus it is optional.

Part of the `appinfo.json` file is the name of the HTML file that serves as the "launch point" for the application, typically `index.html`. Next, that file is loaded and parsed. Any style sheets and JavaScript files referenced in the HTML file (or those listed in `sources.json`) will then be loaded and parsed. This HTML document is responsible for loading the Mojo framework itself and, in the absence of any views being pushed, serves as the view for the stage as well.

THE HOMEBREW SCENE: LIVIN' ON THE EDGE

Palm has gone the same route that Apple pioneered with an online store, the App Catalog. This is the primary way you'll get applications onto your Pre or other webOS device.

However, it's not the only way!

A robust "homebrew" scene has spawned, that is, places you can go to get applications outside the App Catalog written by independent webOS enthusiasts. This scene has made installing applications a breeze with simple desktop utilities that automatically install the applications onto your USB-connected device, as well as an on-device application that can access a homebrew app catalog. I wrote that in lowercase on purpose to distinguish it from Palm's own App Catalog. The homebrew app catalog (called the *app gallery* in fact) is run by other Pre enthusiasts, not Palm.

Now, that all sounds great, but you have to realize there are a couple of significant downsides to this homebrew scene. First, this is not endorsed by Palm. So far, Palm has remained relatively quiet on the topic, allowing the scene to grow without disrupting it. This may or may not continue; we just don't know. However, I have heard rumors of Palm releasing an "official" application to install apps independent of the App Catalog, which would be more than a tacit endorsement of the homebrew scene. I, for one, hope that does indeed come to pass.

Probably the biggest negative, though, is that with the official Palm App Catalog, the applications you find there go through a rigorous process to even make it into the store. Palm makes sure the applications follow proper guidelines and won't ruin your device. No such guarantees are present with homebrew applications, so the risk is entirely yours, and I wouldn't at all be surprised to find that warranties are somehow voided by using homebrew apps.

Still, one of the things that has made Microsoft so successful over the years is being very good to developers and allowing them to really build on top of the platform Microsoft provides. That's exactly what the homebrew scene is doing. My hope is that Palm will, if not officially come out in favor of the scene, at least allow it to continue without hindrance. So far so good on this front, but until Palm gives an official stance either way, we won't know for sure.

Note that I haven't given you any real information on the homebrew scene, such as how to get the apps and that sort of information. That's on purpose. If you choose to enter that scene, you'll have to find the entry point on your own so I don't feel bad if you wreck your brand new Pre! Of course, I'm not giving away any state secrets by saying that finding the homebrew scene is a trivial matter given the power of Google…wink, wink.

Next, Mojo invokes methods on the stage controller, which is a JavaScript object that provides control-layer functions for the stage itself. You provide a stage assistant that the controller delegates calls to in many instances. The first such method invoked, following the constructor of the assistant class itself, is the setup() method. What you do in this method is entirely up to you, but the most typical activity is to push the first scene onto the scene stack, causing it to be shown. Like the stage, the scene you push will have a controller, as well as an assistant, and that assistant also will have a setup() method. The setup() method will be called only when the scene is pushed, not when the user uses the back gesture to return to it. In fact, unless you explicitly destroy a scene, setup() will be called only once.

The activate() method of the stage will next be called, although if you pushed the first scene in setup(), then you likely won't do anything in the activate() method. (Indeed, you don't even have to implement a method of a controller in your assistant that you don't need; Mojo will be just fine without it because there is a default implementation of all of them in the controller.) The activate() method can be called multiple times, any time the scene is brought into view in fact, either because it was pushed or because a scene on the stack above it was popped.

Speaking of popping a scene, any time a scene is popped off the scene stack, the deactivate event will fire, and your scene assistant's deactivate() method will be called.

That covers the basics—the things you'll find yourself using time and again. Other methods will be covered as necessary.

Getting Started with webOS Development

If all of this sounds pretty cool so far (and I presume it does since you bought this book) and you're asking yourself, "But Monty, how much would I have to pay for the privilege of developing a webOS application?"…well, it's time to find out!

In short, getting started developing for webOS couldn't be easier, or cheaper, since it's 100 percent free!

Palm has unleashed upon the world a software development kit (SDK) for exactly that purpose. This SDK contains (nearly) everything you need to write and run webOS applications. I said *nearly* there because there are two prerequisites that you'll need: Java 6 and VirtualBox.

You'll need to have a Java 6 runtime installed first and foremost. You can get that at `http://java.sun.com`. Grab the latest version, and install it on your chosen platform (you can develop on Windows or *nix variants, including Mac).

Throughout this book I'll be talking about development on a Windows platform because that's what I know best. At the same time, I'll try to entirely leave out anything that is platform-specific or point out situations where that is unavoidable and offer suggestions for folks living on the other side of the fence.

Once you have Java installed, it's time to install VirtualBox, which is an x86 virtualization package from Sun that you can find at `http://www.virtualbox.org`. In other words, it allows you to run virtual machines, namely, one for webOS. This allows you to get up and running and developing applications without having to plop down the Benjamins[15] to purchase a real Pre!

Installing both Java and VirtualBox is an exercise is simplicity: execute the installer, follow the prompts (amounting to little more than clicking that Next button a few times), and you'll be all set.

The last piece of the puzzle is the webOS SDK, which you can get at the Palm Developer Network (PND) site: `http://developer.palm.com`. That's not only where to find the SDK but is your one-stop shopping experience for all things webOS development. There you can find message forums to correspond with other developers, documentation of Mojo, articles about webOS development, and much more. You'll want to set up an account when you head over there to download the SDK and visit the site frequently for news about webOS.

The SDK is similarly easy as pie to install, and once that's done, you're ready to rock 'n' roll.

One of the things the SDK includes is a more or less full-fledged webOS (Palm Pre) emulator, as shown in Figure 1-18. In that figure, you can see the operating system starting up, and its Linux underpinnings are readily available. Once the startup sequence ends, you're greeted with a webOS screen as shown in previous figures, and you can begin playing with any of the built-in applications. You'll also have Internet access piggybacked off your PC's connection, so you can use the web browser.

---

[15] *Benjamins*, for those of you outside the United States, refers to the U.S. $100 bill. The phrase "It's all about the Benjamins" has—unfortunately, if you ask me—entered the pop-culture lexicon to basically say "It's all about money." Feel free to insert the name of someone on your country's currency as appropriate!

Figure 1-18. *The webOS (Palm Pre) emulator starting up*

A Proper IDE Makes Things a Lot Easier

Although the SDK, Java, and VirtualBox are all you technically need, there is a way to make life a little easier, and that's to have a proper integrated development environment (IDE). Also on the PDN you can find a plug-in for the popular Eclipse IDE that I highly suggest using.

You'll need to install Eclipse first, of course, which you can get at http://www.eclipse.org. It too comes as a sleek, simple installer to run. Once you have that installed, you'll need to follow the directions on the PDN for how to install the plug-in. (It involves pointing Eclipse at a specific URL and, once again, following the simple instructions.)

What the plug-in will do for you primarily is make creating a new skeleton webOS application as easy as clicking a few buttons, and it also makes running that application in the emulator as easy as clicking another button. The alternative is command-line interactions with the SDK, which work just fine (and I know some people actually prefer that).

■ **Note** Throughout this book I'll be assuming you've installed Eclipse and the plug-in, so I will be describing only that approach. I'm doing this because, first, I think it's the easier approach and, second, there is already good coverage of the command-line interface to the SDK, but not as much of the IDE-based approach, so I feel like I'm doing a greater service to the larger webOS development community by providing this coverage.

As I mentioned, it takes little more than clicking a button to run an application from Eclipse with the plug-in installed, and that, preceded by creating a simple application, is exactly what we'll be doing next.

APTANA

Although 100 percent optional, Palm also suggests installing Aptana Studio in Eclipse, and I echo that recommendation.

Aptana (http://www.aptana.com) is a free plug-in for Eclipse that extends the IDE with capabilities very helpful for web developers, which I want to emphasize is exactly what you are when developing for webOS! In my mind, the single most valuable tool Aptana gives you is JavaScript validation. I personally put the validation view up and docked on the right of my Eclipse window, and that provides me with instant error flags as I'm typing. Simple things such as missing quotes, mismatches braces, and other extremely common errors are instantly shown to me. In fact, when you install Aptana, you'll actually have some choices on what components to install, and I'd suggest the JavaScript editor and validator if nothing else.

Also, although Aptana is free, there is also a professional version that has more features and may well be worth purchasing for you, but that is also 100 percent optional (although note that by default a trial of the professional version will be installed, and you may want to trim things down a bit, as I've done, during and after the installation).

Why Break with Tradition? The HelloWorld Application

Assuming you've gotten all the installations out of the way, let's build ourselves a simple application. If you are already familiar with Eclipse, then much of this will be superfluous, but to be sure as many readers as possible are served by this, I'll assume that you have little or no experience[16] with Eclipse throughout this book.

The first step is, naturally enough, to fire up Eclipse! If this is your first time running it, you'll be asked for a workspace (in fact, by default you'll be asked for the workspace each time, but the first time is when it will be created). This is simply a directory where your code will live. So, specify whatever directory you like and continue.

Once Eclipse starts, assuming this is a newly created workspace, you'll find yourself at a nice welcome screen. You can close this immediately, which will reveal your workbench, as shown in Figure 1-19. In Eclipse parlance, this overall workbench, as I call it, is actually called a *perspective*, and there are numerous types of perspectives that depend on the type of technology and/or tasks you are performing. The Palm plug-in provides a webOS perspective; however, it frankly doesn't provide much benefit at this point aside from some toolbar icons to quickly create a new application or scene. That being said, it's a decent enough starting point, and Eclipse will ask you whether you want to switch to that perspective the first time you create a webOS application. You can modify it, or any other perspective, to your heart's content, so in a sense it doesn't matter what perspective you're working in because you'll likely wind up tweaking it to your liking anyway, but the choice is ultimately yours.

---

[16] I myself am not a regular Eclipse user, so explaining it to you is a good way to reinforce my own knowledge. And no, you may not have a partial refund on the cost of this book on grounds that you're helping me and therefore should get a discount! Nice try, though—LOL.

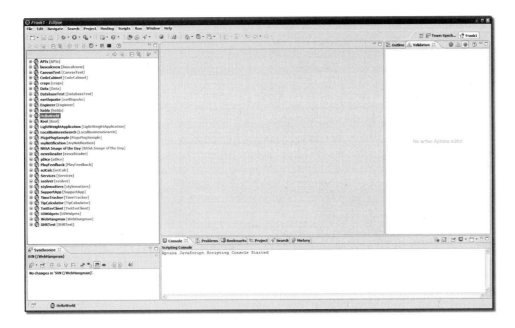

Figure 1-19. *The Eclipse workbench*

What you see will be different from this because I've customized this perspective to how I like it (and I also have a ton of projects in my workspace). You can do so as well, showing and hiding individual views (things like the Validation and Outline tabs you see on the right) and moving tabs around where you want them to be. I suggest saving this perspective so that when you inevitably screw it up somehow by playing around too much, you can recover your preferred organization structure quickly.

To create a new project, all you need to do is select the File menu and then the New option. You'll see a list of things you can create. You'll need to choose Other at the bottom. This will bring you to a pop-up dialog box, as shown in Figure 1-20.

Figure 1-20. *The first step of creating a webOS application in Eclipse*

Select the Mojo Application project type, and click Next. At that point you'll be presented with a second dialog box where you can enter a number of pieces of information that describe the project, as you can see in Figure 1-21. Of the fields you see, only the "Project name" field requires you to enter anything (you can accept the default values for all the others, although something must be entered for each).

Figure 1-21. Entering a name for the new project

Once you click Finish, Eclipse will churn for a few seconds, depending on the speed of your workstation, and eventually you'll see a new project on the left in the Project Explorer tab. If you expand this project, you'll find that its structure, and the files contained within it, matches the directory structure we looked at earlier. This is in fact a complete, fully functional webOS application! To convince yourself of this, you'll need to launch the emulator. You should find an icon for it on your Start menu where the SDK folder was created.

The first time you launch the emulator, it will take a minute or so because the virtual machine representing the Pre has to be installed. Subsequent launches will take only a few seconds. Once the emulator is up and running, you can launch the application. To do so, right-click the project in the Project Explorer, select Run As, and select Palm Application. You'll be greeted with a pop-up, shown in Figure 1-22, asking you to specify the run target.

Figure 1-22. Selecting a run target for the application

It is of course the Palm emulator in this case, so make sure the right option is selected, and click OK. A few seconds later you should see Figure 1-23 appear in the emulator.

Figure 1-23. *The basic application skeleton: it's alive!*

Clearly this application doesn't do a whole lot, but it's the first step you need to take: getting an application up and running in the emulator.

■ **Note** You could at this point run the application on a real Pre. Before you can do that, though, you need to switch the Pre to "developer mode." To do this, you'll need to enter a code on your device, which will expose a new app to switch it to developer mode (do a Google search for *+"Konami code" +"palm pre"*). Once that is done, connect the Pre to your PC via USB, and select a run target of Palm Device instead. Assuming everything has been installed correctly and you've put the Pre into developer mode, the application should run on your Pre. Note that the *Konami code* part is a bit of an Easter egg present in webOS and as such could conceivably be removed in the future. There is an official way to get your app onto the Pre, but this is by far the easier way, so I won't go into the other way; you can find information about it via Google if you need it. Also, you may want to search for the history of the Konami code too—it has a very interesting back story!

Building a Better (Hello) World

Let's now take the next step and make this application just a little more interesting. Let's add a single scene to it, and on this scene let's add a text field the user can type in and a button. When the button is clicked, we'll display an alert message saying "Hello, XXX" where XXX is what the user types in the text field.

The first step is to create the scene. If you want to do this manually, you'll need to create two files: one is the HTML file representing its view, and the other is a JavaScript file that contains the scene assistant. The files need to have specific names in order for Mojo to automatically know about them, and they need to be in specific places in the directory structure. Let's begin with the HTML file. Before you can create this file, you'll need a directory for the scene, so expand the HelloWorld project, and then expand the app directory. You'll see an empty views directory there. Right-click that directory, select

New, and then select Folder. Now you'll need to enter a name for the new directory (or *folder*, as Eclipse likes to call it), and here we'll use sayHello as that name.

With the directory created, you can now create the HTML file for the scene. Right-click the new sayHello directory, and select New and then File. This file must again be named something very specific in order for Mojo to know about it, and that name must be sayHello-scene.html. Once you create that file, Eclipse will open it for editing automatically. Leave it open for the time being.

The next step is to create the scene assistant that assists the controller for this scene. To do this, right-click the assistants directory found under the app directory, and select New and then File. The file name you should enter must be sayHello-assistant.js. Once you've done that, Eclipse will open that file for editing as well, and your workspace should look something like what you see in Figure 1-24.

Figure 1-24. *The HelloWorld application with new directories and files added*

There is an easier way to accomplish all of this, though: simply right-click the project in the Project Explorer view, select New, and select Other (optionally, if you're in the webOS perspective, you'll find an icon on the toolbar for creating a new application or scene, and this will do the same thing). Go to that same Palm group where you went to create the project, and this time select the Mojo Scene option. Simply enter a name for the scene (the name of the project is also required but should have been filled in automatically), and the plug-in will go off and create the directories and files discussed here.

With the files created, we now have to obviously put some "stuff" in there to make it do what we want (there will in fact be some default content in the files created by the plug-in if you went that route, so just overwrite them with what is discussed here). Let's begin by building the view for our new scene. Remember that we're going to have a text field for the user to enter their name in and a button for them to click to see the greeting. The file we need to edit first is the scene's HTML file, so flip to that tab (it should be the first one open in the edit area in the middle with the name sayHello-scene.html), and put this content into it:

```
<br><br>
<div id="txtName" x-mojo-element="TextField"></div>
```

```
<br><br>
<div id="btnGreet" x-mojo-element="Button"></div>
```

Remember I mentioned earlier that a scene's HTML file doesn't contain a full, proper HTML document; instead, it's just a fragment of HTML, as you can see here. Moreover, it's really just plain HTML: two <div>s with some line breaks[17] in between. Now, the <div>s have that special x-mojo-element attribute, of course, so that Mojo can, when it parses this document, create some elements for us, but even with that attribute in play, it's still just basic HTML. Be sure to save these edits before continuing.

The next step is to put some code into the scene assistant, including a model to back up those two UI widgets, namely, the text field and the button. Yes, even at the widget level the MVC architecture is in play! To do this, we'll need to edit the sayHello-assistant.js file and put the following contents into it:

```
function SayHelloAssistant() { };

SayHelloAssistant.prototype.txtNameModel = { value : "" };

SayHelloAssistant.prototype.setup = function() {

  this.controller.setupWidget("txtName",
    { maxLength : 15 }, this.txtNameModel
  );

  this.controller.setupWidget("btnGreet", { }, { label : "Greet Me" } );
  Mojo.Event.listen(this.controller.get("btnGreet"), Mojo.Event.tap,
    this.greet.bind(this)
  );

};

SayHelloAssistant.prototype.greet = function() {

  this.controller.showAlertDialog({
    onChoose : function(inValue) { },
    title : "Greetings!",
    message : "Hello, " + this.txtNameModel.value,
    choices : [
      { label : "Ok", value : "" }
    ]
  });

};
```

Now, this needs a bit of explanation. Simply stated, a scene assistant is a JavaScript class, which means a function. So, the first line creates that function, and once again, "configuration by convention" is in play here, so the name of the class has to be the name of the scene, with the first letter capitalized as well.

Next, we have to add some members to the class, which we do via the prototype of the newly created class. The first member is txtNameModel, which is the model that will be tied to the text field. This

---

[17] Yes, it's ugly, especially to CSS purists, to use line breaks to do layout like that, I know, but I wanted to keep your first time out of the gate as simple as possible.

is a simple object defined with JavaScript Object Notation (JSON) with a single field, value, which not surprisingly is the value of the text field.

Next you add a method to the class, one that you'll see in practically every scene assistant, setup(). This method is called once to set up your scene, so here is where you'll typically configure widgets.

You see, it isn't enough to use the x-mojo-element attribute in the scene's HTML file; you'll also need to programmatically set up the widgets you are using. What this setup really means is you need to tie a model, as well as event handlers, to the widgets. You'll also do some basic configuration, as we're about to see.

Before we continue, I need to point out what this.controller means throughout this code. When you see this.controller, that is a reference to the scene controller for the current scene (a Mojo.Controller.SceneController class). Remember that Mojo spawns a controller for the scene automatically, which then delegates calls to your scene assistant. The controller itself provides functionality that the code in your assistant will need access to; hence, a reference to it is automatically added to your assistant so you can refer to the controller.

The first time we see this used is the first line of code in the setup() method. The call to this.controller.setupWidget() is one of the most common lines of code you'll write, over and over again! This is what defines a given widget that you place in your HTML. This particular line is setting up the text field. The first argument is the ID we assigned to the widget, txtName in this case.

The next argument is a bit of JSON that defines attributes of the widget. Each widget will have a different set of attributes, many optional, and oftentimes you may just have an empty object here if there's no real configuration to do. In this case, I decided to limit the number of characters the user can enter to 15 by setting the maxLength attribute accordingly.

The this argument to the setupWidget() method is the model for the widget. Once again, what goes into the JSON object will depend entirely on the widget you are configuring. Here I've simply given it a reference to the txtNameModel field of the assistant class.

■ **Note** One big gotcha that I'll point out now and likely will again more than once is that changing the model object that a widget points to during the life of the application is nearly always a Very Bad Thing and will lead to you losing a lot of hair as things subtly break in ways that are difficult to track down. You can change the attributes within the model of course, but trying to point a widget to a new model is pretty much a recipe for disaster…trust me, I found this out the hard way!

Note that sometimes you won't need to access the model again, and you can put the JSON inline as the third argument to setupWidget(). I typically prefer that syntax myself, but in this case we'll need access to it, so it has to exist outside the assistant's setup() method and hence the class field in this case.

Following that is another call to setupWidget(), this time to set up the button. In this case, there are no configuration attributes, so we have an empty object passed as the second argument (note that null won't work here). The third argument is the model for the button, and this time we have an attribute called label, which sets the text label shown on the button.

Next we see a call to Mojo.Event.listen(). This is another of the most common methods you'll be using time and again, and its purpose is to set up an event handler on a previously created widget. The first argument to this method is a reference to the widget you want to hook up an event listener to, which is gotten by a call to this.controller.get(), passing it the ID of the button. Because the controller must know about the widget for this to work and since the controller won't know about the widget until you've set it up, that means you can call Mojo.Event.listen() only after a call to this.controller.setupWidget() has been made for the widget you want to hook the event listener to.

The second argument to Mojo.Event.listen() is the type of event to listen for. The event types are defined as pseudo-constants in the Mojo.Event package (JavaScript doesn't have true constants, remember?), and in this case we're listening for a tap event, so `Mojo.Event.tap` is what we want. The third argument is a reference to a callback function that will be called when the event occurs.

The function we're calling here is a method of the scene assistant class, namely, the `greet()` method. So, it might seem like just passing `this.greet` would have been sufficient, and in fact in some situations it would be, but it's not in this case. You see, the problem you encounter is that when the event occurs and the specified function is called, the meaning of the keyword `this` won't be what you expect, which is almost certainly that it refers to the scene assistant instance. Now, if your callback function doesn't actually need the `this` keyword, then you can get away with syntax like `this.greet`.

But, in the callback code here we are using the `this` keyword to get the value of the text field, which is in the `value` attribute of the `txtNameModel` field. So, we need to ensure the `this` keyword has the appropriate *scope*, as it's referred to, and we do this by calling the `bind()` method on the function.

This is a method provided by the Prototype[18] JavaScript library, which is included with the Mojo framework. The `bind()` method provides a specific context to the keyword `this` when the function is executed. For example, say you have a function called `myFunction()`. What does the keyword `this` point to when the function is executed? In JavaScript, the answer depends on what the function is bound to at runtime. Since every function is in fact a property of some object ("naked" objects in the global scope are actually properties of the `window` object), the keyword `this` may not point to what you expect when the function is executed. Many times you need it to point to a specific object, which is where `bind()` comes in. If you do `myFunction.bind(X)`, where X is some object, then when you execute `myFunction()`, the keyword `this` will point to X, regardless of what it might have pointed to without using `bind()`.

I realize that may have sounded a bit complex, but it's actually pretty simple when you look at the code here again. When `greet()` is called in response to the tap event, the `this` keyword will be a reference to the scene assistant, because that's the object that was passed to the `bind()` call, which executed as part of the call to `Mojo.Event.listen()`.

The last bit of code in the assistant is the `greet()` method itself. This uses another method available on the scene controller, `showAlertDialog()`, which pops up a dialog from the bottom of the screen where the user must perform some action. This method is passed a JSON object that defines the dialog box. The first attribute in this object is `onChoose`, which is a function called when the user picks one of the choices available to them. Here there's nothing to do so an empty object is passed. Next is the `title` attribute, which provides the title that will be shown on the dialog box. The `message` attribute is next and is the text of the message shown on the dialog box. Here we concatenate the value entered into the text field by grabbing `this.txtNameModel.value`. Mojo has taken care of updating the model object based on the user input for us. Finally, the `choices` array is a list of buttons that the user can click. Here there's only a single OK button. Each button has a `label` attribute, which is the text displayed on the button, and `value`, which is the value associated with the button and which will be passed to the `onChoose` function.

A Few Final Steps to Make This Work

If you've followed along thus far and tried to run the application in the emulator, you'll discover that it doesn't work yet; all you see is the default text on the stage as before. We're actually missing two other pieces of the puzzle, but before I tell you what they are, let's see how we might debug this situation.

Since the webOS is based on Linux, quite a bit of power is available to us developers. For example, when you're running the emulator, you can actually establish an SSH connection to the emulator and execute shell commands! To do this, use your favorite SSH client and connect to localhost on port 5522 using the username root (no password). Once you do this, you'll find yourself at a shell prompt on the emulator's file system.

─────────────────────────────

[18] It's worth noting that Palm has already said that it might not always be the case that Prototype will be included with Mojo. However, there should be no problem with including it yourself in your applications if that ever happens, so you shouldn't worry one bit about using Prototype in your code.

> ■ **Note** The Palm SDK comes with the popular, but simple, PuTTY client. You can find it in the bin directory where the SDK was installed. PuTTY isn't the most feature-rich client out there, but if you don't have a favorite already, it will certainly get the job done for you.

One of the most useful things you can do is view the log file associated with your application. To do so, go to the /var/home/root directory (cd /var/home/root) and then type the following:

log xxx.yyy.zzz

Figure 1-25 shows an example of such an SSH session watching the execution of our HelloWorld application. I didn't add any log statements (which we'll get to very soon) in the code, however, so all you see are the system-generated messages here.

Figure 1-25. *I'm just sittin' here watchin' the logs go by and by.*

The xxx.yyy.zzz part is the unique ID assigned to your application. This value is stored in the appinfo.json file in the root of the application. This file, as stated earlier, provided Mojo with some needed meta-information about your application. The attributes you'll find in this file by default are described in Table 1-1.

Table 1-1. *Attributes Available in* `appinfo.json`

Attribute	Description
id	This is the unique ID of your application. This should be in the form domain.appName, so com.etherient.codecabinet is an example.
version	This is the version of the application. Must be in the form x.y.z, so 1.0.0 is an example (when you go to package your application for installation onto a Pre, one of the things that can cause that process to break is not following this version format).
vendor	This is the name of the company associated with the application.
type	This will always be the value web (until further notice by Palm).
main	This is the main HTML file representing your stage to load and is typically index.html, which is also the default.
title	This is the title of the application (will be used on the icon in the Launcher).
noWindow	When true, this will be a headless application. Defaults to false.
minicon	This is a smaller PNG file that is used for notifications. Defaults to minicon.png.
icon	The PNG file containing the icon for your application. This is the icon that will appear in the Launcher. Defaults to icon.png. Should be 64×64 pixels in size, 24-bit color. The actual icon content should be around 56×56 pixels (leaving 8 pixels buffer on each side).

So, to view the log for the HelloWorld application, you'll need to type this:

```
log com.yourdomain.helloworld
```

That is the default ID that the new project process created, and although you could of course change it, it's perfectly fine for our purposes here.

Once you enter that command and run the application, you'll see all sorts of messages fly by as webOS, Mojo, and your application do their thing. So, how does this help us debug our application? Well, your first guess is likely that the setup() method of the scene assistant is never executing, so let's test that theory. To do so, add the following as the first line in that method:

```
Mojo.Log.info("########## setup()");
```

Mojo.Log.info() is one of the logging functions available in the Mojo.Log package that just spits out an information-level message, which you'll see as you're viewing the log file.

That is, you'll see it once you add one more file to the application! Add a file named framework_config.json in the root of the project, and put this into it:

```
{
  "logLevel" : 99
}
```

Without doing this, the `Mojo.Log.info()` messages won't make it to the log file because their logging level is higher than the default logging level. This configuration file in general allows you to configure many Mojo framework-level items, one of which is the log level to dump to the log file. A value of 99 will allow all log messages to go through.

Table 1-2 shows all the configuration options available in `framework_config.json`.

Table 1-2. Attributes Available in `framework_config.json`

Attribute	Description
debugEnabled	If true, enables debugging features that include default error handler for service requests; Alt+F for FPS display; Ctrl+Shift+L to log the current scene's HTML; Ctrl+Shift+O to open the Firebug-Lite inspector, if installed; and Ctrl+Shift+V to view the framework version that is in use.
escapeHTMLInTemplates	If true, HTML escapes in any property substitution in templates, which is a good idea.
logEvents	Causes events sent by the framework and mouse events received to be logged at info level.
logLevel	Controls the logging levels: `Mojo.Log.LOG_LEVEL_ERROR (0)`, `Mojo.Log.LOG_LEVEL_INFO (20)`, `Mojo.Log.LOG_LEVEL_WARNING (10)`. Note that the value 99 as used in this application simply means log all levels and is frequently seen in webOS application code during development.
timingEnabled	If true, the timing statistics enable on the scene transitions.
useNativeJSONParser	If true, uses the native JSON parser, if available.

Rerun the application after making these changes, and see whether the log message appears (the hash marks before it are so that it's easy to spot in the output).

DEBUGGING ON A REAL PRE

One of the roadblocks I faced early on was in debugging code running on a real Palm Pre. Specifically, how do I see the same error messages in the log that I described here when working in the emulator? As it turns out, it's a bit trickier than with the emulator, and not very well documented.

The short answer is that in the webOS SDK's bin directory you'll find a program called novacom. This allows you to establish an SSH connection to your Pre when it's hooked up to your desktop via USB. Once you plug your Pre in, you'll get a pop-up asking you what you want to do, whether you want it to be a USB drive, do media syncing, or just charge. Select the Just Charge option, or just leave the prompt up. Then, execute novacom with the command line –t open tty://, and you'll be greeted with a new window with a root@castle: command prompt. From there, type the command tail -f /vat/log/messages | grep xxx where xxx is the name of the application (the ID, more precisely, such as com.etherienet.codecabinet). Now, you'll be able to see those log messages. Note, however, that a change made in version 1.1 of webOS causes Mojo.Log.info messages to not appear, so you'll need to use Mojo.Log.error all the time instead, which do make it to the log file.

Also note that if you leave off the grep portion of that command, you'll see all sorts of messages generated by webOS, not just your application. This can sometimes be useful too, but greping the output focuses you on your application, which is probably what you'll want more times than not.

You'll quickly see that the message never appears, so our scene is never becoming active. This is completely logical: we're never pushing the scene! Remember that Mojo will show the stage, but that's it; anything beyond that we have to do ourselves. Fortunately, that's very easy. Edit the stage-assistant.js file in app/assistants that was created by default. In it you'll find an empty setup() method. You just need to add this single line to that method:

this.controller.pushScene("sayHello");

Just like with our scene assistant, we have a setup() method for the stage, and also just like the scene assistant, Mojo adds a reference to the controller for the stage to our assistant automatically. This controller exposes a pushScene() method, which is what we need to get our scene showing. We pass the name of the scene here, and that's all it takes because we've followed the naming conventions, so Mojo know exactly how to show our scene. It gets pushed onto the scene stack, setup() is called, and the application does what we expect.

Or does it?

We *still* seem to be missing something because if you rerun the application after that change and you're still viewing the log, you'll notice an error message saying that the scene sayHello could not be pushed and that the scene assistant is not defined. But, we did define it, didn't we? Yes, we have, but what we haven't done is told Mojo about it. This is (I promise!) the last step: open up the file sources.json in the root of the project. Add an entry for the scene assistant so that the complete contents of the file now becomes this:

```json
[
    {
        "source": "app\/assistants\/stage-assistant.js"
    },
    {
        "source": "app\/assistants\/sayHello-assistant.js", "scenes": "sayHello"
    }
]
```

The sources.json file can be used to load any arbitrary JavaScript files, just like you can do by including them in an HTML file. One additional bonus, though, is that you can tell Mojo what scenes a given source file contains. By doing that, we can call pushScene() by just passing it the name as specified by the scenes attribute in sources.json.

So, once you make that final change and rerun the application, you should have a working application that does what you see in Figure 1-26.

Figure 1-26. HelloWorld in all its final (ahem) glory

I dare say it's *still* not any sort of award-winning application, but what it does do pretty well is give you most of the basics you'll need to build a webOS application! Believe it or not, if you know nothing more than what you've learned by building this application, so long as you can look up the attribute and model elements that a given widget needs, you can begin building applications right now! They won't be the most robust applications nor will they use the full power of webOS and the Palm Pre, but they could definitely be useful. You have the power, my young apprentice!

Summary

In this chapter, you got a good overview of the technological trends that have brought us to where we are today with the Palm Pre and webOS. We looked at that particular device in some detail but spent most of our time looking at webOS. We looked at the UI metaphors it provides to the user and saw how applications are developed using standard web technologies. We looked at things like the application life cycle; we looked at the components of an application including stages, scenes, and assistants; and of course you got an introduction to the Mojo framework. We learned about the development tools Palm provides, and we looked at how to use them, specifically, the SDK, emulator, and Eclipse plug-in to create our first simple webOS application.

In the next chapter, we'll look at the APIs, services, and widgets that Mojo provides in more detail so that we have the necessary foundation from which to build the applications to come in the subsequent chapters.

CHAPTER 2

The Four, er, Three Horsemen of the Apocalypse

A Survey of Mojo API Packages, Widgets, and Services

In Chapter 1, after a quick initial history lesson, we dived headlong into the world of webOS. We got a feel for how the operating system works and how applications for it are put together. You'll recall that I mentioned three broad categories of facilities at your disposal: the Mojo API, services, and widgets.

Well, this is the chapter in which we dive into these three areas! This will not be an exhaustive, detailed look at every API, widget, and service available, though. That's what the Palm-supplied documentation is for! This chapter will instead be an overview for you to get familiar with what's available and see the basics of using much of it. I'll cover as much as space allows for (my editor would shoot me if I wrote a 200-page chapter, after all!), and I'll definitely cover the things that will be used most frequently in developing webOS applications, but for some parts of Mojo, such as the widgets and services I perceive as a bit less likely to be used, I'll only briefly touch on or skip entirely in some cases.

The idea is that after reading this chapter, you'll have a good general feel for what's available and how to use it, and you can refer to the official Palm documentation for all the details such as all the arguments you can pass to a given method, all the config options for a given widget, and so on (to be sure, you'll see some of that here, but just enough to get the idea). The chapters following this will put this base of knowledge to practical use, which means you'll see more of the details as we go, but this chapter should serve as a solid starting point and even be a good general reference for you to refer to later.

The Mojo API

The Mojo framework is a JavaScript library that provides to you, the application developer, a number of classes and utility functions to both interact with webOS and the device it's running on; it also seeks to make your JavaScript development life a little easier by providing some general-purpose utility-type code too.

Mojo presents an API to you that conceptually is a collection of packages. The term *packages* in JavaScript just means classes (and of course a class in JavaScript means a function). If this is a new concept to you, let me show you some code that explains it:

```
function JavaScript() { };
JavaScript.utils = function() { };
JavaScript.utils.add = function(inA, inB) {
```

```
  return inA + inB;
};
```

```
alert(JavaScript.utils.add(2, 2));
```

This is one approach to coding packages in JavaScript. (There are other ways to accomplish this, but that's a bit out of the scope of this book, and I think the syntax shown here is the clearest way to illustrate how this works.) At the end of the day, we have a JavaScript.utils package that contains an add() method. Underneath it all, though, we have three functions: each is nested inside of another, which is what allows us to use the JavaScript.utils.add() syntax to call the add() method (more precisely, it *necessitates* that call syntax).

■ **Note**   You'll notice that I used the terms *function* and *method* in the text here in a seemingly interchangeable way. In fact, there is a subtle difference. In a language like Java, you have classes, and you have methods. A method cannot exist on its own. In JavaScript, however, all you have is functions. A function acts like a class in Java, and when a function is nested within another, that is conceptually like methods of a class in Java. However, in JavaScript you *can* have "naked" functions. So, when a function is nested within another, I use the term *method*, and when a function stands alone, I call it a *function*. I believe this to be the most accurate and logical nomenclature to use, but I felt it worth talking about here in case the difference is new to you or it wasn't clear from the context of the verbiage here.

This is what you're dealing with when you look at the Mojo API packages. Now, it's also possible in some cases that you'll have something like this:

```
function JavaScript() { };
JavaScript.utils = function() { };
JavaScript.utils.Person = function(inFirstName, inLastName) {
  var firstName = inFirstName;
  var lastName = inLastName;
  this.sayName = function() {
    alert(firstName + " " + lastName);
  };
};
```

```
var p = new JavaScript.utils.Person("Lex", "Luthor");
p.sayName();
```

Here, we have a Person class as part of the JavaScript.utils package, and we can instantiate a new instance of it any time we want. The point is simply that you can have both methods and classes in packages (even though functions are all we're dealing with still).

You can also have purely data members in a package too. For instance:

```
function JavaScript() { };
JavaScript.utils = function() { };
JavaScript.utils.PI = 3.14;
```

```
alert(JavaScript.utils.PI);
```

Although there are no true constants in JavaScript, you could change the value of PI here and thus find yourself a member of the Q Continuum.[1] You can expose what I usually refer to as *pseudo-constants,* like PI here, or just data structures that you intend to be changeable by outside callers (this is pretty infrequent in an API like Mojo).

Just as a matter of curiosity (you in no way, shape, or form need to know this to use Mojo), you can achieve something approaching true constants by doing it this way instead:

```
function JavaScript() { };
JavaScript.utils = function() {
  var PI = 3.14;
  this.getPI = function() { return PI };
};
JavaScript.utils = new JavaScript.utils();
alert(JavaScript.utils.getPI());
JavaScript.utils.PI = 456;
alert(JavaScript.utils.getPI());
```

Here, both alert()s show the same 3.14, proving that the value of PI really is a constant. The downside here is that you need to provide an accessor method, getPI(), rather than just being able to go after JavaScript.utils.PI directly because it is private within the JavaScript.utils package.

■ **Note**   You may find the line JavaScript.utils = new JavaScript.utils(); a bit odd, and indeed, it is! This is needed because without it, when you call getPI(), you'd find that it was undefined. This is because we're just defining the function the first time around but not executing it, which means that getPI() was never "hooked up," so to speak, to the function initially created. By creating a new instance, it executes, and getPI() gets hooked up. Then, the reference to the new instance replaces the reference to the original function, and we get what we want in the end.

With those basics in mind, you know pretty much all you need to know to make use of the Mojo API (in fact, more than you need to know now!). So, let's start exploring what the Mojo API has to offer, beginning with the Mojo.Animation package.

---

[1] In the sixth season episode of *Star Trek: The Next Generation* entitled "True Q," at one point Geordi remarks that, for a second, it seemed like the laws of physics went out the window. At that moment, Q appears and says, "And why shouldn't they be changed; they're so inconvenient!" Clearly, changing PI would have serious implications in the world of physics too!

USE THE SOURCE, LUKE!

One of the best things about JavaScript is that the source code is right there for you. There's no need to reverse-engineer a class file to get (roughly) the original source code, as is the case with Java. There's no trying to convince the authors to give you the source. It's just right there in front of your face (setting aside obfuscation tools, which really just make life a little harder and nothing more).

The Mojo framework, and all the source for it, comes bundled in with your SDK download. There are many times you'll likely need or just want to go look at the source code. A good example is the `Mojo.Char` package discussed in a moment, which the documentation does not fully describe. Only by looking at the source for it will you get the full gist of it.

That being said, as I wrote this chapter, I referred to the Palm documentation for the majority of my information. Since this chapter isn't meant to be an exhaustive look at all of Mojo, anything missing I can point the finger at Palm for! That being said, I will at times refer to the source code directly to give you some insights where it seems necessary.

Also, you will definitely find areas where I say something different from the documentation does, and in those cases I've found discrepancies and am telling you what I found to be reality regardless of what the documentation says! It's worth repeating that Mojo and webOS still have rough edges, and although they are being improved nicely and rapidly, they are still noticeable, especially for us developers

In the end, though, you have the source code, and that's a very big benefit—one you may very well need from time to time as you do webOS development while Palm shores up the official documentation.

Mojo.Animation

This package, as I'm sure will not be surprising for you to learn, is concerned with types of animations. Primarily, support is found here for animating (meaning to change over time) DOM element styles and numeric values.

For example, let's say you want to animate the height of a `<div>` from 20 pixels to 80 pixels over a time period of two seconds. You can accomplish this using the `Mojo.Animation.animateStyle()` method:

```
Mojo.Animation.animateStyle(
  $("divAnimateMe"), "height", "linear",
  {
    currentValue : "20", duration : 2,
    from : "20", to : "80"
  }
);
```

The first argument to this method is a reference to the DOM element to animate (obtained here using the `$()` operator provided by the Prototype library, which is included with the Mojo framework). The second is the name of the attribute to animate (using DOM element naming, *not* JavaScript naming, so `background-color` instead of `backgroundColor`, for example). The third argument is the type of animation curve to use and can be a value of `linear`, `bezier`, or `zeno`. The fourth argument is an object containing options for the animation. The attributes that can be present here are `currentValue`, which is the current value of the attribute being animated (this is optional; by default the current value will be parsed as an integer); styleSetter, which is a function to call to actually set the value (this is optional); from, which is the value to start the animation on; to, which is the value to end the animation on; and duration, which is the number of seconds over which the animation should run.

The Mojo.Animation.animateStyle() method internally makes use of another method in this package, Mojo.Animation.animateValue(). As such, most of the attributes you can pass to this method in its options object can also be passed to Mojo.Animation.animateStyle(). The first argument to this method is a reference to the animation queue to use, which you can get by calling Mojo.Animation.queueForElement() and passing it a reference to the DOM element you're animating. A queue allows for multiple animations to run simultaneously without detriment to the standard 40 frames-per-second (FPS) frame rate that animations run at. The second argument to Mojo.Animation.animateValue() is the type of animation, just like for Mojo.Animation.animateStyle(). The third argument is a function to call at each step change in the animated value. This function will be passed the current value of the property being animated. The final argument is an options argument, just like for Mojo.Animation.animateStyle(). The from, to, and duration attributes are present here too and work in the same way. In addition, there is the onComplete attribute, which is a function to be called when the animation finishes; reverse, which will run the animation in reverse order; and curve, which is the type of animation curve to use.

Speaking of animation curves, there are a couple of constants in Mojo.Animation for this. They are Mojo.Animation.easeIn, which is an animation curve that starts slowly and speeds up; Mojo.Animation.easeInOut, which is a curve that starts slowly, speeds up in the middle, and then slows down at the end; and Mojo.Animation.easeOut, which is a curve that starts quickly and slows down at the end.

■ **Note**   I feel compelled to point out that the Palm documentation for this package is particularly in need of some work. In fact, at the time I wrote this chapter, this part of the documentation contained some outright incorrect information and in fact contradicted itself in the span of a few sentences by stating what the method signatures are and then showing example code that was quite a bit different! I've done the best I can to make sense of this all by examining the actual source code, but I hope the Palm documentation is cleaned up in this area soon because it's definitely confusing.

Mojo.assert(s) and Mojo.require(s)

Within the Mojo namespace itself you'll find a whole batch of methods named Mojo.assertXXX() and Mojo.requireXXX() where XXX is something like Array, Class, or Equal. These are primarily used for debugging purposes, although sometimes they serve a useful purpose in normal program execution.

All of them write an error to the log if their condition isn't met, but with the Mojo.requireXXX() methods, an exception will also be thrown. Table 2-1 lists all these methods.

Table 2-1. *The* assertXXX() *and* requireXXX() *Methods in the Mojo Namespace*

Method	Description
Mojo.assert()	Expression must evaluate to true.
Mojo.assertArray()	Object must be an array.
Mojo.assertClass()	Object must have been constructed with the specified constructor function.
Mojo.assertDefined()	Object must be defined.
Mojo.assertElement()	Object must pass the Prototype library's isElement() test.
Mojo.assertEqual()	Two objects (as compared with ===) must be equal.
Mojo.assertFalse()	Expression must evaluate to false.
Mojo.assertFunction()	Object must pass the Prototype library's isFunction() test.
Mojo.assertMatch()	Value must match specified regular expression.
Mojo.assertNumber()	Value must pass the Prototype library's isNumber() test.
Mojo.assertProperty()	The object to be tested must contain the named property (or array of properties). Note that this is different from an attribute having a value of null, which would *not* cause this assert to be triggered.
Mojo.assertString()	Object must pass the Prototype library's isString() test.

You'll note that I said the table lists *all* the methods, but in fact that isn't the case. I've listed only the Mojo.assertXXX() methods. The reason is that for each of them there is a corresponding Mojo.requireXXX() method. For example, there is a Mojo.requireElement() method that corresponds to Mojo.assertElement(), a Mojo.requireMatch() method that corresponds to Mojo.assertMatch(), and a plain old require() method that corresponds to assert().

Most of these methods, the Mojo.assertXXX() methods and the Mojo.requireXXX() methods alike, have the same method signature. They accept three arguments. The first is the object, or expression depending on the method, that will be evaluated. The second argument is the message to be written out to the log file. This message will be processed as a template into which you can insert dynamic data by way of the third argument, which is a message properties object with attributes to be inserted into the message.

A couple of the methods do have different signatures:

- Mojo.assertClass(), which accepts the object to be tested, the constructor function to test against, the message and the message properties object

- `Mojo.assertEqual()`, which accepts the expected value, the actual value of the variable being tested, the message and the message properties object

- `Mojo.assertMatch()`, which accepts the regular expression to test with, the value to test against the regex, the message and the message properties object

- `Mojo.assertProperty()`, which accepts the object to test, the name (or an array of names) of the properties to test for, the message and the message properties object

Let's see a couple of miscellaneous examples to give you an idea how this works:

```
Mojo.assertFalse(
  1 < 2,
  "#{firstNumber} < #{secondNumber} was TRUE, expected false",
  { firstNumber : 1, secondNumber : 2 }
);
```

This will log the message "1 < 2 was TRUE, expected false" (this will be prefixed with "Warning:" by Mojo) because we're asserting that 1 < 2 is false, but obviously it's true, so the assertion fails. Notice that the values of the attributes `firstNumber` and `secondNumber` are inserted dynamically into the message using the replacement tokens #{firstNumber} and #{secondNumber}. You can of course pass variables as the values of those attributes, which would make a lot more sense since you're probably asserting that some expression based on the current values of those variables is false.

Another example might be this snippet of code:

```
var a = "123";
Mojo.assertArray(a, "a is NOT an array, expected it to be");
```

Since a is a string, the message "a is NOT an array, expected it to be" would be logged. Here, there is no dynamic information being inserted; just the message is enough.

Again, there are corresponding methods, `Mojo.requireFalse()` and `Mojo.requireArray()`, that work the same way, but they would then throw an exception. Which you choose to use depends on the needs of your program.

Another example, this time of the `Mojo.assertProperty()` method, is this:

```
var c = {
  firstName : "Amanda", lastName : "Tapping"
};
Mojo.assertProperties(c, [ "firstName", "age" ],
  "Either firstName or age has no value"
);
```

This will output the message "Either firstName or age is undefined" because the attribute age is not defined on the object. As noted in the table, if age:null was present, the assert would *not* be triggered because this is in fact a test for undefined attributes, not a test for attribute with no value.

One last method you can find in this package is the `Mojo.loadScriptWithCallback()` method. This is a very handy method that will asynchronously load a new JavaScript file and then call a callback function you specify. It works this magic by appending a new <script> tag dynamically to the document.

You may right now be thinking, "Oh! Cool! I can do cross-domain Ajax with this!" and that is indeed true. However, there's no need for that black magic, as you'll see in a project a few chapters from now.

■ **Note** Since, at the time of this writing, there is no way to package a prepopulated database with an application, this provides a decent way to load data only the first time the application is loaded. You would have some code that launches at startup that checks the database. If the initial data isn't there, then you use this method to load a JavaScript file that contains the data to load (maybe in arrays, for example). This would occur only the first time, so the application doesn't incur the cost of loading the JavaScript file each time.

This method accepts three arguments. The first is the path to the source file. The second is the callback function to execute (and it will be called whether loading is successful or fails), and the third is the document to add the script to (the default is the global document, which will typically be exactly what you want it to be).

Mojo.Char

The Mojo.Char package contains some useful constants and methods for dealing with keypress events. For example, although not listed in the documentation, by exploring the source code (it's the keycodes.js file if you're looking for it in the SDK's Mojo framework source code directory structure), you'll find there are a large number of constants defined, such as Mojo.Char.v, Mojo.Char leftArrow, Mojo.Char.sym, and Mojo.Char.period, all having values corresponding to the key codes of those keys. This allows you to identify the key that was pressed in an event handler.

Also in Mojo.Char we find the Mojo.Char.isDeleteKey() method, which accepts a key value (like what's passed to your event handled when a key is pressed) to determine whether it is the Delete key. Likewise, there is a Mojo.Char.isEnterKey() method to check for the Enter key.

This is a simple package, but it saves you the hassle of trying to figure out key codes and come up with your own constants (to be honest, this was a mistake I made early on in my own code before I noticed the Mojo.Char package!).

Mojo.Controller

The Mojo.Controller package is where you find the controllers we've touched on thus far. Recall that your scene assistant gets a reference to the scene controller instance that controls the scene, and I mentioned that there is also an app controller that controls the entire application and a stage controller tied to the stage.

Those controllers live in this package, and we'll look at each individually because there is quite a bit of functionality within them.

Before that, though, I want to touch on a couple of methods that stand alone in this package. The first, Mojo.Controller.errorDialog(), allows you to display a pop-up dialog box with an error message. It's as easy as calling this:

```
Mojo.Controller.errorDialog("An error occurred");
```
The dialog box will have the title Error, and the message you pass to this method will be displayed with a single OK button for the user to tap that dismisses the dialog box.

If you instead need the user to make a decision in response to an error, you can use the Mojo.Controller.showAlertDialog() method:

```
Mojo.Controller.showAlertDialog({
```

```
  onChoose : function(value) {
    if (value == "1") {
      // Do something
    } else {
      // Do something else
    }
  },
  title : "What do you want to do?",
  message : "An error occurred, what do you want to do?",
  choices : [
    { label : "Throw Pre out the window", value : "1" },
    { label : "Jump out of a 5th-story window", value : "2" }
  ]
});
```

The onChoose function allows you to determine the course of action to take based on what the user decides.

If you instead want to display a dialog box that is under your full control, the Mojo.Controller.showDialog() method (the results of which are shown in Figure 2-1) is for you:

```
var helloDialog = this.controller.showDialog({
  template : "hello-dialog", assistant : new HelloAssistant(this),
  preventCancel : true
});
```

Figure 2-1. An example of a custom dialog box

This differs from the other methods in that you can display a much more complex dialog box using it. The template attribute references an HTML file in the app/views directory (named hello-dialog.html in this case) in which you can do more or less anything you can in a scene's HTML file. A dialog box also gets an assistant, just like a scene. All of the same methods you know and love, such as setup() and activate(), are present in this assistant too. The preventCancel attribute, when true, makes it so that the back gestures and other alerts will *not* dismiss the dialog box. The code in the assistant must explicitly dismiss the dialog box, usually in response to some user action.

The one last method in this package is `Mojo.Controller.getAppController()`, and it naturally gets you a reference to the one and only app controller for the running application, which is exactly what we're going to look at next!

Mojo.Controller.AppController

The app controller is the object that is responsible for instantiating the app assistant, if there is one, and provides functionality for managing stages and for dealing with banners and notifications.

You won't execute `Mojo.Controller.AppController` methods directly. Instead, you'll make a call to `Mojo.Controller.getAppController()` and call methods on the returned object. As I describe the following methods, and in fact the methods of the stage and scene controllers as well, I'll simply name the methods themselves sans the packaging details as I've typically done throughout this text, since they refer to a particular instance of a particular controller.

The first method available on the app controller is `closeAllStages()`, which does exactly that: closes all stages associated with the application. Note that the application might still be running in the background, but it would have no UI at that point.

The `closeStage()` method can close a particular named staged, the name of which you pass into it.

If you need to create a new stage and then do something, the `createStageWithCallback()` method is a good choice. The first argument passed to it is either a string that names the stage or an object. In the latter case, the object must contain a `name` property naming the stage. It can also optionally contain an `assistantName` property to specify the stage assistant and a `height` property to specify the height of a pop-up alert. Note that if the stage already exists, then its contents will be replaced.

The `getActiveStageController()` method returns a reference to the controller of the currently active stage.

If you need to know what orientation the screen is currently in, you can use the `getScreenOrientation()` method, which will return one of the values `up`, `down`, `left`, or `right`.

Getting a reference to the controller for a given stage is as easy as calling the `getStageController()` method, passing it the name of the stage you want the controller for. A stage can sometimes take an extended period of time to create (a second or even more). Therefore, if your code uses this method as the application starts up, you are better off using the `getStageProxy()` method instead. This returns to you a proxy object that you can call methods on as if it were the stage itself, and these calls will be delegated to the stage when it is available. Also note that if there is no stage, then `getStageController()` will return null. This is a good way to test whether you should display a dashboard widget for a headless app (I'll discuss these sorts of "background" applications, so to speak, in a later chapter).

The `launch()` method allows you to launch another application. This method accepts four arguments, two of which are required: `appID` is the required ID of the application to launch (this is the `id` `appinfo.json`); `params` is an object whose attributes are parameters that will be passed to the launched application; `onSuccess`, which is optional, is a callback function to call when the application launches; and `onFailure` is also optional and is a callback function to be called if the application cannot be launched.

Managing alerts is another area of functionality provided by this controller. For example, the `removeAllBanners()` method will clear all pending banners from the banner area, minus those already being displayed. The `removeBanner()` method, which takes an optional string naming a category and which your application defines if it has multiple types of banners, removes a single banner. Finally, the `showBanner()` method shows a banner. This method has three arguments. The first can be a string, in which case this is the banner message to display, or an object. In the case of an object, it can have four attributes: `messageText`, which is of course the banner's text; `soundClass`, which is a sound class to use; `soundFile`, which is the path to the sound file to play; and `icon`, which is an icon to display next to the banner message. The second argument, which is optional, is a string that will be passed to the application opened when the user taps the banner message. The final argument, which is optional as well, is the category that the application defines for this message.

Mojo.Controller.StageController

The stage controller is next, and it provides functions typically needed at the stage level, manipulating scenes for the most part.

You can call activate() on an instance to programmatically activate the stage. This comes up in applications with more than one stage. Correspondingly, there is a deactivate() method that does the exact opposite.

A call to activeScene() will get you a reference to the scene controller of the currently active scene.

The getAppController() method returns a reference to the app controller. The getScenes() method returns an array of scene controllers currently on the stack, with the first element being the bottom of the stack. The isActiveAndHasScenese() method returns true if the stage is active and has at least one scene currently pushed onto the stack and returns false otherwise.

The loadStylesheet() method allows you to dynamically load a style sheet into the current stage's document.

The pushScene() and popScene() methods are the two workhorse methods here. The pushScene() method can accept a string that is the name of the scene to push, assuming you've defined it in sources.json. You can also pass an object instead, and this object will contain the name of the scene via the name attribute and can also contain a transition attribute to specify the type of transition to use (one of the constants in the Mojo.Transition package). The swapScene() method is a convenience method that does a simultaneous push of a new scene and pop of the current scene.

Mojo.Controller.SceneController

The scene controller is, in all likelihood, where you'll spend most of your time. Your scene assistant gets a reference to a Mojo.Controller.SceneController instance in the controller field, and through this you have access to a wealth of capabilities.

The first such capability is the enableFullScreenMode() method. Calling this, and passing true to it, enables full-screen mode. This temporarily, while the application runs, does away with the status bar area on the top of the screen. This is called from a particular scene assistant, and it will persist for that scene when it is pushed and popped; you don't have to write code to manage it yourself.

The get() method is a wrapper around the document.getElementById() method we all know and love. Pass it an ID, and you get a DOM reference back. Pass it a DOM reference, and you'll get the same reference back (I'm not sure what the point of that is, other than perhaps being able to write some slightly more generic code, but I digress).

The getSceneController() method allows you to get a reference to the automatically created scene controller associated with the current scene.

The listen() method is a wrapper around the Mojo.Event.listen() method that is slightly more convenient to use. You pass to it as the first argument an ID, or a reference to a DOM node, that you want to listen for events on. The second argument is the type of event to listen for (one of the constants in the Mojo.Event package). The third argument is a reference to a callback function to execute when the event is triggered. The fourth argument, when true, indicates that you want to listen for the events during the capture phase; false means listen for it during event bubbling (if event bubbling is a new term for you, jump ahead a few pages where you'll find a sidebar that discusses it).

The modelChanged() event is one that we'll talk about in more detail later, but in short, it notifies the controller that the model for a widget (generally speaking, the data that backs up that widget) has been updated. This usually involves the widget redrawing itself with the new data.

There is also a popupSubmenu() method that allows you to display a transient menu of choices to the user, but we'll discuss that when we talk about menus more generically later in the chapter.

The serviceRequest() method is also something we'll be looking at in detail later, but in short, it allows you to make calls to the various services that webOS exposes to you, the services that allow you to get at some of the more "low-level" capabilities of the device, its hardware functions, and that sort of stuff. Using it requires little more than a URI to the service you want to call and a JavaScript object containing parameters specific to the service method being called. You can also pass a variable that subscribes you to the service; in other words, a callback function you provide will be called continuously as the service has events to tell you about.

The setDefaultTransition() method is used to set up a transition to be used when pushing and popping scenes. You can also specify the transition to use at the time you push and pop scenes, but you may want a default that you can just "set and forget," and this method allows you to do just that. You pass to it one of the constants found in the Mojo.Transition package, such as Mojo.Transition.crossFade or Mojo.Transition.zoomFade (which is in fact the system default).

The setInitialFocusedElement() is usually called in the scene's setup() method, and it specifies what element should have focus when the scene is first shown. You pass to this an ID, a DOM reference, or null if you want no automatic focus to take place.

The setupWidget() method is the bread and butter of dealing with widgets, and as such we'll see it plenty throughout this book. When you call it, you specify the ID of the widget to set up as specified in the HTML of the scene, you pass it an object containing options specific to the widget in question, and you pass it a reference to another object that serves as the model for the widget. As I said, this will be covered when we talk about widgets, and you'll be seeing a lot of it, so for the moment, this is sufficient knowledge of it I think.

The setUserIdleTimeout() method allows you to set up a timeout that will trigger a function being executed when the user hasn't done anything for some period of time. You could of course code this mechanism yourself without much trouble, but using this method makes it a whole lot easier! The first argument you pass to it is the ID of an element that you want to watch for activity on. Essentially, any activity will reset the inactivity timer. The second argument is the function to call when the inactivity period has expired. The third argument is the number of milliseconds that constitutes inactivity. The last two arguments are booleans that specify whether mouse (or touch) actions constitute user activity and whether key input actions count as activity. By default, both are true.

Note that although you specify a specific element to watch, the idea is that you'll probably specify multiple elements, and activity on any of them will reset the inactivity timeout, so your callback will trigger only when there has been no activity for the specified amount of time on any of the elements being watched.

The setWidgetModel() allows you to point a given widget to a new model. This I don't think really comes up all that often, but it's here if you need it. Just pass it the ID of the widget and the new model, in that order. This, by the way, is the only way you can change a widget's model after it has been set up. Any other way will cause tons of problems in the form of errors in the logs and widgets that don't work as expected.

The useLandscapePageUpDown() method determines whether the swipe gesture, which usually is the back gesture, will instead be taken to mean page up and page down. This typically is only the case in landscape mode, but you could conceivably want it to work that way in portrait mode as well. Passing true means that swipe gestures will be seen as page up and page down events; false makes it register as a back event. Like the enabledFullScreenMode() method, the setting of this persists for the scene, but you must set it individually on each scene as applicable.

Finally, the watchModel() method allows you to set up a callback function that will be triggered when a given widget model changes. You pass to it the model to watch, the owner of the callback function (which might be the keyword this or might be a reference to another object), and of course the function to be called. Typically, this method is used by the framework, and you usually won't need to use it, but I can imagine situations where it could come up, so it's worth knowing about.

Mojo.Depot

Mojo.Depot is a relatively simple wrapper around the HTML5 active records database facilities that allows you to think in terms of objects and not the typical data structures such as tables and records.

Using Mojo.Depot is pretty simple, as the following example demonstrates:

```
var get2 = function() {
  depot.simpleGet("myObject",
    function(inObject) {
      $("divOutput").innerHTML += "Should be empty because " +
        "object was removed: " + Object.toJSON(inObject) + "<br>";
    },
    function() { $("divOutput").innerHTML += "Get2 failed<br>"; }
  );
};

var remove = function() {
  depot.removeSingle("defaultbucket", "myObject",
    function() {
      $("divOutput").innerHTML += "Object removed<br>";
      get2();
    },
    function() { $("divOutput").innerHTML += "Remove failed<br>"; }
  );
};

var get1 = function() {
  depot.simpleGet("myObject",
    function(inObject) {
      $("divOutput").innerHTML += Object.toJSON(inObject) + "<br>";
      remove();
    },
    function() { $("divOutput").innerHTML += "Get failed<br>"; }
  );
};

var add = function() {
  depot.simpleAdd("myObject",
    { firstName : "Burt", lastName : "Reynolds" },
    function() {
      $("divOutput").innerHTML += "Add success<br>";
      get1();
    },
    function() { $("divOutput").innerHTML += "Add failed<br>"; }
  );
};

var depot = new Mojo.Depot({ name : "myDepot" },
```

```
function() {
  $("divOutput").innerHTML += "Create success<br>";
  add();
  },
  function() { $("divOutput").innerHTML += "Create failed<br>"; }
);
```

This perhaps looks a little more complex than it actually is, but that's a result of the asynchronous nature of the calls made to `Mojo.Depot`. Each call has a success and failure callback, which are functions that will be called in those respective situations. Since the flow of the code won't stop when you make these calls, I couldn't simply have done a `Mojo.Depot.simpleAdd()`, followed by a `Mojo.Depot.simpleGet()`, because the second call very well might execute before the first completes, and that would be a Very Bad Thing indeed! So, I create a couple of functions, assign them to variables, and then use those variables within each of the callbacks to execute them at the appropriate times.

It all really starts with the instantiation of a `Mojo.Depot` object near the bottom. The argument passed to the constructor defines the depot, and the only required attribute is `name`, although others can be passed as well:

- `version`: This is the version number used for the HTML5 database (defaults to 1).

- `displayName`: This is the name that would be shown in a UI to the user (this is not currently used).

- `estimatedSize`: This is the size you think the database will wind up being. Although the documentation doesn't say, my supposition is that this will allow the database to be preallocated and make it a bit more efficient.

- `replace`: If true, any existing data will be erased, and the depot will be re-created.

- `filters`: This is an array of strings that objects in the depot can use as filters.

The second argument to `Mojo.Depot()` is the function to call when the creation is successful, and in that case we output a message to `divOutput` in the scene HTML indicating the creation was success, and then the `add()` method is called. If the create fails, the function passed as the third argument is executed, and a message indicating the failure is output (this is the case for all of the depot method calls, so I won't mention the failure callback again).

The `add()` method then uses the `Mojo.Depot.simpleAdd()` method to add an object under the key `myObject`. As you can see, we're dealing with a JSON-defined object, not SQL or database structures, which is the whole point of `Mojo.Depot`. In the success callback, after a message is output, the `get1()` method is called.

The `get1()` method calls the `Mojo.Depot.simpleGet()`, passing it the key to retrieve. The success callback is passed the retrieved object, which we then output to our `divOutput` using the `Object.toJSON()` method that has been added to the `Object` prototype by the Prototype library.

After that, the `remove()` method is called, which calls the `Mojo.Depot.removeSingle()` to remove the object from the depot. This method accepts the key of the object to remove, `myObject` here, but it first takes something called a *bucket*. Buckets are places you can stash objects within the depot. Unfortunately, it doesn't seem possible to add objects to any bucket other than the default bucket, which means that's where we need to remove the object from. The value `defaultbucket` is the value of a hidden field in `Mojo.Depot` that names the default bucket. Unfortunately, since this isn't exposed as a public field, we have no choice but to hard-code the value and hope it doesn't change!

■ **Note**   I think the `Mojo.Depot` package is a perfect example of the sorts of rough edges that development for webOS has at this point. The Palm documentation for this package has some flat-out incorrect information, and I was only able to make this code work by examining the actual Mojo source code. I expect this situation will improve as things proceed, but for now this is the sort of problem you'll sometimes encounter when programming for webOS.

The callback for the `Mojo.Depot.removeSingle()` method makes a call to `get2()`, which tries to retrieve the same object. The message output to the `<div>` shows `null`, indicating that the object really was removed from the depot.

There is also a `Mojo.Depot.removeAll()` method that, as its name implies, removes all object from the opened depot. Also available is a `Mojo.Depot.addMultiple()` and a `Mojo.Depot.getMultiple()` method for adding and getting multiple items at one time. See the documentation for examples of their usage (hint: it's not a whole lot different from the example code shown here!).

Mojo.Event

The `Mojo.Event` package is one of the more important packages in all of the Mojo API and one you'll use quite a bit. It contains two areas to look at: constants and methods.

The constants that it provides each represent a type of event that can be triggered during the lifetime of your application, many of them as a result of user interactions and others because of life-cycle events of the application itself. Some examples include `Mojo.Event.activate`, which is generated when a scene is being activated; `Mojo.Event.tap`, which is triggered when the user taps the screen; `Mojo.Event.listAdd`, which occurs when the special add item in a `List` is tapped, and `Mojo.Event.orientationChange`, which fires when the device is rotated. There are quite a few more, and I suggest a quick hop over to Palm's own Mojo documentation for the rundown of them all. We'll encounter quite a few of them as we explore the projects in the coming chapters.

■ **Note**   I should point out that Palm's documentation does not list all the constants in this package. If you look at the Mojo source code, you'll find that only about half of them are actually listed in the documentation. You'll also see that the source code itself does not contain descriptions of the events. My suspicion is that the constants with no descriptions are things that Palm intends to implement later but hasn't yet or that are so infrequently used that they haven't been properly documented yet. It is certainly true that the events found in the documentation are the ones you'll use probably 99 percent of the time.

All the event constants would be fairly useless if there was no way to listen for a given event, and that's where the `Mojo.Event.listen()` method comes in. This method accepts four arguments, the first of which is a reference to the element to listen for events on, usually retrieved by doing `$("<id>")`. The second argument is the type of event to listen for, and that's going to be one of the previously mentioned constants. The third argument is the function to execute when the event fires. This can be inline or a method of your assistant, or even of another object entirely if you want. This function, when bound with bindAsEventHandler() to a given object (usually the scene assistant), will get a reference to an event object as the first argument, in which you'll find information about the event (in most cases, but not all…sometimes the event object isn't something you care about at all, depending on the event and what you need to do). The final argument is a boolean that, when true, causes the event to be observed during the capture phase.

CAPTURE PHASE VS. EVENT BUBBLING PHASE

Although event propagation isn't a topic specific to webOS development, it very much applies to webOS development.

To begin with, let's define what event bubbling (or *event propagation* as it's often called) actually is. When an event occurs on a DOM element, say the user clicking a <div>, the event first fires an event handler, if one exists, on the <div>. After that, the same event "bubbles up" to the element containing the <div>. Eventually, it bubbles up to the document and ultimately the window. At each step of the way, the event can be handled, and optionally, bubbling can be stopped. This sequence of events can occur in reverse, depending on the environment (in other words, the event begins at the highest level and then propagates down through the DOM hierarchy until it reaches the element that triggered it, which is the last stop). webOS in fact uses this "reverse bubbling order" paradigm.

Any event that is triggered by an element in the DOM of your page goes through a two-phase process to be handled. The first phase is referred to as the *capture phase*.

In this phase, the event is first sent to the document object. It then begins propagating toward the element that actually triggered it. It works its way through the DOM hierarchy on its way to the target element. If any element in between handles the event, it can optionally stop this phase of processing.

The second phase is called the *bubbling phase*, and it occurs after the event has reached (and probably been handled) by the element that triggered it. The element could stop bubbling at this point, but more typically you just let it go. In this phase, the event propagates back toward the document object, hitting each of the intervening DOM nodes in the process.

Typically, you want to hand events in the bubbling phase because you want the target element to get first dibs on the event, so to speak. But, during the capture phase, the event could possibly never reach the triggering element. That's where the fourth argument to Mojo.Event.listen() comes into play. By default it's false, which means the event will hit the document object, then hit the triggering element, and then reverse-propagate back through the nodes between the triggering element and the document object. Setting that flag to true instead means that the event is handled during the capture phase instead.

So, to sum it up: you'll probably infrequently want to set that fourth argument at all; the default will usually be what you want anyway!

Because dealing with focus events on elements is so common, the Mojo.Event.listenForFocus Change() method is available. Pass to it the element to listen for changes and the function to call when a change occurs, and you can deal with both focus and blur in one fell swoop. (Note that there is no explicit `listenForBlur()` method because if you see a focus event for an element, you intrinsically know a blur just occurred on the element that previously had focus.)

Similarly, the `Mojo.Event.listenForHoldEvent()` method can be called to listen for holds. This works with a timer in the background such that if the user lifts their finger before the timer expires, then your callback will not be called because this is not considered a hold event. Pass to this method the element to listen to, the type of down event to initiate the timer, the type of up event to cancel the timer, the function to call when the timer elapses, and the number of seconds (default of one) to use for the timer.

You can cause events to be fired with the `Mojo.Event.send()` method. You pass to this the element to receive the event, the type of event to fire (one of the constants already discussed), an object containing custom events properties and values to send in the event object, and a flag (defaulting to `true`) specifying whether the event's propagation behavior is to bubble (`false` means only the target element will receive it with no bubbling occurring).

A special form of `Mojo.Event.send()` is available in the form of `Mojo.Event.sendKeyDownUpEvents()` for sending key-related events. Pass to this a key description in the form of a Unicode identifier (such as U+0009 for the Tab key) and optionally a reference to the element to target the event to (if not specified, the current `document` object is used). This method sends both a key up and key down event. If you want only one or the other, use the `Mojo.Event.sendKeyEvent()` method instead, which accepts as arguments the key description, the event type (defaults to keydown), and the target element.

Finally, the `Mojo.Event.stopListening()` method is used to remove an event listener from an element. Cleaning up event listens is a good idea because they can be the source of memory leaks in JavaScript if not handled properly. To use this method, you simply pass to it the target element that currently has the listener attached, the type of event listener to remove (one of the event constants), a reference to the function that is currently the callback for the event, and `useCapture` (which is optional and when `true` specifies it is a capture-phase event listener you need to remove).

Mojo.Format

The `Mojo.Format` package contains various utility methods for formatting date, times, numbers, and a few others things.

For example, the `Mojo.Format.formatCurrency()` method accepts as its first argument a numeric value, presumably a monetary amount, and as the second argument either a number, which will be the number of places after the decimal point, or an object. In the case of an object, it can have two attributes: `fractionDigits`, which is the number of places after the decimal point, and `countryCode`, which is a two-letter IETF/ISO 639 code for a country/region that specifies the formatting to use (otherwise, the current locale is used to do this formatting).

The `Mojo.Format.formatDate()` method returns a string representation of a `Date` object and thus takes in a `Date` object as its first argument, and as its second argument it takes either a string or an object. If it's a string, then it must be one of the values short, medium, long, full, or default, which specifies the date format to use. If it's an object, then a number of attributes can be present: date and time, which takes one of the values mentioned earlier to specify the format to use for date and/or time (if only one is specified, then only a date or time will be returned); the format attribute, which acts like setting date and time to the same value; or countryCode, which is a country code as described in the `Mojo.Format.formatCurrency()` method description.

The `Mojo.Format.formatNumber()` method converts a number into a string using options you specify. The first argument is the number to format, and the second can be a number, which is the number of digits after the decimal point, or an object. In the object you can have the `fractionDigits` attribute, which again specifies the number of digits after the decimal point, and `countryCode`, once again the country code to use, as previously described.

The `Mojo.Format.formatPercent()` method formats a number as a percent and returns a string version of it. The first argument is the number to format, and the second is an object that currently only supports the `countryCode` attribute, like the other methods.

The `Mojo.Format.getCurrentTimeZone()` method does exactly what its name says it does: returns to the called a string naming the current time zone.

The `Mojo.Format.isAmPmDefault()` method tells you whether the current locale normally uses 12-hour or 24-hour time. This returns a boolean, `true` when 12-hour time and `false` for 24-hour time. You can optionally pass to this method an object with a single `countryCode` attribute.

Finally, the `Mojo.Format.runTextIndexer()` method is passed a string and what gets returned is that string with all URLs and emoticons replaced with HTML links and images. In other words, it transforms the input string into HTML.

Mojo.Function/Mojo.Function.Synchronize

The `Mojo.Function` package really only has two things in it: the method `Mojo.Function.debounce()` and the class `Mojo.Function.Synchronize`. Let's look at each of these.

The `Mojo.Function.debounce()` method deals with a nasty situation that can sometimes arise when you have a function that can be called many times over a given period of time, but you really want to react to it only once. The term *debounce* is used in this case, and it comes from our friends in the hardware business! It turns out that when you press a mechanical switch, the single, smooth action that we perceive can oftentimes be a series of very small bounces of the mechanical mechanism. This results in a repeated opening and closing of an electrical pathway. Debouncing circuits take care of this situation, and the same thing can arise in software.

For example, as you resize a browser window, a resize event will fire numerous times. However, you probably only want your code to react to the resizing once it's complete. How do you know when that happens, though? That's where the idea of debouncing comes in. Simply stated, you keep track of those essentially intermediate events that fire, and when they stop for some specified period of time, the code continues under the assumption that the event has completed.

So, how do we use `Mojo.Function.debounce()` to do this? Here's a very simple example:

```
var wrapper = Mojo.Function.debounce(undefined,
  function(inValue) {
    $("divOutput").innerHTML = inValue;
  }, 2
);
for (var i = 0; i < 101; i++) {
  wrapper(i * 2);
}
```

What's happening here is that the call to `Mojo.Function.debounce()` wraps around a given function and returns to us a wrapper function. We call this wrapper function in place of the function that has been wrapped. The first argument to `Mojo.Function.debounce()` is a reference to a function that will be called with each call to the wrapper. This is optional, however, so you can pass `undefined`, as shown in the example. The second argument is a function that will be called after some period of time when no intermediate calls have occurred. Here I've put that function inline, but you don't need to write it that way if you don't want to do so. The third argument is the amount of time, in seconds, to wait.

So, let's walk through this. First, we call `Mojo.Function.debounce()` and wrap it around the inlined function. This gets us a function reference by the variable `wrapper`. Then, we have a loop that calls `wrapper()` a number of times, passing it a number. The first time `wrapper()` is called, a timer is kicked off behind the scenes. Each subsequent time it's called, that timer gets reset. So, while that loop is executing, the timer is continually reset. Eventually, when the loop ends, that timer starts counting for two seconds. Once two seconds has elapsed, that means there's been no calls to wrapper() in that amount of time, so now the inlined function is executed, and the last value passed to wrapper() is written out to a <div> in the scene's HTML. Only the value 200 will show up, but none of the values from zero to 199 will, because those invocations of wrapper() are essentially debounced out of existence, so to speak.

The other thing in this package is Mojo.Function.Synchronize, which is a class you'll instantiate to use. The idea here is that if you have a batch of asynchronous calls to make, be they Ajax calls or system services requests, you may have some other function that you want to call only after the asynchronous calls complete. Although you could track this all yourself of course, this class provides all the plumbing for doing it automatically.

An example usage is this:

```
var synchronizer = new Mojo.Function.Synchronize({
  syncCallback : keepGoing
});
var wrappedCallback1 = synchronizer.wrap(someAsychronousCallback1);
var wrappedCallback1 = synchronizer.wrap(someAsychronousCallback2);
doAsychronousThing1(wrappedCallback1);
doAsychronousThing2(wrappedCallback2);
```

Assuming that doAsychronousThing1() and doAsychronousThing2() take the arguments passed to them and use them as callbacks, then when the asynchronous requests complete and both callbacks have been executed, only then will keepGoing() be executed. The same function-wrapping paradigm as we saw with Mojo.Function.debounce() is in play here.

This can be an especially handy trick to use when you're making Ajax requests because sometimes you want to treat a couple of separate requests functionally as a batch, and this allows you to do so.

Mojo.Log

Logging in an application is the bread and butter of debugging. For all the fancy debuggers we have today with all their nifty-keen breakpoints and watch expressions, sometimes just being able to dump some text out to a file, or a console, and watch it go by as we execute the program is the best way, and that's exactly what this package is all about.

Within this package you'll find three constants: Mojo.Log.LOG_LEVEL_ERROR, Mojo.Log.LOG_LEVEL_INFO, and Mojo.Log.LOG_LEVEL_WARNING. The names of those constants also tell you that there are three levels of logging severity available to you: error, info, and warning. Errors are meant to signify critical failures where the program cannot continue. Info is for general informational messages. Warning is for situations where something unexpected and potentially bad has occurred but doesn't need to stop program execution.

■ **Note** Interestingly, there doesn't appear, at present at least, to be any situation where you'd actually need these constants. I assume there are some situations, but I didn't come across any during the writing of this book. Still, it's good to know they are there if you need them.

One nice thing about the Mojo.Log implementation is that it shouldn't slow down program execution much, if at all. There is some intelligence built into the API so that additional string objects are not constructed unless the logging level is such that the message will make it to the output. Most logging implementations actually construct the output string first and *then* check to see whether the message should be logged, thereby incurring string construction overhead that is just thrown away. Mojo.Log doesn't do that, so logging statements in your program should be very cheap.

Using logging is simple, and we saw a bit of it in Chapter 1. You have three methods available to you to print log statements: Mojo.Log.info(), Mojo.Log.warn(), and Mojo.Log.error(). Their names obviously determine what level the message is logged at. If, for instance, you call Mojo.Log.info() but the current log level says that nothing below errors should be logged, then your informational message won't be logged. Note that defining what level your application is logging at is done by changing the logLevel attribute in your framework_config.json file, as described in Chapter 1.

■ **Note**   You can in fact pass a variable number of arguments to all of these logging methods, and Mojo will concatenate them all together. If an argument is an object, its toString() return value will be concatenated.

There are a couple of other methods in this package that can come in handy. One is Mojo.Log.logProperties(). This will dump all the properties of an object. Its signature is as follows:

```
Mojo.Log.logProperties(object, name, includePrototype);
```
where object is the object to log, name (optional) is the name to display for the object, and includePrototype (optional) is a boolean (defaulting to false) that says whether you want to see properties from the object's prototype as well.

Similar to Mojo.Log.logProperties is Mojo.Log.propertiesAsString(), which accepts an object and the optional includePrototype arguments like Mojo.Log.logProperties does. This one returns a string listing all the members of the object, other than functions.

Mojo.Model

The Mojo.Model package contains a handful of utility functions for dealing with data in JSON objects.

The first is Mojo.Model.decorate(), which allows you to create what's called a *decorator object*. In simplest terms, this is a clone of an existing object that you can then add properties to without impacting the original. A bit of example code will explain this pretty clearly I suspect:

```
var obj1 = {
  firstName : "Frank"
};
var decObj = Mojo.Model.decorate(obj1, { lastName : "Zammetti" });
decObj.middleName = "William";
```

If you were to display the contents of decObj.firstName, decObj.middleName, and decObj.lastName concatenated together, the results would be "FrankWilliamZammetti" because obj1 has been copied, and the properties from the second object passed to Mojo.Model.decorate() have been copied into it, and then the middleName property has been added to it after the fact. Now, if you try to do the same thing for obj1, you'd find that middleName and lastName are undefined, thus proving that the original object was not impacted.

The `Mojo.Model.encrypt()` and `Mojo.Model.decrypt()` methods go hand in hand. The first will, using a given key as the first argument, encrypt a passed-in string (the second argument) and return a base64-encoded, Blowfish-encrypted version of it. The later method will of course return the original string given the key (the first argument) and the encrypted version of the string (the second argument).

Finally, the `Mojo.Model.format()` method is a powerful, multipurpose method for formatting data. The first argument you pass to it, the model, is an object containing data attributes to be formatted. The second argument is an object where the names of the attributes present match the attributes in the model, and the values of the attributes are functions that format the corresponding model attribute. The result returned from these functions are added as attributes to the object returned by `Mojo.Model.format()` and are named for the attribute they format with the string "Formatted" appended. Like `Mojo.Model.decorate()`, you can also, as the third argument, pass a object, the attributes of which are copied to the decorated returned object before the formatters are executed.

Once again, a bit of example code should make this all very clear:

```
var model = { firstName : "frank", lastName : "zammetti" }
var decObj = Mojo.Model.format(model,
  {
    firstName : function(inData) { return inData.toUpperCase(); },
    middleName : function(inData) { return inData.toUpperCase(); },
    lastName : function(inData) { return inData.toUpperCase(); }
  },
  { middleName : "william"}
);
Mojo.Controller.getAppController().showBanner({
  messageText : decObj.firstNameFormatted + " " + decObj.middleNameFormatted +
    " " + decObj.lastNameFormatted,
  soundClass : "alerts" }, {}, ""
);
```

The result of this code would be a banner message at the bottom of the screen saying "FRANK WILLIAM ZAMMETTI." Notice that it is all uppercase, while the original data is all lowercase, proving that the formatter functions executed. As you can see, the name of the attribute where the formatted value is found has the text "Formatted" appended to it. The original values are still available in decObj under their original names.

Mojo.Model.Cookie

The `Mojo.Model.Cookie` package is technically part of the `Mojo.Model` package. However, if you look in the Palm documentation, at the time of this writing at least, you'll actually see `Mojo.Cookie` listed. If you tap it for details, though, you'll find that it's actually `Mojo.Model.Cookie`. I suspect this is just a little bit of documentation cleanup that someone needs to do, but I listed this separately anyway in deference to the Palm documentation.

Cookies are a ubiquitous and well-known data storage mechanism in the world of web applications, and webOS provides this support, as one would expect from a web technology–based operating system! The `Mojo.Model.Cookie` package is actually a class that you'll instantiate to represent a cookie.

For example, say we want to store the name of our user in a cookie. We might name the cookie userName. So, to work with that cookie, we'd do the following:

```
var userNameCookie = new Mojo.Model.Cookie("userName");
```

Then, if we want to retrieve the value stored in the cookie, we simply do the following:

```
var cookieValue = userNameCookie.get();
```

Now, this can return null if the cookie doesn't yet exist or has no value stored in it, so we can check for that condition if the logic of our code needs to do so. For example, let's say we want to write a default value to the cookie if it hasn't been set yet. So, we can add some more code after the previous:

```
if (!cookieValue) {
  userNameCookie.put("default username");
}
```

Now, if at some point we want to get rid of this cookie, all we need to do is this:

```
userNameCookie.delete();
```

Note that calling delete() will just clear out the value; the userNameCookie object is still valid, and we can call get() and put() (end even delete() if we want) on it again.

This is a pretty simple interface to cookies, and it's just about the easiest way to store data in your application, so it's good to know about it, especially for small bits of information.

■ **Note**   I don't know about you, but I frankly found the API design here a little odd. It seemed weird to me to create a Mojo.Model.Cookie object and only then read, write, or delete the cookie. It seems like a layer of abstraction that doesn't really need to be there. But, this is a matter of opinion, and once you get past the little bit of weirdness there (if like me you experience any in the first place), it's obviously a pretty clean and simple interface anyway, so I'm not complaining or anything (not a lot anyway!)

We'll see cookies being used in the next chapter in the first of the six applications to come, but there's really not much beyond what's shown here.

Mojo.Service

Although we will be looking at the available services later in this chapter, it is in fact the Mojo.Service package that contains your single point of entry to any of those services. This package contains a single method, Mojo.Service.Request(), and it is that single method that you'll be using to access services.

You will in fact use it indirectly because you'll be calling this within the context of a scene, and the scene's controller exposes a servicesRequest() method that is a backdoor way of getting to Mojo.Service.Request().

We'll get into the details of services in the section later dedicated to them. For now, just tuck this information away in your brain for quick retrieval later!

Mojo.Transition

This package is rather sparse but contains some constants you'll want to know about. Here you'll find four constants to be precise: Mojo.Transition.crossFade, Mojo.Transition.defaultTransition, Mojo.Transition.none, and Mojo.Transition.zoomFade. These constants are used when you push or pull a scene (using the transition attribute optionally passed to it) to specify the type of transition animation you want. These constants may come into play in other situations as well, but this is the primary purpose of them.

The Mojo.Transition.crossFade transition is a quick and fairly subtle transition where one scene is faded out while another is simultaneously faded in, which is why it's called a *cross fade.*

The Mojo.Transition.zoomFade transition combines the crossFade transition with a quick zoom in or out (depending on whether a scene is being pushed or popper). This is (currently) the system default transition and so Mojo.Transition.defaultTransition equals Mojo.Transition.zoomFade (but if future updates of webOS change the default transition, that would no longer be true).

The Mojo.Transition.none constant is used when you want no transition between scenes, so they simply appear and disappear immediately.

Mojo.View

The Mojo.View package provides functionality to the developer for dealing with fragments of HTML and scene views markup. A scene has one main HTML file that provides the static structure for that scene, but there are usually a number of dynamic templates, which are just fragments of HTML, used to render dynamic content into the scene (as items in a List widget, for example). There are also some basic bits of functionality that a developer may need access to in order to manipulate the view, and this is what you'll find in this package.

For example, the Mojo.View.advanceFocus() method can automatically set focus on the next focusable element within a given container. Feed to this method a reference to the containing element, and focus will be advanced (or set on the first focusable element if none currently has focus). Related to this is Mojo.View.makeFocusable(), which also receives a reference to an element, and it makes it a focusable element by adding a tabindex value of zero to it. The Mojo.View.makeNotFocusable() method removes that tabindex value, thereby making the element not able to automatically have focus. There is also a Mojo.View.getFocusableList() that, when passed an element reference, returns a list of all its children that are focusable. Finally, Mojo.View.getFocusedElement() returns to you a reference to the element that currently has focus within a specified container element.

The Mojo.View.convertToNode() method takes in a string of HTML and returns to you a DOM element created from "rendering" that node (virtually rendering it; nothing gets put on the screen by calling this method). If the HTML you pass in results in more than one element being created, that is, <div><div>Hello</div></div>, then only the top-level element, the first <div> here, for example, is returned. By contrast, the Mojo.View.convertToNodeList() returns a list of nodes from a string of markup.

The Mojo.View.render() method is a workhorse that allows you to generate HTML based on a template and some dynamic data to insert into it. For example, say you have an HTML file in your views directory named myTemplate.html. To render its HTML with data inserted into it, you could call the following:

```
var content = Mojo.View.render({ object : { firstName : "John", lastName : "Sheridan" },
  template: "myTemplate"})
$("someElement").innerHTML = content;
```

The call to Mojo.View.render() reads in the template file and then inserts into it the data found in the object pointed to by the object attribute. This uses replacement tokens in the template in the form #{firstName} to know where to insert the data. The content generated by this call can then be inserted into the DOM, as shown.

The object passed to Mojo.View.render() defines options for the call. The object attribute is the object to pull the data from. You can also pass an attributes attribute, which will be used to provide data when a given token name isn't found in object. You can also pass an array of formatter functions to format the attributes before insertion (see the discussion of Mojo.Model.format() for an explanation of this). The template attribute is of course the path to the template to use. You can also pass an attribute named collection, which will be an array of objects (like the object attribute). In this case, each of the objects in collection is processed against the template, and all of the individual resultant bits of markup are concatenated together and returned. Related to this is separator, which specifies another template to use to render markup between each item of the collections array (that is, you could render an <hr> element between each <div> generated by the processing).

The method Mojo.Event.visible() returns true if the element passed to it is visible (as well as all its ancestors), false otherwise.

Finally, there is the Mojo.Event.requiresProperties() method. You pass to this method a reference to an element, a target object with properties to check for, and another object with property names. So, given that DOM element and a target object, the element will be hidden if the value of any of the named properties in the third argument object is undefined or has a value of false in the target object.

Mojo.Widget

The Mojo.Widget package is naturally where all the UI widgets live. This deserves its own larger section, though, and that's where we're headed next.

Building a User Interface: Widgets

Although each widget has its own config options, they all follow a general outline that I'll, uh, *outline*, here! In Chapter 1 you saw how simple Button and TextField widgets could be added to a scene's layout HTML as a plain old <div> and then set up, transformed if you will, into a webOS widget by virtue of some JavaScript. As it happens, all the widgets follow that same basic idea. What's more, all of them follow another basic pattern: they each have config options and a model, and they (usually) have event handlers hooked up to them.

In code, the basic skeleton is this:

```
this.controller.setupWidget("AAA",
  { /*Config Options*/ },
  { /*Model*/ }
);
Mojo.Event.listen(this.controller.get("AAA"),
  Mojo.Event.BBB,this.CCC.bind(this)
);
```

With this basic structure, you can get any widget to work. The value AAA is the ID of the <div> tag in the scene's HTML, and BBB is one of the event constants for the event you want to listen for. Note here that I'm showing the config options object and the model objects inline, but more typically the model will be either global-scoped or, more usually, a member of the scene assistant class this widget is set up in so that you can get the value of a widget easily from the code for the scene. Likewise, although I show the event callback function as a member of the scene assistant class, you'll sometimes want to just put it inline in the Mojo.Event.listen() method call. For me, that decision comes down to how much code we're talking about, for the most part. If it's really just a line or two of code, putting it inline doesn't hurt my head much. Anything more substantial, and I'll tend to externalize it. Also, I'm more likely to use inline code when doesn't need access to members of the scene assistant. In the end, though, this decision is yours to make and is largely a matter of style (although most developers, I think it's safe to say, will find it cleaner style-wise to have the handler outside the Mojo.Event.listen() call).

For the reason that this basic skeleton is so ubiquitous when setting up widgets, from here on out I'll only show instances where a given widget deviates from this skeleton in a significant way. Otherwise, you can take the previous snippet of code and happily go off setting up widgets to your heart's content (with the help of the widget descriptions to follow, or the Mojo documentation itself, to give you the specific config options, model attributes, events, and methods for the widget in question).

Also as we saw in Chapter 1, the x-mojo-element attribute on the <div> is the key to letting Mojo know this <div> is to be a widget. Each of the widgets has a corresponding x-mojo-element value, as well as a set of config options and model attributes. The Palm documentation spells all this out for each widget and also lists the events that a widget produces and that you can listen for.

In addition, a widget frequently exposes methods that allow your code to manipulate the widget in different ways. You can call these methods any time you want, so long as you have a reference to the widget. You might think that the call to setupWidget() would return that reference, but that isn't the case (although I'd bet good money that Mojo will be updated at some point to do that because it's pretty logical). For the time being, this.controller.get("AAA") is the call to make to get that reference, again passing in the ID of the widget in place of AAA.

As we explore the widgets available, I'll explain most of the config options, model attributes, events, and methods available for each widget. Again, though, this isn't meant to be an exhaustive look at the widgets; it's just a general overview for you to get the gist of what's available to you.

One idea that applies to many of the model attributes for many of the widgets is that you can tell Mojo what the name of the attribute is. For example, the Button widget has an attribute in the model that determines whether the Button is disabled. By default, the attribute name is disabled. If you want to call it ZaphodBeeblebrox[2] instead, you can add the config option disabledProperty:ZaphodBeeblebrox, and from then on you can add ZaphodBeeblebrox:false to the Button's model to disable it. As we look at the widgets, I'll only point out the default attribute names, since in general my feeling is they shouldn't be changed without a good reason. You know you can, though, so if you're feeling a little crazy, go for it!

Something else that is common is updating the model for a widget after creation. This of course comes up frequently, and it's always done in the same basic way:

```
this.controller.modelChanged(XXX);
```

The value of XXX will be a reference to the model that was used when the widget was set up. I know I mentioned this in Chapter 1, but I'll say it again: if you try to point a widget at a whole new model object after setup, you'll be in for a world of hurt! Updating what's in the model and telling the controller that the model was updated (thereby telling the widget too) is perfectly fine, but it has to be the same object. This is because Mojo adds some attributes to the model for internal usage, and if it doesn't find them present during a call to modelChanged(), then things won't work, and it'll usually fail in subtle, difficult-to-debug ways, so don't do it, m'kay?

Calling modelChanged() updates the UI automatically as applicable, so there's no work for you to do there. Notice that you aren't even telling modelChanged() what widget is being updated; it knows that internally (probably from those extra attributes that get added, but I didn't check on that, and it doesn't really matter so long as it works!).

And now, let's get to some widgets!

---

[2] Zaphod Beeblebrox is a character from the popular Hitchhiker's Guide to the Galaxy series of books (and movies). Zaphod shares three of the same mothers with one of the lead characters from the series, Ford Prefect. The direct descendants of Zaphod are also the direct ancestors of his father, because of an unfortunate accident with a time machine and a contraceptive device. Try wrapping your brain around that one!

Button

x-mojo-element="Button"

The Button widget, along with the List widget, is one of the two main workhorses of webOS applications. You'll likely wind up seeing more Button and List widgets than any other kind by a wide margin.

A Button is of course not unlike any other button you've ever seen, and it works like any other: you tap it, and something happens.

A Button can have a number of different styles, as you can see in Figure 2-2 (it'll be difficult to tell on the printed page, but trust me, the last two buttons are red).

Figure 2-2. *Buttons can show off some style too!*

Like all the webOS widgets, you can even make it look drastically different if you want by styling it with CSS. You'll see some of that in the projects to come, but without even going into the CSS, Mojo gives you some nice styling options just by applying the appropriate style classes to it.

A Button accepts a label config attribute, which is the text displayed on the button. It also accepts a type attribute, which can be one of the values Mojo.Widget.defaultButton, which is the default if type isn't specified and makes it a basic Button, or Mojo.Widget.activityButton, which adds a spinner when the Button is tapped. A Spinner is another type of widget used to indicate activity, but we'll get to that later.

The model for a Button can contain a buttonClass attribute that names the style classes to apply to the button. This attribute can contain multiple style classes, just like the class attribute of a <div>, and if you specify a value, you'll want to make sure to include palm-button so as to maintain the basic Button styling. You can then add affirmative to make the button green or negative to make it red, which are standard webOS styles for Button widgets and should be used to help indicate the function of the Button (in other words, a red Button might be appropriate for an action that is permanent, like a deletion of some sort). The disabled attribute, when true, will make the Button unreactive to user interaction and will have a slightly different look to it to indicate this.

CheckBox

x-mojo-element=" CheckBox"

A CheckBox is a way for a user to make a yes/no decision on a specific option, something like "Are you married?" Figure 2-3 shows this pretty ubiquitous UI widget.

Figure 2-3. A CheckBox by any other name is…a CheckBox!

The CheckBox's config options include the trueValue and falseValue attributes, which tell what values will be found in the model's value member when the CheckBox is selected or not, respectively. The model has value and disabled, nothing more.

The only event the CheckBox triggers is Mojo.Event.propertyChanged, and this is the case for many of the widgets. The event object passed to your callback will include a value attribute with trueValue or falseValue in it, plus a model attribute that is a reference to the CheckBox's model supplied when the widget was set up.

The CheckBox exposes no method, so that, my friend, is just about all there is to a CheckBox!

ToggleButton

x-mojo-element=" ToggleButton"

The ToggleButton widget is another take on a check box that is, to most people I suspect, a more visually pleasing UI metaphor. It's really designed specifically for on/off decisions, while a CheckBox can be applied to other binary decisions. Figure 2-4 shows an example of the ToggleButton widget. As you can see, it visually models a physical toggle button, making it a conceptually nice UI metaphor for a user because its usage is pretty self-evident.[3]

---

[3] Unless you're living in Amish country and don't have electricity, in which case it won't be so obvious…oh, and I suspect you aren't reading this book in that case either!

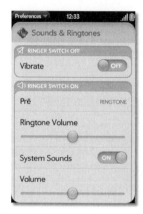

Figure 2-4. *The* `ToggleButton`*: the vibrate option was before it, before it was against it.*

The `ToggleButton` has many of the same config options as the `CheckBox` does. In addition to the `trueValue` and `falseValue` options, there are also `trueLabel` and `falseLabel` options, which let you have text other than the default "on" and "off" (so, although I said this widget is really kind of meant for on/off decisions, clearly you aren't limited to that).

Aside from those, the config options, as well as the model attributes, events (`Mojo.Event.propertyChanged`), and methods (none), are the same as `CheckBox`, and you work with a `ToggleButton` the same basic way.

RadioButton
x-mojo-element=" RadioButton"
A `RadioButton` is a group of mutually exclusive options that the user must choose from. When one option is selected by a tap, the others are deselected. In Figure 2-5 you can get an idea of what this looks like.

Figure 2-5. *The* `RadioButton`*, shown given an answer typical of your spouse*

The config options for a RadioButton, most importantly, has a choices attribute. This is an array in the following form:

```
[
  { label : "YES", value : "1" },
  { label : "NO", value : "2" },
  { label : "MAYBE", value : "3" },
]
```

The values can be anything you like and any type. In the model you have the usual value and disabled attributes, with value being one of the values from choices. The Mojo.Event.propertyChanged event is fired as usual, providing you the value in the incoming event, as well as a reference to the model. No methods are exposed for this widget.

ListSelector

RadioButton and CheckBox widgets are great when you have a simple binary choice for the user to make, but oftentimes they really need to choose from a number of options. In such a situation, the ListSelector might be a good choice (I say "might" because there's the List widget too, but we'll get to that later). You can see the ListSelector in Figure 2-6. There are four of them showing there: STATUS, TRANSPORT, WORK, and TEST.

Figure 2-6. *The ListSelector widget, in all its glory*

Each of them has a current value: Away, m1ghtyat0m, Assiduous, and sun-cmd, correspondingly. The user interacts with it by clicking the label, which is the text with the arrow next to it, and a list of options pops up. The user then checks off the option they want to set for that item. This list can scroll if there are too many options to display.

Just like the RadioButton, a ListSelector's config options include a choices array attribute, and it uses the same form as the RadioButton. In addition, the multiline option, when true, means that long choices will wrap rather than being truncated at the edge of the pop-up list.

Interestingly, you can have choices in both the config options as well as the model for the widget. The documentation says that if the choices can change after the ListSelector is set up, then you should use the model; otherwise, they should go in the config options, and I dare say that makes perfect sense! Beyond that, you have the usual value and disabled model attributes to deal with.

The usual Mojo.Event.propertyChanged event is present here, and like many other widgets, there are no methods to call on a ListSelector.

DatePicker

x-mojo-element=" DatePicker"

The DatePicker widget is a very nice webOS-specific UI element for selecting a date, specifically a month, a day, and a year. It breaks the date up into those three components and allows the user to select each and choose from a list, avoiding them having to type anything. Figure 2-7 shows this widget. The first part shows the DatePicker as it appears initially, and the subsequent three images show each of the three components of it being tapped to reveal the selection list (which can be scrolled by dragging to reveal more options).

Figure 2-7. *<lowBrowHumor>Pick a date, not your nose, with the DatePicker</lowBrowHumor>*

The DatePicker's config options include a labelPlacement attribute. This impacts the DATE text you see on the left (which you specify via the aptly named label attribute). The value of labelPlacement can be Mojo.Widget.labelPlacementLeft or Mojo.Widget.labelPlacementRight to put the text to the left or to the right of the DatePicker. The month, day, and year attributes allow you to specify whether those components of the DatePicker will be displayed. All three by default are set to true.

In the model you'll find a single date attribute that is a JavaScript Date object. You can set this initially (or after the fact) to populate the DatePicker with the specified date.

Mojo.Event.propertyChanged is the only event this widget fires, like the CheckBox. Also like the CheckBox, there are no methods for you to call.

TimePicker

x-mojo-element=" TimePicker"

The TimePicker is just like the DatePicker but is obviously for selecting times! In Figure 2-8 you can clearly see the similarity and that the method of interaction is the same.

Figure 2-8. TimePicker: picking the time, not your...ah, never mind

As for as coding it, the config options include the same `label` and `labelPlacement` attributes as for the `DatePicker`, but of course the `month`, `day`, and `year` attributes are *not* present. What you'll find in their place, though, is a `minuteInterval` attribute, which defines the interval seen between the selections in the list (5 by default).

In the model you'll find a `time` attribute, as opposed to `date` for the `DatePicker`. However, just like the `DatePicker`, it's a JavaScript `Date` object. Obviously, everything but the time component is ignored.

No methods are exposed by this widget for you to call, and the usual `Mojo.Event.propertyChanged` is the only event fired by it.

IntegerPicker
x-mojo-element=" IntegerPicker"
The `IntegerPicker` widget is essentially a single field of a `DatePicker` but made generic for selecting a number. Similarly, though, you tap the field, a list appears, and the user can scroll it and ultimately make a selection. Figure 2-9 shows this widget as it initially displays and then what the user sees when they tap it.

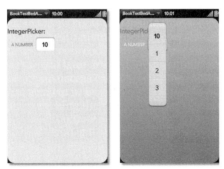

Figure 2-9. The IntegerPicker, when typing a number is simply too hard

Working with an `IntegerPicker` is child's play. Its `label` and `labelPlacement` config options work just like those of the `DatePicker`. The `min` and `max` config options allow you to set the low and high bounds from which the user can choose, and the `padNumbers` option, when `true`, will pad out numbers so that they are always the same number of digits as the largest allowable number (so, 001, 050, and 500 if min is 1 and max is 500, for example); false (the default) will not.

The Mojo.Event.propertyChanged event is again present, as is the value attribute in the model. Like the DatePicker again, no methods are callable on an IntegerPicker.

List

x-mojo-element=" List"

The List widget is one of, and possibly *the*, most powerful and often-used widget in the webOS arsenal. Palm's webOS was in a sense designed with the List widget in mind because of its interaction method. A List can be scrolled by flicking up or down on it, and that scrolling obeys the laws of physics, inertia specifically, so it's a very rich and obvious way for a user to look at a list of information.

Figure 2-10 shows a couple of examples of a List. The first is a basic List, the second shows that you can make a List much more robust because you can specify a template to use for rendering each item and therefore you can make it look however you like, and the third shows that the List can have other widgets nested within it, which makes it extremely powerful since you can edit items in place, and more.

Figure 2-10. The much-loved, oft-overworked List *widget, shown in three different flavors*

A List can have static data, supplied at the time you set it up inline with the call to setupWidget(), or you can supply data in the model or dynamically add items to it as the flow of your application requires. The List also inherently supports a method for deleting items, so you don't have to develop that interaction model yourself, nor do you have to build UI components for it.

The applications in this book will make extensive use of the List widget, so we won't go into all the details of its usage here. However, some basic usage information is of course a good idea.

A simple List can be set up with the following code, beginning in the scene's view HTML:

```
<div id="listID" x-mojo-element="List"></div>
```
Then, you'll need a model for the List:

```
var listModel = { items : [
  { data : "Item 1" },
  { data : "Item 2" },
  { data : "Item 3" }
```

```
] };
```

Finally, set up the widget similarly to how all others are set up:

```
this.controller.setupWidget("listID", {
  addItemLabel : "Add...",
  swipeToDelete : true,
  itemTemplate : "myList/list-item"
}, listModel);
this.controller.listen("listID", Mojo.Event.listTap, itemTapped.bind(this));
this.controller.listen("listID", Mojo.Event.listAdd, addTapped.bind(this));
this.controller.listen("listID", Mojo.Event.listDelete, itemDeleted.bind(this));
```

The data in the model is what is rendered initially, but you can add items to the array at any time to update the model if you need to add items. The List widget can have an item at the bottom that the user can tap to add a new item, and you can define the label that will be seen with the addItemLabel config options. The swipeToDelete option allows the user to swipe right to left to delete an item. The itemTemplate attribute names the HTML file that will be used to generate the markup for each item. A very simple example of one is this:

```
<div class="row textfield" x-mojo-tap-highlight="momentary">
  <div class="title">
    #{data}
  </div>
</div>
```

For each item, a <div> is generated, and some Mojo-supplied style classes are applied. Inside this <div> is another <div>, and this is where the data is shown. Here we've used a replacement token, #{data}, that says that the data attribute of the item being rendered from the items array of the model for the widget should be inserted. As you can see, since you are just generating HTML, you aren't limited in what you can do; virtually anything you can think of can be put into a List in this manner, including new widgets (which you'll of course have to set up in your code too).

In addition to these config options, some others are available. The listTemplate is similar to the itemTemplate attribute except that listTemplate allows you to generate markup around the List itself. The preventDeleteProperty names an attribute that will be found on each item in the model, and if this attribute is set to true, then that particular item will not allow deletion, although other items in the List may. This of course matters only if swipeToDelete is set to true. In addition, the autoconfirmDelete attribute, when true, will cause a Delete button and an Undo button to be rendered in place of the item being swiped so the user can confirm the deletion (when false, the deletion occurs without this confirmation). The reorderable attribute, when set to true, allows the user to drag and drop List items to put them in the desired order.

The emptyTemplate attribute allows you to render some HTML when the List is empty.

The dividerTemplate and dividerFunction attributes work together to put dividers between groupings in the List. The dividerTemplate attribute specifies the HTML file that will render the divider, while the dividerFunction references a function that will be called for each item in the model. The function should return a label string for the item. The List takes care of rendering a divider any time the label value is different between two consecutive items (therefore it is important that items are grouped within the model).

In the model you'll find just an items attribute, which is the data to render in the List. This is an array of objects, and the objects can contain any data you like. Your item template will make use of this data however you specify it to do so.

The List fires a number of events, a couple of which you see in the example code being listened for. These events include Mojo.Event.listChange, which is triggered when the data model changes; Mojo.Event.listTap, triggered by an item being tapped as it's passed the object from the items array as the value attribute of the event object; Mojo.Event.listAdd, triggered when the add item is tapped; Mojo.Event.listDelete, triggered when an item is swiped for deletion (and when it has been confirmed if autoconfirmDelete is true) and is also passed the object being deleted; and Mojo.Event.listReorder, triggered when an item is moved and is passed the item, as well as the starting and index indexes in the items array, as the toIndex and fromIndex attributes on the incoming event object.

A number of methods are exposed by the List widget. The focusItem() method can be called to set focus on a given item. The showAddItem() method can be called to show the add item, if you initially weren't showing it but need to dynamically turn it on after the fact. The getLength() method can be called to tell you how many items are in the list.

FilterField

x-mojo-element=" FilterField"
The FilterField widget gives you a nice, consistent UI approach to filtering the content the user is viewing. The way it works is that the user clicks off any UI widget so that nothing has focus and then simply starts typing. A box appears at the top of the screen, as shown in Figure 2-11, where they can enter some text to filter by.

Figure 2-11. The FilterField, doing its filtering best

Each keypress results in a function that you specify being called, at which point you should implement the logic to filter whatever it is the user is looking at. For instance, you may have a list of names in a List widget, and when the user types, you filter that List to only show names beginning with what they enter.

A FilterField has a config option delay, which specifies the number of milliseconds between keypresses to wait before firing your specified filter function (defaults to 300 milliseconds). You can also specify a filterFieldHeight attribute to set how tall in pixels you want the FilterField to be at the top of the screen when it appears.

In the model you'll find a disabled attribute that, when true, means that keypresses will not trigger the FilterField popping up.

The events that the FilterField triggers are Mojo.Event.filter, which will be called after the amount of time that is specified by delay and will be passed the currently entered value in the FilterField as the filterString attribute of the incoming event object, and

Mojo.Event.filterImmediate, which is sent on every keypress and otherwise works the same as Mojo.Event.filter.

Three methods are available on the FilterField. open() programmatically causes the FilterField to appear, and close() programmatically closes it. Finally, the setCount() method specifies the number to be shown in the results bubble on the right of the FilterField. This will normally be called as part of the work done by your filter function (the event handler for one of the two events) to show how many items match the currently entered value.

FilterList

The FilterList widget is a combination of a List and a FilterField. Palm has gone through the trouble of combining these two things that in many cases go together like the proverbial peanut butter and chocolate! In case you can't imagine, Figure 2-12 is what this looks like.

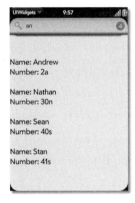

Figure 2-12. A List can be filtered too using the FilterList.

Basically, this is exactly what you would think it is in terms of programming: all of the config options, model attributes, events, and methods from the List and FilterField widgets are available as part of the FilterList widget.

TextField
x-mojo-element=" TextField"
A TextField, like a Button, is a UI widget you are probably already familiar with, and Palm's take on it isn't much different, as you can see in Figure 2-13.

Figure 2-13. *Text entry is made simple (and fun!) with the* TextField *widget.*

For such a simple widget, it has quite a few config options, though! The first is hintText, which is some text that is initially displayed in the TextField but that is *not* the same as the value of the TextField. The multiline attribute, which defaults to false, allows for text wrapping and multiple lines of input, which means you can use a TextField like a <textarea> in HTML as well.

The charsAllowed attribute is a reference to a function that will be called on each keypress that you supply to determine whether a given character is allowed. Return true for those that are or false for those that aren't.

The autoFocus attribute, when true (and not the default false), means that the field will gain focus when the scene is pushed. Obviously, only a single widget in the scene should have this attribute set to true.

The modifierState attribute, which takes a value of Mojo.Widget.numLock or Mojo.Widget.capsLock, indicates the initial state of those modifiers, so if you're expecting numbers as input, you can set Mojo.Widget.numLock to lock the keyboard onto numbers (the user can always switch it off).

The growWidth attribute, defaulting to false, says that the TextField can grow horizontally as the user types when set to true instead. This is kind of the opposite of setting multiline to true if you think about it! Related to that is autoResizeMax, which sets the widest the TextField can become.

The enterSubmits attribute, defaulting to false, says that the Enter key acts as a "submit," meaning that the model is updated then, instead of when the field loses focus, which is what happens by default.

The limitResize attribute will stop the height of the TextField from growing when multiline is set to true and will instead scroll. This attribute defaults to false. The holdToEnable attribute, false by default, will allow the user to tap, briefly hold, and then release a disabled TextField to enable it.

The focusMode attribute indicates what happens when the TextField gains focus. A value of Mojo.Widget.focusSelect means that any existing text will be selected when the TextField gets focus, Mojo.Widget.focusInsertMode means typed text will be inserted where the cursor is by default if there is existing text, and Mojo.Widget.focusAppendMode positions the cursor at the end of existing text and adds new entries to it.

The changeOnKeyPress attribute, when set to true instead of the default false, will fire the Mojo.Event.propertyChanged event (which, by the way, is the only event this widget fires) on every keypress, instead of just when focus is lost as it usually does.

The maxLength attribute allows you to limit how much the user can enter (there is no limit unless you set this to something).

The requiresEnterKey attribute, normally false, will make the user have to press the Enter key when set to true to fire the Mojo.Event.propertyChanged event. The holdToEdit attribute will make it so that a tap means ignore when set to true instead of the default false, which makes a tap on the TextField recognized as the user wanting to enter something.

The emoticons attribute, if true, allows emoticons like ☺ and ☹ to be entered (false by default). The autoReplace attribute turns on the SmartTextEngine services of PalmSysMgr, which by default is turned on and replaces text like "dont" with "don't" as the user likely intended. Finally, the textCase attribute defines the capitalization of TextField. A value of Mojo.Widget.steModeSentenceCase (the default) capitalizes the first letter of the first word of a sentence automatically, Mojo.Widget.steModeTitleCase capitalizes the first letter of every word, and Mojo.Widget.steModeLowerCase performs no capitalization.

The model for a TextField includes just a value attribute and a disabled attribute, like most widgets we've seen.

A TextField exposes a number of methods for your usage. The focus() method puts focus onto the field, and the blur() method removes focus from it (triggering the Mojo.Event.propertyChanged event, unless config options make that not happen). The getValue() method returns the plain-text value of the TextField, and setValue() sets it (note that getValue() and setValue() is the same as accessing the TextField's model directly, and for my money, I prefer the model access method, but YMMV[4]). The getCursorPosition() method returns to you an object containing two attributes, selectionStart and selectionEnd, describing where the cursor is and what's selected (if the values are the same, then no text is selected). Conversely, setCursorPosition accepts two arguments, start and end, that allows you to select text in the TextField.

PasswordField

x-mojo-element=" PasswordField"

The PasswordField is a specialized form of a TextField for entering sensitive information, most usually a password. As the user types, the previous characters entered are replaced with some character, usually an asterisk, so that they're hidden. Figure 2-14 shows this widget in action.

---

[4] YMMV is an Internet/texting shortcut that stands for Your Mileage May Vary. There are tons of these abbreviations in use by the cool kids: FTW is For The Win (usually seen after a seemingly slam-dunk response in an online argument that's nowhere near a slam-dunk), IANAL is I Am Not A Lawyer (what people who have no real knowledge of the legal system say when making comments that imply they do), and AFAIK is As Far As I Know (what I say to my wife when she asks whether there's any gas left in the car and I know there's *just barely* enough to get to the nearest gas station!)

Figure 2-14. I suspect not good enough for the CIA, but good enough for us: the `PasswordField` widget

Since it is just a specialized `TextField`, if you guessed that its API in terms of config options, model attributes, events, and methods is similar, you'd be correct. In point of fact, they appear to be exactly identical! So, we get off easy this time! There are really no details to discuss here that weren't discussed in the `TextField` section.

RichTextEdit
x-mojo-element=" RichTextEdit"
Another form of text entry field is the `RichTextEdit` widget. With this widget you can add some formatting to text, bold, italics, and underlining to be specific. Figure 2-15 shows what this looks like.

Figure 2-15. I wish I were as rich as the `RichTextEdit` widget!

The `RichTextEdit` widget uses options found on the Edit application menu that are enabled explicitly by the application (by default they aren't there).

It also happens to be just about the easiest widget to describe in terms of programming because it literally has no config options, only a `value` model attribute and a `disabled` model attribute, and no methods! Otherwise, you set it up just like you would a `TextField`, and you're off to the races.

ProgressBar
x-mojo-element=" ProgressBar"
Long-run operations require the UI to show the user progress; otherwise, they justifiably get antsy and even wonder if the application has crashed. It's kind of a shame that so many people seem to be under the impression that applications crashing all the time is the normal way computers work, but I digress.

The `ProgressBar` widget, which you can see in Figure 2-16, is one of a couple of options webOS gives you for fulfilling this need. The `ProgressBar` is simply a bar that fills up over some period of time as an operation runs.

Figure 2-16. Makin' progress with the ProgressBar

Using the ProgressBar is very simple. The config options it supports include title, for specifying the text shown on the ProgressBar; image, which allows you to put an image on the ProgressBar; icon, which is a CSS class for displaying an icon on the ProgressBar; and iconPath, which is the path relative to the application's path where the icon is found. Now, interestingly, the default style of the ProgressBar basically nullifies all four of those attributes because there isn't room for any of those things on it! You could hack the style sheets if you wanted, though, and that's why the attributes are supported, to allow you to do just that.

In the model we have a couple of attributes: value is the current value of the ProgressBar, between zero and one; and width allows you to force the width of the ProgressBar to a size you choose. You can also do this as a result of your styles and layout in the scene's HTML.

Actually making the ProgressBar fill up is a simple matter of updating the value in the model and informing the controller of the model change, as was previously discussed. The value is between 0 and 1, with 0 being empty and 1 being completely filled up. There is also a reset() method to set the value back to 0.

The ProgressBar fires a Mojo.Event.progressComplete when it reaches 1. This is useful when you have an interval that is updating the ProgressPill in the background, which is a common way to make the ProgressBar fill up.

ProgressPill
x-mojo-element=" ProgressPill"
The ProgressPill is a more robust version of the ProgressBar, allowing for text inside the part of the widget that fills up, icons on it, and even clickable elements to abort the operation. Figure 2-17 shows a simple ProgressPill in action.

Figure 2-17. The big brother of the ProgressBar is such a pill: the ProgressPill widget.

Programming the ProgressPill is just like programming the ProgressBar; however, the title, image, icon, and iconPath config options have an effect on the ProgressPill. In addition, there is a titleRight attribute, which allows you to put a label on the right side of the ProgressPill.

The same model attributes are present, as well as the same methods, and the Mojo.Event.progressComplete event fires for the ProgressPill too. In addition, a Mojo.Event.progressIconTap will be fired if the user clicks the icon on the ProgressPill, and the typical thing to do (but not necessarily the only thing that can be done) is to cancel the operation in progress.

Spinner
x-mojo-element=" Spinner"
The Spinner is another nice way to show that activity is taking place that the user needs to wait for. It is different from the ProgressBar and ProgressPill in that, usually, it represents a blocking operation, that is, one that the user cannot abort. A Spinner is a big animated circle, as you can see (minus the animation naturally!) in Figure 2-18.

Figure 2-18. Hurry up and wait with the Spinner!

A Spinner can, and frequently does, show up as part of buttons. In addition, you can create a custom Spinner graphic and use that instead of the default circle if you want.

In the config options you'll find the spinnerSize attribute, which takes Mojo.Widget.spinnerSmall or Mojo.Widget.spinnerLarge. Small is the default, which is 32×32 in pixels; the large is 128×128. The fps attribute controls the number of frames per second, which effectively controls the speed of the spinning (the default is 10).

The model includes an attribute named spinning, which is a boolean that determines whether the Spinner is spinning (true) or not (false). To help control this, three methods are available: start(), which starts the Spinner spinning; stop(), which stops it from spinning; and toggle(), which starts it if it's currently stopped or stops it if it's currently spinning. There are no events to deal with for this widget.

Slider
x-mojo-element=" Slider"
The Slider widget, shown in Figure 2-19, is a way to let a user choose a value within an allowed continuum of values. The user can tap and hold on the knob and slide it left and right. They also can click somewhere on the Slider, and the knob will jump there, and the value will change to what corresponds to that location on the bar.

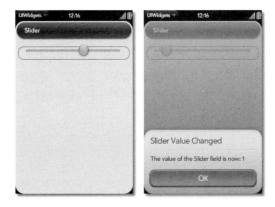

Figure 2-19. *The more you move that knob, the more you're slip-slidin' away.*[5]

The Slider uses two config options to determine the range of the values the user can choose between: minValue and maxValue. You can wind up getting decimal values, however. Simply divide the difference between minValue and maxValue by the width of the Slider to determine the value of each step, and you'll see that it's very easy to get something other than a whole number. Since this is usually not want you want, you can also supply the round attribute, set to true, to round the current value to the nearest whole number.

---

[5] This is a reference to the Paul Simon song "Slip Slidin' Away." My dad is a big fan, and this just serves to prove to him that all those years he's been trying to get me to listen to and appreciate his music, I *was* in fact paying attention!

In the model you'll find a value attribute holding the current value, and that's it. There are no methods exposed by the Slider, and the only event this widget fires is the usual Mojo.Event.propertyChanged.

Drawer

x-mojo-element=" Drawer"

The Drawer widget is an organizational element. With it you can group content together in drawers, very much like a file cabinet. The user can open one Drawer by clicking a button (or any other UI interaction you like or programmatically in response to some trigger) to reveal the content within it, which can be as simple or as complex as you like (that is, just some basic HTML or a bunch of other widgets). Figure 2-20 shows a simple example of the Drawer (note that the Button isn't technically part of the Drawer, although this is probably the usual way you'll see a Drawer used).

Figure 2-20. *The Drawer widget (socks and...other things...not included)*

You can have as many Drawer widgets as you like, and they aren't related to one another in the sense that opening one does not automatically close others (although, since you supply the code that opens and closes them, you could do this if you wanted). Although having a Button right above a Drawer is typical, you could use any other UI element you like, and it could be anywhere, not just on top of the Drawer, or in fact you could have no visual means for a Drawer to be opened or closed and instead do it all through code.

To use this widget, you simply create a <div> with an x-mojo-element value of Drawer. The content within this <div> is what's inside the Drawer. Usually you'll see a Button declared right before the Drawer, but that's not, strictly speaking, required.

The config options object for this widget has an unstyled attribute. When set to true, styles typical of a Drawer will not be added, allowing you to use the Drawer strictly for its hide and show functionality. The content of the Drawer will still be contained with the DOM structure of a Drawer as usual, so you still get the animated opening and closing, for example, but none of the visual styling.

The Drawer widget has no events associated with it.

Each Drawer has a model associated with it and within this model is an open attribute. When true, the Drawer is open, and it is closed when false. You can set this attribute directly and call the controller's modelChanged() method if you want.

Another way to open and close a Drawer is to use the three methods of this widget. The first is setOpenState(). Pass it true to open the Drawer, and pass it false to close it. The getOpenState() will tell you the current state of the drawer (true or false), and toggleState() will simply open the Drawer if currently closed or close it if currently open.

ImageView
x-mojo-element=" ImageView"
The ImageView widget provides a user-friendly way to view an image, or series of images. The user can flick left and right to cycle through multiple images and can zoom in on the image being viewed. Figure 2-21 shows a basic example of this widget.

Figure 2-21. The ImageView widget (if a Palm Pre images itself, does that make it self-aware?!?)

The config options for the ImageView include limitZoom. When this attribute is true, the ImageView will not allow the user to zoom into the image like they normally can with the pinch and expand gestures (that's when they put two fingers on the image and spread them apart to zoom in or pinch them together to zoom out).

■ **Note** There are also a couple of options including highResolutionLoadTimer, extractFSParams, lowResExtractFSParams, and noExtractFS, which I am frankly unable to determine the proper uses for! The documentation is sparse on them, and looking at the code for the widget itself doesn't shed much light on the situation. The Palm-supplied UIWidgets example app demonstrates this widget (that's what the screenshot is from in fact), but in the code these aren't used (noExtractFS is in the config options, but it's commented out). They clearly have to do with the fact that the ImageView supports both a low-res (thumbnail) and a high-res version of a given image, but how you use them I am frankly unable to determine.

What I *can* determine, though, is how to set images in the ImageView: use the leftUrlProvided(), centerUrlProvided(), and rightUrlProvided() methods. The image currently being viewed is always the center image; those the user can flick left or right to see are the other two. Each of these methods accepts two arguments. The first is the application-relative path to the image, and the second is the application-relative path to a thumbnail version of the image. The second argument appears to be optional.

Note that you don't set the images in the config options, or the model, as you might expect. Instead, you set up the ImageView and *then* call those three methods as applicable. In the model there is also onLeftFunction and onRightFunction attributes, and these reference callback functions that will fire when the user flicks left or right.

So, let's say you have seven images you want to show. You'd set up the ImageView and then call leftUrlProvided() to show the third image, centerUrlProvided() to show the fourth image, and rightUrlProvided() to show the fifth image. Then, when the user flicks left, your onLeftFunction would fire, and you'd call leftUrlProvided() to show the fourth image, centerUrlProvided() to show the fifth image, and rightUrlProvided() to show the sixth image. Once you reach the situation where rightUrlProvided() is setting the seventh image and the user flicks left again, then your onLeftFunction would simply not change the images because that's the end of the sequence.

You can also listen for the Mojo.Event.imageViewChanged event, which will fire any time the image changes as a result of a user flick.

Finally, in addition to those three methods, there is also a getCurrentParams() method, which returns to you an object containing the attributes imageWidth and imageHeight, focusX and focusY (the user can pan the image, and this tells you the center point of that pan), sourceImage (the path to the image being viewed), scale (the scale factor if the user has zoomed in), and sourceWidth and sourceHeight (appears to be the width and height of the image with zoom taken into account, so the size of the image as it currently exists on the screen).

WebView
x-mojo-element=" WebView"

The WebView widget allows you to embed a web page in a scene. The widget might take up the whole scene's card, or it might just be a small portion of it, as shown in Figure 2-22.

Figure 2-22. The WebView widget (hey, nice web site, wonder who that is?!?)

The config options object for this widget requires you to specify the url attribute only, The others are all optional and include the following: virtualPageHeight and virtualPageWidth, which gives a virtual size to the browser embedded within the WebView widget; minFontSize, which is the minimum font size that will be allowed to be shown on the page; iterrogateClicks, which will cause a

Mojo.Event.webViewLinkClicked event to be fired in the application whenever a link is clicked in the WebView widget; and showClickedLink, which will style clicked links with a gray background and border.

There are no attributes associated with the WebView widget in the model, so just pass an empty object for the model.

A number of events are fired by this widget including Mojo.Event.webViewLoadStarted, Mojo.Event.webViewLoadProgress, Mojo.Event.webViewLoadStopped, and Mojo.Event.webViewLoadFailed, which are all involved with tracking the progress of the web page being loaded. The Mojo.Event.webViewTitleChanged event will fire if the title of the document in the WebView widget is changed. Mojo.Event.webViewScrollAndScaleChanged will be called any time the page is scrolled or scaled. Mojo.Event.webViewUrlRedirect is called if a redirect is encountered on the page. Other events are fired as well; see the documentation for the complete list.

The WebView widget also exposes quite a few methods for your use. The clearCache() and clearCookies() methods are for clearing the browser cache and cookies, respectively. The goBack() and goForward() methods are for programmatically going back or forward in the browser's history. The setBlockPopups(), passed true, disallows pop-ups. The saveViewToFile() method is used to save an image of the current WebView, and it accepts a file name as the first argument and optionally four more arguments specifying a region of the current view. The stopLoad() method allows you to abort loading of the current page. The focus() and blur() methods allow you to set focus to or remove focus from the WebView widget. The clearHistory() method, like clearCache() and clearCookies(), is a per-WebView widget way to clear history (cookies and cache are also tied to a given WebView instance). Like events, a few more methods are available, and the documentation will list them all for you.

Menus

With webOS, you have two types of menus available to you: the application menu and pop-up menus. The application menu is the ubiquitous menu seen in the upper-left corner of all applications, shown in Figure 2-23. Now, whether there is anything visible in the menu or not (in fact, whether it opens when tapped or not) is at the discretion of you and your application code.

Figure 2-23. The application Menu (mmmm, menu...I'm hungry all of a sudden!)

You set up an application menu just like you do any widget except for the part about a <div> in the scene's HTML. That part is dropped entirely. Instead, you'll just need a config options object and a model, like so:

```
var appMenuAttributes = {
  omitDefaultItems : true, richTextEditMenu  : true
};
var appMenuModel = {
  visible : true,
  items : [
    Mojo.Menu.editItem,
    { label : "Preferences...", command : "preferences-CLICK" },
    { label : "About Code Cabinet...", command : "aboutCodeCabinet-CLICK" }
  ]
};
```

Then, you call setupWidget() with them:

```
this.controller.setupWidget(Mojo.Menu.appMenu, appMenuAttributes, appMenuModel);
```

Your menu is then active for that scene. Each scene can set up its own version of the application menu if necessary, so you can tailor the content of the menu as appropriate.

Note the two config options present. omitDefaultOptions turns off the default Edit and Help menu items, and the richTextEditMenu option turns on the Edit menu items for the RichTextEdit widget: bold italic and underline. The items array is an array of the items found on the menu. The first item here, Mojo.Menu.editItem, is a constant that specifies to put the Edit menu there (since omitDefaultOptions is true, we have to do this to show the Edit menu). The rest of the items are other menu items. The command attribute is the string that will be associated with a given menu item.

In your stage assistant, you add a handleCommand() method. This is called when any of the menu items is clicked. It is passed an event object, which you should check to be sure it is of type Mojo.Event.command. If it is, you'll find a command attribute in it with the string corresponding to the command attribute of the clicked item, and your code can do whatever is necessary for that function.

■ **Note**   There's actually a bug in this code, which is in fact a known bug in Mojo (which may be corrected by the time you read this): you cannot specify omitDefaultOptions at the same time as richTextEditMenu. The omitDefaultOptions setting overrides the other, and the fact that Mojo.Menu.editItem is in the items array doesn't matter. In other words, at the time of this writing, there is no way to have only an Edit menu; either you get Edit and Help or you get neither.

The other type of menu is a pop-up menu, and this is meant for quick, transient choices by the user, usually tied to some UI interaction, such as a button click. Showing a pop-up menu is similar to the application menu but different, of course:

```
this.controller.popupSubmenu({
  onChoose : function() {
    // Handle taps
  },
  items : [
    { label : "Peanut Butter", command : "pb" },
    { label : "Chocolate", command : "choc" }
  ]
```

```
});
```

With a pop-up menu, there are no default options to deal with; it's just what you put in the `items` array, and since a pop-up menu isn't tied to the stage, the callback handler is part of the call to `popupSubmenu()` (whether you make it inline like this or a method on your assistant is up to you).

You can also specify a `placeNear` attribute and give it a reference to a DOM node, in which case the pop-up menu will appear near that element. You should also set `manualPlacement` to `true` when using `placeNear` (or optionally, just set `manualPlacement` to `true` with no value for `placeNear` to center the pop-up menu on the screen). The `toggleCmdAttribute` takes one of the command values from the `items` array and is used to specify that item to have a check mark next to it to show a current value. Optionally, you can use the `chosen` attribute on one of the items in the `items` array, set to `true`, to get the same effect.

Hey, Can I Get Some Service Around Here?

A service is an on-device server that presents to you various resources, data, or virtually anything else that could be served. Any time you access a service, you'll be specifying a uniform resource locator (URL) to this method, along with other information.

When we looked at the `Mojo.Service` package earlier, we saw the `Mojo.Service.request()` there, and we learned that, usually, you will use it indirectly because you'll be calling this within the context of a scene, and the scene's controller exposes a `servicesRequest()` method that is a backdoor way of getting to `Mojo.Service.Request()`.

For example, say you want to get the system time. You can do so using the service at the URI `palm://com.palm.systemservice`, which exposes system-level services of various kinds (we'll see what is offered later in this chapter).

■ **Note**   Note the use of the `palm://` as the protocol. This denotes a local device-based service.

The syntax for calling that service is as follows:

```
this.controller.serviceRequest("palm://com.palm.systemservice",
  {
    method : "time/getSystemTime",
    parameters : { },
    onSuccess : function(inResp) {
      $("divOutputGood").innerHTML = "TIME: " + Object.toJSON(inResp);
    },
    onFailure : function(inResp) {
      $("divOutputBad").innerHTML = "ERROR: " + Object.toJSON(inResp);
    }
  }
);
```

As you can see, the first argument to the method is the URI of the services you're calling. The second argument is an object that contains the options for the specific method of the service you want to execute. The `method` attribute, with a value of `time/getSystemTime` here, is the method used to get the current system time. The `parameters` attribute would contain any parameters specific to the method; in this case, there are none, so we just pass an empty object. The onSuccess attribute is a reference to a function that will be called when a successful response is received. In this case, we just dump the response into a <div> in the scene for display (the Object.toJSON() method gives us back a string representation of an object, so it's suitable for display). The same thing is done in the onFailure callback, which, as I'm sure you can guess, is called if the service request isn't successful. Figure 2-24 shows the result of this execution.

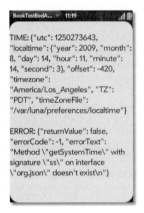

Figure 2-24. *A service request, both successful and not successful*

A third possible argument, which can be a simple boolean or an object, can be used to specify what to do when an error occurs. If you pass true, then the services will be "resubscribed" if an error occurs, which is a fancy way of saying it will be called again after a brief delay. If you pass an object, then it can provide some options for the request, including the resubscribe attribute that, when set to true, does the same "resubscribe on error" trick as just described, and the useNativeParsed attribute that, when true, will request the use of a native JSON parser, if available.

Application Manager
palm://com.palm.applicationManager
As it happens, the Application Manager service is perhaps the most important service of them all, which is the reason I'm discussing it first. This service allows you to launch a given resource, some sort of file on the local file system or a remote resource via HTTP/HTTPS, and have the operating system launch it with the appropriate handler application.

For example, if you want to view a GIF on your web site, a call to this service will open the image viewer application to show it. You don't have to know specifically the application that handles the type of resource being opened.

This service also allows you to launch another application specifically, so if you'd prefer the web browser show the image, you can do that as well.

There are two methods exposed by this service: open() and launch(). The difference is simply that open() will open the appropriate application given a resource, and launch() will launch a specified application, optionally opening a given resource in the process. In other words, for launch() you'll need to know which application you want to launch, and for open() you leave the decision to the OS.

Using either one is just like previously described:

```
this.controller.serviceRequest("palm://com.palm.applicationManager", {
  method : "open",
  parameters : {
    target : "xxx",
    onSuccess : function() { /* Do something */ },
    onFailure : function() { /* Do something else */ }
  }
});
```

The target attribute of the parameters object is the URI to the resource to load. The URI begins with a command prefix, which can be any of the following: mailto, im, sms, contact, chatWith, opencontact, mojave, http, https, data, tel, rtsp, mobi, mapto, maploc, or sprinttv. These commands map to specific applications; for instance, opencontact maps to the Contacts app, sms maps to the Messaging application, and mobi maps to the Video Player application.

You can also specify a file command type to reference a local file. In that case, webOS uses the extension to determine the application to open.

If the command is http or https, the first thing done is to retrieve the HTTP header, and then an attempt is made to determine the data type from that. If a match is found, then the resource is downloaded, and the appropriate application is launched. If there is no header or the type cannot be determined, then the resource is downloaded, and then the extension is used to determine the type. If this still doesn't yield an application type, then an error is thrown.

You can also specify onSuccess and onFailure handler functions as part of the parameters object. What gets passed to onSuccess is an object with two attributes: processId, which is the process ID of the launched application, and returnValue, which will be true. For onFailure, the object contains an errorText attribute describing the failure reason and returnValue, set to false this time.

The launch() method is called similarly to open() except that instead of a target attribute you'll now supply in the parameters object an id parameter, which is the ID of the application you want to open, and params, which is an object of parameters specific to the target application. The onSuccess and onFailure paradigm is in play here as well. The list of application IDs can be found in the Mojo documentation, but just for examples, com.palm.app.browser is for the web browser, com.palm.app.docviewer is for the document viewer, and com.palm.app.videoplayer is for the video player.

Let's look at a quick example of using the launch() method:

```
this.controller.serviceRequest("palm://com.palm.applicationManager", {
  method : "launch",
  parameters :  {
    id : "com.etherient.codecabinet"
    params : "whatever you want"
  }
});
```

In this example, I've given you a clue about something: notice the ID specified? If you were to jump ahead a chapter, you'd find that the ID specified here is the ID of the application in that chapter. Yes, it's true: you aren't limited to Palm-supplied applications! You can launch your own the same way, no problem at all.

Accounts

palm://com.palm.accounts/crud

The Accounts service is a path into the Palm Synergy capabilities of webOS. *Synergy* is the name given to the capability to merge various types of data together into one coherent view, such as contacts from multiple sources (such as your Google address book, Facebook account, and corporate Exchange servers) and e-mails from multiple accounts. This is a big selling-point of webOS and the Palm Pre because, on the device, you see one combined list, with duplicates eliminated, regardless of where the information came from. This capability extends to other application such as messaging, where you can have SMS conversations with a person mixed in with an AOL IM session, and it looks like one continuous conversation, based on the person you're communicating with.

This combining is done virtually on your phone; the data is not physically combined on any servers anywhere.

From an application development standpoint, you can create accounts that can then be used by your application or other Synergy applications. For example, you could create a new contacts account with this code:

```
this.controller.serviceRequest("palm://com.palm.accounts/crud", {
  method : "createAccount",
  parameters : {
    accountId: "MrRogersNeighborhood",
    username : "Mr. Rogers", domain : "www.myneighborhood.com",
    displayName : "Mr. Rogers Neighborhood",
    icons: { largeIcon: undefined, smallIcon: undefined },
    dataTypes : [ "CONTACTS" ], isDataReadOnly : false
  }
});
```

If you execute that code and then go into the Contacts application, you'll find that the account "Mr. Rogers Neighborhood" shows up there.

You could then update this account by using the updateAccount method. With it you can change the displayName, icons, and isDataReadOnly attributes (you'll need to know the accountId value to use this). You could delete the account by using the deleteAcount method, which takes in the accountId and optionally the dataTypes to delete (note that the account, as well as all associated data, is deleted).

The listAccounts method lets you list all the accounts created by a given application, and the getAccount allows you to retrieve an account given an accountId.

Alarms

palm://com.palm.power/timeout

The Alarms service allows you to set alarms using the Real Time Clock (RTC) in the device. An alarm can signal the user at a preset time or at an interval from the current time. An alarm can wake the device up, but by default they do not.

Two types of alarms are supported: Monotonic, which are alarms that go off at an interval from the time it is set in the future (but not more than 24 hours in the future), independent of clock changes, and Calendar alarms, which go off at a fixed date and time and have no 24-hour limit. An alarm will wake up your application, or relaunch it, at the specified time. To make your application work with an alarm, you need to add a handleLaunch() method to your app assistant that handles the parameters passed to the application (which include the parameters you pass as part of the service request so set up the alarm) and then calls stageController.activate() to bring your application to the foreground.

Only a single alarm can be active for an application, so if you set one, any previous alarm will be overridden. If the alarm does not wake the device, as is the case by default, and the device is not on when the alarm goes off, notification will be given to the user the next time they turn it on. Reboots of the device do not impact alarms; they will continue to trigger as expected. Lastly, the resolution of an alarm is plus or minus two seconds, so if you need true real-time accuracy, you're out of luck!

The service exposes two methods for you: set and clear. The set method accepts a number of attributes. The first is at, which is used to create a calendar-type alarm. The format for this value is mm/dd/yyy hh:mm:ss. If you want an interval-type alarm, then you'll instead use the in attribute, which is in the form hh:mm:ss and is how far in the future the alarm should trigger. These two attributes are mutually exclusive.

The key attribute is the identifier for the timeout and is in the form xxx.yyy.zzz.timer, where xxx.yyy.zzz is the ID of your application. The wakeup attribute, if true, causes the alarm to wake the device. The params attribute can also be specified, and this is any information you want to pass to your application when the alarm goes off.

Finally, the uri attribute is used to trigger an application launch when the alarm goes off. This would be the URI for the Application Manager service.

Let's take a look at some code for this, since it's a tad different from many of the other services:

```
this.controller.serviceRequest("palm://com.palm.power/timeout", {
  method : "set",
  parameters : {
    at : "02/17/2010 16:00:00",
    wakeup : true,
    key : "com.etherient.codecabinet.timer",
    uri : "palm://com.palm.applicationManager/open",
    params : {
      id : "com.etherient.codecabinet",
      params : {
        message : "Alarm triggered"
      }
    }
  }
  onSuccess : this.handleSuccess.bind(this),
  onFailure : this.handleFailure.bind(this)
});
```

Here, an alarm will be triggered on February 17, 2010, at 4 p.m. When this happens, the Code Cabinet application (from the next chapter) will be launched, and the message "Alarm triggered" will be sent to its handleLaunch() method. The device will be woken up if asleep when the alarm triggers.

Now, if we want to cancel this alarm before it triggers, that's where the clear method comes into play. It simply needs the value of the key attribute used when set was called, passed in the parameters object, and the alarm will be deleted. Easy enough!

Audio

See Application Manager

An application can launch an audio file to be played by the application associated with it by using the Application Manager service's open() method. The Pre supports many common audio formats including MP3, AAC, AAC+, eAAC+, AMR-NB, QCELP, and WAV (LPCM, ADPCM, uLaw, and aLaw).

■ **Note**   OK, frankly, to me, only MP3 and WAV I'd consider common in that list, but hey, that's just me!

When calling the open() method, you pass it the URI to the resource to play in the form
http://audio-file or http://audio-file or rtsp://audio-file. You can alternatively use the launch()
method instead, which will launch the appropriately application into its starting scene if the resource at
the specified URI is not found.

Browser
See Application Manager
Like the Audio service, the Browser service rides the coattails of the Application Manager service's
open() method. Simply specify a properly formed URL as the target attribute of the parameters object
passed to open(), and the web browser will pop up, and the site will be loaded.

Calendar
palm://com.palm.calendar/crud
The Calendar service is, as I'm sure you can guess, how you work with entries in the calendar database
on your device. You can only access records created by your application however, for security reasons.
With this service, you can create, update, delete, and list calendar entries, events, and attendees.

Three primary objects are dealt with when using this service: attendee, calendar, and event.

The attendee object has the attributes email, name, and organizer (if the attendee named by the name
attribute is the organizer of the event). All three are optional.

The calendar object has the attributes calendarId, externalId, name, and trackChanges. The
calendarId and name attributes are required. The trackChanges attribute, when true, marks a change
made to a calendar so that it is tracked, and a call to the getChanges method, which we'll talk about
shortly, will return this calendar record in its results.

The event object is for a specific event with a calendar. It includes an allDay attribute, which, when
true (defaults to false), marks the event as a full-day event. The optional attendees attribute lists the
attendee object of those attending the event. The location attribute specifies, optionally, the location of
the event. The note attribute, which is optional, allows you to have some notes associated with the event.
The subject attribute is the title of the event (although optional, I suspect you'd always have something
for this attribute). Finally, startTimestamp and endTimstamp are the starting and ending times of the event
correspondingly, and their values are in milliseconds (time since Unix epoch).

The methods available for this service include the createCalendar method, which includes the
accountId parameter (the account to tie this record to, as described for the Accounts service), and the
calendar object to define the calendar. It returns a calendarId, which you will need going forward to
work with the calendar.

The getCalendar returns a calendar object for a given calendarId (you'll also need the accountId for
this). The listCalendars method returns an array of calendar objects of all the calendars for a given
accountId.

The updateCalendar method takes in a calendar object and allows you to modify an existing
calendar. The deleteCalendar method takes in a calendarId and deletes it (you can optionally specify the
trackChange parameter, set to true, so that the calendar will still be returned when calling the getChanges
method).

The createEvent, getEvent, listEvents, updateEvent, and deleteEvent methods all work just like their calendar counterparts but at the event level. Their interfaces are essentially identical; just replace all calendar-related objects with event versions, and you are, by and large, good to go. A simple example of using this service might be as follows:

```
var myEvent = {
  eventId : "123", calendarId : "meetings", subject : "Project Status",
  startTimestamp : new Date().getTime(),
  endTimestamp : new Date().getTime() + 3600000,
  allDay : false, note : "I can't miss this!", location : "My office",
  attendees : [], alarm : "none"
};
this.controller.serviceRequest("palm://com.palm.calendar/crud", {
  method : "createEvent",
  parameters: {
    calendarId : "meetings", event : myEvent
  },
  onSuccess : this.handleSuccess.bind(this),
  onFailure : this.handleFailure.bind(this)
});
```

The startTracking method sets up monitoring of a given account so that you can then use the getChanges method, which returns all the changes to the account since the call to startTracking. When you are all done making changes, call the doneWithChanges method, and all changes to the account will be forgotten. Note that the call to getChanges is incremental until you call doneWithChanges. This means the first time you call it, it may tell you that event A has changed, and the next time it may tell you that event B has changed, but it will *also* still tell you that event A has changed too, so your code has to be smart enough to recognize an already reported change (or call doneWithChanges to reset things).

Connection Manager
palm://com.palm.connectionmanager

The Connection Manager service supplies, currently, a single getstatus method that gives you information about the current connectivity state of the device. This is of course very important information that your application can use to do things such as cache data changes until connectivity is available and then sync the changes to a remote data store, and so on.

This method takes no parameters and returns to you a number of attributes on the response object. One is isInternetConnectionAvailable, which is a simple boolean. Note that it doesn't tell you the connection method, simply whether an Internet connection is available. Three other attributes are present as well: btpan, wan, and wifi. These are objects that provide information about the current Bluetooth, WAN, and Wi-Fi connections, respectively.

The btpan object contains the attributes ipAddress, panUser (the name of the Bluetooth PAN client connected to the device), and state, either connected or disconnected.

The wan object contains the attributes ipAddress, network (unknown, unusable, gprs, edge, umts, hsdpa, 1x, or evdo), and state, just like in btpan.

Finally, the wifi object contains the attributes bssid (basic service set identifier), ipAddress, ssid (service set identifier), and state.

Contacts

palm://com.palm.contacts/crud

The Contacts service allows your application access to the contacts database maintained in your Pre. These contacts play into the whole Synergy framework and so will appear in the combined list in the Contacts application, just like any other.

To work with this service, you'll be working with a number of objects. The first is Address, which has the attributes streetAddress, city, state, zipCode, country, label (0=home, 1=work, 2=other, and in the case of more there is a customLabel attribute that allows you to set a label for the type of address it is), and freeformAddress (but this is an output-only field unfortunately).

There is of course a Contact object, and it has a large number of attributes. Not all are listed here, but here's a flavor for what's available: firstName, lastName, birthday, addresses (a collection of Address objects), jobTitle, pictureLoc (a small 50×50 pixel image), spouse, suffix, nickname, and notes.

The ContactSlice object is a slimmed-down version of Contact and is used when listing contacts. Instead of getting all information for all contacts, you'll get a collection of ContactSlice objects with the attributes companyName, displayText, firstName, lastName, middleName, id, nickname, pictureLoc, prefix, and suffix. Since you get the id, you can of course retrieve the full Contact record to get at all the data.

The CustomField object is used to define custom fields for a contact. It is a simple object with two attributes: name and value.

The EmailAddress object is used to store information about an e-mail address. It has customLabel and label attributes, like the Address object does, as well as a value attribute (the e-mail address itself).

There is an IMName object that supplies information about messaging details for a contact. This object has the attributes customLabel and label, as well as serviceName (with one of the values gmail, aol, msn, yahoo, jabber, or icq[6]) and value, which is the username on that particular IM service.

The PhoneNumber object provides details on a given phone number for a contact and as such has a label, customLabel, and value attribute, just like the EmailAddress object and others.

Finally, the URL object provides information on a web address tied to a contact. This object has only two attributes: label and url.

Moving on to the available services, the first we find is listContacts. Send to this the parameters accountId, filter (which finds matches based on the firstName, lastName, and companyName fields), limit (the maximum number of matches to return), and offset (used to scroll through a large set of results little by little). This method returns an array of ContactSlice objects.

The getContact method is also available; you pass to it an accountId and an id of a contact record, and you'll get back the full Contact object.

The createContact method allows you to create a contact record. Pass to it an accountId and an Account object with the data for the contact to create. Available for this method is also a trackChange parameter, which, when true, allows you to make calls to getChanges, another method available. This works like change tracking as described for the Calendar service. Similarly to that service, there is also a startTracking method and a doneWithChanges method that work the same way.

There is also an updateContact method and a deleteContact method, which do precisely what you think they do! Pass to them both an accountId, an account record id, and in the case of updateContact, a Contact record, and the data will be updated, or the record will be deleted. Both of these support change tracking as well.

To put this into context, let's look at a simple example:

---

[6] Interestingly, at the time of this writing, webOS supports only the AOL and Gmail IM services. I guess we can draw some reasonable conclusions on what will be available in the future (in fact, what may be available already by the time you read this!)

```
this.controller.serviceRequest("palm://com.palm.accounts/crud", {
  method : "listAccounts",
  parameters : { },
  onSuccess : function(inResponse) {
    var myContact = {
      firstName : "Richard", lastName : "Belzer"
    };
    this.controller.serviceRequest("palm://com.palm.contacts/crud", {
      method : "createContact",
      parameters : {
        accountId : inResponse.list[0].accountId,
        contact : myContact
      },
      onSuccess : this.handleSuccess.bind(this),
      onFailure : this.handleFailure.bind(this)
    });
  },
  onFailure : function() { }
});
```

Here, we use the `listAccounts` method to retrieve a list of accounts available on the device. Next, in the `onSuccess` callback, a new contact is created. Although there's a lot of information we could populate in the account object, `firstName` and `lastName` are sufficient for a simple example. Next, the `createContact` method is used to add the contact to the first account in the returned list. Although this example certainly doesn't show all this service has to offer, it begins to give you an idea of its usage.

Document Viewers
See Application Manager

The Document Viewers service is another of those "I'm not going to do any *real* work because Application Manager already does it for me!" services, like Audio and Browser, that uses the Application Manager service to do its dirty work.

Once again, use the `open()` method, pointing it at the resource you want to open, and the DocView application will be launched, allowing common document types to be viewed including txt, doc/docx (Microsoft Word), xls/xlsx (Microsoft Excel), and ppt/pptx (Microsoft PowerPoint).

GPS
palm://com.palm.location

The GPS service provides location awareness to your application. The service provides various levels of accuracy and continuous location fixes for tracking purposes and can even do reverse location, which means it can return a location for a given longitude and latitude. This service respects the terms of service that the user opts into in order to use location services (or will not return data if the user has opted out of its location service usage).

The service provides three easy-to-use methods, beginning with the `getCurrentPosition` method. This method accepts three optional parameters, the first of which is `accuracy`. This is a number from 1 to 3. 1 is high-accuracy (100mt or less), 2 is medium-accuracy (350mt or less), and 3 is of course low accuracy (more than 350mt). The default is medium. The `maximumAge` parameter allows your program to accept a cached position value up to x seconds old where x is the value of the parameter. A value of 0, or not specifying it at all, means a new position fix should be supplied at that time. Finally, `responseTime` specifies how long your program will wait for a position fix. It accepts one of three numeric values: 1 means immediate but no more than five seconds, 2 means between five and twenty seconds, and 3 means greater than twenty seconds.

It is important to realize that a call to this service will usually not be immediate; therefore, setting responseTime, while optional, is a real good idea! If responseTime elapses with no response, the onFailure handler will fire with an errorCode of one.

Another important possible value for onFailure's errorCode is six, which means permission denied, in other words, the user opted out of the location services. Your code should always check for these two conditions and can check for other errorCode values (2 means position is unavailable, 5 means location services are off, and 7 means the application already has a pending request).

The onSuccess handler receives an object with the following attributes: heading is the compass azimuth in degrees, horizAccuracy and vertAccuracy are the horizontal and vertical accuracy values in meters, latitude and longitude are the current location fix, timestamp is the milliseconds value when the fix was achieved, and velocity is how fast the device is moving in meters per second.

The startTracking method allows your application to subscribe for continuous position fix callbacks. It will only fire, however, if the service determines that the position of the device has changed. Using this method is very similar to the getLocation method, except that the only input parameter is the subscribe attribute, set to true. The object returned to onSuccess is new with each fix, and onFailure returns the same errorCode values as getPosition, except that a value of four can also be returned, which indicates that no more position fixes will be sent to the application.

When you call startTracking, it returns to you a handle to a tracking session. To stop tracking, call the cancel() method on that handle.

The final method is getReverseLocation. To use this, pass to it in its parameters a latitude and a longitude in degrees. What is returned is an object with an address attribute, which is a user-readable, full-string version of the address corresponding to the location. Each of the lines is separated with a semicolon.

This service will be used in the project in the next chapter, so if you'd like to jump ahead briefly and take a look, it's fine by me!

Maps

See Application Manager

The Map service uses the Application Manager to launch an application that can deal with maps, which is Google Maps currently (although conceivably that could change at some point, but come on, it's Google, so that's unlikely!).

When you call the open() method, you'll specify the target attribute of the parameters object. The value of this attribute must adhere to the Google Maps parameters format. This is a fairly robust expression language created by Google for mapping purposes. You can find full details at http://mapki.com/wiki/Google_Map_Parameters, but a simple example might be q=pizza&near=52.123N,2.456W

Using the launch() method, however, is probably the better approach. In that case, the parameters object will have an id value of com.palm.app.maps, and the params object can contain some information about the location you want to open, beginning with location. This is an object containing information about the point where you want to perform a query. The attributes of this object include acc, which is the accuracy in meters; age, which is the age of the location fix in seconds; and lat and lng, the latitude and longitude, respectively. Here's an example of using this to search for pizza around a given location:

```
this.controller.serviceRequest("palm://com.palm.applicationManager", {
  method : "open",
  parameters : {
```

```
    id : "com.palm.app.maps",
    params : {
      location : {
        lat : 37.759568992305134, lng : -122.39842414855957, acc : 1
      },
      query : "pizza",
    }
  }
);
```

Aside from location, you can also specify layer, which can activate selective overlays (currently on a value of t, for traffic, is supported). The query attribute allows you to perform a keyword search for information around a given location (although more typically it will probably just be a search term, such as *pizza*, because it's probably clearer to use the location attribute instead). The type attribute takes a value of either m for map (the default) or k for satellite and is the view you want to see. Finally, the zoom attribute is a value from 1 to 18 that is the zoom level to show the map at. Of course, if you don't specify a query, then the map will open around the location you specify, which oftentimes is all you want to happen.

Messaging
See Application Manager
The Messaging service is really just a way to launch the Messaging application using our good friend the Application Manager service's launch() method with an id of com.palm.app.messaging. In the params object, you can pass some information including attachment, which is a path to a file to attach to the message; composeAddress, which is a mobile telephone number to send the message to; messageText, which obviously is the message you want to send; and personId, which is the ID of a contact if you want to chat with that person.

Phone
See Application Manager
The Phone service allows you to place a call from your application or trigger launching of the phone application. It uses the Application Manager service's open() and launch() methods to accomplish this.

The open() method takes a target attribute in the parameters object, which is in the form tel://dialstring, where dialstring is the phone number to dial.

In contrast, using the launch() method just brings up the phone dialer application without prepopulating a phone number. The id value to use in this case is com.palm.app.phone.

Photos
See Application Manager
The Photos service is used to view images in the /media partition of the device. To use it, call the launch() method of the Application Manager service with the id value com.palm.app.photos in the parameters object, and the photo viewer application will be launched.

■ **Note**   The documentation seems to contradict itself with regard to this service. In one place, it says you can specify a target URI to open—point to an image, in other words—and it also says you can specify an album ID to open a given photo album. However, in another part (and in the services example application found in the SDK's examples directory), it says and shows that this service takes in no parameters, which implies you cannot do either of those things! I'm not sure which is correct, frankly, although the evidence seems to say you can only launch the photo viewer application and nothing more.

System Properties

palm://com.palm.preferences/systemProperties

The System Properties service allows you to get information about the device and the operating system running on it. To use this service, you simply make a service request to the URI shown here, use its get method, and pass in the key of the system value you want to retrieve. Currently, the only supported value is com.palm.properties.nduid, which returns to you the unique ID of the device.

Use the onSuccess event handler to get the value. This handler will be passed the key that was requested and its value in a response object.

■ **Note**   Interestingly, the documentation says that you shouldn't use this unique ID to identify a user, and the reasoning is solid: a phone can be bought, sold, or replaced at any time, and if your application ties data to the unique ID, then someone else may have access to that data. Given this state of affairs, it seems as though this is a slightly useless piece of information to be able to retrieve, doesn't it? Presumably, though, down the road there will be other system parameters available to us application developers, so the services itself will be valuable.

System Service

palm://com.palm.systemservice/time

The System Service service (yes, I know that sounds odd!) is a general set of methods that allow an application to access various system settings.

Even though I said it provides a set of methods, at the time of this writing it in fact has only one: the getSystemTime method. Obviously this gets the current time, but it's more functional than that actually. You call it at the URI shown here, using getSystemTime as the value of the method attribute. Then, point the onSuccess attribute to a callback handler that will receive a response object. This object will have the following attributes: localtime, which is an object with the fields year, month, day, hour, minute, and second; offset, which is a number specifying the number of minutes off from UTC (can be negative for time zones west of UTC); timezone, which is literally the system's current time zone (see this page for information on what this value looks like: http://www.gnu.org/software/libc/manual/html_node/TZ-Variable.html); and utc, which is the number of seconds since the Unix epoch (midnight of January 1, 1970 UTC).

Note that onFailure is not necessary with this service because the call will always succeed, so long as the service is running (and there's probably a bigger problem if it's not!).

Remember when I said this method was a bit more functional than simply giving you the time? This functionality comes in the form of the subscribe attribute in the parameters object. If this is set to true, then your application will receive notifications via repeat calls to the specified onSuccess handler, whenever the time zone changes and/or the system time changes by a "significant" amount (significant being currently defined as five minutes). This is a great "set it and forget it" approach to allowing your application to handle time zone changes automatically, if that's something that is important to how your application functions.

System Sounds
palm://com.palm.audio/systemsounds
The System Sounds service allows you to play a number of predefined system sounds from your application. This gives the user some nice audio feedback to events that they should be aware of as your application runs.

The playFeedback is the method you'll call on this service, and in the parameters object you'll specify a name attribute, which is one of the following names: appclose, back_01, browser_01, card_01, card_02, card_03, card_04, card_05, default_425hz, delete_01, discardingapp_01, down2, dtmf_0, dtmf_1, dtmf_2, dtmf_3, dtmf_4, dtmf_5, dtmf_6, dtmf_7, dtmf_8, dtmf_9, dtmf_asterisk, dtmf_pound, error_01, error_02, error_03, focusing, launch_01, launch_02, launch_03, pagebackwards, pageforward_01, shuffle_02, shuffle_03, shuffle_04, shuffle_05, shuffle_06, shuffle_07, shuffle_08, shuffling_01, shutter, switchingapps_01, switchingapps_02, switchingapps_03, tones_3beeps_otasp_done, unassigned, and up2. Note that these names are subject to change, but I find it unlikely that Palm will change them given that people are now building applications based on them. Of course, the sounds themselves could be changed even if the names stay the same too.

Video
See Application Manager
An application can launch a video file to be played by the application associated with it by using the Application Manager service's open() method. The Pre supports many common audio formats including H.264, MPEG4/H.263, and AAC (AAC-HE, AAC-HEv2, AAC-LC, and AAC-LTP) and supports containers such as M4A, M4V, MOV, MP4, 3G2, and 3GP.

The same comments about using the Audio service apply to the Video service as well. In addition, though, the parameters passed to open() can include an optional thumbURL attribute where a thumbnail is displayed while the larger video loads, as well as an optional videoTitle that is the name of the video displayed to the user.

View File
See Application Manager
The View File service piggybacks on the Application Manager service just as the Audio and Video services do, and it works in essentially the same way. The URI you specify in the call to open() can be in the form file://filepath.ext if viewing a local file or an HTTP address to open a remote file. In the latter case, the file will first be downloaded before the appropriate viewing application, if one exists, is launched.

Email
See Application Manager
The Email service provides your application with a way to send e-mails. Like many other services, interacting with it is via the Application Manager service.

When you call this service, specify a method of open. Then, in the parameters object, use an id of com.palm.app.email. The params object inside parameters can include a number of attributes, all of which are optional. account is the ID of an existing e-mail account from which to send the message (if not specified, the default account is used). attachments is an array of objects containing an attribute fullPath that tells the e-mail application where the files to attach are (you can also optionally include an displayName and mimeType attribute for each). recipients is an array of recipient objects that has the attributes contactDisplay, which is the name to display for the recipient; role, which is an integer where 1 is To, 2 is CC, and 3 is BCC; type, which is optional and if specified should have a value of email; and value, which is the well-formed e-mail address for the recipient. Finally, summary is the subject of the e-mail, and text is the body of the message.

You can also, if you prefer, skip all that complexity and instead just include a target attribute in the parameters object, the value of which is a well-formed mailto: URL, as specified by RFC2368.

Accelerometer

The Accelerometer service is actually different from the other services because this service communicates in a somewhat proactive way with your application. Instead of making a service request, your code will instead listen for events triggered by this service. These events include rotation events (when the user rotates the device from portrait mode to landscape mode), shake events (when the user quite literally shakes the device), and raw accelerometer data (useful for games and such).

To deal with orientation events, the first step is to enable your stage to be rotatable. To do so, execute this code in your setup code:

```
if (this.controller.stageController.setWindowOrientation) {
  this.controller.stageController.setWindowOrientation("free");
}
```

When the device is rotated, webOS will automatically rotate your stage. Now, your application of course needs to be able to handle this, potentially redrawing its UI, for example. To deal with this, you'll need to listen for the orientationchange event:

```
this.controller.listen(document, "orientationchange",
  this.handleOrientation.bindAsEventHandler(this)
);
```

The incoming event object will include an attribute position with a value from 0 to 5 that indicates the orientation (0=face up, 1=face down, 2= normal portrait, 3=upside down, 4=left side-down landscape, and 5=right side-down landscape). You'll also get a roll attribute, which is the right-handed rotation around the x-axis, and pitch, which is right-handed rotation around the y-axis (both in degrees).

■ **Note**   This is the first time I've used the `bindAsEventHandler()` method. This is a method added to the Function prototype by the Prototype library specifically for event handlers. It, like the `bind()` method, ensures that the keyword `this` has the appropriate context inside the event handler (as defined by you when you call it), but it also ensures that the first argument passed to the handler is an event object. Frequently, you don't need the event object, in which case `bindAsEventHandler()` is really no different from using `bind()`. Also, in some situations I've found that `bind()` will still get the event object as expected. In short, if you need the event object in your handler, I'd suggest using `bindAsEventHandler()` to be safe. Otherwise, `bind()` will work just fine (and you should be able to always use `bindAsEventHandler()` if you want; just remember that the first argument will always be an event object, even if it's an empty, useless object).

For shake events, three events are in fact involved: `shakestart`, `shaking`, and `shakeend`. These are triggered exactly when their name implies that they are, and you can listen to all three if you want. However, in practice, most times you'll really need to listen only for the `shaking` event, unless you have some specific task to do before and after that. The `sharestart` and `shakeend` events are called only once, while `shaking` is called repeatedly at roughly one-second intervals, so how you use them will of course depend on your needs. The incoming event includes a `magnitude` attribute to tell you how hard the device is being shaken (ideally not too hard, or you may wind up getting a "flew into wall" event right before a "needs to go for repairs" event!)

Finally, raw accelerometer data is available by listening for the `acceleration` event. This event fires at a rate of 4Hz whenever the device is in motion. The incoming event object includes three attributes, `accelX`, `accelY`, and `accelZ`, which combined tell you the acceleration along the x-, y-, and z-axes in g's.[7]

Camera

Using the Camera service, an application can allow the user to take a picture by launching the Camera application. The calling application can specify the file name to save the picture as, or the Camera application can do it. Once the capture is complete, the calling application resumes control.

This service is a bit different from the others because you don't actually use the `servicesRequest()` method to interact with it. Instead, you effectively push the scene from the Camera application, like so:

```
this.controller.stageController.pushScene(
  { appId : "com.palm.app.camera", name : "capture" },
  { sublaunch : true, filename : "myPicture.jpg" }
);
```

Yes, it's true, if you know the name of the scene in another application, you can push it, just like it was a scene in your own application. You simply need to specify the `appId` attribute in the object passed as the first argument to `pushScene()` and the `name` of the scene to push, and you're all set.

---

[7] I was going to use the term *g-force* here, but I didn't want to leave you with the unfortunate image of that recent *G-Force* movie about the talking secret-agent gerbils! Then again, if you're around my age and grew up with Saturday morning cartoons, you more likely would have thought of G-Force from *Battle of the Planets*, which is a *far* cooler cultural reference!

■ **Note**   All subsequent arguments to `pushScene()` are passed to the application and scene being launched, so the second object with the attribute `sublaunch` is something specific to the Camera application's capture scene that tells the application that control should be returned to the calling application after taking the picture. The file name as well specifies the file name to save the picture as, which is optional.

Mojo Messaging Service

The Mojo Messaging Service is a robust mechanism for push notifications providing a mechanism for the device to interact with cloud-based (read: Internet-based) data providers. This service allows your application to avoid polling the remote source for data changes, which can be a battery killer and a waste of bandwidth. Instead, the device can subscribe to changes at the remote site, and those changes will be pushed to the device as necessary.

This service is a fairly complex beast and pretty obviously requires server-side cooperation. Because of this, I'm going to defer discussion of it until Chapter 7, when we'll write an application, including that server-side infrastructure, to use this service.

■ **Note**   It is also worth noting that this service is currently in beta and therefore could change between the time of this writing and the time it's finalized. I think the basics will remain the same, though, so it should be a worthwhile exercise.

Summary

In this chapter, we soared like an eagle over the Mojo framework and explored the API, widgets, and services it has to offer. This provides us with a solid base of knowledge from which to build the applications in the remaining chapters of this book. We saw how to use a lot of it, which gives us a general idea how to use all of it (just the details from method call to method call change).

Speaking of the remaining chapters—the next chapter is the first of five chapters each focused on building a real (and I hope, useful!) webOS application. The first one we'll tackle will provide us code monkeys with a place to store snippets of code…a cabinet, of sorts!

PART 2

The Projects

A computer once beat me at chess, but it was no match for me at kickboxing.

—Emo Philips

In a room full of top software designers, if two agree on the same thing, that's a majority.

—Bill Curtis

Commenting your code is like cleaning your bathroom: you never want to do it, but it really does create a more pleasant experience for you and your guests.

—Ryan Campbell

It's better to wait for a productive programmer to become available than it is to wait for the first available programmer to become productive.

—Steve McConnell

Some people, when confronted with a problem, think "I know, I'll use regular expressions." Now they have two problems.

—Jamie Zawinski

Why are you so quick to jump to the conclusion I'm crazy? That I'm dangerous, I'm out of control? [pause] It's 'cause I'm kinda acting that way, aren't I?

—Doctor Daniel Jackson, *Stargate SG-1*

CHAPTER 3

■■■

A Place for Your Stuff:
Code Cabinet

An Application for Developers to Store, Organize, and Find Snippets of Code

I'm a code monkey,[1] and in all probability you are too (otherwise you're probably reading the wrong book!). As a primate programmer, I have bits of code floating around that I reuse over and over again, and after 25+ years of doing this programming thing, I have quite a few—enough so that keeping them all organized is difficult.

That's where Code Cabinet comes in! With this application, we have an on-the-go solution for storing those snippets, categorizing them, and even getting them out of our Pre and delivered to our virtual doorstep so we can use the snippets of code in our daily working lives.

In this chapter, we'll create our first full-scale webOS application (assuming you've read the chapters in order, that is!), and it's a good starting point because it's not an overly complex application, but it touches on most of the basics and a bit beyond that.

So, let's get right to it and talk about the features this application will have.

What Does This App Do Anyway?

As I began to think about what a tool for organizing snippets of code should be able to do, a number of obvious features jumped out at me. An application of this nature pretty much *has* to do certain things, while others are optional (but that's what the "Suggested Exercises" section at the end of this chapter is for!).

For now, though, I'll talk about the features we'll be implementing and give just a rough idea of what might be involved.

- The user should be able to create categories in which to place code snippets. Categories are the main organizational unit in the application.

- The user will generally navigate by selecting a category from a List (which will include a count of snippets in the category), which then reveals all the snippets within it in another List. Selecting a snippet will bring the user to another view where the snippet details are.

---

[1] The term *code monkey* is meant to be a reference to a great song by the artist Jonathan Coulton. If you've never heard this very funny song, rush over to http://www.jonathancoulton.com/ and check it out; it's a laugh riot for anyone in the IT industry. Jonathan has tons of other great material as well…so, on second thought, finish reading this chapter first because you might wind up being on his site for a while!

- Each snippet should contain a whole bunch of information fields about it, including a name, a brief description, the author, the e-mail address of the author, and a field to store a reference to a URL where the snippet was found. We'll also need a way to enter the snippet's code, of course, as well as some notes about it. We'll also allow entering up to five keywords for the snippet for searching (more on search shortly!). Let's have some fun and make the fields where we enter the code and the notes support rich-text capabilities such as bold, underline, and italics.

- Since there are a fair number of fields for each snippet, we'll use a Drawer widget to organize it a bit, grouping some fields together in one Drawer and other fields in other Drawers.

- Let's provide a mechanism to search for snippets. The user will be able to search on any of the snippet fields, and the search will be across all categories.

- The user should be able to simply delete categories (and all the snippets in them) and individual snippets. For categories, let's use the swipe gesture of a List, but for snippets let's use a Button (the reason the two are different should be clear when we look at the basic flow through the application).

- Let's also allow for e-mailing a snippet, because otherwise it'll be a bit tough to get a snippet into a project elsewhere!

- The application should provide at least some minimum preferences for the user to play with. Specifically, let's allow them to change the default sort order when listing snippets, based on a couple of different fields. These preferences will be stored in cookies, since that's simple and the data size isn't large.

- The snippet data will be stored in a SQLite/HTML5 database, since the amount of data will be much larger than preferences. Besides, a relational database will make the organizational structure of the categories and snippets pretty natural.

Those are the capabilities this application will provide in a nutshell and a general idea of how we'll pull them off.

Planning the Application

Any time you work on a webOS application, a great place to start is to sketch the basic flow through the various views the application will have and also produce some very simple, low-fidelity mock-ups[2] of what each scene will look like. This is explicitly meant to be as quick and dirty as possible, so if you have a whiteboard handy, that's a great tool. If you have some notebooks, those will work too. Hand sketching is a fantastic way to conceptualize a UI without getting into details that can trip you up if you try to think about them too early. Especially with a webOS application, where scene transitions are at the core of how applications work, this approach works especially well.

---

[2] This diagram was done with a tool called Balsamiq Mockups (http://www.balsamiq.com/products/mockups), which is a great little Adobe AIR application. It's a cross between Visio and hand drawing because it lets you create diagrams like Visio, but the components you manipulate have a hand-drawn look. I think this is a good compromise between the two; you get something a little more robust and good looking for the boardroom, but still something kind of low-fidelity.

Figure 3-1 shows a basic navigation model that describes all the scene transitions possible and shows a rough diagram of each of the scenes.

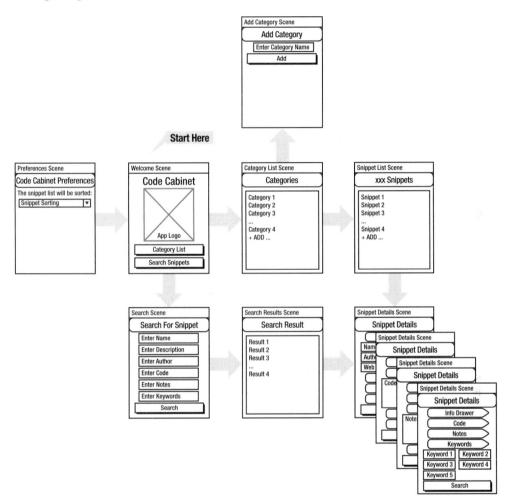

Figure 3-1. *A "whiteboardish" sketching of the scene flow of the application*

All the action starts in the middle (roughly) with the Welcome scene. This is the first scene that will be pushed when the application starts. It has a big, honkin' logo in the middle, a title up top, and two Buttons.

The first Button is the Category List Button that leads, following the arrow going to the right, to the Category List scene. From there, the user can create a new category by tapping the Add item at the bottom of the List, which leads (following the arrow going up) to the Add Category scene. The only flow is back from there to the Category List scene.

Alternatively, the user can tap a category, which brings up the Snippet List scene, off to the right. From here, the user can tap a snippet and get to the Snippet Details scene. Figure 3-1 shows show four layered images here, which is meant to indicate that it's one scene but has multiple possible permutations, such as Drawer widgets, which is the case here.

Going back to the Welcome scene, the other possible flow, following the down arrow, is a result of tapping the Search Snippets Button. This leads to the Search scene. The user enters some search criteria there and taps the Search Button. This leads to the right and the Search Results scene (assuming there are results to display and snippets to search).

From there, the user can tap a snippet in the search results and, continuing to follow the flow to the right, winds up in the same Snippet Details scene as when looking at the list of snippets in a category.

The Preferences scene is off to the left with no arrows from it because this appears as a result of selecting Preferences from the application menu. It's not, as is the case for all the other scenes, part of the application flow, at least not in my mind (which is a scary place indeed!).

I also want to mention that not shown in this diagram is the e-mail application that can be launched from the Snippet Details scene. Since it's in another application, I decided not to show it, but it's worth noting that it would be off to the right from the Snippet Details scene if I were to add it to the diagram.

So, that's the basic navigational structure behind this application and a rough idea of what each of the component scenes looks like. Now, let's get into some actual code and starting building this thing!

■ **Note** Naturally, this chapter is describing constructing an application that already exists and that you should have by now downloaded as part of the source code bundle for this book. I wouldn't ask you to type in all this code! But, just play along and pretend like you're building this from scratch, because that's how I'll generally present it. Also, note that I have condensed a lot of the source code presented here in terms of spacing and removing all comments, just to save space on the printed page. However, when you look at the real code, you'll see that it's formatted nicely (I think so at least!) and has I believe very good commenting throughout. This will apply to all the code to come in the rest of the book too.

Creating the Skeleton

The first step is to create a basic application skeleton that we can build from, and this is most easily accomplished using the Palm-supplied Eclipse plug-in. When you create this project, you'll be asked for a number of pieces of information. Enter **CodeCabinet** for the project name and for the title, **Etherient** for the vendor, **com.etherient.codecabinet** for the ID, and **1.0.0** for the version. In fact, whatever you type in for the project name is automatically replicated into the title and ID fields; however, I personally prefer the ID field to be all lowercase (for no particular reason frankly; I just think it looks better!), so you should really only have to change that value. You could enter different values here if you wanted, of course, but this is part of that "playing along as if you are building the application from scratch" game I mentioned. In fact, these values are what you'll find in the downloaded source code.

After the project is created, you'll need to create a couple of scenes. This is a simple matter of right-clicking the project, selecting New, and then selecting Other. Navigate to the Palm webOS group, and select Mojo Scene. You'll be prompted for a name. You'll need to do this a total of eight times, once for each of the following scenes: categoryAdd, categoryList, preferences, search, searchResults, snippetDetails, snippetList, and welcome. Once you've done that, you'll find that the resulting project structure is what you see in Figure 3-2.

Figure 3-2. The application's directory structure and file contents

For each of the scenes, the Mojo scene wizard has created a scene assistant in the app/assistants directory, and it has created a directory named after the scene in app/views. In each of those directories is an HTML file that is the view for the scene. If you open sources.json in the root of the project, you'll also note that the appropriate JavaScript file was added so that it is loaded when the application starts.

The wizard has even created the most basic code required to make a scene work, so you could at this point run the application. However, since no scene is pushed, all you'll see is the stage. The contents in all the JavaScript and HTML files that were generated will be overwritten by the code to come, but at this point you have the basic application skeleton created and ready to go!

Exploring the Data Model

With the application skeleton out of the way, let's take a quick detour and think about the data model that will back up the application. All the snippets the user can enter will be stored in the HTML5 database facility that webOS provides. This is a SQLite-based relational database with the HTML5 database façade in front of it, providing us with a pretty simple API to work with databases, tables, and the data in them.

For this application, only two tables are really needed: a categories table and a snippets table. Database design is of course an expansive topic, and you can usually architect the data layer in a number of ways. I typically try to use the simplest structure I can come up with, even if it isn't necessarily the most efficient. There is of course a trade-off that has to go on here because if you don't consider efficiency at all, you'll wind up with a data layer that performs like a dog or that has tons of redundant data taking up space (actually, this nearly always leads to poor performance, so the two concerns are very much interrelated). For this application, though, having two simple tables is a pretty obvious structure and one I don't think you could improve on *too* much.

Be that as it may, Figure 3-3 shows the information about the first of the two tables, the categories table. This table is very simple—just one field! The name of the category is really all we need. It will serve as the key value to which snippet records will be tied.

■ **Note** These database diagrams are screen captures from the Firefox extension SQLite Manager (https://addons.mozilla.org/en-US/firefox/addon/5817). It's a great tool that allowed me to simply create the databases and do a screen capture of them. This is a really nice, simple way to get all the information about the table in one place, without having to spend any time drawing diagrams. You see, sometimes laziness is a *good* thing!

Figure 3-3. The structure of the categories table

The snippets tables is next, and it has a bit more meat to it, as you can see in Figure 3-4.

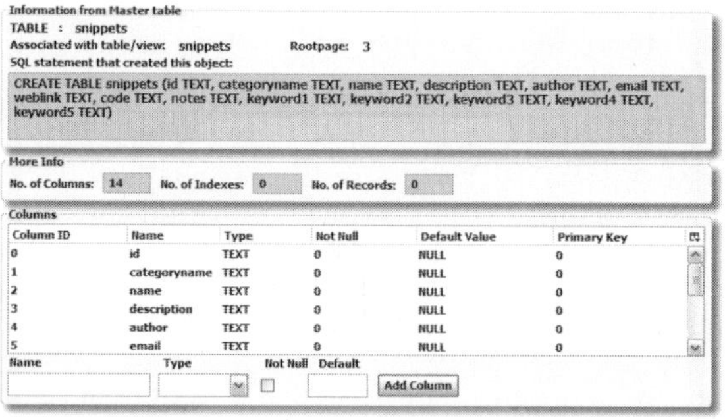

Figure 3-4. The structure of the snippets table

The one unfortunate thing about the SQLite Manager extension is that the list of rows in the table is a fixed height, so you have to scroll to see all the fields this table has. Fortunately, the SQL used to create the table, which includes all the information about each field, is shown above that.

The fields in this table map to the pieces of information to be stored about a snippet as described in the "What Does This App Do Anyway?" section, and I suspect they are all pretty self-evident as to what information they are meant to contain.

Configuring the Application

Three files make up the configuration of this application; two are required (and autogenerated by the New Project Wizard), and a third is optional but convenient during development.

The appinfo.json File

The appinfo.json file is one of the two required files, and if you entered the values as described earlier (or simply downloaded the source bundle), you'll see that the contents match what you entered, as shown in Listing 3-1.

Listing 3-1. The appinfo.json File

```
{
  "id": "com.etherient.codecabinet",
  "version": "1.0.0",
  "vendor": "Etherient",
  "type": "web",
  "main": "index.html",
  "title": "CodeCabinet",
  "icon": "icon.png"
}
```

There shouldn't really be any surprises there. This file contains the values entered in the wizard, plus some default values for type (which, as previously stated, for the time being is always web); main (generally index.html unless you have reason to change it), which points to the main stage's HTML file; and icon, which will at this point have a default wizard-supplied application icon.

The sources.json File

The second required file, which like appinfo.json is autogenerated, is sources.json, which lists the JavaScript files that make up the application and the scenes within them (if any). Listing 3-2 shows this file. If you created the application from scratch, note that your version will look a little different because it will have a different quoting structure and will use escape characters. I've edited this version into a form I prefer (again, not for any particular reason, other than I try to avoid escape characters whenever possible because I think it makes the code just slightly harder to mentally parse).

Listing 3-2. The sources.json File

```
[
  { "source" : "app/assistants/stage-assistant.js" },
  { "source" : "app/assistants/welcome-assistant.js",
    "scenes" : "welcome" },
  { "source" : "app/assistants/categoryAdd-assistant.js",
```

```
      "scenes" : "categoryAdd" },
  { "source" : "app/assistants/categoryList-assistant.js",
      "scenes" : "categoryList" },
  { "source" : "app/assistants/snippetDetails-assistant.js",
      "scenes" : "snippetDetails" },
  { "source" : "app/assistants/snippetList-assistant.js",
      "scenes" : "snippetList" },
  { "source" : "app/assistants/search-assistant.js", "scenes" : "search" },
  { "source" : "app/assistants/preferences-assistant.js",
      "scenes" : "preferences"  },
  { "source" : "app/assistants/searchResults-assistant.js",
      "scenes" : "searchResults" },
  { "source" : "app/CodeCabinet.js" },
  { "source" : "app/DAO.js" }
]
```

Note the last two entries: CodeCabinet.js and DAO.js. You'll notice they don't have the scenes attribute associated with them like all the others do. That is simply because they are not scene assistants; they are just some other JavaScript files that are part of the application. Listing them in sources.json means they will be loaded automatically and we don't have to use <script> tags in index.html (which is another way you could load them). I prefer having all the imports in one place, and sources.json fits the bill nicely.

Also notice that the scenes added with the wizard automatically have the appropriate elements added to this file. That wizard truly does set up the *complete* skeleton for a scene. All you have to do is push the scene, and it'll work, thanks to the work done by the wizard.

The framework_config.json File

The final file, which has to be manually added to the root of the project, is framework_config.json. This one is entirely optional, and the New Project Wizard therefore doesn't create it for you. However, it does help make debugging and development a bit easier. Listing 3-3 shows the contents of this file.

Listing 3-3. The framework_config.json File

```
{
  "logLevel" : 99
}
```

As previously discussed in chapter 1, setting logLevel to 99 ensures we'll see all Mojo.Log.xxxx() messages in the log file for the application.

Global-Scope Code

The first two real source files I'll cover are CodeCabinet.js and DAO.js. These represent what you might call "core" code, which is code that lives in global scope and isn't tied to any one particular scene.

The CodeCabinet.js File

The CodeCabinet.js file contains a single class, not surprisingly named CodeCabinet, that contains some code needed across scenes. Let's begin by looking at the constructor function:

```
function CodeCabinet() {

  this.sortOrderCookie = new Mojo.Model.Cookie("CodeCabinet_snippetSortOrder");

  var storedSortOrder = this.sortOrderCookie.get();
  if (!storedSortOrder) {
    this.sortOrderCookie.put("name_asc");
  }
}
```

We need a cookie in which to store the user's preferred snippet sort order, and that's what this code sets up. The name of the cookie is CodeCabinet_snippetSortOrder, so we create a new Mojo.Model.Cookie using that name. The get() method is then called on that object to find out what sort order was previously set by the user. If that method call returns null, then the if statement is hit, and we call put(), passing it a default value name_asc, meaning sort the snippets by name in ascending order.

Next, we have some code that sets up your application menu:

```
this.appMenuAttributes = { richTextEditMenu  : true };
this.appMenuModel = {
  items : [
    { label : "About Code Cabinet...", command : "aboutCodeCabinet-TAP" }
  ]
};
```

The richTextEditMenu attribute in the object containing the options for the menu, when set to true as it is here, adds the Bold, Italic, and Underline options to the Edit menu so that when the user is entering code or notes about a snippet, they can use those rich-text features. (Note that those items are disabled unless focus is on a RichTextEdit widget, and they are enabled automatically in that situation.) The model for the menu includes a new item, About Code Cabinet. The command attribute specifies the string that will be passed to the menu event handler so we can tell that the user tapped that option.

Figure 3-5 shows what the application menu looks like given this set of configuration information. It's just a standard webOS application menu, with the addition of the About Code Cabinet option.

Figure 3-5. The glorious Code Cabinet application menu

After that there are two attributes:

```
this.currentCategory = null;
this.currentSnippet = null;
```

These hold a reference to an object with information about the currently selected category, if any, and the currently selected snippet, if any. We'll see these used later.

Following this is what appears to be (and in fact is!) a model for a List widget:

```
this.lstSnippetListModel = { items : [ ] };
```

This is the model for the List showing snippets in a selected category. This field is on the CodeCabinet object, as opposed to being in the scene that has the List in it, because it is needed from more than one scene (you'll see why later). Although it would have been possible to have it present in the JavaScript file for one scene and access it from another scene, I felt that, architecturally, it was more logical to have something shared in what is essentially a shared location.

Similarly, a couple of other models are shared in the same way:

```
this.searchFieldModels = {
    txtName : { value : "" },
    txtDescription : { value : "" },
    txtAuthor : { value : "" },
    txtCode : { value : "" },
    txtNotes : { value : "" },
    txtKeywords : { value : "" }
};
```

In this case, we have six models, one for each of the search fields, nested inside a container object. This is in no way required, but I prefer having things that are related grouped in some way, as with the containing object searchFieldModels here.

This is the final line of code in this file:

```
var codeCabinet = new CodeCabinet();
```

This of course is instantiating an instance of the CodeCabinet class. The global variable codeCabinet is how we'll access the models and other fields throughout the rest of the code in the application.

The DAO.js File

The DAO class is a data access object (DAO) that contains the functions the application code calls on to access the database. This keeps the data access code separate from the rest of the application code so that, for example, if we wanted to store this information on the server, we could just modify the DAO methods to call a server instead of writing to a local database. Among other things, this is a key component of being able to have an application that can gracefully work offline as well as online (not a concern in this application, but, as a bit of foreshadowing, in later chapters it will be!)

These are the first two lines of code in this class:

```
this.db = null;
var databaseName = "CodeCabinet";
```

The db field is a reference to the open database the application will use. This reference will be populated in the init() method, which we'll be looking at shortly. The databaseName field is simply that: the name of the database the application will use.

■ **Note** Since the ID of the application must be unique, it would probably be smart to use that ID value as the database name as well. I didn't do that here just to show that there's no requirement along those lines that you need to follow; it's entirely up to you, and you aren't limited to a single database either, if your application's needs demand something else.

Following these two lines are a batch of lines that define the SQL statements that are used in this application. These are just string variables, but instead of listing the code, I went with Table 3-1 instead, which is a little more concise and to the point. Most of these statements have question marks in them, which is where data will be dynamically inserted when the statements are used. Note too that all but one of them ends with the GO; directive. I found out the hard way that without that, your database accesses won't always work properly, even if they will in other SQLite environments (and the one without that directive in fact *does* have it but in a slightly different way, which you'll see a little later).

Table 3-1. The SQL Statements Used in This Application

DAO Class Field	SQL	Description
sqlCreateCategoriesTable	CREATE TABLE IF NOT EXISTS categories (name TEXT); GO;	This is used to create the categories table, used in the init() method.
sqlCreateCategory	INSERT INTO categories (name) VALUES (?); GO;	This inserts a new category with a given name into the categories table. It is used in the createCategory() method.
sqlRetrieveCategories	SELECT c.name, (select count(name) from snippets where categoryname=c.name) as snippetCount FROM categories c ORDER BY c.name; GO;	This returns a list of categories, as well as the number of snippets within each, ordered by name. This is used in the retrieveCategories() method.
sqlDeleteCategory	DELETE FROM categories WHERE name=?; GO;	This deletes a category with a given name from the categories table. It is used in the deleteCategory() method.

Table 3-1. *The SQL Statements Used in This Application (continued)*

sqlCreateSnippetsTable	CREATE TABLE IF NOT EXISTS snippets (id TEXT, categoryname TEXT, name TEXT, description TEXT, author TEXT, email TEXT, weblink TEXT, code TEXT, notes TEXT, keyword1 TEXT, keyword2 TEXT, keyword3 TEXT, keyword4 TEXT, keyword5 TEXT); GO;	This is used to create the snippets table. It is used in the init() method.
sqlCreateSnippet	INSERT INTO snippets (id, categoryname, name, description, author, email, weblink, code, notes, keyword1, keyword2, keyword3, keyword4, keyword5) VALUES (?, ?, ?, ?, ?, ?, ?, ?, ?, ?, ?,?, ?, ?); GO;	This inserts a new snippet into the snippets table, given the data for the snippet. It is used in the createSnippet() method.
sqlRetrieveSnippetsInCategory	SELECT * FROM snippets where categoryname=? ORDER BY	This returns all the details for all snippets in a given category, ordered by what the user has set in their preferences. This is used in the retrieveSnippets() method.
sqlRetrieveAllSnippets	SELECT id, categoryname, TRIM(name) AS name, TRIM(description) AS description, TRIM(author) AS author, TRIM(email) AS email, TRIM(weblink) AS weblink, TRIM(code) AS code, TRIM(notes) AS notes, TRIM(keyword1) AS keyword1, TRIM(keyword2) AS keyword2, TRIM(keyword3) AS keyword3, TRIM(keyword4) AS keyword4, TRIM(keyword5) AS keyword5 FROM snippets ORDER BY	This retrieves all the details for all snippets, trimming all the searchable fields, ordered by what the user has set in their preferences. This is used in the retrieveSnippets() method, specifically when performing a search.
sqlUpdateSnippet	UPDATE snippets SET name=?, description=?, author=?, email=?, weblink=?, code=?, notes=?, keyword1=?, keyword2=?, keyword3=?, keyword4=?, keyword5=? WHERE id=?; GO;	This updates the details of an existing snippet. All the details are updated, whether they have different values or not. This used in the updateSnippet() method.

Table 3-1. The SQL Statements Used in This Application (continued)

sqlDeleteSnippet	DELETE FROM snippets WHERE id=?; GO;	This deletes a snippet given an ID (all snippets have a unique ID). This is used in the deleteSnippet() method.
sqlDeleteSnippetsInCategory	DELETE FROM snippets WHERE categoryname=?; GO;	This deletes all the snippets in a given category. This is used in the deleteCategory() method (when a category is delete, so too are all the snippets in it).

Initializing the DAO

The DAO class follows the basic create, retrieve, update, delete (CRUD) structure of most DAOs, but even before getting into the CRUD method, there is the init() method to talk about:

```
this.init = function() {

  this.db = openDatabase(databaseName, "", databaseName, 65536);
  this.db.transaction((function (inTransaction) {
    inTransaction.executeSql(sqlCreateCategoriesTable, [], function() { },
      dao.errorHandler);
    inTransaction.executeSql(sqlCreateSnippetsTable, [], function() { },
      dao.errorHandler);
  }));

};
```

This method will be called from the stage's setup() method, which is effectively the entry point into the application. Its first task is to open the database using the openDatabase() method that is available automatically in global scope. This accepts as arguments the name of the database (the value of the databaseName field here), the target version of the database (an empty string here, which means any version is acceptable), a display name for the database (not currently used by webOS, but here it's the databaseName value again), and the estimated size of the database. Although a database can grow beyond this size, you should generally make as reasonable a guess as you can for this value.

■ **Note** A few notes are in order here. First, HTML5 databases are limited to 1MB. Should you need a database larger than that, you can specify the database name with a prefix of ext:, which will cause the database to be created in the mass media partition of the Palm Pre (which is where data such as music and wallpapers and such are stored). Your database can then be any size you want…up to the size available obviously. Sorry, no unlimited multidimensional quantum entanglement-based storage…yet! Second, on the version argument, this is an application-defined schema version. If you specify a version number and a database doesn't existing matching both the name *and* version, then a new database is created. This is meant to enable smooth transitions when your schema needs to change.

The reference to the opened database is stored in the class db field. Next, the two tables we need are created, if they don't already exist.

Executing a SQL query requires you to execute a transaction against the database. This is done with the aptly named transaction() method on the opened database referenced by db. A call to this method can take up to three arguments. The first is the transaction callback, which is a function that will execute the steps involved in the transaction. After that you can specify a function to execute if an error occurs, and you can specify a third to execute if the transaction is successful.

Within the transaction callback function, you will execute some number of executeSql() methods called on the transaction object passed into the function. The executeSql() method accepts as arguments a SQL string to execute, an array of values to insert in place of any question mark tokens in the SQL statement, a function to execute if the call is successful, and one to execute if it results in an error.

So, in the init() method, we're executing two SQL statements, sqlCreateCategoriesTable and sqlCreateSnippetsTable. Neither of these has any dynamic data, so an empty array is passed as the second argument. There's nothing special we need to do when and if these calls are successful, so a do-nothing function is the third argument, and for error handling we have a common errorHandler() method on the DAO class, which you'll learn about later, but that's the fourth argument for both of these method calls.

Creating a Category

Next up is the createCategory() method, used to create a new category from the Add Category scene:

```
this.createCategory = function(inCategoryName) {

  this.db.transaction((function (inTransaction) {
    inTransaction.executeSql(sqlCreateCategory, [ inCategoryName ],
      function() { }, dao.errorHandler);
  }));

};
```

This is the same sort of code we saw in init(); however, this time there is dynamic data to be inserted into the SQL, namely, the name of the category to create, so that value is the one element in the array passed as the second argument.

Retrieving Categories

The next method is the retrieveCategories() method, which is used to list all the categories in the Category List scene:

```
this.retrieveCategories = function(inCallback) {
```

```
    this.db.transaction((function (inTransaction) {
      inTransaction.executeSql(sqlRetrieveCategories, [ ],
        function(inTransaction, inResultSet) {
          var results = [ ];
          if (inResultSet.rows) {
            for (var i = 0; i < inResultSet.rows.length; i++) {
              results.push(inResultSet.rows.item(i));
            }
          }
          inCallback(results);
        }, dao.errorHandler
      );
    }));

};
```

I wanted what gets returned here to not be inherently tied to the underlying storage mechanism; I wanted instead to get a simple array of objects back, where each object contains the data describing a category. So, inside the success callback, the code iterates over the rows attribute of the inResultSet object that is passed into the function. Assuming there is in fact a rows attribute, meaning there are categories to deal with, then for each we call the item() method of it, which returns a simple JavaScript object with fields matching those of the table, and push that object onto an array.

Now, we have a bit of a problem here: some application code made a call to retrieveCategories(), but you'll notice that all of this database code is asynchronous, meaning that there is no way the caller of retrieveCategories() can ever get data back from it immediately. Instead, what happens is that the caller passes in a reference to a callback function as the inCallback argument. Then, in the success callback, the function referenced by inCallback is called, and the array generated in the success callback is passed to it. Yes, what we have here is a callback calling a callback, which is a bit confusing! Understanding it is a matter of understanding the fundamental asynchronous paradigm in play.

One way to make this simpler would have been to pass inCallback as the third argument to executeSql(). That way, the caller of retrieveCategories() specifies the function to call upon success of the SQL execution. The problem with that approach is that the application code now needs to have knowledge of the underlying storage mechanism, which means it has to know that the second argument it will be passed is a ResultSet. It also has to know that inside that object is a rows field and that to get data on a given row it needs to call the item() method of the rows element, passing it a row index. This is bad because it's intermingling the data access code with the application code, making it far more difficult to change the storage mechanism later. Instead, just a simple array is generated from the inline success callback function, and then that success callback calls the callback sent in by the caller of retrieveCategories(), passing that array to it. By adding that one level of indirection, we maintain a good separation of layers and make switching the storage mechanism later a lot easier.

Deleting a Category

Well, that was a bit of a tangent, but I think a necessary one, because this is a model you'll see repeated in most of the applications in this book. I hope it makes sense to you at this point because we're going to see a lot more of it very soon! For now, though, here's the deleteCategory() method, which is considerably more straightforward:

```
this.deleteCategory = function(inCategoryName) {

  this.db.transaction((function (inTransaction) {
    inTransaction.executeSql(sqlDeleteSnippetsInCategory, [ inCategoryName ],
      function() { }, dao.errorHandler);
    inTransaction.executeSql(sqlDeleteCategory, [ inCategoryName ],
      function() { }, dao.errorHandler);
  }));

};
```

Ah, yes, that's a lot simpler! Deleting a category means also deleting all the snippets within it, so there are two SQL statements to execute: sqlDeleteSnippetsInCategory and sqlDeleteCategory. Both have the category name inserted into them, so that's the only element passed in the second argument array.

Creating a Snippet

The createSnippet() method is next, and it too is fairly simple:

```
this.createSnippet = function(inSnippetDescriptor) {

  this.db.transaction((function (inTransaction) {
    inTransaction.executeSql(sqlCreateSnippet, [
      inSnippetDescriptor.id, inSnippetDescriptor.categoryname,
      inSnippetDescriptor.name, inSnippetDescriptor.description,
      inSnippetDescriptor.author, inSnippetDescriptor.email,
      inSnippetDescriptor.weblink, inSnippetDescriptor.code,
      inSnippetDescriptor.notes, inSnippetDescriptor.keyword1,
      inSnippetDescriptor.keyword2, inSnippetDescriptor.keyword3,
      inSnippetDescriptor.keyword4, inSnippetDescriptor.keyword5
    ], function() { }, dao.errorHandler);
  }));

};
```

The difference between this method and, say, deleteCategory(), is really just that there is a lot more data dynamically inserted into the SQL statement; hence, the array passed as the second argument has a lot more elements. All the data comes from the inSnippetDescriptor object passed into the function, which has fields matching the fields in the snippets table.

Retrieving Snippets

The next method up for exploration is about the most complex one in the whole DAO class: the retrieveSnippets() method:

```
this.retrieveSnippets = function(inCategoryName, inCallback) {

  var sql = sqlRetrieveAllSnippets;
  var params = [ ];
```

```
if (inCategoryName) {
  sql = sqlRetrieveSnippetsInCategory;
  params = [ inCategoryName ];
}
```

The only reason this method is more complicated than the rest is because it is used in two situations: when showing the list of snippets in the Snippet List scene and also when showing search results in the Search Results scene. Because of this dual use, the SQL statement used will vary, and it depends on whether the inCategoryName argument is null or not. When it's null, all snippets across all categories are being requested, which is the case when doing a search. So, that's the default SQL statement pointed to by the sql variable. This statement has no dynamic data, so by default the params variable points to an empty array. Now, if inCategoryName isn't null, then instead we point sql to sqlRetrieveSnippetsInCategory and point params to an array containing inCategoryName.

One more bit of complexity is in play here, and it's the reason neither of these SQL statements has the GO; directive at the end:

```
var storedSortOrder = codeCabinet.sortOrderCookie.get();
var sortInfo = storedSortOrder.split("_");
switch (sortInfo[0]) {
  case "newest":
    sql += "id DESC;";
  break;
  case "oldest":
    sql += "id ASC;";
  break;
  case "name":
    sql += "name " + sortInfo[1].toUpperCase() + ";";
  break;
  case "author":
    sql += "author " + sortInfo[1].toUpperCase() + ";";
  break;
}
sql += " GO;";
```

The sort order is dependent on the preference setting chosen by the user, so we have to dynamically append the appropriate order by clause to the SQL statement. To do this, we call codeCabinet.sortOrderCookie.get() to get the current sort order. Next, we split() that value. The value can be one of name_asc, name_desc, author_asc, author_desc, newest, or oldest. So, we switch on the first element of the array generated by the call to split(). This tells us what field to sort on. For the values newest and oldest, the field to sort on is the id field, because those values always increase as snippets are added. For those two values, they themselves determine whether the sort is ascending or descending. For name and author, however, the second element of the split()-generated array determined the sort order. Finally, the GO; directive is appended to complete the SQL statement.

After that, the same sort of execution occurs, as we've seen before:

```
this.db.transaction((function (inTransaction) {
  inTransaction.executeSql(sql, params,
    function(inTransaction, inResultSet) {
      var results = [ ];
      if (inResultSet.rows) {
        for (var i = 0; i < inResultSet.rows.length; i++) {
          results.push(inResultSet.rows.item(i));
```

```
          }
        }
        inCallback(results);
      }, dao.errorHandler
    );
  }));
```

The same sort of marshaling to an array is done, and the same sort of callback-calling-a-callback paradigm is at work as what we saw earlier, so there's probably not much more to be said about it.

Updating a Snippet

The next method is the updateSnippet() method:

```
  this.updateSnippet = function(inSnippetDescriptor) {

    this.db.transaction((function (inTransaction) {
      inTransaction.executeSql(sqlUpdateSnippet, [
        inSnippetDescriptor.name, inSnippetDescriptor.description,
        inSnippetDescriptor.author, inSnippetDescriptor.email,
        inSnippetDescriptor.weblink, inSnippetDescriptor.code,
        inSnippetDescriptor.notes, inSnippetDescriptor.keyword1,
        inSnippetDescriptor.keyword2, inSnippetDescriptor.keyword3,
        inSnippetDescriptor.keyword4, inSnippetDescriptor.keyword5,
        inSnippetDescriptor.id
      ], function() { }, dao.errorHandler);
    }));

  };
```

This is nearly identical to the addSnippet() method; the only real difference is that the inSnippetDescriptor.id value is at the end here vs. the beginning in addSnippet(). A look at the two SQL statements reveals the reason: the ID of the snippet to update is part of the where clause in the case of updating a snippet.

Deleting a Snippet

Deleting a snippet is achieved via the deleteSnippet() method:

```
  this.deleteSnippet = function(inID) {

    this.db.transaction((function (inTransaction) {
      inTransaction.executeSql(sqlDeleteSnippet, [ inID ], function() { },
        dao.errorHandler);
    }));

  };
```

I'd be willing to bet that's exactly what you would have expected it to look like at this point! In fact, I certainly *hope* it was!

Handling Errors

The final method to explore in the DAO class is one we've seen reference to everywhere else, namely, the errorHandler() method:

```
this.errorHandler = function(inTransaction, inError) {

  Mojo.Controller.errorDialog(
    "DAO ERROR - (" + inError.code + ") : " + inError.message
  );

};
```

```
var dao = new DAO();
```

Astute readers will at this point proclaim that the error handling in this application is not very robust, and I'm not about to argue the point! All we're doing here is calling on the Mojo.Controller.errorDialog() function to display the error message to the user. There's no attempt at recovery and no real graceful degradation of some sort; things simply don't work. In reality, there's probably not a whole lot more you *could* do here, other than build some sort of retry mechanism that maybe exits the application after three failed attempts. I'm not sure that's really any more robust, though. In any case, feel perfectly free to enhance the error handling any way you see fit; I won't complain!

Setting the Stage

For this application, a single stage is all we need, and in fact there's not a whole lot to it. Let's begin with the view HTML, which is in index.html in the root of the project and about as simple as it gets:

```
<?xml version="1.0" encoding="UTF-8"?>
<!DOCTYPE html PUBLIC "-//W3C//DTD XHTML 1.1//EN"
  "http://www.w3.org/TR/xhtml11/DTD/xhtml11.dtd">
<html xmlns="http://www.w3.org/1999/xhtml" xml:lang="en">
  <head>
    <title>Code Cabinet</title>
    <script src="/usr/palm/frameworks/mojo/mojo.js" type="text/javascript"
      x-mojo-version="1" />
    <link href="stylesheets/codecabinet.css" media="screen" rel="stylesheet"
      type="text/css" />
  </head>
  <body></body>
</html>
```

It is, in fact, really just the usual import of mojo.js, plus importing the style sheet for the application. There's no actual content in the <body>, which is pretty typical of a stage's view HTML (and certainly typical of the applications in this book).

However, there are definitely some things going on in the stage's assistant, found in the app/assistants/stage-assistant.js file, beginning with the definition of the StageAssistant class and its first method, setup():

```
function StageAssistant() { };
```

```
StageAssistant.prototype.setup = function() {
  dao.init();
  this.controller.pushScene("welcome");
};
```

This is effectively the entry point into the application because it is the first bit of code executed at startup (technically, there is an optional application assistant that would if present be executed first, but in the absence of that assistant, the `setup()` method of the stage assistant is the first thing executed). The first thing that is done is to call `init()` on the DAO instance that is created as a result of the DAO.js file being loaded (remember, it's in sources.json, so it gets loaded automatically, and the last line of it is to instantiate an instance of the DAO class). Once that's done, the Welcome scene is pushed, and the UI appears to the user.

In the `StageAssistant` class, we also find the method `handleCommand()`, which is what gets triggered when the application menu is activated. I'll break this method up a bit into more easily digestible chunks, beginning with this one:

```
StageAssistant.prototype.handleCommand = function(inEvent) {

  switch (inEvent.type) {

    case Mojo.Event.commandEnable:
      switch (inEvent.command) {
        case Mojo.Menu.prefsCmd:
          inEvent.stopPropagation();
        break;
      }
    break;
```

The `inEvent` argument is the event object generated by the operating system describing the menu event. Within it is a `type` attribute that tells us what type of event occurred. One of these types is the `Mojo.Event.commandEnable` event, which occurs when a menu item is enabled. You'll recall from your look at `CodeCabinet.js` that each menu item has a `command` attribute associated with it. This is true of the default items as well. The `inEvent` object also has a `command` attribute, and interrogating this attribute gives us the `command` value of the item that is being dealt with. Putting this information together reveals that we can determine when the default Preferences menu item is being enabled by looking for the `Mojo.Event.commandEnable` as the value of the `inEvent.type` attribute and then looking for the `Mojo.Menu.prefsCmd` as the value of the `inEvent.command` attribute.

This helps because what happens is that these events are propagating through something called the *commander chain*. This is an array, ordered like a stack, of handlers at various levels (application, stage, and scene controller). As an event propagates, the handlers that have been registered with the commander chain get a chance to handle the event as they see fit. They can also just ignore the event and let it continue to propagate.

What happens for the default Preferences and Help menu items is that they get disabled by a handler higher up in the commander chain. To enable it, we need to stop that from happening, and the way to do that is to call `inEvent.stopPropagation()` when we recognize the Preferences item is being enabled. That way, the handler that would execute after this event doesn't get a chance to disable it because propagation is stopped dead in its tracks.

The next bit of code in the `handleCommand()` method is this:

```
case Mojo.Event.command:
```

```
    switch (inEvent.command) {
      case "aboutCodeCabinet-TAP":
        this.controller.activeScene().showAlertDialog({
          onChoose : function(inValue) {},
          title : "Code Cabinet v1.0",
          message : "From the book " +
            "'Practical webOS Projects With the Palm Pre' " +
            "(Apress, 2009, ISBN-13: 978-1-4302-2674-1). " +
            "Copyright 2009 Frank W. Zammetti. All rights reserved. " +
            "A product of Etherient: http://www.etherient.com",
          choices : [
            { label : "Ok", value : "" }
          ]
        });
      break;
      case Mojo.Menu.prefsCmd:
        this.controller.pushScene("preferences");
      break;
    }
  break;

  }

};
```

This time we're looking for the Mojo.Event.command as the event type. This occurs when a menu item is tapped, so when we detect that, we can then look at the value of the inEvent.command attribute to tell which menu item was tapped.

The first value we might see is aboutCodeCabinet-TAP. In this case, we need to display the About dialog box. To do so, we use the showAlertDialog() method of the scene controller. Since this could occur on any scene in the application, we need to request a reference to the current scene's controller by using the activeScene() method of the stage controller (referenced by this.controller). The showAlertDialog() method takes in an object that describes what we want to happen. The onChoose attribute is the function to execute when the user chooses one of the options listed in the choices array. Here we have only one option, an Ok button, and there's no work to be done, so onChoose is an empty function (the dialog box will be automatically dismissed for us, so there's no code to do that here). The title and message attributes are the title and message shown in the dialog box, respectively. In Figure 3-6 you can see this About dialog box for yourself.

Figure 3-6. Since Code Cabinet can tell you about itself, does that make it self-aware and therefore a threat to destroy the human race?!?

The other value we might see for `inEvent.command` is `Mojo.Menu.prefsCmd`, in which case we just need to push the Preferences scene.

A Matter of Style

In the `stylesheets` directory of the project, you can find the file `codecabinet.css`. Rather than look at the entire contents of this style sheet now, I'll weave in discussions of the styles it contains as they are encountered in the code. I think seeing this style information in context will be more beneficial than the alternative, but certainly you should be aware that the file is there because we just saw it imported as part of the stage's view definition HTML file.

One style is more general in nature, though, so let's look at that here:

```
body.palm-default {
  background-color : #ffffff;
}
```

This sets the background color or all scenes to pure white (by default it's a slightly off-white color). This is done so that the shadow on the title graphic blends in better. Since the graphic was created with a pure white background in mind, it would wind up having a slight halo effect around it without the scene being pure white (remove this style and run the application in the emulator to see what I mean). That just wouldn't look so hot!

■ **Note** This is actually an example of something to *not* do! A pure white background is a usability faux pas because it's harder on the eyes, which is, one would think, why Palm decided to make the default color slightly off-white. I did it here, partially because I didn't want to regenerate the graphic using the off-white color as its basis but also to demonstrate how to change the background color of all scenes, which is something you may want to do at some point…just not to pure white!

A Scene-by-Scene Account

Now it's time to start looking at each of the scenes as shown in Figure 3-1 earlier. Some of them are a bit complex, but others are simple, such as the first one: the Welcome scene.

Welcome Scene

The Welcome scene is the one you see when the application starts. It's the first one pushed by the code in the stage controller's setup() method. Figure 3-7 depicts this scene.

Figure 3-7. The Welcome scene, bold and beautiful!

It's fairly simple; it contains just two images (the title and the big filing cabinet) and two Buttons at the bottom.

The View HTML

The markup that makes up its view, in the app/views/welcome/welcome-scene.html file, is quite concise:

```
<br>
<center>
  <img src="images/title.gif" />
  <img src="images/welcomeIcon.png" vspace="20" />
  <div id="welcome_btnCategoryList" x-mojo-element="Button"></div>
  <div id="welcome_btnSearch" x-mojo-element="Button"></div>
</center>
```

Two <img> tags take care of the title and the filing cabinet, and two <div>s with the x-mojo-element attribute value Button takes care of the Buttons. As previously mentioned, a scene's HTML isn't a complete HTML document; it's just a fragment, because it gets essentially included into a proper HTML document generated by the framework when the scene is constructed.

The Scene Assistant

The assistant for this scene, found in app/assistants/welcome-assistant.js, is similarly pretty simple, but I'm going to chunk it up a bit to cover it in detail, starting with this bit:

```
function WelcomeAssistant() { };

WelcomeAssistant.prototype.setup = function() {

  this.controller.setupWidget(Mojo.Menu.appMenu, codeCabinet.appMenuAttributes,
    codeCabinet.appMenuModel);

  this.controller.setupWidget("welcome_btnCategoryList", { },
    { label : "Category List" }
  );
  Mojo.Event.listen(this.controller.get("welcome_btnCategoryList"),
    Mojo.Event.tap, this.categoryList.bind(this)
  );

};
```

WelcomeAssistant is the JavaScript object we're creating here to be the assistant for this scene, and the first thing it contains is the setup() method, which most scenes will have. It is called by the framework when the scene is pushed to allow us a chance to do any sort of setup before the scene is shown to the user. The first bit of setup, which will be the case for all the scenes, is to set up the application menu. To do so, we call the setupWidget() method of the controller associated with this scene (pointed to by this.controller). To this method we pass the ID of the widget to set up (in this case, the constant Mojo.Menu.appMenu provided by Mojo), the attributes for the menu (the codeCabinet.appMenuAttributes object we saw earlier), and the model for the menu (codeCabinet.appMenuModel).

Following that we set up the first of our two Buttons. The first argument, the ID, is the ID on the <div> in the scene's HTML. There are no attributes to set, so we pass an empty object as the second argument. The third argument, the model for the Button, contains just a single attribute: label, which is of course the text on the Button.

The next thing to do is to attach an event handler to the Button. The first argument passed to the Mojo.Event.listen() method is a reference to the widget to attach the event to, which is retrieved by calling the get() method on the scene controller, passing it the ID of the widget. The second argument is the type of event to listen for, Mojo.Event.tap in this case, which handles touch-screen tap events. The final argument is a reference to the function that will be called when the event occurs, in this case the categoryList() method of the scene assistant.

The Search Button is set up in the same way, so I'm not showing that code here. The only difference is the label and the function to be called when the Button is tapped (search() in that case).

The event handlers for those Buttons are as follows:

```
WelcomeAssistant.prototype.categoryList = function() {
  Mojo.Controller.stageController.pushScene("categoryList");
};
```

```
WelcomeAssistant.prototype.search = function() {
  Mojo.Controller.stageController.pushScene("search");
};
```

As you can see, they do nothing but push the appropriate scene, the Category List scene for the first Button and the Search scene for the second Button.

Category List Scene

The next scene to look at is the Category List scene, which is shown when the first Button in the Welcome scene is tapped. Figure 3-8 shows an example of this scene.

Figure 3-8. The Category List scene (and no, I don't still code in FoxPro!)

As you can see, it's a List widget, with the categories listed, and beside each is an icon and the number of snippets in that category. There is also an Add item at the bottom of the List for adding a new category.

The View HTML

The view HTML for this scene is quite simple and is found in the file app/views/categoryList/categoryList-scene.html. The content of this file is as follows:

```
<div id="main" class="palm-hasheader">
  <div class="palm-header">Categories</div>
</div>

<div id="categoryList_lstCategoryList" x-mojo-element="List"
  style="display:none;"></div>

<div x-mojo-element="Spinner" id="categoryList_divSpinner"
  class="spinnerClass" style="display:block;"></div>
```

The first <div> is the title pill that says Categories. The title pill is a very common UI element seen very frequently in webOS applications. It is constructed by having a <div> with the Mojo-supplied style class palm-hasheader applied, as well as having the specific id main (if either of these is missing or they do not have the correct values, the content of the scene, the List widget in this case, will appear behind the pill to begin with). Inside that <div> is another with the class palm-header, which provides the actual visual look of the pill (without this, you'll just see plain text there). The textual content of the inner <div> is the title shown on the pill.

After that is another <div> with the x-mojo-element attribute with a value of List. This is the List widget that will show the categories. Notice that the style attribute is used to hide the List. This is done because the next element is another Mojo widget, the Spinner. This will appear when the List is being populated and is initially shown. The style class applied to it, spinnerClass, has the following values:

```css
.spinnerClass {
  position : absolute;
  left : 96px;
  top : 110px;
}
```

This serves to center the Spinner on the scene.

■ **Note** An Excel spreadsheet is available on the Palm Developer Network site that lists the style classes provided by Mojo. Unfortunately, at least at the time of this writing, that list is incomplete and doesn't do a whole lot to tell you how, when, and why to use certain styles. At this point in time, looking at example code and flat-out copying it is just about the only good way to get a handle on these styles. Of course, I hope this book provides you with that information and those examples, but it's definitely an area that the Palm documentation needs some work in.

The Scene Assistant

The scene assistant, found in app/assistants/categoryList-assistant.js, begins with the following code:

```javascript
function CategoryListAssistant() { };

CategoryListAssistant.prototype.lstCategoryListModel = { items : [ ] };

CategoryListAssistant.prototype.setup = function() {

  this.controller.setupWidget(Mojo.Menu.appMenu, codeCabinet.appMenuAttributes,
    codeCabinet.appMenuModel);

  this.controller.setupWidget("categoryList_divSpinner",
    { spinnerSize : "large" }, { spinning : true }
  );
```

The CategoryListAssistant object is created, and then an object is added under the field name lstCategoryListModel. This is the model object for the List. It starts out with no items in it, so the items attribute is just an empty array.

After that is the ubiquitous setup() method. The first thing done, like in the Welcome scene, is to set up the application menu. After that, the Spinner is set up. The spinnerSize attribute is set to a value of large, since we want the larger 128×128 Spinner. In the model we start the Spinner spinning immediately. This means that when this scene is pushed, since the List is hidden, the Spinner will initially be seen and will be spinning while the List is being populated.

Speaking of the List, that's the next thing we find code for:

```
this.controller.setupWidget("categoryList_lstCategoryList", {
  addItemLabel : "Add...",
  swipeToDelete : true,
  itemTemplate : "categoryList/list-item"
}, this.lstCategoryListModel);
this.controller.listen("categoryList_lstCategoryList", Mojo.Event.listTap,
  this.selectCategory);
this.controller.listen("categoryList_lstCategoryList", Mojo.Event.listAdd,
  this.addCategory);
this.controller.listen("categoryList_lstCategoryList", Mojo.Event.listDelete,
  this.deleteCategory.bind(this));
```

The attributes object contains the addItemLabel attribute, with the text to show for the Add item at the bottom. Since we want the user to be able to delete items by swiping them from right to left, the swipeToDelete attribute needs to be set to true. The itemTemplate attribute specifies the HTML file that will be used to render each item in the list. We'll look at that template at the end, so as to not break our train of thought here.

The lstCategoryListModel object is passed as the third argument to setupWidget(), thereby associating that model object with the List widget.

After that, three events handlers are attached. The first handles taps on a category, the second handles when the Add item is tapped, and the third handles when an item is being deleted. In fact, this last one is listening for an event triggered after the user has confirmed the deletion because, by default, buttons labeled Delete and Cancel will appear in place of the swiped item to allow the user to confirm or cancel the deletion. It's nice that we get that for free; our code has to be concerned only with actually doing the delete.

The activate() assistant method is next, and this is called any time the scene becomes active, after setup(), which is called only once, is executed:

```
CategoryListAssistant.prototype.activate = function() {

  $("categoryList_divSpinner").show();
  $("categoryList_lstCategoryList").hide();
  this.lstCategoryListModel.items = [ ];
  dao.retrieveCategories(this.processResults.bind(this));

};
```

■ **Note** The $() function is one of the functions that the Prototype library provides (although it may look odd, $ is in fact a valid JavaScript function name). This function retrieves a reference to a named DOM node (via its id attribute). Prototype provides a number of similarly named functions for various common operations such as this. Check out the Prototype documentation if you are new to the library to see what it has to offer.

Here, the Spinner is shown, and the List is hidden (note the user of the $() operator, provided by the Prototype library, which is a more robust version of the document.getElementById() method). This is redundant the first time the scene is shown since the markup already does this, but it has to be done for subsequent activations, such as when the user does the back gesture from the Snippet List scene. After that, the items array in the List's model is cleared, and then the retrieveCategories() method of the DAO is called. We pass to this method a reference to the processResults() method, which will execute when the SQL query is compete. The method for that code is as follows:

```
CategoryListAssistant.prototype.processResults = function(inResults) {

  for (var i = 0; i < inResults.length; i++) {
    this.lstCategoryListModel.items.push(inResults[i]);
  }
  this.controller.modelChanged(this.lstCategoryListModel);
  $("categoryList_divSpinner").hide();
  $("categoryList_lstCategoryList").show();

};
```

Recall that retrieveCategories() returns an array of objects, each representing one row in the categories table. So, we iterate over that array and push each item into the just-emptied items array in the List's model. Once that's done, we need to inform the controller that the model has changed for the List, so we call this.controller.modelChanged(), passing it the model. The List will be automatically updated on the screen with the new data at this point, but of course it's hidden at this point, so the only task left is to hide the Spinner and show the List.

Now, remember those three event handlers attached to the List? Well, it's time to examine them, beginning with the selectCategory() method, which is the one called when the user taps a category:

```
CategoryListAssistant.prototype.selectCategory = function(inEvent) {
  codeCabinet.currentCategory = inEvent.item;
  Mojo.Controller.stageController.pushScene("snippetList");
};
```

The currentCategory field of the codeCabinet object gets a reference to the selected category, which is passed in as the value of the item attribute in the inEvent object. This is one of the objects returned by the call to dao.retrieveCategories(). Once that's done, the Snippet List scene is pushed, which will make use of that object to load the snippets for the category.

That's getting ahead of things, though; we still have two event handlers to look at, and next up is addCategory(), the one executed when the user taps the Add item at the bottom:

```
CategoryListAssistant.prototype.addCategory = function() {
  Mojo.Controller.stageController.pushScene("categoryAdd");
```

```
};
```

All this handler needs to do is push the Add Category scene, actually named `categoryAdd`, and its job is done.

Deleting a category is the final function to look at, and it's handled by the `deleteCategory()` method:

```
CategoryListAssistant.prototype.deleteCategory = function(inEvent) {
  dao.deleteCategory(inEvent.item.name);
  this.lstCategoryListModel.items.splice(inEvent.index, 1);
};
```

Remember that this gets called only after the user confirms the deletion. The confirmation is done automatically and looks like what you see in Figure 3-9.

Figure 3-9. Confirmation of deleting a category (nice, since it wipes out the snippets too!)

So, the `dao.deleteCategory()` method is called, passing in the name of the category. Once again, the `inEvent` object contains an `item` attribute, which is the object for the selected category, which means there is a `name` attribute to it (since `name` is the name of the field in the categories table, which is what this object was created from).

■ **Note** We don't seem to need to inform the controller of the model change when deleting a `List` item. I was a bit surprised by this, but it seems that it is done automatically by the framework. Cool—less work is good in my book!

With all that code out of the way, let's jump back slightly to the template for the `List` items, as found in the `app/views/categoryList/list-item.html` file:

```
<div class="palm-row" x-mojo-tap-highlight="momentary">
  <div class="palm-row-wrapper textfield-group">
    <div class="title">
```

```
      <div class="palm-dashboard-icon-container catSnipListIconContainer">
        <div class="dashboard-newitem categoryListSnippetCountContainer">
          <span class="categoryListSnippetCount">#{snippetCount}</span>
        </div>
        <div class="palm-dashboard-icon categoryListIcon"></div>
      </div>
      <div class="categoryListTitle truncating-text">#{name}</div>
    </div>
  </div>
</div>
```

This is once again just an HTML fragment. It's a somewhat complex structure that uses quite a few framework-supplied styles and a few custom ones. In general, when creating a List, you'll start by copying the list template for an existing List, be it one you've created yourself previously or one from an example, and modify it as necessary. That's exactly what I've done here. Since this can be treated as a template for future lists, let's look at the styles that I've modified to make this List unique.

The first is catSnipListIconContainer, applied to the container that contains the icon image shown in the List. This style class is as follows:

```
.catSnipListIconContainer {
  height : 54px;
  margin-top : 6px;
  padding-right : 10px;
}
```

The height of the icon is 48 pixels, so by setting the height of its container to 54 pixels and then pushing it down 6 pixels with margin-top, the icon is effectively centered vertically on the line. Setting padding-right to 10 pixels ensures that the text on the line isn't bumping up against the icon.

The categoryListSnippetCountContainer style class is meant to move the little bubble where the snippet count for a given category appears so that it is superimposed over the icon.

```
.categoryListSnippetCountContainer  {
  position : relative;
  left : 4px;
}
```

As the number in the bubble increases, it will be pushed to the left naturally, but this style ensures its position looks good.

The categoryListIcon class is what puts the category icon itself on the List item. This is just a background image specification—nothing fancy.

```
.categoryListIcon {
  background : url(../images/icoCategory.png) center no-repeat;
}
```

Finally, the categoryListTitle class styles the text of the category name:

```
.categoryListTitle {
  font-size : 18px;
  color : #000000;
  position : relative;
```

```
  top : 4px;
}
```

It also pushes the text down 4 pixels from its natural position in the layout flow, which makes it appear vertically centered better.

One interesting built-in style used here is the `truncating-text` class. Its job is to ensure that long category names get truncated at the right edge of the list item instead of it wrapping. This is important to keep the `List` looking good and, more specifically, to ensure each line item is the same height.

Finally, note the replacement tokens used in this template: `#{snippetCount}` is the text shown in the bubble and is the number of snippets in the category, and `#{name}` is the name of the category. These replacement tokens are of course what makes this template useful in generating the markup used to render the `List`.

Category Add Scene

When the user taps the Add item on the category `List`, the Add Category scene is pushed, which is shown in Figure 3-10.

Figure 3-10. *Creating a new category (simple, but effective)*

It's a simple scene, with just a single `TextArea` and a `Button`.

The View HTML

The view HTML for this scene in the file `app/views/categoryAdd-scene.html` is as follows:

```html
<div id="main" class="palm-hasheader">
  <div class="palm-header">Add Category</div>
</div>

<div class="palm-group">
  <div class="palm-group-title">Enter category name</div>
  <div class="palm-list">
    <div class="palm-row single">
```

```
    <div class="palm-row-wrapper textfield-group"
      x-mojo-focus-highlight="true">
      <div class="title">
        <div id="categoryAdd_txtCategoryName"
          x-mojo-element="TextField"></div>
      </div>
    </div>
  </div>
</div>
</div>

<div id="categoryAdd_btnAdd" x-mojo-element="Button"></div>
```

A title pill is present in this scene, just like in the Category List scene. Below that is a big chunk of markup, which is a batch of nested <div> elements. This is another of those "just copy this going forward and treat it like a template" kinds of deals, because going into the details of each style class used here would not be very useful. The result of all of this markup and styling is what's important, and that's that we get a TextField surrounded by a frame with a title above it, which is a typical way to present TextField widgets in a webOS application.

Below that is the single Button widget, so there's nothing new there.

The Scene Assistant

The scene assistant, app/assistants/categoryAdd-assistant.js, is fairly simple, beginning with creating the CategoryAddAssistant, setting up a field on it, and setting up the typical setup() method:

```
function CategoryAddAssistant() { };

CategoryAddAssistant.prototype.txtCategoryNameModel = { value : "" };

CategoryAddAssistant.prototype.setup = function() {

  this.controller.setupWidget(Mojo.Menu.appMenu, codeCabinet.appMenuAttributes,
    codeCabinet.appMenuModel);

  this.controller.setupWidget("categoryAdd_txtCategoryName",
    { focusMode : Mojo.Widget.focusSelectMode, maxLength : 30 },
    this.txtCategoryNameModel
  );

  this.controller.setupWidget("categoryAdd_btnAdd", { },
    { label : "Add", buttonClass : "affirmative" }
  );
  Mojo.Event.listen(this.controller.get("categoryAdd_btnAdd"), Mojo.Event.tap,
    this.add.bind(this)
  );

};
```

The txtCategoryNameModel is the model object for the TextField where the user enters the new category's name. It has a value attribute that is initially empty. Within the setup() method, we have the same code to set up the application menu as we've seen before, as well as a call to setupWidget() to set up the TextField. The focusMode attribute in the widget's attribute object specifies the value Mojo.Widget.focusSelectMode so that when the widget gains focus, its current value will be highlighted (which means when the user starts typing, the value is overwritten). The maxLength attribute specifies that the entered name can be no longer than 30 characters.

The Button the user taps to add the category is then set up. The buttonClass attribute in the Button's model specifies a style of affirmative, which is used on Buttons to make them green and, usually, to indicate a positive response (alternatively, the negative style class makes the Button red to indicate a negative response).

The Button's Mojo.Event.tap event is tied to the add() method of the CategoryAddAssistant:

```
CategoryAddAssistant.prototype.add = function() {

  if (this.txtCategoryNameModel.value &&
    this.txtCategoryNameModel.value.strip() != "") {
    dao.createCategory(this.txtCategoryNameModel.value);
    this.controller.stageController.popScene();
  } else {
    Mojo.Controller.errorDialog(
      "I'm sorry but you must enter a name for this category."
    );
  }

};
```

First, a check is done to make sure the user entered something. This is done by checking the value attribute of the model associated with the TextField. If it's not null and is not empty once the strip() method removes whitespace from both ends, then the createCategory() method of the DAO is called, passing the name they entered. This writes a new record to the categories table. At that point, all that's left to do is to pop this scene off the scene stack, revealing the Category List scene below it. As previously discussed, the activate() method of that scene will fire as a result of this, causing the category List widget to be updated to show the newly added category.

If the user didn't enter anything, then the Mojo.Cotnroller.errorDialog() method is called to show a pop-up message indicating that a name is required.

Snippet List Scene

This Snippet List scene is, to a large extent, similar to the Category List scene, as you can see for yourself in Figure 3-11. The Snippet List scene is what appears when the user taps one of the categories in the category list.

Figure 3-11. *A list of snippets in the FoxPro category (I swear, I really don't do FoxPro anymore!)*

To save a little time and space, let's just look at the differences between these two scenes.

The View HTML

The app/views/snippetList-scene.html file is nearly identical to the app/views/categoryList-scene.html file, really just differing in the IDs of elements and the text in the header pill naturally. Take a look for yourself if you don't believe me. ☺

The Scene Assistant

The SnippetListAssistant found in app/assistants/snippetList-assistant.js too isn't very different, at least early on. The setup() method sets up the application menu, Spinner and List, just like in the Category List scene. For the List in the scene, however, the swipeToDelete attribute is *not* present because the deleting of snippets is done from the Snippet Details scene that appears when a snippet is selected from this scene. Therefore, there is no handling of the Mojo.Event.listDelete event here.

One thing that is a bit different, however, is the activate() method:

```
SnippetListAssistant.prototype.activate = function() {

  $("main-hdr").innerHTML = codeCabinet.currentCategory.name + " Snippets";
  $("snippetList_divSpinner").show();
  $("snippetList_lstSnippetList").hide();
  codeCabinet.lstSnippetListModel.items = [ ];
  dao.retrieveSnippets(codeCabinet.currentCategory.name,
    this.processResults.bind(this));

};
```

The header pill needs to include the name of the selected category, so the innerHTML contents of the main-hdr <div> is updated to the value of the name attribute of the currentCategory object pointed to by the codeCabinet.currentCategory field. This, you'll recall, is set when a category is selected on the Category List scene.

The list of snippets is retrieved, and we have a processResults() method again that populates the list. That method is also nearly identical to the Category List scene, although the template used is different:

```
<div class="palm-row" x-mojo-tap-highlight="momentary">
  <div class="palm-row-wrapper textfield-group">
    <div class="title">
      <div class="palm-dashboard-icon-container catSnipListIconContainer">
        <div class="palm-dashboard-icon snippetListIcon"></div>
      </div>
      <div class="snippetListTitle truncating-text">#{name}</div>
      <div class="snippetListDescription truncating-text">#{description}</div>
    </div>
  </div>
</div>
```

This time there is no snippet count to show, so that part of the markup is removed, and this time we show a second line of text that is the description of the snippet. The snippetListIcon has a different background image so that there is a little bit of a visual difference between the two List widgets. Other than those differences, the two templates don't differ much either (which further proves my point that it's a good idea to copy an existing template and then modify it as necessary).

When a snippet is selected, the selectSnippet() method is executed:

```
SnippetListAssistant.prototype.selectSnippet = function(inEvent) {

  codeCabinet.currentSnippet = inEvent.item;
  Mojo.Controller.stageController.pushScene("snippetDetails");

};
```

A reference to the object of the selected snippet is recorded in codeCabinet.currentSnippet, and then the Snippet Details scene is pushed, which, like this scene referencing the codeCabinet.currentCategory object, will reference codeCabinet.currentSnippet to populate the details.

When the Add item is selected, the addSnippet() method is called, which simply pushes the Snippet Details scene as well, but before doing so it sets codeCabinet.currentSnippet to null. Therefore, the Snippet Details scene, based on whether codeCabinet.currentSnippet is null, serves as the scene for both adding a new snippet and viewing (and potentially modifying) an existing snippet, and that scene is where we're headed next!

Snippet Details Scene

The Snippet Details scene allows you to view details of a selected snippet, as well as enter a new snippet. It contains all the fields of data that are stored about a snippet, all organized into Drawers so as to not seem totally overwhelming as would probably be the case if it were just one big, long list. In Figure 3-12 you can see part of this scene (even with the Drawers there is too much for one screen, so you have to scroll down to see the rest).

Figure 3-12. The first few fields of the Info Drawer in the Snippet Details scene

Although there is a pretty large volume of code in both the view HTML and the assistant for this scene, a lot of it is highly redundant, and because of this, you'll see an ellipsis where I've left out repetitive bits of code in an effort to shrink it down a bit in print. Rest assured, I haven't cut anything out that isn't redundant!

The View HTML

The view HTML file, namely, app/views/snippetDetails-scene.html, begins with a header pill as has been the case in other scenes and then leads into the first of four Drawers, the Info Drawer:

```
<div id="main" class="palm-hasheader">
  <div class="palm-header">Snippet Details</div>
</div>

<div id="snippetDetails_btnInfoDrawer" class="palm-button">Info</div>
<div id="snippetDetails_drwInfo" x-mojo-element="Drawer">
  <div class="palm-group">
    <div class="palm-group-title">Name</div>
    <div class="palm-list">
      <div class="palm-row single">
        <div class="palm-row-wrapper textfield-group"
          x-mojo-focus-highlight="true">
          <div class="title">
            <div id="snippetDetails_txtName" x-mojo-element="TextField"></div>
          </div>
        </div>
      </div>
    </div>
  </div>
</div>
...
```

```
</div>
```

A Drawer by itself is just a container, not a whole lot different (save for some automatic styles applied) from a plain old <div>. Where a Drawer becomes an interactive UI element is when you "attach" to it some other widget, say a Button, to allow the user to open and close the Drawer. I put "attach" in quotes there because there's nothing truly attaching the Button to the Drawer; indeed, it doesn't have to be a Button at all, and it could be far away from the Drawer in the UI, although a Button right above the Drawer makes a lot of sense, and it is what you'll most commonly see. So, that's why you see a Button declared right above the <div> with the x-mojo-element value Drawer, which is the Drawer itself. That Button will open and close the Drawer when tapped (assuming the appropriate handler code is attached to it, which it is, as we'll see).

Inside the Drawer we find a number of TextField elements, all wrapped up in the same fairly verbose markup and style structure as you saw in earlier scenes. I've shown only the first such field, the Name field, but where the ellipsis is, there are actually four other fields, Description, Author, eMail, and Web Link, all of them using the same basic markup as for the Name field.

After those fields comes the second of the four Drawers in this scene, this one enclosing the Code RichTextEdit field:

```
<div id="snippetDetails_btnCodeDrawer" class="palm-button">Code</div>
<div id="snippetDetails_drwCode" x-mojo-element="Drawer">
  <div class="palm-list">
    <div class="palm-row single">
      <div class="palm-row-wrapper textfield-group"
        x-mojo-focus-highlight="true">
        <div class="title">
          <div id="snippetDetails_rteCode"
            x-mojo-element="RichTextEdit" style="height:200px;"></div>
        </div>
      </div>
    </div>
  </div>
</div>
```

As you can see, it's only a little different from the Info Drawer. The difference is really in the RichTextField's surrounding markup: there is no <div> with a class of palm-group, nor is there a <div> with the class palm-group-title. This changes the visual style by removing the rounded look that the TextField elements get and also removes the border and title from around it.

The Notes Drawer is very nearly identical to the Code Drawer, just differing in title and element IDs.

Note that both the Code and Notes Drawers use RichTextEdit widgets, as you can see in Figure 3-13. With RichTextEdit, you can apply some "richness" to the text you enter, including bold, italic, and underline.

Figure 3-13. *The Notes Drawer, now opened, with some rich text entered*

You apply those text styles by selecting the appropriate option in the Edit menu of the application menu, as shown in Figure 3-14. If you select Bold, then all the text entered from that point on will be bold until you tap the Bold menu item again to toggle it off.

Figure 3-14. *The Edit menu options, as used in the Code Drawer's RichTextEdit widget*

The Keywords Drawer is, frankly, just more of the same! This Drawer contains five TextField widgets, one for each keyword allowed to be associated with a snippet. I'm going to skip showing the HTML snippet for this because what we just looked at for the Info Drawer pretty effectively covers it as well. What I *will* do, however, is show you this Drawer and the TextField widgets within it (see Figure 3-15).

Figure 3-15. The Keywords Drawer and some keywords entered

Each of the TextFields has an ID of snippetDetails_textKeywordZ, where Z is 1 through 5. That's truly the only difference, aside from the text on the Button, of course.

The last bit of markup in the scene's HTML is for the Buttons at the bottom:

```
<table width="100%">
  <tr>
    <td width="33%"><div id="snippetDetails_btnSave"
      x-mojo-element="Button"></div></td>
    <td width="34%"><div id="snippetDetails_btnSend"
      x-mojo-element="Button"></div></td>
    <td width="33%"><div id="snippetDetails_btnDelete"
      x-mojo-element="Button"></div></td>
  </tr>
</table>
```

A <table> is used to allow the Buttons, all three of them, to float across the screen. The Buttons themselves will size horizontally to their container, a table cell in this case, so this is a nice, easy way to lay out three Buttons in a row (you can see these Buttons a page or two ago in Figure 3-13). Note that the Buttons automatically have some padding on the sides of them, so they won't get all bunched up together when doing this. There's no limit to how many Buttons you could put in a row technically, although their labels certainly represent a limit, but more important, so does usability: if they're much smaller than this, they are not good tap targets (generally, 48×48 pixels is the smallest reasonable target).

The Scene Assistant

The SnippetDetailsAssistant, housed in the app/assistants/snippetDetails-assistant.js file, begins with a bit of interesting code:

```
function SnippetDetailsAssistant() { };

SnippetDetailsAssistant.prototype.drawerModels = {
  info : { open : true,
    fields : {
```

```
          txtName : { value : "" },
          txtDescription : { value : "" },
          txtAuthor : { value : "" },
          txtEMail : { value : "" },
          txtWebLink : { value : "" }
        }
      },
      code : { open : false, fields : {
        rteCode : { value : "" }
      } },
      notes : { open : false, fields : {
        rteNotes : { value : "" }
      } },
      keywords : { open : false,
        fields : {
          txtKeyword1 : { value : "" },
          txtKeyword2 : { value : "" },
          txtKeyword3 : { value : "" },
          txtKeyword4 : { value : "" },
          txtKeyword5 : { value : "" }
        }
      }
    }
};
```

The drawerModels object contains within it a bunch of other model objects, one for each Drawer to be exact. Then, within the model object for a given Drawer there is some number of other model objects, one for each of the fields in that Drawer. I'd say this is a bit of an atypical approach, but I wanted to demonstrate that it was possible; there's nothing to stop you from nesting objects like this, which implicitly tells you that webOS won't complain if you add custom attributes to a model object, which is nice to know because it means you can tie any custom data you like to a given widget without having to carry around a whole separate object for it; just use the model object that you need anyway!

The nesting like this is just a code organization approach, one you may like or not. I kind of like the idea of everything being contained within one object like this, but YMMV.

After that are two other model objects, one each for the Delete Button and the Send Button (which sends the snippet via e-mail):

```
SnippetDetailsAssistant.prototype.btnDeleteModel = {
  label : "Delete", buttonClass : "negative buttonfloat",
  disabled : true
};


SnippetDetailsAssistant.prototype.btnSendModel = {
  label : "Send", buttonClass : "buttonfloat", disabled : true
};
```

The sharp-eyed reader will at this point wonder why there are only two model objects but three Buttons. The simple answer is that only these two ever need to be disabled, and the other (the Save Button) is always enabled. These two will be disabled when creating a new snippet.

The setup() method is next:

```
SnippetDetailsAssistant.prototype.setup = function() {

  this.controller.setupWidget(Mojo.Menu.appMenu, codeCabinet.appMenuAttributes,
    codeCabinet.appMenuModel);

  this.controller.setupWidget("snippetDetails_drwInfo", { },
    this.drawerModels.info);
  Mojo.Event.listen(this.controller.get("snippetDetails_btnInfoDrawer"),
    Mojo.Event.tap,
    function() {
      this.drawerModels.info.open = !this.drawerModels.info.open;
      this.controller.modelChanged(this.drawerModels.info, this);
    }.bind(this)
  );
```

The application menu, like all scenes, is set up first. Then, the Info section Drawer is set up, and a
Mojo.Event.tap event handler is attached. This is where the Drawer becomes interactive: when tapped,
the handler for the Button flips the open attribute in the model for the Drawer, and
this.controller.modelChanged() is called, which opens or closes the Drawer as dictated by the new value
of the open attribute. All the Drawer Buttons work in the same way.

Within the Info Drawer are a number of TextField widgets, such as the Name field:

```
  this.controller.setupWidget("snippetDetails_txtName",
    { focusMode : Mojo.Widget.focusSelectMode, maxLength : 30 },
    this.drawerModels.info.fields.txtName
  );
...
```

This is the same sort of setup we've seen previously, and there are a number of others just like it for
the rest of the fields in this Drawer. The Code and Notes Drawers have only a single RichTextEdit widget
within them, but they are set up just like these are. There are no configuration attributes associated with
the RichTextEdit widget, and the model just has the usual value attribute.

The Keyword fields are set up just slightly differently:

```
  for (var i = 1; i < 6; i++) {
    this.controller.setupWidget("snippetDetails_txtKeyword" + i,
      { focusMode : Mojo.Widget.focusSelectMode, maxLength : 15 },
      this.drawerModels.keywords.fields["txtKeyword" + i]
    );
  }
```

Because there are five of them, all identical, a little loop was in order to save my fingers from typing
too much! The actual TextField configuration is just like all the others, though.

The final bit of work the setup() method needs to accomplish is to set up the three Buttons at the
bottom: Save, Send, and Delete. We'll just look at the code for the Save button:

```
  this.controller.setupWidget("snippetDetails_btnSave", { },
    { label : "Save", buttonClass : "affirmative buttonfloat" }
  );
  Mojo.Event.listen(this.controller.get("snippetDetails_btnSave"),
    Mojo.Event.tap, this.saveSnippet.bind(this)
```

```
);
```

Yep, just like any other Button! One new addition, however, is the use of the `buttonfloat` style for the `buttonClass` attribute (in addition to the `affirmative` style class, which we've seen before). The `buttonfloat` class is needed to make sure the Buttons look correct when put in a row like these are.

The Delete Button has the `negative` style applied it instead of `affirmative`, and the Send Button has neither of those. Aside from that, and of course what method is called for a tap event, they look just like that bit of code.

Following the `setup()` method is the `activate()` method, called whenever the scene becomes current. This has some work to do to determine whether a new snippet is being created or whether an existing one is being viewed and/or edited.

```
SnippetDetailsAssistant.prototype.activate = function() {

  if (codeCabinet.currentSnippet) {

    for (var dm in this.drawerModels) {
      for (var f in this.drawerModels[dm].fields) {
        if (f == "rteCode") {
          this.controller.get("snippetDetails_rteCode").innerHTML =
            codeCabinet.currentSnippet.code;
        } else if (f == "rteNotes") {
          this.controller.get("snippetDetails_rteNotes").innerHTML =
            codeCabinet.currentSnippet.notes;
        } else {
          this.drawerModels[dm].fields[f].value =
            codeCabinet.currentSnippet[f.toLowerCase().substr(3)];
          this.controller.modelChanged(this.drawerModels[dm].fields[f]);
        }
      }
    }

    SnippetDetailsAssistant.prototype.btnDeleteModel.disabled = false;
    this.controller.modelChanged(
      SnippetDetailsAssistant.prototype.btnDeleteModel);
    SnippetDetailsAssistant.prototype.btnSendModel.disabled = false;
    this.controller.modelChanged(
      SnippetDetailsAssistant.prototype.btnSendModel);
```

If `codeCabinet.currentSnippet` points to a snippet object, then an existing snippet was just selected from either the Snippet List scene or the Search Results scene. In this case, we need to populate the data in the `TextFields` and `RichTextEdit` fields. This is another reason I chose to nest all the model objects: it makes this bit of code a bit more generic.

It begins by iterating over all the Drawer models, so we'll see four iterations of this loop. Inside that loop, it iterates over the fields in the Drawer. For each, it checks to see whether it is the Code or Notes `RichTextEdit` fields. The reason for this is that these two fields get their values set differently than all the `TextField` widgets. For a `RichTextEdit`, you need to set the `innerHTML` of the widget. The appropriate field from the `codeCabinet.currentSnippet` object is retrieved and inserted in that manner.

For all the `TextFields`, though, what happens is the `value` of the model object is updated. There is a little bit of black magic here because the name of the field in the model, which is the value of the loop variable `f`, begins with the string `txt`. This needs to be removed because the name of the field to get the value from in the current snippet object doesn't have that prefix. That's where the substr(3) comes into play: it gets rid of the Hungarian Notation[3] prefix, thereby giving us the correct field name in the model object to set. Once that's done, our friend this.controller.modelChanged() is called, again using the loop index variables to pass in the correct model object.

Finally, the Buttons are dealt with. When viewing/editing an existing snippet, the Delete and Send Buttons need to be enabled, so their models are changed to reflect that. Remember that the Send Button is always enabled, so there's nothing to do there.

Now, the else branch of the if statement that this method began with handles the case where we're creating a new snippet:

```
for (var dm in this.drawerModels) {
  for (var f in this.drawerModels[dm].fields) {
    if (f == "rteCode") {
      this.controller.get("snippetDetails_rteCode").innerHTML = "";
    } else if (f == "rteNotes") {
      this.controller.get("snippetDetails_rteNotes").innerHTML = "";
    } else {
      this.drawerModels[dm].fields[f].value = null;
      this.controller.modelChanged(this.drawerModels[dm].fields[f]);
    }
  }
}

SnippetDetailsAssistant.prototype.btnDeleteModel.disabled = true;
this.controller.modelChanged(
  SnippetDetailsAssistant.prototype.btnDeleteModel);
SnippetDetailsAssistant.prototype.btnSendModel.disabled = true;
this.controller.modelChanged(
  SnippetDetailsAssistant.prototype.btnSendModel);
```

As you can see, it looks substantially the same. The only real difference is that instead of pulling values from the codeCabinet.currentSnippet object and inserting it into the fields, we are inserting blanks (into the RichTextEdits anyway; the value attribute of the models for the TextFields are set to null, which has the same effect). The Buttons are disabled this time around, since only Save is a valid operation at this point.

The final block of code in this method applies to both scenarios and so is outside the if statement:

```
this.drawerModels.info.open = true;
this.drawerModels.code.open = false;
this.drawerModels.notes.open = false;
this.drawerModels.keywords.open = false;
this.controller.modelChanged(this.drawerModels.info, this);
this.controller.modelChanged(this.drawerModels.code, this);
this.controller.modelChanged(this.drawerModels.notes, this);
```

---

[3] Hungarian Notation is a fairly common technique in programming that some people like and some people totally hate. The idea is that you append a no-more-than-three-character prefix to a variable that tells you what type it is or what kind of object it represents. The prefix txt here refers to a TextField. The Code and Notes RichTextEdit widgets have the prefix rte instead. I am one of the people who likes this technique on the grounds that, in my opinion, it helps to make code self-documenting.

```
this.controller.modelChanged(this.drawerModels.keywords, this);
```

This ensures that the Info Drawer begins opened while all others are initially closed.

When the Save Button is tapped, the saveSnippet() method is what gets executed. We'll chunk this up a bit to make swallowing it a little easier.

```
SnippetDetailsAssistant.prototype.saveSnippet = function() {

  if (!this.drawerModels.info.fields.txtName.value ||
    this.drawerModels.info.fields.txtName.value.strip() == "" ||
    !this.controller.get("snippetDetails_rteCode").innerHTML ||
    this.controller.get("snippetDetails_rteCode").innerHTML.strip() == ""
  ) {
  Mojo.Controller.errorDialog(
    "I'm sorry but you must enter at least a name and code for this snippet."
  );
  return;
  }
```

This first chunk of code is responsible for doing a little data entry checking to ensure that both a name and some code have been entered for this snippet. If either, or both, is blank, then Mojo.Controller.errorDialog() is used to inform the user that they must enter something in these fields. The method is terminated at this point.

If they entered something, though, then the following chunk of code executes:

```
var snippetDescriptor = {
  id : new Date().getTime(), categoryname : codeCabinet.currentCategory.name,
  name : this.drawerModels.info.fields.txtName.value,
  description : this.drawerModels.info.fields.txtDescription.value,
  author : this.drawerModels.info.fields.txtAuthor.value,
  email : this.drawerModels.info.fields.txtEMail.value,
  weblink : this.drawerModels.info.fields.txtWebLink.value,
  code : this.controller.get("snippetDetails_rteCode").innerHTML,
  notes : this.controller.get("snippetDetails_rteNotes").innerHTML,
  keyword1 : this.drawerModels.keywords.fields.txtKeyword1.value,
  keyword2 : this.drawerModels.keywords.fields.txtKeyword2.value,
  keyword3 : this.drawerModels.keywords.fields.txtKeyword3.value,
  keyword4 : this.drawerModels.keywords.fields.txtKeyword4.value,
  keyword5 : this.drawerModels.keywords.fields.txtKeyword5.value
};
```

This is simply creating an object (called a snippetDescriptor object), populating in it fields with names matching the columns in the snippets table, and giving them values from the models behind the TextFields and RichTextEdits. Note the id field, which gets its value from the current time, thereby giving every snippet created a unique ID (unless the user goes back in time and manages to create a snippet at the exact same millisecond as they previously did…which I suppose is inevitable given temporal physics, but I digress).

Here is the actual code that does the save branches based on whether the snippet is new or not:

```
if (codeCabinet.currentSnippet) {
  snippetDescriptor.id = codeCabinet.currentSnippet.id;
  dao.updateSnippet(snippetDescriptor);
```

```
      Mojo.Controller.getAppController().showBanner({
        messageText : "Snippet update successful", soundClass : "alerts" },
        {}, "");
    } else {
      dao.createSnippet(snippetDescriptor);
      Mojo.Controller.stageController.popScene();
    }
```

For existing snippets, the autogenerated ID has to be overridden with the ID from the codeCabinet.currentSnippet object. Then, it's just a call to dao.updateSnippet(), passing in the snippetDescriptor. The showBanner() method of the AppController class is used to display a nonintrusive banner message at the bottom of the screen indicating the save was successful.

For a new snippet, the snippetDescriptor is simply passed to the dao.createSnippet() method, and the Snippet Details scene is popped. Once the Snippet List scene appears again, its activate() method fires, and the List is updated, including the new snippet.

The user has the option of e-mailing the snippet as well, which results in the e-mail application being launched and prepopulated with some data, as shown in Figure 3-16.

Figure 3-16. Sending a snippet as an e-mail opens the e-mail application with autogenerated content.

The code behind this is in the send() method:

```
SnippetDetailsAssistant.prototype.send = function() {

  var description = codeCabinet.currentSnippet.description
  if (!description) { description = "N/A"; }
  var author = codeCabinet.currentSnippet.author
  if (!author) { author = "N/A"; }
  var email = codeCabinet.currentSnippet.email
  if (!email) { email = "N/A"; }
  var weblink = codeCabinet.currentSnippet.weblink
  if (!weblink) { weblink = "N/A"; }
  var keyword1 = codeCabinet.currentSnippet.keyword1
  if (!keyword1) { keyword1 = "N/A"; }
  var keyword2 = codeCabinet.currentSnippet.keyword2
```

```
    if (!keyword2) { keyword2 = "N/A"; }
    var keyword3 = codeCabinet.currentSnippet.keyword3
    if (!keyword3) { keyword3 = "N/A"; }
    var keyword4 = codeCabinet.currentSnippet.keyword4
    if (!keyword4) { keyword4 = "N/A"; }
    var keyword5 = codeCabinet.currentSnippet.keyword5
    if (!keyword5) { keyword5 = "N/A"; }
    var notes = codeCabinet.currentSnippet.notes
    if (!notes) { notes = "N/A"; }

    this.controller.serviceRequest("palm://com.palm.applicationManager", {
      method   : "launch",
      parameters : { id : "com.palm.app.email", params: {
        summary : "Your code snippet has arrived",
        text :
          "Hello from Code Cabinet!<br><br>" +
          "The following snippet was sent on " + new Date() + ":<br><br>" +
          "Category: " + codeCabinet.currentCategory.name + "<br>" +
          "Name: " + codeCabinet.currentSnippet.name + "<br>" +
          "Description: " + description + "<br>" +
          "Author: " + author + "<br>" + "eMail: " + email + "<br>" +
          "Web Link: " + weblink + "<br>" +
          "Keywords: " + keyword1 + "," + keyword2 + "," + keyword3 + "," +
            keyword4 + "," + keyword5 + "<br><br>" +
          "Notes:<br>" + notes + "<br><br>" +
          "Code:<br>" + codeCabinet.currentSnippet.code + "<br><br>" +
          "Have a great day!"
      } }
    });

};
```

First all the data from the current snippet is retrieved, and then it's checked to see whether it's empty. If it is, the string "N/A" is used in its place. Once that's done, the serviceRequest() method of the scene controller is called. The Application Manager service is used to launch the Email application. The params object inside the parameters object contains a summary attribute, which is the subject of the e-mail, and then the text attribute is the body of the e-mail, constructed using simple string concatenation.

The final method in this assistant is the deleteSnippet() method:

```
SnippetDetailsAssistant.prototype.deleteSnippet = function() {

  this.controller.showAlertDialog({
    onChoose : function(inValue) {
      if (inValue == "yes") {
        dao.deleteSnippet(codeCabinet.currentSnippet.id);
        Mojo.Controller.stageController.popScene();
      }
    },
    title : "Confirm Delete",
    message : "Are you sure you want to delete this snippet?",
    choices : [
```

```
      { label : "Yes", value : "yes", type : "affirmative"},
      { label : "No", value : "no", type : "negative"}
    ]
  });

};
```

First, an alert dialog box is shown with the showAlertDialog() method of the scene controller, resulting in the pop-up in Figure 3-17.

Figure 3-17. *Getting confirmation of snippet deletion*

This dialog box has two Buttons, as defined by the choices config attribute. The callback function just looks for the value of the Yes button because if No is tapped, the dialog box will be automatically dismissed and there's nothing for us to do. When Yes is tapped, however, it's a simple matter of calling dao.deleteSnippet(), passing the ID of the current snippet, and then popping the scene. Once again, the Snippet List scene's activate() method fires, updating the List, which no longer includes the snippet that was just deleted.

Search Scene
The Search scene is next; this scene of course is where the user enters criteria to search for snippets. You can see it in Figure 3-18.

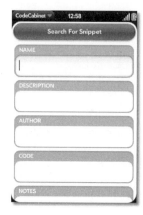

Figure 3-18. *Search criteria to find snippet(s)*

In large measure, this mimics the Snippet Details scene, at least in terms of the fields it contains, since all of them (except for eMail and Web Link) are searchable. The only substantive difference is that instead of five separate keyword fields, here there is one Keywords field, and therefore the user can enter multiple keywords separated by a comma.

The View HTML

The view HTML is located at app/views/search/search-scene.html. Its contents, truncated to remove redundancy, are as follows:

```
<div id="main" class="palm-hasheader">
  <div class="palm-header">Search For Snippet</div>
</div>

<div class="palm-group">
  <div class="palm-group-title">Name</div>
  <div class="palm-list">
    <div class="palm-row single">
      <div class="palm-row-wrapper textfield-group"
        x-mojo-focus-highlight="true">
        <div class="title">
          <div id="search_txtName" x-mojo-element="TextField"></div>
        </div>
      </div>
    </div>
  </div>
</div>
...
<div id="search_btnSearch" x-mojo-element="Button"></div>
```

Only one of the entry fields is shown here, and like has been the case with previous scenes, the rest are just duplicates of this code, with IDs changed. It's just a simple TextField, something that should pretty much be old hat by now!

The Scene Assistant

The SearchAssistant class, defined in app/assistants/search-assistant.js, has the usual stuff in the setup() method that we've become quite accustomed to:

```
function SearchAssistant() { };

SearchAssistant.prototype.setup = function() {

  this.controller.setupWidget(Mojo.Menu.appMenu, codeCabinet.appMenuAttributes,
    codeCabinet.appMenuModel);

  this.controller.setupWidget("search_txtName",
    { focusMode : Mojo.Widget.focusSelectMode, maxLength : 30 },
    codeCabinet.searchFieldModels.txtName
  );
...
  this.controller.setupWidget("search_btnSearch", { },
    { label : "Search", buttonClass : "affirmative buttonfloat" }
  );
  Mojo.Event.listen(this.controller.get("search_btnSearch"), Mojo.Event.tap,
    this.search.bind(this)
  );

};
```

All the TextFields are set up like the Name field is here, because that in turn is set up very much like previous TextFields have been, so we won't dwell on that. Nor will we dwell on the Search Button setup because, again, it's nothing new by now. We will, however, check out the code behind the search() method, called when the Search Button is tapped:

```
SearchAssistant.prototype.search = function() {

  if ((!codeCabinet.searchFieldModels.txtKeywords.value ||
    codeCabinet.searchFieldModels.txtKeywords.value == "") &&
    (!codeCabinet.searchFieldModels.txtCode.value ||
    codeCabinet.searchFieldModels.txtCode.value == "") &&
    (!codeCabinet.searchFieldModels.txtName.value ||
    codeCabinet.searchFieldModels.txtName.value == "") &&
    (!codeCabinet.searchFieldModels.txtAuthor.value ||
    codeCabinet.searchFieldModels.txtAuthor.value == "") &&
    (!codeCabinet.searchFieldModels.txtDescription.value ||
    codeCabinet.searchFieldModels.txtDescription.value == "") &&
    (!codeCabinet.searchFieldModels.txtNotes.value ||
    codeCabinet.searchFieldModels.txtNotes.value == "")) {
    Mojo.Controller.errorDialog(
      "I'm sorry but you must enter at least one search " +
        "criteria in order to perform a search."
    );
    return;
  }
```

```
    Mojo.Controller.stageController.pushScene("searchResults");

};
```

A quick sanity check is done to ensure the user entered something in at least one field. If they haven't, they are politely informed that they need to do so via a dialog box displayed using `Mojo.Controller.errorDialog`. Assuming they've entered something, though, the Search Results scene is pushed, which is where the real action is with regard to searching, and what we're looking at right…now!

Search Results Scene

The Search Results scene, visually, looks virtually identical to the Snippet List scene, as you can see by gazing at Figure 3-19.

Figure 3-19. Search Results scene. Just tap a result to see the snippet details.

The user can tap a snippet to bring up its details or gesture back to return to the Search scene.

The View HTML

Being nearly identical to the snippet list, if you expect the scene markup in `app/views/searchResults/searchResults-scene.html` to be also nearly identical, you're right:

```
<div id="main" class="palm-hasheader">
  <div class="palm-header">Search Results</div>
</div>

<div id="searchResults_lstSearchResultsList" x-mojo-element="List"
  style="display:none;"></div>

<div x-mojo-element="Spinner" id="searchResults_divSpinner"
  class="spinnerClass" style="display:block;"></div>
```

A header pill with the title Search Results, a `List` widget (initially not shown), and a `Spinner` widget (initially shown) are all we need.

The Scene Assistant

Now we come to the scene assistant for the Search Results scene, found in
app/assistants/searchResults-assistant.js. There is certainly some meat on these bones, so let's get
to it:

```
function SearchResultsAssistant() { };

SearchResultsAssistant.prototype.lstSearchResultsModel = { items : [ ] };

SearchResultsAssistant.prototype.setup = function() {

  this.controller.setupWidget(Mojo.Menu.appMenu, codeCabinet.appMenuAttributes,
    codeCabinet.appMenuModel);

  this.controller.setupWidget("searchResults_divSpinner",
    { spinnerSize : "large" }, { spinning : true }
  );

  this.controller.setupWidget("searchResults_lstSearchResultsList", {
    itemTemplate : "searchResults/list-item"
  }, this.lstSearchResultsModel);
  this.controller.listen("searchResults_lstSearchResultsList",
    Mojo.Event.listTap, this.selectSnippet);

};
```

Again, this is largely similar to the Snippet List scene's assistant because, after all, it's really just the
same listing of snippets. So, we have the model for the List, initially with an empty items array, as a field
of the assistant. The application menu is set up like always, and then the Spinner is created. Finally, the
List is set up, using the template app/views/searchResults/list-item.html. We're going to skip looking
at that template entirely because it is identical to the one for the snippet list. If you need to refresh your
memory, jump on back there to take another look and then continue.

The activate() method is next:

```
SearchResultsAssistant.prototype.activate = function() {

  $("searchResults_divSpinner").show();
  $("searchResults_lstSearchResultsList").hide();
  this.lstSearchResultsModel.items = [ ];
  dao.retrieveSnippets(null, this.processResults.bind(this));

};
```

First, we make sure the Spinner is showing and the List is hidden so that the user has some visual
indication of activity while the search is carried out. Next, the items array in the List's model is cleared,
and finally the dao.retrieveSnippets() method is called. Note that the first argument to that method,
which is the name of the category to get snippets for, is null. This indicates to that method that *all*
snippets across *all* categories should be returned.

When the DAO method completes, it calls our specified callback method, processResults(), which
we'll look at in chunks, owing to its length:

```
SearchResultsAssistant.prototype.processResults = function(inSnippets) {

  if (!inSnippets || !inSnippets.length) {
    this.controller.showAlertDialog({
      onChoose : function(inValue) {
        this.controller.stageController.popScene();
      },
      title : "Nothing To Do",
      message : "There are no snippets to search.  How about you go " +
        "create a few??",
      choices : [
        { label : "Ok", type : "affirmative"}
      ]
    });
    return;
  }
```

The first thing we do is check to see whether we got any results from the DAO method. If there are no results, then there are no snippets yet created, so we inform the user of that fact using the showAlertDialog() of the scene controller. After that, we abort the method's execution.

Once past that initial check, we know that we have some snippets, so now the job is to figure out which ones match the search criteria entered by the user.

```
var matches = [ ];

var snippetName = codeCabinet.searchFieldModels.txtName.value ?
  codeCabinet.searchFieldModels.txtName.value.strip().toLowerCase() : null;
var snippetDescription = codeCabinet.searchFieldModels.txtDescription.value ?
  codeCabinet.searchFieldModels.txtDescription.value.strip().toLowerCase() :
  null;
var snippetAuthor = codeCabinet.searchFieldModels.txtAuthor.value ?
  codeCabinet.searchFieldModels.txtAuthor.value.strip().toLowerCase() : null;
var snippetCode = codeCabinet.searchFieldModels.txtCode.value ?
  codeCabinet.searchFieldModels.txtCode.value.strip().toLowerCase() : null;
var snippetNotes = codeCabinet.searchFieldModels.txtNotes.value ?
  codeCabinet.searchFieldModels.txtNotes.value.strip().toLowerCase() : null;
var snippetKeywords = codeCabinet.searchFieldModels.txtKeywords.value ?
  codeCabinet.searchFieldModels.txtKeywords.value.strip().toLowerCase() :
  null;
```

The first step is to get the entered values for all the fields that can be searched on. For each, we strip() whitespace off the ends and convert the entered values to all lowercase so that, combined with the code after this, we can have a case-insensitive search. If no value was entered for a given field, then the value is set to null. Six variables—snippetName, snippetDescription, snippetAuthor, snippetCode, snippetNotes, and snippetKeywords—now contain the trimmed, all-lowercase versions of the search criteria entered by the user.

With that out of the way, it's time to scan through the snippets returned by the DAO method:

```
for (var i = 0; i < inSnippets.length; i++) {

  var matched = "";
```

```
    if (snippetName) {
      if (inSnippets[i].name.toLowerCase().indexOf(snippetName) != -1) {
        matched += "T";
      } else {
        matched += "F";
      }
    }
```

For each of the possible search fields, we check to see whether the user entered a value. For example, we check to see whether snippetName has a value. If it does, then we grab the name field from the next snippet in the result list, convert it to lowercase, and then see whether the value the user entered appears anywhere in the snippet's name. If it does, we add a letter T to the variable matched; otherwise, we add an F. The idea here is that since the user can enter multiple criteria and a matching snippet must match on all entered criteria, then by adding a T or an F to this variable we can check at the end to see whether there are only Ts in the string. If there are, then the snippet matches. If there are any Fs, then it's not a match.

The remaining searchable fields are checked in the same manner as name, until we get to the keywords, which require some different logic:

```
    if (snippetKeywords) {
      var a = snippetKeywords.split(",");
      var foundAny = false;
      for (var j = 0; j < a.length; j++) {
        var nextKeyword = a[j].strip().toLowerCase();
        if (nextKeyword != "") {
          if (inSnippets[i].keyword1.toLowerCase() == nextKeyword ||
            inSnippets[i].keyword2.toLowerCase() == nextKeyword ||
            inSnippets[i].keyword3.toLowerCase() == nextKeyword ||
            inSnippets[i].keyword4.toLowerCase() == nextKeyword ||
            inSnippets[i].keyword5.toLowerCase() == nextKeyword) {
            foundAny = true;
          }
        }
      }
      if (foundAny) {
        matched += "T";
      } else {
        matched += "F";
      }
    }
```

For the keywords, the first step is to split() the string entered by the user so that we get an array of the keywords (words separated by commas) that they want to search for. Next, we iterate over the resultant array, and for each we strip() and convert to lowercase the next keyword entered. We then check all five of the separate keyword fields in the snippet object with the keyword entered, and if any match, the flag foundAny is set to true. After the iteration over the tokenized keywords string is completed, we check foundAny. If it's true, then we add a T to matched; otherwise, we add an F.

Finally, we do that check I mentioned previously:

```
    if (matched.indexOf("F") == -1) {
      matches.push(inSnippets[i]);
```

```
      }

   }
```

As long as there are no Fs in the `matched` string, then the snippet object is pushed onto an array of matching records.

That closes out the iteration over the snippet objects returned by the DAO, so now we check to see whether we have found any matching snippets:

```
if (matches.length > 0) {
  for (var i = 0; i < matches.length; i++) {
    this.lstSearchResultsModel.items.push(matches[i]);
  }
  this.controller.modelChanged(this.lstSearchResultsModel);
  $("searchResults_divSpinner").hide();
  $("searchResults_lstSearchResultsList").show();
} else {
  Mojo.Controller.getAppController().showBanner({
    messageText : "No snippets found matching criteria",
    soundClass : "alerts" }, {}, ""
  );
  this.controller.stageController.popScene();
}

};
```

If we have, then we push each of them into the `items` array in the model for the `List`, call `modelChanged()` to get the `List` updated on the screen, hide the `Spinner`, show the `List`, and we're done! If no results were found, however, then a banner notification is shown saying no matches were found, and the scene is popped, returning the user to the Search scene. You can see this banned notification in Figure 3-20.

Figure 3-20. Banner message when no matching snippets are found

Only a single method remains to look at in this assistant, and that's the selectSnippet() method, executed when the user taps a snippet in the result list:

```
SearchResultsAssistant.prototype.selectSnippet = function(inEvent) {
  codeCabinet.currentSnippet = inEvent.item;
  Mojo.Controller.stageController.pushScene("snippetDetails");
};
```

Just like from the Snippet List scene, the codeCabinet.currentSnippet variable is pointed to the object containing the information for the snippet, and the Snippet Details scene is pushed.

Preferences Scene

The final scene to visit in our Code Cabinet exploration is the Preferences scene. This scene, seen in Figure 3-21, is seen[4] when the user selects Preferences from the application menu.

Figure 3-21. *The Preferences scene*

There's only one preference at the user's disposal, but sometimes one is enough!

The View HTML

The scene's view markup, found in app/views/preferencesView/preferencesView-scene.html, is a relatively simple bit of markup:

```
<div class="palm-page-header">
  <div class="header-icon preferences"></div>
  <div class="header-text">Code Cabinet Preferences</div>
```

---

[4] Dig that fancy homophone action? It's always fun to see how many words that sound alike but are spelled differently (aka homophones or homonyms) you can string together and yet still have a coherent, accurate sentence! I suppose it's not as cool as possible because *seen* is used twice, but a quick Google search didn't turn up a third form of the word, so let's go with it anyway!

```
</div>

<div class="palm-row">
  <span style="position:relative;left:4px;top:18px;">
    The snippet list will be sorted:
  </span>
</div>

<div class="palm-list">
  <div class="palm-row">
    <div id="preferences_snippetsSortOrder" x-mojo-element="ListSelector"></div>
  </div>
</div>
```

The palm-page-header style gives us a header style different from the header pill present in other scenes. This is a style common to Preferences scenes in many webOS applications. Within the first <div> is another with the style classes header-icon and preferences applied. This is a bit of custom styling, extending the Palm-supplied styling for icons on a header:

```
.header-icon.preferences {
    background : url(../images/preferencesIcon.png) no-repeat;
}
```

Yep, it's nothing but a background image; that's how the icon winds up on the header.

After the header we have a <div> with the style palm-row. The purpose of this is to get a divider line below the text, which that style includes. Within the <div> is a <span> that is bumped to the right and down a bit from where it would normally have appeared in the page flow. This gets it off the edge of the screen and also puts some space between the top of it and the header.

Finally, a ListSelector widget is wrapped inside two <div>s. The outer <div> has the palm-list style as well so that there is a line below it. The result of this, plus the <div> surrounding the text label, is that the ListSelector has a subtle gray divider line above and below it, which I thought looked better and also serves to separate the widget from the text label a bit.

The Scene Assistant

The PreferencesAssistant, in the file app/assistants/preferencesScene-assistant.js, begins, as most of our assistants have, with the basic object construction, some class-level fields, and a setup() method:

```
function PreferencesAssistant() { };

PreferencesAssistant.prototype.snippetsSortOrderModel = { value : null };

PreferencesAssistant.prototype.setup = function() {

  var storedSortOrder = codeCabinet.sortOrderCookie.get();
  this.snippetsSortOrderModel.value = storedSortOrder;

  this.controller.setupWidget("preferences_snippetsSortOrder",
    { label: "Snippet Sorting",
      choices: [
        { label : "By Name ASC", value : "name_asc"},
```

```
        { label : "By Name DESC", value : "name_desc"},
        { label : "By Author ASC", value : "author_asc"},
        { label : "By Author DESC", value : "author_desc"},
        { label : "Newest First", value : "newest"},
        { label : "Oldest First", value : "oldest"}
      ]
    }, this.snippetsSortOrderModel
  );
  Mojo.Event.listen(this.controller.get("preferences_snippetsSortOrder"),
    Mojo.Event.propertyChange, this.orderChanged.bind(this)
  );

};
```

The setup() method is primarily responsible for setting up our ListSelector widget, but before that can be done, we first retrieve the current sort order as stored in the codeCabinet.sortOrderCookie that we saw created (and populated with a value, either a default or read in from a stored cookie) in the CodeCabinet.js code. This value is inserted into the snippetsSortOrderModel's value field, which is the model that backs the ListSelector.

Then, the ListSelector itself is set up in a fashion typical of all widgets. The attributes for the widget include a label attribute, which is the text shown on the right that the user taps to see the list of options, and choices, which is the list of choices that appear when the label is tapped. Each of them has a text label attribute and a value attribute, and you'll notice that those values match the possible values stored in the cookie as discussed earlier. Figure 3-22, by the way, shows the ListSelector when expanded.

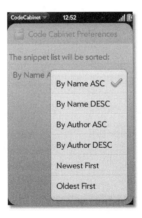

Figure 3-22. *There may only be one preference, but there are a lot of choices for it!*

The ListSelector has a single event, Mojo.Event.propertyChange, being listened for. When it occurs, it fires the orderChanged() method:

```
PreferencesAssistant.prototype.orderChanged = function() {
  codeCabinet.sortOrderCookie.put(this.snippetsSortOrderModel.value);
};
```

This simply calls the put() method on the cookie stored in codeCabinet.sortOrderCookie, passing it the newly selected value from the model of the ListSelector, and that's literally all there is to Preferences!

Suggested Exercises

As I mentioned at the beginning of this chapter, the features built into this application represent the basics of what such an application should do, with perhaps just a few things a bit beyond the basics. However, there is clearly more that could be done in an application like this, so I offer a few suggestions to you, as I'll do at the end of each application chapter, for things that would make the application better. More important, implementing these suggestions will enhance your hands-on knowledge and experience in developing webOS applications in a way that, I hope, is a little easier on you than writing an application completely from scratch.

- Although perhaps a bit more advanced, how about automatic color coding of snippets in accordance with rules for a given language? Allowing the user to modify the rules for a given language and store them as preferences would be a plus (and likely you wouldn't be able to store that in cookies owing to the likely size of the database, so some HTML5 database work is probably in order).

- Try to rework the code so that it doesn't simply refresh the lists after adding a category or snippet (or modifying a snippet). This was a design choice I made (a) because it was the most time-efficient way to implement it and (b) so that I could make this suggestion! There's really no need to do a refresh like this, though; you should be able to manipulate the list's data in memory at the same time you update the database.

- Make the Web Link field active such that when you tap it (or an icon next to it?), you open the e-mail application with that address in the To field.

I'm sure you can think of plenty on your own, but this should give you a good start.

Summary

In this chapter, we built an application for storing, organizing, and finding snippets of code that all programmers tend to keep. We saw for the first time in the context of a "serious" application the basics of webOS development including stages, scenes, assistants, and controllers. We saw in action a number of webOS widgets including Buttons, Lists, Drawers, Menus, ListSelectors, and Spinners. We saw how to store data in cookies for preferences, and we saw how to store more robust data in the SQLite/HTML5-based database infrastructure provided by the operating system. We saw how to launch another application and feed it data for sending e-mail.

Perhaps most important, in the end, we built an application that should prove useful to any programmer out there!

In the next chapter, we'll build an application that for the first time allows us to interact with services beyond our mobile device—out in the cloud, as the saying goes. In the process, we'll put together another application that has real-world usage scenarios, and we'll learn a bunch of new stuff and continue exercising our newfound webOS development knowledge!

■■■

A Gateway to Industry: Local Business Search

An App That Uses Web Services to Find Businesses in the Users' Current Location

The Palm Pre is a great phone all by itself. Add to it a bunch of applications, and you have yourself a powerful little computer right there in your pocket all the time.

But, this Internet thing seems to have some staying power too. You wouldn't have thought so a year or two ago when it could have gone either way. (If I have to tell you those last two sentences were sarcasm, then you're reading the wrong wise-cracking author!) Wouldn't it be great if there was a way to mix the power of the Pre, and webOS of course, with the vast amount of data available on the Internet?

Yes, indeed it would be, and indeed that's what we're going to do in this chapter! We'll learn how we can access some existing web services made available by one of the most well-known companies on the Internet, namely, Yahoo! We'll use these services to build an application to find businesses in a given area (presumably your "local" area, but in reality you can use it to find businesses anywhere).

We'll also see how we can build an application with a fairly different look and feel from other applications we've built, and we'll see a bunch of new webOS facilities in the process.

What's This App Do Anyway?

Let's get the silly terminology out of the way first, shall we? What we're actually creating here is called a *mashup*. A mashup, as these types of web apps have come to be known, is basically a web site or application that takes content from multiple sources (usually via some sort of public programmatic interface—a remote API, in other words) and integrates it all into a new experience, that is, a new application.

The term *mashup* might sound a bit silly (it does to me!), but it's the term that's been applied to what is at its core an extremely powerful vision: people provide various services and data over the Internet via a well-defined programmatic interface, and anyone can come along and combine them to create applications. In other words, we're talking about a relatively simple, open, platform-agnostic service-oriented architecture (SOA).

MORE ON SOA

The idea of SOA has been gaining steam over the past few years. Most notably, the concept of web services has been evolving rapidly over that time. However, the meaning of that term has been evolving as well. People now often consider things such as the Yahoo! services that will be used in this application to be web services, even though they don't use the full web services stack (that is, SOAP, WS-Security, and all the other specifications that can go along with it).

Whatever line of demarcation you choose to use, the bottom line is that you're developing using an SOA, which means you have loosely coupled components that expose a remote service interface that, usually, is platform- and language-agnostic and can therefore be married together in nearly limitless ways.

The benefits of this approach are numerous. The simple fact that you aren't generally tied to any particular technology or language is a big one. The ease with which updates can be done, assuming the interface doesn't change, is another big one (this is the same reason people love web apps in general). The ability to use all sorts of automated tools to both create and consume services is another (although this isn't always a good thing, if those tools become a crutch that allows you to not understand what you're doing). Realizing the goal of building your application on top of established standards is another. Reusing existing assets and therefore increasing the speed with which solutions can be delivered is another (some would argue this is the biggest benefit). There are plenty more; these are just some that come to mind immediately.

You've probably heard the term *mashup* before, just like you've almost certainly heard the term *Web Services* before too. Web Services are sometimes involved to create mashups. However, Web Services, as most people mean when they use the term, can be pretty complicated beasts! The types of things you deal with when working with web services are SOAP; Universal Description, Discovery, and Integration (UDDI) directories; and Web Services Description Language (WSDL) documents—not to mention a whole host of other specifications. Although there's nothing that says that stuff can't be involved when writing a mashup, typically they aren't. There are other techniques available for writing mashups, as we'll soon see.

Notice when I wrote *Web Services* in the last paragraph that both words were capitalized. That is meant to refer to the more "proper" Web Services using the technologies described in that paragraph. More generically, however, is the term *web services* (note the absence of capitalization) that really just refers to an API that you can call on remotely via the Internet. It is this class of web services that we'll be exploiting in this application.

Getting back to the term *mashup* for a moment, it also refers to a web app that, by and large, runs within your browser (as opposed to one that primarily runs on a server, as in typical web site architecture). In fact, for many people, *mashup* implies a JavaScript-based application that can run locally with no server interaction (aside from loading it in the first place, which is actually optional too) and calling on remote servers for data and services to perform their tasks. The term *mashup* has generally come to mean browser-based JavaScript clients aggregating content through public APIs from various companies and vendors to form new applications. These APIs are often referred to as *web services*, and even though they may not truly be web services in the sense of using the full technology stack (the whole alphabet soup of terms I threw around earlier), they still fulfill the same basic goal as those types of web services. They provide services and function over a network (specifically, the Web), so calling them *web services* isn't too far-fetched anyway.

Since a webOS application is a web application, as you well know by now, applying the term *mashup* to certain webOS applications doesn't seem like much of a stretch to me at all. Also, since all webOS applications run within a web browser (albeit one you don't really see as such), they too stay in line with the idea of a JavaScript-based application running locally in a browser. To me, the definition fits more or less perfectly!

So, now we know we're going to be building a mashup here and we know we're going to be using some remote APIs to accomplish it, so let's discuss some of the features the application will have and some of the main functions it will perform:

- By using a remote service provides by Yahoo!, we will be able to perform a search for businesses given an address or some components of a location. We'll be able to see a List of search results and select one to view in more detail, including the address, phone number, web site, and average user ratings.

- We'll also be able to view a map of the location around the business and be able to zoom in and out of that map. These maps will also be provided by Yahoo!

- We can save a selected business as a favorite so that we can quickly call up its details later. These favorites will be stored in a local Depot.

- The user will also be able to launch the built-in Google Maps application using the longitude and latitude of a given business so that the user can get directions if they want.

- The application will be "dark," literally using the "dark" theme that Palm provides for applications with dark backgrounds. We'll add just a little bit of visual flair by allowing the user to choose a background (even some animated ones!).

Now let's have a look at the web services we'll use to pull this off and look at how we're going to be calling on them.

AJAX

AJAX, as I'd be willing to bet my dog you know already (well, not really—my wife and kids will kill me if I gave away the family dog, although my wallet would thank me), stands for Asynchronous JavaScript and XML. This acronym describes a method for a JavaScript-based client application to interact with a server to retrieve data that does not result in immediately redrawing the currently viewed page. This is termed an *out-of-band* request because it's outside the normal page-to-page flow through a typical web site or web application.

The curious thing about AJAX, though, is that it doesn't have to be asynchronous (but virtually always is), doesn't have to involve JavaScript (but virtually always does), and doesn't need to use XML at all (and more and more frequently doesn't). It's more of a theoretical way to approach the problem of how to retrieve data from a server without having to reload the entire page, which is the whole point of AJAX! This innovation allowed for a whole new class of applications to be built, making AJAX in many ways a powerful force in the world of web development (a super-hero of sorts, as shown in Figure 4-1).

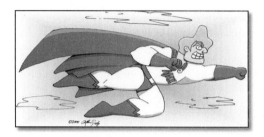

Figure 4-1. *If you ever wanted to know what a programming technique would look like as a person, there you go!*

■ **Note** AJAX is a technique that was originated by a guy name Jesse James Garrett of Adaptive Path (www.adaptivepath.com). I am fighting my natural urge to make the obvious outlaw jokes here! Mr. Garrett wrote an essay in February 2005 (you can see it at www.adaptivepath.com/publications/essays/archives/000385.php) in which he coined the term AJAX.

Now, you'll notice that I wrote that as AJAX. That's actually very significant. You see, nowadays, the term *Ajax* is different from the acronym. The distinction is that AJAX refers to the communication mechanism that allows for out-of-band partial-page refreshes most commonly using something called the XMLHttpRequest object. That's a JavaScript object that allows you to make HTTP requests to a server, get some data back, and process it in some way, most frequently resulting in part of the page being changed. Note the difference between this and the basic function of a browser: the data you get via an AJAX request requires your code to do something with it, whereas the browser normally requests an HTML page from the server and simply displays it in its entirety.

The term *Ajax*, however, is much broader. In effect, Ajax really refers to what many of us prefer to call rich Internet applications (RIAs). Ajax now refers to applications that have AJAX interactions with a server but that also have fancy UIs, have graphical effects, and are typically very interactive. Those same AJAX requests are what allows Ajax, or RIAs. You've likely heard the term Web 2.0 as well, which in most regards means the same thing as RIA and, nowadays, Ajax.

Now, in the case of webOS, things are somewhat different, but at the end of the day, not all *that* much. You see, there is still the opportunity to make AJAX requests, but since webOS applications are inherently pretty fancy in terms of UI and of course are quite interactive in nature most of the time, the broader term *Ajax* makes a lot of sense in this context too.

So, although this application will make use of AJAX the communication technique, it is in effect also what many would these days call an Ajax application.

The Trouble with AJAX

That's all well and good, but there's one huge fly in the ointment here, and that's that AJAX requests adhere to what's called the *same-domain policy*. Simply stated, an AJAX request can be made only to the same domain that served the HTML document trying to make the request. This is a fairly simple, but effective, security measure. It for the most part gets around a number of hacking exploits that would otherwise allow a malicious user to do all manner of nasty things with your browser. This is a topic that is quite a bit broader than what I could cover in a book not focused on that topic, but suffice it to say that the same-domain policy is, generally speaking, a good thing, at least in terms of security.

However, in terms of using remote systems to obtain data, it's a very, very bad thing. In fact, in normal web applications there are all sorts of fancy tricks to get around this policy (which of course introduces security problems, but I digress).

Since a webOS application is effectively "served" by the operating system, then if this same-domain policy exists in the webOS environment too, we're going to have to use those same sorts of hacks to get at the remote data we need for this application.

As it happens, Palm recognized what this limitation would mean and decided that the easier course of action would be to remove the same-domain policy restriction. As it turns out, you can make AJAX requests to any remote domain you want, without restriction. Although this does arguably have implications in terms of security, the fact is that it makes a whole class of modern applications possible.

Actually making an AJAX request is a simple thing to do because the Prototype library provides a very simple API for making such requests. We'll see that code later as we explore the application, but I'll give you a bit of a preview by telling you that it comes down to a single easy-to-use function. All the plumbing code that we'd otherwise have to deal with is rolled up in Prototype nice and neat and hidden from us. Trust me, you're going to love this!

Meet the Yahoo! Web Services

Before we can get to the application code, there's one more thing we need to look at, and that's the Yahoo! Web Services we're going to use.

But, before you can even go look at the web services, we need to get some paperwork out of the way first.

Most API services in general require you to register to use their APIs, and Yahoo! is no exception. Every time you interact with the Yahoo! services, you need to pass an appid parameter (as part of a number of parameters you'll need to pass). The value of this parameter is a unique identifier assigned to your application. Not passing this value, or passing an invalid value, will result in the call failing. Before you can play with the application in this chapter, you will have to register and get your own ID. It's a painless process that you can go through by accessing the following page:

http://api.search.yahoo.com/webservices/register_application

You should plug your own ID into the LocalBusinessSearch.js file (in the aptly named appID field) before you spend time with the application, just so you are playing nice with Yahoo! I'll use XXX in the following sections when referencing appid to indicate that you should plug your ID in there.

Some limitations are associated with using the APIs in terms of request volume, but the upper limit is so high as to not be a realistic concern for your adventures with this application. In any case, the limits are based on requests made from a given IP address over a 24-hour period, so even if you run over the limit, just try again tomorrow, and you should be good to go. If you are intent on building a production-level application by using these services, you will need to consult with Yahoo! for other registration options that allow for high volumes. Again, for our purposes, the number of requests allowed is more than sufficient.

The Yahoo! Search Service

Yahoo! offers some very nice search services that you can play with, and one of them is the Yahoo! Local Search service. It enables you to search for businesses in a given geographic location. For each search result, the service provides a plethora of information, including the business location, contact information (phone number, web site, and so forth), and user rating information.

Using this service requires you to access a given URL, for example:

```
http://local.yahooapis.com/LocalSearchService/V3/localSearch?↵
appid=YahooDemo&query=pizza&zip=90210&results=2
```

The appid used here is a common one that Yahoo! uses in its own examples, which means you can load this URL into your browser and get a proper response.

The parameters you pass are probably pretty obvious, but in case they aren't, the query parameter enables you to specify a keyword to search for, zip is just a U.S. zip code to center the search around, and results is the maximum number of results you want to return.

If you paste that into the address bar of your web browser, you'll see that what you get back is an XML document. That's pretty nifty on its own, but if you've ever dealt with XML in JavaScript, you know that it isn't the most pleasant experience. Thankfully, Yahoo! provides a great alternative: simply append output=json as a query parameter, and you'll get a response back in JavaScript Object Notation (JSON) instead. Here is the result of doing so:

```
{"ResultSet":{"totalResultsAvailable":"1037","totalResultsReturned":"2",↵
"firstResultPosition":"1","ResultSetMapUrl":"http:\/\/maps.yahoo.com↵
\/broadband\/?q1=Beverly+Hills%2C+CA+90210&tt=pizza&tp=1","Result":[{↵
"id":"20478419","Title":"California Pizza Kitchen","Address":↵
"207 S Beverly Dr","City":"Beverly Hills","State":"CA","Phone":↵
"(310) 275-1101","Latitude":"34.064568","Longitude":"-118.399254",↵
"Rating":{"AverageRating":"4","TotalRatings":"88","TotalReviews":"62",↵
"LastReviewDate":"1213312430","LastReviewIntro":"its ok same pizza at ↵
every location its ok same pizza at every location"},"Distance":"2.07",↵
"Url":"http:\/\/local.yahoo.com\/info-20478419-california-pizza-kitchen-↵
beverly-hills","ClickUrl":"http:\/\/local.yahoo.com\/info-20478419-↵
california-pizza-kitchen-beverly-hills","MapUrl":"http:\/\/maps.yahoo.com↵
\/maps_result?q1=207+S+Beverly+Dr+Beverly+Hills+CA&gid1=20478419",↵
"BusinessUrl":"http:\/\/www.cpk.com\/","BusinessClickUrl":"http:\/\/↵
www.cpk.com\/","Categories":{"Category":[{"id":"96926225","content":↵
"Salad Restaurants"},{"id":"96926243","content":"Pizza"},{"id":"96926155",↵
"content":"Californian Restaurants"},{"id":"96926190","content":↵
"Italian Restaurants"},{"id":"96926234","content":"Carry Out & Take Out"},↵
{"id":"96926236","content":"Restaurants"},{"id":"96926238","content":↵
"Sandwiches"}]}},{"id":"31216257","Title":"Pizza Rustica","Address":↵
"231 N Beverly Dr","City":"Beverly Hills","State":"CA","Phone":↵
"(310) 550-7499","Latitude":"34.067488","Longitude":"-118.3998","Rating":↵
{"AverageRating":"5","TotalRatings":"4","TotalReviews":"3",↵
"LastReviewDate":"1158242113","LastReviewIntro":"Rustica but good!"},↵
"Distance":"1.87","Url":"http:\/\/local.yahoo.com\/info-31216257-pizza-↵
rustica-beverly-hills","ClickUrl":"http:\/\/local.yahoo.com\/info-↵
31216257-pizza-rustica-beverly-hills","MapUrl":"http:\/\/maps.yahoo.com↵
\/maps_result?q1=231+N+Beverly+Dr+Beverly+Hills+CA&gid1=31216257",↵
"BusinessUrl":"http:\/\/www.pizzarusticala.com\/","BusinessClickUrl":↵
"http:\/\/www.pizzarusticala.com\/","Categories":{"Category":{"id":↵
"96926243","content":"Pizza"}}}]}}
```

Now, obviously, that's not really meant for human consumption (although it is human-readable, it's certainly not pleasant to read). The nice thing, though, is that the Prototype API we'll use to make this same request as part of the application will automatically turn this into an object graph for us, so all we know is that we made a request and we got back some JavaScript objects to deal with. That's very cool indeed!

The set of data returned by the service is pretty large, and a lot of it won't be used in this application, but if you cruise on over to `http://developer.yahoo.com/search/local/V3/localSearch.html`, you can get all those details, plus a lot more, about this particular service. It's without question a handy API to be able to access.

The Yahoo! Map Image Service

Yahoo! is also going to be providing the maps that you can see in the application (yes, take a break and go play with the application a bit now!). Yahoo! Maps is a service that has been around for a while, even before a public AJAX-accessible interface was provided for it. It enables you to get maps for a given address, as well as access other features, such as traffic and local places of interest. The API Yahoo! provides a number of different services, but for our purposes, we'll be focusing on the Map Image service.

The Yahoo! Maps Map Image API enables you to get a reference to a graphic of a map generated according to the parameters you specify in your request. You may specify latitude and longitude or an address in your request.

This service is referenced via a simple HTTP request, such as the following:

```
http://local.yahooapis.com/MapsService/V1/mapImage?appid=XXX&output=json&↵
latitude=34.064568&longitude=-118.399254
```

The `latitude` and `longitude` parameters specify the center of the area we want a map for, and the `appid` is once again your registered application ID. If you go ahead and paste that into the address bar of your web browser, assuming you plug in your own application ID, you'll see the following response:

```
{"ResultSet":{"Result":"http:\/\/gws.maps.yahoo.com\/mapimage?MAPDATA=↵
9JKfWOd6wXUraXtLboL_09kxYUGyR24vwm2OMX8jMnWdjwOBh456gOUVFvHROYzBnPGSvYbAJL↵
XMpX74E.hyU53LdJLVHwie6oOw_nrSdaCvS1xv53ANiNSawgbEGnXhFo.B_h.Nw9tCaa2EjjP↵
j7lA-&mvt=m&cltype=onnetwork&.intl=us&appid=hNGwI8XV34FmZYlnbFS3Ga2jw3w8RG↵
scRq2ETnrRtO3QlHcRMy86NqYb._TIgvZ5&oper=&_proxy=ydn,xml"}}
```

What you've gotten back includes a reference to an image now sitting on Yahoo!'s servers. If you pluck out the following URL:

```
http://gws.maps.yahoo.com/mapimage?MAPDATA=↵
9JKfWOd6wXUraXtLboL_09kxYUGyR24vwm2OMX8jMnWdjwOBh456gOUVFvHROYzBnPGSvYbAJL↵
XMpX74E.hyU53LdJLVHwie6oOw_nrSdaCvS1xv53ANiNSawgbEGnXhFo.B_h.Nw9tCaa2EjjP↵
j7lA-&mvt=m&cltype=onnetwork&.intl=us&appid=hNGwI8XV34FmZYlnbFS3Ga2jw3w8RG↵
scRq2ETnrRtO3QlHcRMy86NqYb._TIgvZ5&oper=&_proxy=ydn,xml
```

and put that in the address bar of a web browser, you'll see an image that is a map of the Beverly Hills area of California, as shown in Figure 4-2.

So, using this API is really a two-step process: call the API to request the map, and then access the returned URL to retrieve the generated map. A typical usage scenario, and in fact the way you'll find it done in the application, is to point an `<img>` element at the returned map URL.

Like with the local search API, there are other parameters you can pass in, but only three more will be of interest in this application: image_width, image_height, and zoom. The first two allow us to specify the size of the image we want back, and the third specifies what zoom level we want the image to be at. The value of this parameter goes from 1 to 12, with 1 being street level and 12 being country (region really) level.

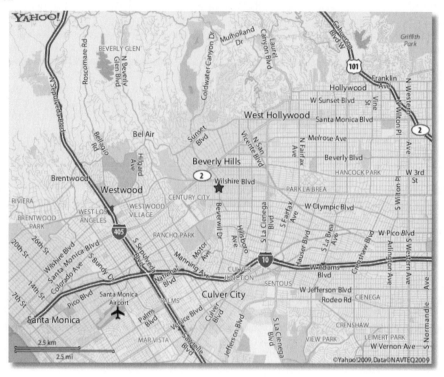

Figure 4-2. The map resulting from accessing the URL in the example

As with the local search service, I encourage you to examine the Yahoo! Maps APIs (http://developer.yahoo.com/maps/rest/V1) because they can definitely do more than this application demonstrates. This is about all we need for the purposes of this chapter, though, so you're now armed with all the knowledge you need to go forth and dissect this application!

Planning the Application

This application has a few more scenes than the previous application did, so diagramming the flow through it is a very good idea, and Figure 4-3 is the result of that effort.

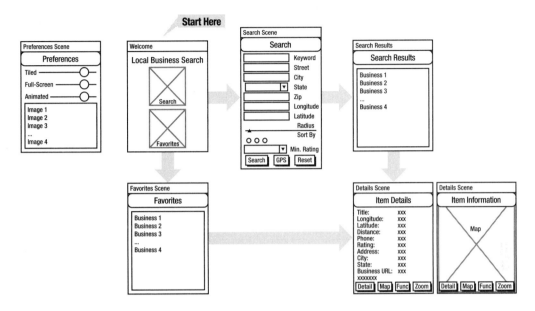

Figure 4-3. *A whiteboardish sketching of the scene flow of the application*

As with the previous application, we start with a Welcome scene. From there, the flow can follow three paths.

The first path is the most common, which is performing a search. Clicking the search button (which isn't a Button as we've come to know per se, but we'll get to that later). This leads to the aptly named Search scene. The user enters their search criteria here, or uses the GPS button to get their current location via GPS, and then clicks the search button to initiate the search. This leads to the Search Results scene.

The user can then scroll through the List, which displays the title of the business, the distance in miles from the specified search location, and the number of stars the business is rated as, and can then click an item to pull up its details. This results in the Item Details scene being displayed.

The Item Details scene is in a sense two scenes put together. There is the table of details about the business, including a link to its home page (if it has one) that when clicked causes the site to be loaded in the browser application. The user can also flip to the map view by clicking the Map menu button at the bottom. The map is displayed, but this isn't a scene transition as the map is just an <img> element that is initially hidden in the Item Details scene's HTML. The user can also use the menu button at the bottom to launch the built-in Google Maps application to map the longitude and latitude for the business. This allows them to get directions, among other things, that Google Maps offers.

Alternatively, the user can click the Favorites button from the Welcome scene and be led down a different flow. The Favorites scene is pretty much identical to the Search Results scene, and clicking an item leads to the very same Item Details scene as from Search Results. The user can also delete items from the favorites List with a swipe, unlike the Search Results scene.

The final flow is for preferences. This simply leads to the Preferences scene, where the user can select an alternate background image for the application.

Creating the Skeleton

If you were to create this application from scratch, you would again use the Palm-supplied application wizard to do so and then add to it six scenes. The directory structure at the end of that process would look like Figure 4-4.

Figure 4-4. *The application's directory structure and file contents*

As with the previous application, I've left the images directory collapsed because it would make this image a bit too tall for the printed page. However, I don't want to deprive you of information, so Table 4-1 describes the images you'll find in that directory.

Table 4-1. *The Images in the* images *Directory*

File Name	Description
backgroundXX.gif	There are actually 19 files beginning with background and ending with a number where you see XX here. These are the background images the user can choose from.
btnFavorites.png	This is the image for the Favorites button (the big heart) on the Welcome scene.
btnSearch.png	This is the image for the search button (the binoculars) on the Welcome scene.
icoPreferences.png	This is the icon for the header of the Preferences scene.
LocalBusinessSearch.png	This is the title graphic on the Welcome scene.

my-scene-fade-bottom-dark.png	This is used to provide a fade effect over the bottom elements on the Search Results and Favorites scenes to indicate there are more items below.
ratingX.png	These are a total of six files, where X is a number from 0 to 5. These are the star images in the search results and favorites for business ratings.

The my-scene-fade-bottom-dark.png image will be discussed in more detail later, but the rest are, I hope, pretty self-explanatory and won't require further explanation.

The Data Model

In the previous application, we were dealing directly with the HTML5 database facility, which means we were responsible for the structure of the database, what tables were present in it, and everything. With this application, however, we'll be using the Depot facility.

Depot is just an API wrapper around HTML5's relational store, though, which means that those details are handled for us. All we need to do is store and load plain old JavaScript object, and the Depot API takes care of how it's actually stored in the database, how it's retrieved, and so on.

Therefore, in effect, there *is no data model for this application!* At least, there's none that we explicitly know about or define ourselves.

As you'll see as we explore the code, there are two types of objects that will be stored in the Depot. One is an object that contains all the data for a given favorite business, and the other is an object containing user preferences. The code for working with the Depot is quite simple and, in many regards, not a whole lot different from the SQLite code we saw in the previous application, minus the need to muck around with all that icky SQL anyway!

Application Configuration

The three configuration files in this application are, just like in the previous chapter's project, appinfo.json, sources.json, and framework_config.json.

appinfo.json

The appinfo.json file for this application is not much different from that in the previous application, as you can see for yourself in Listing 4-1.

Listing 4-1. The appinfo.json File

```
{
  "id": "com.etherient.localbusinesssearch",
  "version": "1.0.0",
  "vendor": "Etherient",
  "type": "web",
  "main": "index.html",
  "title": "Local Business Search",
  "icon": "icon.png"
```

```
}
```

The only real differences are the `id` and `title` attributes, but otherwise it's identical, and there certainly are no surprises here.

sources.json

We load most of our JavaScript in the `sources.json` file, as shown in the previous chapter. Listing 4-2 shows the contents of this file.

Listing 4-2. The `sources.json` File

```
[
    {
      "source" : "app/LocalBusinessSearch.js"
    },
    {
      "source" : "app/assistants/stage-assistant.js"
    },
    {
      "source" : "app/assistants/welcome-assistant.js", "scenes" : "welcome"
    },
    {
      "source" : "app/assistants/search-assistant.js", "scenes" : "search"
    },
    {
      "source" : "app/assistants/searchResults-assistant.js",
      "scenes" : "searchResults"
    },
    {
      "source" : "app/assistants/favorites-assistant.js", "scenes" : "favorites"
    },
    {
      "source" : "app/assistants/details-assistant.js", "scenes" : "details"
    },
    {
      "source" : "app/assistants/preferences-assistant.js",
      "scenes" : "preferences"
    }
]
```

As you can see, just like in the previous chapter, we load the `LocalBusinessSearch.js` file containing some global, shared code and then all the assistants in the app/assistants directory.

framework_config.json

Finally, the `framework_config.json` file, shown in Listing 4-3, has just the one attribute we've come to expect.

Listing 4-3. The framework_config.json File

```
{ "logLevel" : 99 }
```
As always, this file is optional, and you can adjust the logLevel as you see fit.

Global-Scope Code

In this application there is a single global-scope class, LocalBusinessSearch, and it is found in the LocalBusinessSearch.js file.

LocalBusinessSearch.js

The LocalBusinessSearch class is built much like we built the CodeCabinet class in the previous application. At the end of this source file, a single instance of the class is instantiated and available as the variable localBusinessSearch.

Within this class, we find a number of data fields that allows for sharing some data across scenes. These fields are summarized in Table 4-2.

Table 4-2. The Fields of the LocalBusinessSearch Class

Field	Description
appID	This is the application ID you registered with Yahoo! for. You'll need to plug your ID in here to play with the application.
searchWebServiceURL	This is the URL for the Yahoo! Local Search service.
mapWebServiceURL	This is the URL for the Yahoo! Map Image service.
currentBusiness	This is a reference to the currently selected business. This references the object returned by the search service that contains all the data about the business.
zoomLevel	This is the zoom level that the map is currently being viewed at. This is needed because when the Pre is rotated, we need to request a new version of the map image from Yahoo!, and to do that, we need to know what zoom level it's currently viewed at.
searchParams	This is an object that contains the parameters entered by the user on the Search scene. This is needed by the Search Results scene and therefore needs to be in a shared location.
searchInProgress	This is a flag that tells us when a search is in progress. This is used to stop a transition back from the Item Details scene to the Search Results scene triggering another search call.
favorites	This is the collection of favorites the user has stored.

Table 4-2. *The Fields of the LocalBusinessSearch Class (continued)*

preferences	This is an object containing the preferences the user has set (just the selected background image at this time).
lastOrientation	This field holds the value corresponding to the last recorded orientation of the device, whether portrait, landscape, upside down, and so on.
appMenuAttributes	This consists of the attributes for the application menu.
appMenuModel	This is the model for the application menu.

Those fields are the first thing we find in the constructor of the class, and after that we find a couple of statements to be executed upon instantiation.

Opening the Depot

The first such statement is a block of code responsible for setting up the Depot. This chunk of code is as follows:

```
this.depot = new Mojo.Depot(
  { name : "LocalBusinessSearch", version : 1, replace : false },
  function() {
    localBusinessSearch.depot.simpleGet("favorites",
      function(inObject) {
        if (inObject) {
          if (localBusinessSearch.doesObjectHaveAttributes(inObject)) {
            localBusinessSearch.favorites = inObject;
          }
        }
      },
      function(inTransaction, inResult) {
        Mojo.Controller.errorDialog("Failure reading favorites: " +
          inResult);
      }
    );
    localBusinessSearch.depot.simpleGet("preferences",
      function(inObject) {
        if (inObject) {
          localBusinessSearch.preferences = inObject;
        }
        document.body.style.background =
          "url(images/" + localBusinessSearch.preferences.background +
          ".gif) center center";
      }
    );
  },
  function(inTransaction, inResult) {
```

```
    Mojo.Controller.errorDialog("Error opening favorites depot: " + inResult);
    localBusinessSearch.depot = null;
  }
);
```

To use the Depot, we first instantiate a new instance of it. The first argument passed to the constructor is an object containing the name of the Depot (LocalBusinessSearch), the version (1), and whether any existing Depot under that name should be replaced (no in this case).

The second argument passed to the constructor is a function to execute when the Depot is successfully created (or opened if it already exists). In this callback function, we call the simpleGet() method (which is a convenience wrapper around a couple of the Depot methods we'd otherwise have to use specifically) to retrieve an object under the key "favorites" (the first argument). The second argument to simpleGet() is a callback function for when the object is retrieved. This also gets called if no such object is found, but that's considered a successful outcome, which is what this callback is for. If the returned object isn't null, then we call a helper function that is a member of LocalBusinessSearch named doesObjectHaveAttributes(). This method is as follows:

```
this.doesObjectHaveAttributes = function(inObject) {

  var hasAttributes = false;
  for (var a in inObject) {
    hasAttributes = true;
    break;
  }
  if (hasAttributes) {
    return true;
  } else {
    return false;
  }

};
```

As you can see, it's a simple test to determine whether the passed-in object has any attributes. This is necessary because if the user saves some favorites but then explicitly deletes them via the UI, the object for favorites will still be in the Depot, but it won't have any attributes (because, as we'll see later, each favorite becomes an attribute of this object). The favorites field of the localBusinessSearch object should be null to indicate there are no favorites, rather than being just an empty object. Since it is by default null, that means we want to point it to the object returned by the simpleGet() call only if the object has attributes.

The third argument passed to the simpleGet() method is a function to handle various failures during the retrieval. In this case, we just use Mojo.Controller.errorDialog() to display an error dialog box showing the error information returned by the Depot API.

A second simpleGet() call is made to retrieve an object under the key "preferences." This contains the preferences for the user, namely, what background image they selected. Because the preferences field of localBusinessSearch contains a default object (with a single attribute background with a value background19), we want to replace that object only if one is retrieved from the Depot (none would be if the user never selected a background). Otherwise, the default would be used since the if block would be skipped. The success callback updates the background style attribute of the global document object to point to the appropriate image file. This affects all scenes since they are part of the same overall HTML document.

Now, if the Depot couldn't be opened or created for any reason, then the failure callback function at the end of that code block executes. This simply ensures that the depot field of localBusinessSearch is null. Later we'll use this to ensure we don't try to save favorites and preferences (but the rest of the application should still be usable).

Is the Internet Out There?!?

After the Depot is dealt with and after that doesObjectHaveAttributes()helper method, we find another helper method that will be used throughout the code, checkConnectivity():

```
this.checkConnectivity = function(inAssistant, inSuccessCallback,
  inFailureCallback) {

  inAssistant.controller.serviceRequest("palm://com.palm.connectionmanager", {
    method : "getstatus",
    parameters : { subscribe : false },
    onSuccess : function(inResponse) {
      if (inResponse.isInternetConnectionAvailable) {
        inSuccessCallback();
      } else {
        inAssistant.controller.showAlertDialog({
          onChoose : function() { inFailureCallback() },
          title : "Error",
          message : "Internet connection not avalailable",
          choices : [ { label : "Ok", value : "ok" } ]
        });
      }
    },
    onFailure : function() {
      inAssistant.controller.showAlertDialog({
        onChoose : function() { inFailureCallback() },
        title : "Error",
        message : "Internet connection not avalailable",
        choices : [ { label : "Ok", value : "ok" } ]
      });
    }
  });

};
```

The job of this method is to use the Connection Manager service to determine whether an Internet connection is currently available. As I'm sure you can guess, this will be used before an AJAX request is made. This method is passed in a reference to the current assistant as inAssistant, as well as references to two functions. The inSuccessCallback will be called if Internet connectivity is available, while inFailureCallback will be called if it's not.

The serviceRequest() method of the controller associated with inAssistant is called, and we're using the getstatus method of the Connection Manager service in this case. We don't want to subscribe for updates, so subscribe is set to false in the parameters object.

■ **Note** Although I didn't offer this as a suggestion at the end of the chapter, it might be fun to subscribe for updates from this service and have it set some flag or something whenever it changes. That way, the code before the AJAX calls can interrogate the flag rather than calling the service manually. In effect, it would do the same thing; you'd just be using the subscription feature instead of, effectively, implementing it manually as the code exists now.

The third argument to the serviceRequest() method is the function to execute upon successful return from the service. All it does is check the isInternetConnectionAvailable attribute of the response object. If it's true, the inSuccessCallback() is called. If it's false, then an error dialog box is shown saying no connection is available. Since this is called before each AJAX call, the result is that the message will be seen whenever the user tries to perform a search or manipulates the map (that is, zooming or rotating the device), which requires a new map image request.

When the user dismisses the error dialog box, the inFailureCallback function is called. This gives us an opportunity to clean things up, change the UI, and do whatever needs to happen in this case.

Although a failure response from the service probably should never happen under most normal circumstances, it is handled in the same way as no connectivity being available. I think this makes sense since connectivity is most likely not available if we can't even get the status about it!

Setting the Stage

The stage in this application, like in many others, is very bare; it just contains the, pardon the pun, bare essentials! You can see this for yourself in Listing 4-4. However, there *is* in fact one interesting thing to note…take a look at that <body> tag.

Listing 4-4. The Stage HTML: Nothing Fancy—Just One Interesting Bit!

```
<?xml version="1.0" encoding="UTF-8"?>
<!DOCTYPE html PUBLIC "-//W3C//DTD XHTML 1.1//EN"
  "http://www.w3.org/TR/xhtml11/DTD/xhtml11.dtd">

<html xmlns="http://www.w3.org/1999/xhtml" xml:lang="en">

  <head>

    <title>Local Business Search</title>

    <script src="/usr/palm/frameworks/mojo/mojo.js" type="text/javascript"
      x-mojo-version="1" />

    <link href="stylesheets/localbusinesssearch.css" media="screen"
      rel="stylesheet" type="text/css" />

  </head>

  <body class="palm-dark"></body>
```

```
</html>
```

In the previous application, the background of the application was white, and all of the elements on top of it were of course darker in nature. This is what Palm calls the "light theme." This is the default look of a webOS application. However, it's not the only look.

The built-in Tasks application, for example, uses what's called the "dark" theme, and it's just that: it's a theme based on a dark background and elements above it designed to complement that. You can switch your application to use this theme just by adding the palm-dark class to the <body> element, as is done here. This filters down (remember the cascading part of Cascading Style Sheets?) and applies to all the elements of all the scenes of your application.

Now, although that is really all you *have* to do to use this theme, it's likely not all you'll need to do because there may be elements that don't work well on a dark background, and you'll be responsible for figuring out how to deal with that. It may just be some style changes, perhaps some new images, and so on. You might find, however, that everything looks fine with the dark theme, in which case you're golden. There are a few elements of this application that will need to be addressed for this theme, but we'll discuss them as we encounter them. For now, know that adding that class attribute activates the theme; that's the pertinent point here.

■ **Note** You can make starting up your application quicker by adding the theme attribute to appinfo.json with a value of light. This informs webOS that you won't be using the dark theme, so those styles won't be loaded, making application startup a little quicker. It's not required at all, as the previous application shows, but without this setting, the styles will be loaded even though they won't be used. Waste not, want not, I always say!

The stage assistant in this application is a bit more interesting than many, and we'll break it down to discuss it here. Let's start with this opening salvo:

```
function StageAssistant() { };

StageAssistant.prototype.setup = function() {

  if (this.controller.setWindowOrientation) {
    this.controller.setWindowOrientation("free");
  }

  this.controller.pushScene("welcome");

};
```

The first scene is pushed, as we know is the usual job of the stage assistant, but before that, we have something new. By calling the setWindowOrientation() method of the stage controller and passing it a value of free, we activate the ability for the user to rotate the device. When this occurs, webOS will automatically rotate the stage for us. So, the application can be viewed in the usual portrait mode or landscape mode. Let me reiterate that there isn't anything special we have to do beyond this one setting; webOS handles the rotations for us, redrawing the screen as necessary. Now, as we'll see later, we do in fact have some other work to do when rotation events occur, but it's entirely optional and dependant on the needs of the application.

■ **Note** Most examples you see of this shows the call to `setWindowOrientation()` wrapped in a check to be sure it exists. To be bluntly honest, I'm not sure why this is! I did some research and couldn't come up with an answer. My guess, however, is that rotation won't be available on some platforms, in which case the method may not be either. In any case, I see no harm in such a check, which is why you see it done here. Also note that this same method allows you to explicitly set the orientation of your application (you can pass in a value of `up`, `down`, `left`, or `right` to do so).

With `setup()` out of the way, we now have to deal with the application menu, which this application has, just like the previous one did. The code for handling the commands generated by taps on this menu is very much like what we saw in that application as well, really with only one difference:

```
StageAssistant.prototype.handleCommand = function(inEvent) {

  switch (inEvent.type) {

    case Mojo.Event.commandEnable:
      switch (inEvent.command) {
        case Mojo.Menu.prefsCmd:
          if (localBusinessSearch.depot) {
            inEvent.stopPropagation();
          }
        break;
      }
    break;

    case Mojo.Event.command:
      switch (inEvent.command) {
        case "about-TAP":
          this.controller.activeScene().showAlertDialog({
            onChoose : function(inValue) {},
            title : "Local Business Search v1.0",
            message : "From the book " +
              "'Practical webOS Projects With the Palm Pre' " +
              "(Apress, 2009, ISBN-13: 978-1-4302-2674-1). " +
              "Copyright 2009 Frank W. Zammetti. All rights reserved. " +
              "A product of Etherient: http://www.etherient.com",
            choices : [
              { label : "Ok", value : "" }
            ]
          });
        break;
        case Mojo.Menu.prefsCmd:
          this.controller.pushScene("preferences");
```

```
            break;
        }
        break;

    }
};
```

The only real difference is in the handling of the `Mojo.Menu.prefsCmd` command. As we know, this is handled to allow us to enable the Preferences item by stopping propagation of the `Mojo.Event.commandEnable` event, as previously discussed. However, in this case, we wouldn't want that menu item to be available if the Depot wasn't opened successfully. There are all sorts of ways this could have been dealt with: pop an error message when the menu item was clicked, show a message when the user tried to select a background on the Preferences scene (when we try to save it to the Depot), and so on. However, I felt the more elegant approach was to just disable Preferences altogether. So, the line that stops the event propagation, thereby allowing the menu item to be enabled, is wrapped in a check of the depot field of the `localBusinessSearch` object. If that field is `null`, the code in the `if` check will be skipped, so the menu item will be disabled as usual.

A Matter of Style

The style sheet for this application is a fairly simple affair, and there's just one new bit that needs some discussion. First however, is something you *have* seen before:

```
.header-icon.preferences {
    background : url(../images/icoPreferences.png) no-repeat;
}
```

This is the icon for the header of the preferences view, just like in the previous application. The new bit is coming right up now, though:

```
.cssSceneFadeBottom {
    position : fixed;
    bottom : 0px;
    z-index : 50000;
    height : 54px;
    width : 100%;
    background : url(../images/sceneFadeBottomDark.png) bottom center repeat-x !important;
    -webkit-palm-mouse-target : ignore;
}
```

When you have a `List`, it of course will frequently (otherwise, why is it a `List`?!?) have more items than can be displayed on one screen. However, if the `List` is dynamically populated, like for the search results in this application, you don't know that when you create the `List`. So, how does the user know there is more content down below the bottom edge of the screen, without actually scrolling it?

Palm offers a simple but elegant solution: the scroll fader. What you do is you superimpose a semitransparent image over the bottom of the `List`. This results in a few pixels at the bottom being a little dimmer (and a bit blurry, to my eyes at least). This gives a visual clue to the user that there's more down there (kind of floating in the ether, so to speak, which is kind of what it looks like to me). To pull this off, you just need an appropriate image, and as it happens, the SDK comes with some as part of the Style Matters sample application. There is a version for light themes and one for dark themes, so we need the one for dark themes here. You simply create a style that is applied to a <div>, and this style fixes the position of the <div> to the bottom of the screen (position:fixed) and sets a z-index on it so that it is higher than anything else in the scene. Give it the appropriate background image, and make sure its width and height are such that it covers a bit of the bottom and the desired effect is achieved. Note that the -webkit-palm-mouse-target:ignore attribute is necessary; otherwise, an item obscured by the fader would be unclickable. There's a little bit of markup that goes along with making the fader work, but we'll see that a little later.

When rendering the search results and favorites Lists, the next two styles are used:

```
.cssListTitle {
  font-size : 18px;
  color : #ffffff;
  position : relative;
  top : -10px;
}
```

The cssListTitle is the larger text in the list for the title of the business. Since we have a dark theme going here, the color of the text is pure white, so it shows up well. The position of the text is offset a little bit upward so that it, in conjunction with the details, winds up looking nicely centered in the row. Speaking of the details:

```
.cssListDetails {
  font-size : 14px;
  color : #d0d0d0;
  margin-bottom : -20px;
  line-height : 28px;
  position : relative;
  top : -22px;
}
```

As in the previous application, the text is colored a fairly dark gray, which still shows up pretty well in the dark theme but is different enough from the title to differentiate it. The margin-bottom, line-height, position, and top attributes all serve to position it nicely right below the title text, but combined with that title, it's nicely centered in the row.

When the details for a selected business are displayed, there are a series of text labels next to the data elements, and those labels are styled with the cssDetailsLabel class:

```
.cssDetailsLabel {
  font-weight : bold;
}
```

Yep, it's nothing but making the text bold so that it stands out from the data. That data, incidentally, will get the default styling for text in the scene, so there's no work to do there, save for one particular field:

```
.cssDetailsURL {
  font-size : 75%;
}
```

If the business data contains a URL, it is displayed in the details. However, because a URL has no spaces in it, if it's too long, it will get clipped by the edge of the screen (the user can scroll the scene, but that's frankly a bit ugly to me). To help alleviate this situation, I decided to make the URL text only 75 percent of the default text size. Except for rather long URLs, this should avoid that clipping, in most cases at least.

A Scene-by-Scene Account

As with the previous application, we'll explore each scene in turn, and also like that application, some of them (two, specifically) are quite a bit beefier than the others. We'll start slow and easy, though, with the Welcome scene.

Welcome Scene

The Welcome scene is what the user sees upon first launching the application, and if you've read this chapter linearly and haven't played with the application yet (for the love of all that is good in the world, why not?!?), then Figure 4-5 is the first look you're getting at the application.

Figure 4-5. A "Choose Your Own Caption" adventure: (a) who turned out the lights? (b) what is the Matrix?

Hmm, that looks a bit different from the last application, that's for sure! Now, digital paper isn't here yet, so you can't see animation on the printed page. But, if you could (or if you've played with the application a bit), you'd know that the background shown here is actually moving! Yes, it's the effect from the popular (well, the first one anyway) Matrix series of movies. This is one of those things that reinforces the notion that a webOS application is indeed a web application: you've no doubt seen web sites with animated backgrounds that achieve that effect by using an animated GIF as the background image. Well, this is the same! There's no code to write and no complicated animation logic to deal with.

---

[1] "Choose Your Own Caption" is a reference to the popular (in years past) Choose Your Own Adventure series of books. If you're too young to remember them, here's the gist: it's a book where every few pages you have a decision to make that branches you to a different page somewhere else in the book. The outcome of the story depends on the decisions you make. Yes, kids, this is long before we had video games, back when we read by the light of the fireplace and our biggest problem in life was when Pa would be home with our freshly killed dinner!

You simply set a background image using an animated GIF, and you're off to the races (quite literally if you found a GIF with running horses!)

Granted, an animated background is really just an interesting, and potentially very annoying, visual effect. It serves no real purpose for the application, because it indeed could get in the way. That's why the preferences allow the user to change this, but I digress until a bit later on that.

The other big difference here is the two big, honking images right smack in the middle of the screen. These are in fact buttons, but not in the sense of Button widgets. They are just two big graphics that are clickable, but they serve the same purpose as the Buttons on the Welcome scene of the previous application. Once again, this demonstrates how you can "go off the reservation," so to speak, and do practically anything with a webOS application that you can with a plain old web site in terms of HTML, CSS, JavaScript, and layout (for better or worse—you decide!)

The View HTML

The HTML for this scene's view is quite simple, as shown in Listing 4-5.

Listing 4-5. The Welcome Scene's View HTML

```
<center>
  <img style="position:relative;left:5px;" vspace="20"
    src="images/LocalBusinessSearch.png" />
  <br>
  <img id="btnSearch"
    style="position:relative;left:5px;" vspace="20" width="128" height="128"
    src="images/btnSearch.png" />
  <br>
  <img id="btnFavorites"
    style="position:relative;left:5px;" vspace="20" width="128" height="128"
    src="images/btnFavorites.png" />
</center>
```

Yep, not much to it at all. In fact, there are just three <img> elements centered on the page. Once interesting note here: remember I said the two big graphics were clickable? Well, where's the event handler code for that? Ah, good catch on your part! That's actually done in the scene assistant, which is next.

The Scene Assistant

The scene assistant, as most of them do, begins very innocently:

```
function WelcomeAssistant() { };

WelcomeAssistant.prototype.orientationBind = null;
```

The orientationBind field is something we'll come back to because it'll make no sense out of context. So, let's continue to the setup() method:

```
WelcomeAssistant.prototype.setup = function() {

  this.controller.setupWidget(Mojo.Menu.appMenu,
```

```
    localBusinessSearch.appMenuAttributes, localBusinessSearch.appMenuModel);

  Mojo.Event.listen($("btnSearch"), Mojo.Event.tap,
    function() {
      Mojo.Controller.stageController.pushScene({
        name : "search", transition : Mojo.Transition.crossFade
      });
    }
  );
  Mojo.Event.listen($("btnFavorites"), Mojo.Event.tap,
    function() {
      Mojo.Controller.stageController.pushScene({
        name : "favorites", transition : Mojo.Transition.crossFade
      });
    }
  );

};
```

We have an application menu once again for this application, and it's set up in the same way as we have seen in the past. The next block of code, though, answers the question asked before about the event handlers for the clickable images.

The `Mojo.Event.listen()` method, which we've seen numerous times now, hooks up the event handlers to the graphics. You see, these don't have to be used on widgets; they can be used on any DOM node on the page. We're still dealing with a `Mojo.Event.tap` event, and the handler code is in-lined here. All they do is push the Search or Favorites scene, respectively, but there's something new and exciting about that even!

Previously, we just passed the name of the scene to the `pushScene()` method, but here we're passing an object. This object contains a `name` attribute, so that's not much different, but it also contains a `transition` attribute. This defines the way we want to transition to the new scene visually. Although Palm recommends using the `Mojo.Transition.zoomFade` transition, which is the default, when moving between scenes, I decided to use the `Mojo.Transition.crossFade` transition this time, just to be different.

■ **Note** Palm recommends using the default `zoomFade` transition when transitioning between scenes lower or higher in the hierarchy and using the `crossFade` transition when going between scenes at the same level. For example, this means that going from the Welcome scene to the Search scene should use the `zoomFade` transition, while going to search results should probably use `crossFade`. As shown by this application, however, there's no technical reason to do this; it's up to you ultimately.

Dealing with Orientation Changes

Now we come back to that `orientationBind` field, as well as the handling of device orientation change events, brought to us by way of the `activate()` method:

```
WelcomeAssistant.prototype.activate = function() {
```

```
    this.orientationBind = this.handleOrientation.bind(this);
    Mojo.Event.listen(document, "orientationchange",
        this.orientationBind
    );

};
```

When the device is rotated, assuming a call to setWindowOrientation() was made and was passed a value of free, then the OS will generate orientationchange events. We can listen for those on the document object, which is where they register. The Mojo.Event.listen() method is again used, this time binding to the document object. There is no Mojo.Event.XXX constant for the orientation change event currently, however, so you have to use the literal string orientationchange for the name of the event to listen to.

You'll notice, however, that there is something going on even before the event binding. We've seen the bind() method called numerous times before, but never on its own like this. You see, when you call bind() on a function, a new function is actually created that wraps the one you're binding. Oftentimes this doesn't matter much, but in this case it does.

The reason it matters is because of the deactivate() method:

```
WelcomeAssistant.prototype.deactivate = function() {

    Mojo.Event.stopListening(document, "orientationchange",
        this.orientationBind
    );

};
```

The reason we have to stop listening for this event will become clear a bit later, but rest assured, we need to stop listening for this event when the Welcome scene is deactivated (that is, when the user goes to the Search scene or Favorites scene). To do this, we call on the Mojo.Event.stopListening() method. This method takes the object that was being listened to, the event that was being listened for, and the function that was the callback registered to handle the event.

The problem is that every single time you call bind() on a function, you get a *new* generated function (this is usually referred to as "creating a bind"). This means that if we try, for instance, to pass this.handleOrientation.bind(this) to Mojo.Event.listen() and then do the same for the call to Mojo.Event.stopListening(), the callback function will actually be different each time. The end result is that the handleOrientation() function will continue to be called even after the call to stopListening() because it would have failed to detach the listener.

The solution is that before the call to Mojo.Event.listen(), we call bind() on the callback function, handleOrientation(), and store the reference to the returned function in the orientationBind field of this assistant. Then, in deactivate(), we can pass that same reference to Mojo.Event.stopListening(), and the event listener will be detached as expected.

In fact, it's actually better to create this bind one time, in the setup() method for example, and not do it every time. This will be more efficient in the long run, especially if you're talking about something that will happen frequently. In the case of the Welcome scene, I don't envision the user going back to it too often over the course of an execution of the application, so I'm willing to accept the slight inefficiency (and besides, it lets me tell you all about this now!). Still, if it's something that will happen frequently, creating the bind once is a very good idea indeed.

Now, when an orientation event occurs, when the user rotates the device on its axis, the handleOrientation() method is executed:

```
WelcomeAssistant.prototype.handleOrientation = function(inEvent) {

  if (inEvent.position > 1 &&
    inEvent.position != localBusinessSearch.lastOrientation) {

    localBusinessSearch.lastOrientation = inEvent.position;

    var btnSearch = $("btnSearch");
    var btnFavorites = $("btnFavorites");

    switch (inEvent.position) {
      case 2: case 3:
        btnSearch.setAttribute("width", "128");
        btnSearch.setAttribute("height", "128");
        btnFavorites.setAttribute("width", "128");
        btnFavorites.setAttribute("height", "128");
      break;
      case 4: case 5:
        btnSearch.setAttribute("width", "64");
        btnSearch.setAttribute("height", "64");
        btnFavorites.setAttribute("width", "64");
        btnFavorites.setAttribute("height", "64");
      break;
    }

  }

};
```

As stated earlier, the actual rotation of the scene occurs automatically, but in this scene we have an interesting problem: the graphics are so large that when rotated into landscape mode, the favorites image is cut off! My simplistic solution here is to make the graphics half as large when in landscape mode, which solves the problem.

So, the first thing done in this method is to see whether the new position of the device, as stated by the position attribute of the incoming event object, is greater than 1. A value of 0 or 1 corresponds to the device being flat on its back or upside down, and there's nothing for us to do in those cases. This same logic also checks to see whether the new orientation is different from the last orientation recorded by way of the lastOrientation field of the localBusinessSearch object. This is necessary because this method will actually get called every second or so, regardless of whether the device's orientation changes. It would, however, be a waste of energy to resize the graphics if the orientation hasn't changed, so we avoid that with this logic.

Next, we get references to the two button graphics and then enter into a switch statement. The first case covers values of 2 and 3 for the position, which are portrait values (one is the device held normally; the other is when it's held upside-down but still in portrait orientation). In this situation, we change the width and height of the buttons to their usual 128-pixel size. When in landscape mode (values of 4 and 5), we halve them to 64 pixels instead.

Search Scene

When the user clicks the binoculars graphic on the Welcome scene, they are magically transported to the Search scene. Here they can enter some search criteria to find some businesses. This scene is what you see in Figure 4-6.

Figure 4-6. *Getting ready to perform a search. Note the dark theme in use.*

This has quite a different look to it, primarily because of the dark theme being used but also because of some other stylistic choices made in its construction. There are a couple of new widgets here, and of course that GPS button at the bottom points to a new service in play, so let's start tearing it apart, shall we?

The View HTML

The scene's view HTML begins, like most do, with a header:

```
<div id="main" class="palm-hasheader">
  <div class="palm-header">Search</div>
</div>
```

There's nothing new there, but after that is something definitely new:

```
<div class="palm-scrim" id="search_divScrim" style="display:none;">
  <div id="search_divSpinner" x-mojo-element="Spinner"></div>
</div>
```

Now, we've seen the Spinner plenty of times, of course, but never enclosed in a <div> like this. As you'll recall in the previous application, when the Spinner was shown, it was just a <div> being flipped in and out of view. It's actually the same here, but with the addition of something called a *scrim*.

A scrim is simply a semitransparent element, a <div> usually, that obscures the parts of the UI that cannot be interacted with. In this case (and probably most typical with a scrim), the entire scene is obscured, with a Spinner on top of it to indicate activity.

In this scene, the scrim (and Spinner) comes into play when the application is trying to get a GPS fix. In this situation, we don't want the user interacting with the search fields, so the scrim is shown, with the Spinner on top, and the components behind the scrim are rendered untouchable.

All it takes to turn a plain old <div> into a scrim is to add the palm-scrim class to it. This class applies the appropriate semitransparency and sizes and positions it properly. You still need to set display:none on it initially and show it as appropriate, though.

After the scrim, we find a series of TextField declarations, only one of which is shown here for the sake of brevity:

```
<div class="palm-row">
  <div class="palm-row-wrapper">
    <div class="textfield-group" x-mojo-focus-highlight="true">
      <div class="title">
        <div class="label" style="color:#babaff;">Keyword</div>
        <div id="search_txtKeyword" x-mojo-element="TextField"></div>
      </div>
    </div>
  </div>
</div>
...
```

For the most part, this is similar to the TextField markup we've previously seen. One big difference is the label that you see to the right of the TextField. This is just a <div> with the label class applied to it. I also manually have set the color of the field to a medium shade of blue so that it stands apart from the white entered text. Also, since the TextField isn't wrapped in as much container markup as we've previously seen, it has a more plain kind of look to it, but it's a look that I think works a little better with the dark theme.

The other fields that aren't shown are very much the same, but then we find another that is slightly different:

```
<div class="palm-row">
  <div class="palm-row-wrapper">
    <div class="textfield-group" x-mojo-focus-highlight="true">
      <div class="title">
        <div class="label" style="color:#babaff;">State</div>
        <div style="width:220px;" x-mojo-element="ListSelector"
          id="search_lsState"></div>
      </div>
    </div>
  </div>

</div>
```

Here we're using a ListSelector to allow the user to choose a state. The width of the <div> that becomes the widget is explicitly set here so that it doesn't run into the label and also so that it stretches across most of the screen, which I found to look better.

Next up we have the markup for the radius Slider:

```
<div class="palm-row" style="height:80px;">
  <div class="palm-row-wrapper">
    <div class="textfield-group" x-mojo-focus-highlight="true">
      <div class="title">
```

```
        <div class="label" style="position:relative;top:-4px;color:#babaff;"">
          Radius (<span id="search_radius">5</span> miles)
        </div>
        <div x-mojo-element="Slider" id="search_sldRadius"
          style="position:relative;top:44px;height:80px;"></div>
      </div>
    </div>
  </div>
</div>
```

Much of the markup is typical and not unlike the previous widgets' markup. The label is interesting, however, in that it's a <div> with a <span> embedded in it. The <span> is where the current value of the Slider will be inserted because, by default, there is no display of the value of a Slider. This way, the user knows what value they are entering with the widget. Some positioning is done to ensure that the label appears above the Slider. The problem I ran into is that I couldn't get the size of the Slider to be limited so that it could be directly to the left of the label, as all the other fields are. So, I compromised a bit and just positioned it above the Slider a bit, which I think looks pretty good and side-steps the issue.

■ **Note** I'm not sure if this was something I just couldn't figure out or if it's a flaw with the Slider widget. Perhaps, if you have time, you can play with it a bit and let me know if you find a way to make it work! It may well just be a style setting I missed (that's exactly what it *should* be, but finding the right class is sometimes not as easy as you'd like it to be). Hey, nobody's perfect, right?!?

The <div> that becomes the Slider is itself pushed down 44 pixels to make this layout work. By default it actually would overlap the divider line between this field and the previous field, which definitely looked bad.

There are a few more fields mixed in here, but they are much like others, so I've cut them out. The final one, which is a little different, is for the Sort By RadioButton:

```
<div class="palm-row" style="height:100px;">
  <div class="palm-row-wrapper">
    <div class="textfield-group">
      <div class="title">
        <div class="label"
          style="position:relative;top:-4px;color:#babaff;"">Sort By</div>
        <div x-mojo-element="RadioButton" id="search_rbSortBy"
          style="position:relative;left:-10px;top:-14px;"></div>
      </div>
    </div>
  </div>
</div>
```

A RadioButton isn't declared any differently than any other Mojo widget, but I again had to play some positioning games to make it look different. Just like with the Slider, it doesn't seem possible to put the label directly to the right of the RadioButton, so I pushed the label up above the RadioButton as with the Radius Slider. I also needed to nudge the RadioButton's <div> down a bit and left a bit so that it didn't run into the label and also so that it didn't run up to the right edge of the screen, which it seemed to want to do.

■ **Note** It might not be politically correct to say, but I've found that these sorts of "nudging" CSS tricks are often the most expedient way to get the layout just the way you want. I have no doubt that there are more elegant ways to accomplish things or style overrides that would work, and as you've seen, there's certainly some of that throughout this book. When you have deadlines looming, though, whether for writing a book or on the job, sometimes you need something that Just Works, and these sorts of quick-and-dirty CSS tricks are often exactly that. I don't feel bad doing them here and there, and I don't think you should either!

The Scene Assistant

Now we come to the assistant for the Search scene, and this is one of the two big ones, both in terms of amount of code and complexity, but it's also a bit more interesting than some others! Let's begin with this bit:

```
function SearchAssistant() { };

SearchAssistant.prototype.searchModels = {
    keyword : { value : null },
    sortBy : { value : null },
    minimumRating : { value : null },
    street : { value : null },
    city : { value : null },
    state : { value : null },
    zip : { value : null },
    radius : { value : null },
    longitude : { value : null },
    latitude : { value : null }
};
```

Well, we know what that's all about at this point: searchModels contains the models for each of the search fields.

Did you notice that there are some buttons running across the bottom of this scene? If you had guessed they were Button widgets, you'd be wrong. Well, you'd be *directly* wrong, meaning they aren't Buttons in our code, but they probably are behind the scenes.

To be precise, they are part of what's called a *command menu*. A command menu has a model, just like the application model we know and love:

```
SearchAssistant.prototype.commandMenuModel = {
    items : [
        { label : "Perform Search", command : "search" },
        { label : "GPS", command : "gps" },
        { label : "Reset", command : "reset" }
    ]
```

```
};
```

A command menu is a collection of buttons across the bottom of a scene. They hover above the scene, are semitransparent, and are automatically hidden and shown by the OS when the application is "cardified" or brought to the foreground. Each element in the items array inside the command menu's model becomes a button on the menu (items can also be grouped to create a sort of radio button–type thing, but we'll see that in the Item Details scene). Here we just have three individual elements. Each has a label or icon attribute, depending on whether you want the item to be a textual button or a button with just an icon on it. Each also has a command attribute, which defines the value that will be passed to the function called whenever one of these are tapped (similar to how the application menu works).

▨ **Note** There is also something called a *scene menu*, which is very much like the command menu except that it runs across the top of the scene. That type of menu isn't used in this application but will be in a future application.

With those couple of fields out of the way, we can set up the scene:

```
SearchAssistant.prototype.setup = function() {

  this.controller.setupWidget(Mojo.Menu.appMenu,
    localBusinessSearch.appMenuAttributes, localBusinessSearch.appMenuModel);

  this.controller.setupWidget("search_divSpinner",
    { spinnerSize : "large" }, { spinning : true }
  );
```

The application menu is set up like always, and the Spinner is set up as we've seen before too. Note that the scrim doesn't need to be set up here because it's not a widget; it's just a <div> with a specific styling applied.

Following that is a number of blocks of code, one for each of the search criteria fields. The first is for the keyword field:

```
  this.controller.setupWidget("search_txtKeyword",
    { focusMode : Mojo.Widget.focusSelectMode, maxLength : 30,
      textCase : Mojo.Widget.steModeLowerCase },
    this.searchModels.keyword
  );
```

This is mostly standard TextField setup, but this is the first time we're seeing the textCase attribute in use. By default, a TextField capitalizes the first letter entered, but in this case there's no point in that, so setting this attribute of Mojo.Widget.setModeLowerCase turns that behavior off.

The next widget that's set up is the sort by RadioButton:

```
  this.controller.setupWidget("search_rbSortBy",
    { choices : [
      { label : "Distance", value : "distance" },
      { label : "Title", value : "title" },
      { label : "Rating", value : "rating" }
```

```
    ] },
    this.searchModels.sortBy
  );
```

The choices available for this RadioButton are hard-coded into the attributes of the widget since they never change.

The minimum rating IntegerPicker is next:

```
  this.controller.setupWidget("search_ipMinimumRating",
    { min : 0, max : 5, label : " " },
    this.searchModels.minimumRating
  );
```

The IntegerPicker allows us to easily pick a number between 0 and 5. It normally has a label attribute that puts the label to the left of the widget, but since the markup contains the label to the right, a single space is the value for the label attribute.

After this is the setup for the street and city fields, but we'll skip them in favor of something more interesting, the state field:

```
  var stateVals = [
    "Alabama", "Alaska", "Arizona", "Arkansas", "California", "Colorado",
    "Connecticut", "Delaware", "Florida", "Georgia", "Hawaii", "Idaho",
    "Illinois", "Indiana", "Iowa", "Kansas", "Kentucky", "Louisiana",
    "Maine", "Maryland", "Massachusetts", "Michigan", "Minnesota", "Mississippi",
    "Missouri", "Montana", "Nebraska", "Nevada", "New Hampshire",
    "New Jersey", "New Mexico", "New York", "North Carolina", "North Dakota",
    "Ohio", "Oklahoma", "Oregon", "Pennsylvania", "Rhode Island",
    "South Carolina", "South Dakota", "Tennessee", "Texas", "Utah", "Vermont",
    "Virginia", "Washington", "West Virginia", "Wisconsin", "Wyoming"
  ];
  var stateChoices = [ ];
  for (var i = 0; i < stateVals.length; i++ ) {
    stateChoices.push({
      label : stateVals[i], value : stateVals[i]
    });
  }
  this.controller.setupWidget("search_lsState",
    { choices : stateChoices, label : " " },
    this.searchModels.state
  );
```

A ListSelector is used to present the user with a scrollable list of states to choose from. The stateVals array contains the source data, which is then used to populate the stateChoices array, where each item in that array is an object with a label attribute and a value attribute. They happen to have the same values here, but that of course doesn't have to be true of a ListSelector's data (I'd say usually it won't be the case). The label attribute here, like for the minimum rating field, is a single space so that it has no automatic label.

The zip code field is next, but like for the street and city, they're skipped since showing that code would be a bit redundant. The one point of interest, about the zip code field specifically, is that it allows only numbers to be entered, as is reasonable for a zip code field. To accomplish this, the modifierState config attribute is set to a value of Mojo.Widget.numLock. The other value frequently seen for this config option is Mojo.Widget.capsLock, which initially locks the TextField to all capitalized letters.

Since we're not going to look at those widgets, we'll get to the radius Slider now:

```
this.controller.setupWidget("search_sldRadius",
  { minValue : 1, maxValue : 1000, round : true, modelProperty : "value" },
  this.searchModels.radius
);
Mojo.Event.listen(this.controller.get("search_sldRadius"),
  Mojo.Event.propertyChange, function() {
    $("search_radius").innerHTML = this.searchModels.radius.value;
  }.bind(this)
);
```

The Slider can have a value from 1 to 1,000, and by setting the round attribute to true, we ensure we'll always get whole numbers. Notice that the Mojo.Event.propertyChange event is handled so that the current value of the Slider's model van be inserted into the search_radius <span> that we saw earlier so the user can see the value they are selecting. One unfortunate thing is that the propertyChange event fires only once the user lifts their finger off the screen, so the value isn't really updated in real time. I'm hoping that's something that will be available in a future version of Mojo.

Like a number of other fields, the longitude and latitude fields, which would appear next in the code, are being skipped here. However, what we won't skip is this:

```
this.controller.setupWidget(Mojo.Menu.commandMenu, null,
  this.commandMenuModel);

this.clear();
```

The command menu is set up much like the application menu is and much like any other widget is. Finally, when we're all done, the clear() method is called, which ensures that the entry fields are clear and/or have default values in them.

Handling Commands

With setup() out of the way, the next thing to examine is the method that is called to handle the command events generated by the command menu:

```
SearchAssistant.prototype.handleCommand = function(inEvent) {

  if (inEvent.type == Mojo.Event.command) {
    switch (inEvent.command) {

      case "search":
        this.search();
      break;

      case "reset":
        this.clear();
      break;
```

This is actually only the first part of the handleCommand() method. The rest of it we'll look at in the next section. The Search and Clear buttons simply call on search() and clear() methods, respectively, so that's all there is to the first two case statements.

Getting a GPS Fix

The third case statement in the handleCommand() method's switch statement handles when the GPS button is clicked:

```
case "gps":
  $("search_divScrim").show();
  this.controller.serviceRequest("palm://com.palm.location", {
    method : "getCurrentPosition",
    parameters : { maximumAge : 60 },
    onSuccess : function(inResponse) {
      $("search_divScrim").hide();
      switch (inResponse.errorCode) {
        case 0:
          this.searchModels.longitude.value = inResponse.longitude;
          this.searchModels.latitude.value = inResponse.latitude;
          this.controller.modelChanged(this.searchModels.longitude, this);
          this.controller.modelChanged(this.searchModels.latitude, this);
          break;
        case 1: case 2: case 3:
          Mojo.Controller.errorDialog(
            "Timeout waiting for GPS fix.  Are you indoors, or is " +
            "your view of the sky obstructed?"
          );
          break;
        case 5: case 6:
          Mojo.Controller.errorDialog(
            "GPS fix cannot be retrieved because Location Service is " +
            "off, or you have not accepted the terms of use."
          );
          break;
        case 7: case 8:
          Mojo.Controller.errorDialog(
            "The application already has a pending request, or has " +
            "been temporarily blacklisted."
          );
          break;
      }
    }.bind(this),
    onFailure : function(inResponse) {
      $("search_divScrim").hide();
      switch (inResponse.errorCode) {
        case 1: case 2: case 3:
          Mojo.Controller.errorDialog(
            "Timeout waiting for GPS fix.  Are you indoors, or is " +
            "your view of the sky obstructed?"
          );
```

```
        break;
      case 5: case 6:
        Mojo.Controller.errorDialog(
          "GPS fix cannot be retrieved because Location Service is " +
          "off, or you have not accepted the terms of use."
        );
      break;
      case 7: case 8:
        Mojo.Controller.errorDialog(
          "The application already has a pending request, or has " +
          "been temporarily blacklisted."
        );
      break;
      }
    }
  });
break;
```

Although it's fairly lengthy, a lot of it is error handling, so it looks more complex than it really is. The first task performed is to show the scrim and Spinner. Calling the show() method on the object returned by $("search_divScrim") accomplishes the task because the Spinner is nested within that <div>.

After that, the serviceRequest() method is used to call on the GPS service, its getCurrentPosition method specifically. The parameters object for this call includes the maximumAge parameter, set to 60, as in 60 seconds. This means that a cached location up to a minute old is acceptable as a response.

If we get a successful response, then the scrim is hidden, and the errorCode field of the returned response object is checked. If the value is 0, then we get a location, in which case the models for the longitude and latitude fields are updated.

A number of errorCode values greater than 0 can be returned to the success callback, and you can see that they are handled via error dialog boxes. Likewise, the service call can result in failure, and there are a number of possible causes. I won't go through all the reasons this call can fail (or return a nonzero success errorCode) because I think the case statements and the text of the error messages spell it out pretty well for you.

In Figure 4-7 you can see an example of one such error outcome.

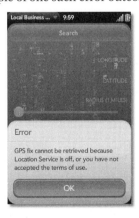

Figure 4-7. If GPS worked indoors, I think the radiation involved would cause our heads to explode.

Clearing the Search Fields

The end of the setup() method and when the user clicks the Clear button is as follows:

```
SearchAssistant.prototype.clear = function() {

  this.searchModels.keyword.value = "";
  this.searchModels.sortBy.value = "distance";
  this.searchModels.minimumRating.value = 0;
  this.searchModels.street.value = "";
  this.searchModels.city.value = "";
  this.searchModels.state.value = "";
  this.searchModels.zip.value = "";
  this.searchModels.radius.value = 5;
  this.searchModels.longitude.value = "";
  this.searchModels.latitude.value = "";

  for (var f in this.searchModels) {
    this.controller.modelChanged(this.searchModels[f], this);
  }The clear() method, called at

};
```

The value in the models for all the search fields are cleared, or set to default values, and then the searchModels object is iterated. For each member, we call modelChanged() so the screen is updated accordingly. Pretty straightforward, I'd say!

Performing a Search

The final method in this assistant is the search() method, and although it's somewhat lengthy, it's fairly simple. Still, we'll chunk it up a bit:

```
SearchAssistant.prototype.search = function() {

  if (this.searchModels.keyword.value == "") {
    Mojo.Controller.errorDialog("You must enter a keyword to search for.");
    return;
  }
```

The method starts with a couple of simple validation checks. The first is to ensure a keyword is entered, because otherwise there's nothing to search for! An error dialog box is shown if the field is blank and the method is aborted.

```
  if (this.searchModels.street.value == "" &&
    this.searchModels.city.value == "" &&
    this.searchModels.state.value == "" &&
    this.searchModels.zip.value == "" &&
    this.searchModels.longitude.value == "" &&
    this.searchModels.latitude.value == "") {
    Mojo.Controller.errorDialog(
      "You must enter a location to search around " +
```

```
      "(just zip code at a minimum)."
    );
    return;
  }
```

The next check is around the location components of a search. In short, *some* location must be entered, be it a street address, a zip code, or a longitude and latitude. Just a zip code is the absolute minimum that is required.

```
  if (this.searchModels.street.value != "" &&
    (this.searchModels.city.value == "" ||
     this.searchModels.state.value == "")) {
    Mojo.Controller.errorDialog(
      "When street is entered you must also enter city and state."
    );
    return;
  }
```

If the user entered a street, then the city and state both become required (but interestingly, *not* the zip code, as per the search service's rules). That's what the previous check is for.

One final check is required:

```
  if ((this.searchModels.longitude.value != "" &&
     this.searchModels.latitude.value == "") ||
    (this.searchModels.longitude.value == "" &&
     this.searchModels.latitude.value != "")) {
    Mojo.Controller.errorDialog(
      "When either longitude or latitude is entered, they both must be entered."
    );
    return;
  }
```

When longitude or latitude is entered, they both must be entered, since a search with only one is invalid.

Finally, with the validation out of the way, we can begin preparing for the inevitable AJAX call.

```
  localBusinessSearch.searchParams = {
    appid : localBusinessSearch.appID, output : "json", results : 20,
    query : this.searchModels.keyword.value,
    sort : this.searchModels.sortBy.value,
    minimum_rating : this.searchModels.minimumRating.value,
    street : this.searchModels.street.value,
    city : this.searchModels.city.value,
    state : this.searchModels.state.value,
    zip : this.searchModels.zip.value,
    radius : this.searchModels.radius.value,
    longitude : this.searchModels.longitude.value,
    latitude : this.searchModels.latitude.value
  };
```

The searchParams object contains all the parameters required to make the call work. Since the actual AJAX call that uses this will be done by the Search Results scene, we set the searchParams field of the localBusinessSearch object to it so the Search Results scene can get at it. As you can see, most of them come from the models of the search criteria fields. However, there are a couple that don't, namely, appid and output. The appid and output parameters are basic to using the Yahoo! services, as previously discussed. The results attribute is also specific to this service, and it determines how many results we want back (assuming there even are that many). The maximum value allowed by the service for a single call is 20 (if there are more than 20 results, then you would have to call the service again, passing a value to tell it the last results you got, and it will fill in the next 20 after that, and so on).

Once that object is constructed, we can perform the final task:

```
localBusinessSearch.searchInProgress = true;
Mojo.Controller.stageController.pushScene({
  name : "searchResults", transition : Mojo.Transition.crossFade
});

};
```

The searchInProgress flag is set to true so that the Search Results scene knows to perform the search (and the AJAX call specifically), and then that scene is pushed. Once again we see the Mojo.Transition.crossFade effect being used explicitly.

Search Results Scene

When a search is initiated from the Search scene, the Search Results scene is pushed, and the actual code that makes the search happen, including the AJAX call, is found here. This scene, which you can see in Figure 4-8, uses a scrim, like the Search scene, to obscure the UI while the search is in progress.

Figure 4-8. *Running a search. Note the usage of the scrim to obscure the UI.*

That fact is a bit less important here since alternatively the List would have just been hidden while the Spinner was shown, as shown in the previous application, but I thought this was better if for no other reason than consistency with the previous scene.

The View HTML

The scene's view HTML is quite simplistic, as you can see in Listing 4-6.

Listing 4-6. The searchResults-scene.html File

```
<div id="main" class="palm-hasheader">
  <div class="palm-header">Search Results</div>
</div>

<div class="palm-scrim" id="searchResults_divScrim" style="display:none;">
  <div id="searchResults_divSpinner" x-mojo-element="Spinner"></div>
</div>

<div class="cssSceneFadeBottom" x-mojo-scroll-fade="bottom"></div>

<div id="searchResults_lstSearchResults" x-mojo-element="List"></div>
```

A header, a scrim with a `Spinner` within it, and a `List` makes up the main content, all of which we've seen before.

There's also that `<div>` with the class `cssSceneFadeBottom`, which we discussed a little bit earlier. This is what makes the `List` fade off at the bottom to indicate to the user that there is more content down below the edge of the screen. Adding the custom `x-mojo-scroll-fade` attribute with a value of `bottom` is also necessary to make this work (you can have a fade at the "top" too if you want, but since the header obscures the list, it winds up looking a bit redundant to my eyes). The CSS we looked at earlier takes care of the rest.

The Scene Assistant

Next we'll look at the Search scene's scene assistant, beginning with this bit:

```
function SearchResultsAssistant() { };

SearchResultsAssistant.prototype.lstSearchResultsModel = { items : [ ] };
```

If you've seen one `List` mode, you've seen them all, more or less, and that's what we have here. Next is the setup() method:

```
SearchResultsAssistant.prototype.setup = function() {

  this.controller.setupWidget(Mojo.Menu.appMenu,
    localBusinessSearch.appMenuAttributes, localBusinessSearch.appMenuModel);

  this.controller.setupWidget("searchResults_divSpinner",
    { spinnerSize : "large" }, { spinning : true }
  );

  this.controller.setupWidget("searchResults_lstSearchResults", {
```

```
        itemTemplate : "searchResults/list-item"
    }, this.lstSearchResultsModel);
    this.controller.listen("searchResults_lstSearchResults",
        Mojo.Event.listTap, this.selectBusiness);

};
```

The application menu is set up like always, as is the Spinner. The results List is then set up, using the list-item.html files as its item template, which is shown in Listing 4-7.

Listing 4-7. The list-item.html File

```html
<div class="palm-row" x-mojo-tap-highlight="momentary">
  <div class="palm-row-wrapper textfield-group">
    <div class="title">
      <div class="cssListTitle truncating-text">#{Title}</div>
      <div class="cssListDetails">
        #{Distance} Miles
        <img src="images/rating#{Rating.AverageRating}.png" hspace="10" />
      </div>
    </div>
  </div>
</div>
```

The template is pretty simplistic. The stars you see in the List in Figure 4-9 are a result of a number being inserted for the #{Rating.AverageRating} token to form the complete name of one of the six graphics files containing the star images. The object that is used by this template is one of the objects from the Result array in the object returned by the Yahoo! search service. These objects have a Rating field, which within it has an AverageRating field (among others that aren't used in this application). This is interesting because it shows, for the first time, that you can have as rich an object hierarchy within each of the objects processed by a List template, and you can drill down through it with your tokens just as you would in JavaScript code. This means that you aren't limited to a flat object in your List templates, which is definitely a useful thing to know!

Figure 4-9 shows the result of this template being evaluated with some search results.

204

Figure 4-9. *Some search results. My, the stars look lovely this evening!*

Activating the scene is what we come to next, and this is where the real action takes place:

```
SearchResultsAssistant.prototype.activate = function() {

  if (!localBusinessSearch.searchInProgress) {
    return;
  }
```

You'll recall I mentioned the searchInProgress field briefly earlier, and now we can see how it's used. Because the scene can come into view as a result of a search being initiated as well as the user swiping back from the Item Details scene that we have yet to look at, this activate() method can be called in those two situations. In the later, we wouldn't want to do the search a second time, so by checking this flag and aborting activate() if it's true, we accomplish that goal.

The next task is to show the Spinner:

```
$("searchResults_divScrim").show();
```

Remember that the Spinner is embedded within the scrim, so it's the scrim's <div> that we need to call show() on. Next, the List is cleared:

```
this.lstSearchResultsModel.items = [ ];
this.controller.modelChanged(this.lstSearchResultsModel, this);
```

With those UI preliminaries out of the way, it's time to perform the first of our AJAX requests:

```
localBusinessSearch.checkConnectivity(this,
  function() {
    new Ajax.Request(
      localBusinessSearch.searchWebServiceURL, {
        method : "get", evalJSON : "force",
        parameters : localBusinessSearch.searchParams,
        onSuccess : this.processResults.bind(this),
        onFailure : function(inTransport) {
          $("searchResults_divScrim").hide();
          Mojo.Controller.errorDialog("FAILURE: " + inTransport.status +
            " - " + inTransport.responseText);
        },
        onException : function(inTransport, inException) {
          $("searchResults_divScrim").hide();
          Mojo.Controller.errorDialog("EXCEPTION: " + inException);
        }
      }
    );
  }.bind(this),
  function() {
    this.controller.stageController.popScene();
  }.bind(this)
);
```

```
};
```

The `localBusinessSearch.checkConnectivity()` method that we saw earlier kicks things off. Once again, this accepts as its first argument a reference to the scene assistant making the call—a function to call if connectivity is available and one to call if it isn't. The former is where the AJAX call is made from.

The `Ajax.Request()` method is provided by the Prototype library, and it's quite simple to use. All you do is pass it as the first argument the URL of the service you want to call, which here is the value of the `localBusinessSearch.searchWebServiceURL`, and then an object that contains all the parameters of the call. This object includes some prototype-specific attributes. The `method` attribute tells us what HTTP method to use, get in this case. The `evalJSON` attribute, when set to `force`, tells Prototype that we want a response that it recognizes as JSON to be evaluated so that we'll have a true JavaScript object as a result.

The `parameters` attribute references the `searchParams` object we saw earlier, and these are the parameters specific to the service you're calling. After that are `onSuccess` and `onFailure`. They reference functions to be executed when the call returns successfully or when it fails. In the failure case, the scrim is hidden, and an error dialog box is shown with information passed in via the `inTransport` object. This is an object that Prototype generates, which includes not only the response from the server but other metainformation about the call, one of which is the `status` field, which is typically used when a failure occurs. The `responseText` attribute is also used, and this is the literal text response the service sent back.

There is also an `onException` handler. The difference between this and `onFailure` is that `onFailure` is called when the service call succeeds, but the response isn't something Prototype recognizes and can handle. You can consider these "soft" errors in the sense that they are usually errors returned by the service for error conditions that are anticipated.

The `onException` handler, on the other hand, is when an HTTP error occurs or the call fails in a catastrophic way for any other reason. When this occurs, in addition to the transport object, you also get a JavaScript exception object, so we can display details about what happened in the error dialog box.

When Internet connectivity isn't available, the error dialog box is shown by the `checkConnectivity()` method, and then the final block of code is called, which pops the Search Results scene, putting the user back at the Search scene.

Of course, at this point I'm sure you realize I skipped how a successful response from the service is handled. That's done in the briefly mentioned `processResults()` method, which is our next stop.

Handling Returned Search Results

Handling the response from the server means of course populating the `List`, but there are some things that have to be done before then, beginning with a quick check:

```
SearchResultsAssistant.prototype.processResults = function(inTransport) {

  localBusinessSearch.searchInProgress = false;

  if (inTransport.responseJSON.ResultSet.totalResultsAvailable == 0) {
    this.controller.showAlertDialog({
      onChoose : function(inValue) {
        this.controller.stageController.popScene();
      },
      title : "Nothing Found",
      message : "No businesses were found matching your search critera",
      choices : [
        { label : "Ok", type : "affirmative"}
```

```
    ]
  });
  return;
}
```

This ensures there were some results to display. If there are none, then Figure 4-10 is what the user will see.

Figure 4-10. *No matches found. What exactly where you searching for, you naughty person?!?*

Another condition that can occur is if there are more than 20 matches. In this case, the following code kicks in:

```
if (inTransport.responseJSON.ResultSet.totalResultsAvailable > 20) {
  this.controller.showAlertDialog({
    onChoose : function(inValue) {
      this.controller.stageController.popScene();
    },
    title : "Too Many Matches",
    message : "More than 20 matches were found.  Please try to narrow " +
      "the search (reducing the radius value is a good way).",
    choices : [
      { label : "Ok", type : "affirmative"}
    ]
  });
  return;
}
```

Note that in both of these situations the scene is popped once the user dismisses the dialog box. This way, they are back at the Search scene and can attempt to narrow their search a bit. Figure 4-11 shows the result of this condition.

Figure 4-11. Too many resutls available

Now, if both of those conditions are avoided, then we populate the List from the results returned by the service call:

```
for (var i = 0; i < inTransport.responseJSON.ResultSet.Result.length; i++) {
  this.lstSearchResultsModel.items.push(
    inTransport.responseJSON.ResultSet.Result[i]
  );
}
this.controller.modelChanged(this.lstSearchResultsModel, this);
```

Remember that Prototype has nicely converted the response to a JavaScript object for us because the response was recognized as being in JSON form, so the responseJSON field of inTransport is how we get at the resultant object. Within this object we find that there is a ResultSet object, and within that is a Result array (this is what the Yahoo! service provides; it's nothing the code here is generating). So, it's a simple matter to iterate over that array and push() each item of the array into the items array in the model for the List, and we're good to go. All that remains is to hide the scrim, and the user can then interact with the List.

Handling User Selection of a Search Result

When the user taps one of the items in the List, it's time to show the details for that business. In this case, the selectBusiness() method fires, which is what was attached in setup() to the Mojo.Event.tap event of the List:

```
SearchResultsAssistant.prototype.selectBusiness = function(inEvent) {

  localBusinessSearch.currentBusiness = inEvent.item;

  Mojo.Controller.stageController.pushScene({
    name : "details", transition : Mojo.Transition.crossFade
```

```
    });

};
```

All it takes is to record the selected item by pointing the localBusinessSearch.currentBusiness field to the object passed in as inEvent.item and then pushing the Item Details scene, which is our next stop.

Item Details Scene

The Item Details scene is perhaps the most complex, and probably the most interesting, of the scenes. In Figure 4-12 you can get an idea what this scene looks like.

Figure 4-12. If you've carefully looked at these examples, you'll realize how much I love pizza!

There are actually two different views within this scene, and this is just one of them, showing the details of the selected business. The other shows the map of the business. The command menu at the bottom—specifically, the two grouped buttons on the left side—allow you to flip between the views.

The View HTML

The view HTML is just some straightforward HTML, even more straightforward than a lot of other scenes' HTML:

```
<div id="main" class="palm-hasheader">
  <div class="palm-header">Item Information</div>
</div>
```

We have a header like always at the top and then the following:

```
<table border="0" cellpadding="0" cellspacing="0" width="100%"
  id="details_tblDetails">
  <tr>
    <td valign="top" class="cssDetailsLabel">Title: </td>
```

```
  <td width="100%" id="details_Title"></td>
</tr>
...
<tr>
  <td valign="top" class="cssDetailsLabel">Business URL: </td>
  <td> </td>
</tr>
<tr><td colspan="2" class="cssDetailsURL" id="details_BusinessUrl"></td></tr>
</table>
```

Yep, that's just a plain old table. I've cut out most of the rows, since they look just like the row for the business's title that you see here. The second column of each row is where the data from the `localBusinessSearch.currentBusiness` object will be inserted. The last one, where the URL for the business will be inserted, assuming the business has one, spans both columns, since the label for that data element is situated above it on the previous row.

```
<img id="details_map" style="display:none;position:absolute;" />
```
The map that is displayed when the user clicks the Map button is just an `<img>` element, initially hidden as you can see. So, either the `<table>` or the `<img>` is showing, depending on whether the user is viewing the details of the business or the map of the business, so I'm pretty sure you can guess what the code behind those two buttons is going to look like!

The Scene Assistant

The scene assistant opened with the usual constructor and a single field:

```
function DetailsAssistant() { };
```

```
DetailsAssistant.prototype.orientationBind = null;
```

You'll recall our discussion in the Welcome scene of the orientation event handling and how we had to have the bind wrapped around the event handler shared so that we could deactivate the listener later. The same sort of concern is present with this scene because there's some work involved when the user rotates the device.

```
DetailsAssistant.prototype.commandMenuModel = {
  processEvents : true,
  items : [
    { toggleCmd : null,
      items : [
        { label : "Details", command : "details" },
        { label : "Map", command : "map" }
      ]
    },
    { icon : "new", submenu : "functions" },
    { icon : "search", submenu : "zoom", disabled : null }
  ]
};
```

The command menu's model is next, and it is similar to that of the Search scene, with one neat difference. The first element of the `items` array in the model is itself an object with an `items` array. The two elements in this second `items` array are the buttons themselves, defined just like any other we've seen. Also present in this object is a `toggleCmd` attribute. These two things combined allow us to group two buttons together and determine which is "toggled." Initially, neither is, which is why the value is `null`.

Also note that the second two elements of the `items` array (the one directly nested under the model) use the `icon` attribute as opposed to the `label` attribute as the others do. These reference the name of style classes that have background images defined on them. The `new` and `search` styles are ones built in to webOS, which is why you don't see them defined in the style sheet of the application. Arguably, the `new` icon isn't the best choice for this second menu, which contains some generic functions the user can perform, but it was the best choice I could fine.

The third element, the search button, can be disabled depending on whether the map is currently in view, so there is a `disabled` attribute on it. Note that this button isn't for doing a search; it's actually for zooming in and out of the map image. However, the icon for search is a magnifying glass, so I thought it fit the notion of zooming just fine.

You can glimpse this scene in Figure 4-13. I've also at this point clicked the command menu so you can see what options are available in it.

Figure 4-13. *The command menu (perhaps not the best icon choice there, but you'll cope!)*

Speaking of those options, you'll notice that the last two elements of the `items` array in the model for the command menu have a `submenu` attribute in them. As the name itself implies, that sets us up to have another menu, a pop-up menu in this case, appear when the buttons are clicked. Like the other menu types we've seen, a pop-up menu has a model behind it, and the one for the functions menu is thus:

```
DetailsAssistant.prototype.functionsSubMenuModel = {
  items : [
    { label : "Add To Favorites", command : "addToFavorites",
      disabled : function() {
        if (localBusinessSearch.depot) {
          return false;
        } else {
          return true;
```

```
      }
    }()
  },
  { label : "Open In Google Maps", command : "openInGoogleMaps" }
  ]
};
```

That's basically like the other menus we've seen, but notice the `disabled` attribute. The Add To Favorites function needs to be disabled if the Depot wasn't opened at application startup, so we have some logic built in here. Notice the syntax here: we have a function defined inline, and immediately after its definition we have (). This results in this function being executed when the `functionsSubMenuModel` object is evaluated. The code in this function checks to see whether `localBusinessSearch.depot` is null. If it's not, then `false` is returned, which becomes the value of the `disabled` attribute for the menu item, so Add To Favorites is active. If `depot` is null, then `true` is returned, and the menu item is disabled. This immediate execution of an inline function is a powerful technique that is a nice trick to have in your toolbox, one that JavaScript developers aren't always aware of in my experience.

As for the functions button, the zoom button is a submenu, so it too has a model associated with it:

```
DetailsAssistant.prototype.zoomSubMenuModel = {
  items : [
    { label : "Street", command : "zoom1" }, { label : "2", command : "zoom2" },
    { label : "3", command : "zoom3" }, { label : "4", command : "zoom4" },
    { label : "5", command : "zoom5" }, { label : "6", command : "zoom6" },
    { label : "7", command : "zoom7" }, { label : "8", command : "zoom8" },
    { label : "9", command : "zoom9" }, { label : "10", command : "zoom10" },
    { label : "11", command : "zoom11" },
  { label : "Country", command : "zoom12" }
  ]
};
```

This just has a series of numbers, bookended by two words, which correspond to the possible zoom levels the user can choose from when viewing the map.

Next we have to set up the scene:

```
DetailsAssistant.prototype.setup = function() {

  this.controller.setupWidget(Mojo.Menu.appMenu,
    localBusinessSearch.appMenuAttributes, localBusinessSearch.appMenuModel);

  this.controller.setupWidget(Mojo.Menu.commandMenu, null,
    this.commandMenuModel);

  this.controller.setupWidget("functions", null,
    this.functionsSubMenuModel);

  this.controller.setupWidget("zoom", null, this.zoomSubMenuModel);

};
```

Along with setting up the application menu, the command menu is set up. The pop-up menus for functions and zoom also have to be set up, and they are done in the same way as the command menu itself.

Activating and Deactivating the Scene

Activating the scene is the next task, and because there's quite a bit going on here, we'll break it up into bit-sized morsels for your chewing pleasure:

```
DetailsAssistant.prototype.activate = function() {

  this.orientationBind = this.handleOrientation.bind(this);
  Mojo.Event.listen(document, "orientationchange",
    this.orientationBind
  );
```

Just like in the Welcome scene, we need to listen to orientation change events, and once again we have that binding issue to worry about, so the same sort of code seen before is done here.

After that, we need to set up our command menu, and since this scene might not be activating for the first time, we have to reset the UI:

```
  this.commandMenuModel.items[0].toggleCmd = "details";
  this.controller.modelChanged(this.commandMenuModel, this);
  this.commandMenuModel.items[2].disabled = true;
  this.controller.modelChanged(this.commandMenuModel, this);
```

We start by ensuring that the details button is the one selected in the group of two buttons to the left. Setting the `toggleCmd` attribute to the command associated with the button we want selected and calling `modelChanged()` does that job. We also need to disable the zoom button since that should be available only when the map is showing. Since it's the third element in the `items` array of the model, `items[2]` gets us to the right element, and then we just set its `disabled` attribute to `true` and update the model.

```
  localBusinessSearch.zoomLevel = 6;
```

When the map is showing and the user rotates the device, we'll need to request a new version of the map from the Yahoo! Map Image service. To do that properly, we need to know what zoom level the map is currently being viewed at. This information is stored in the `localBusinessSearch.zoomLevel` field. The default zoom level, as defined by the web service, is 6, so we set that initial value here.

Next, we request the initial map image:

```
  this.getMap();
```

We'll get into the `getMap()` method soon, but for now it's enough to say that it calls the web service to request the initial map image and updates the `<img>` tag to point to it when the response comes back.

Next, the details for the business are populated:

```
  $("details_Title").innerHTML = localBusinessSearch.currentBusiness.Title;
  $("details_Longitude").innerHTML =
    localBusinessSearch.currentBusiness.Longitude;
  $("details_Latitude").innerHTML =
    localBusinessSearch.currentBusiness.Latitude;
  $("details_Distance").innerHTML =
```

```
      localBusinessSearch.currentBusiness.Distance;
    $("details_Phone").innerHTML = localBusinessSearch.currentBusiness.Phone;
    var ratingVal = localBusinessSearch.currentBusiness.Rating.AverageRating;
    $("details_Rating").innerHTML = (isNaN(ratingVal) ? 0 : ratingVal);
    $("details_Address").innerHTML = localBusinessSearch.currentBusiness.Address;
    $("details_City").innerHTML = localBusinessSearch.currentBusiness.City;
    $("details_State").innerHTML = localBusinessSearch.currentBusiness.State;
    var BusinessUrl = localBusinessSearch.currentBusiness.BusinessUrl;
    if (BusinessUrl) {
      BusinessUrl = "<a href=\"" + BusinessUrl + "\">" + BusinessUrl + "</a>";
    } else {
      BusinessUrl = "";
    }
    $("details_BusinessUrl").innerHTML = BusinessUrl;

};
```

There's nothing fancy here: it's just the `innerHTML` of the table cells in the second column of the table being updated with the various fields from the object for the selected business. Since this object is directly taken from the service response earlier, the field names are defined by Yahoo! and not our application, but that's fine.

When the scene is deactivated, we have one thing to accomplish:

```
DetailsAssistant.prototype.deactivate = function() {

  Mojo.Event.stopListening(document, "orientationchange",
    this.orientationBind
  );

};
```

Just like the Welcome scene, we need to stop listening for orientation change events. Earlier I alluded to this being necessary. The reason it's necessary, there as well as here, is that if the user is viewing a business and rotates the device, if the listener on the welcome view fires at the same time as the listener for this scene, the code in the two effectively conflict (because they are reading and setting the same field in `localBusinessSearch` that stores the orientation), and things go south in a hurry. It's not a concurrency issue per se; since JavaScript is single-threaded, there's no problem in that regard. The problem that does exist, however, is that one of the handlers fires first and updates the orientation value. Then when the second handler fires, it doesn't work as expected because it will think the orientation hasn't changed because of the previous handler having updated the last orientation. Since this value must be different from the orientation in the incoming event object to the handler for it to register the orientation change at all, we have a problem Houston (to paraphrase Tom Hanks[2] a bit!).

Believe me, I found this out the hard way! Stopping the listener for the orientation change events on these scenes when they aren't the top scene is the right thing to do to avoid Very Nasty Things.

---

[2] This is a reference to the movie *Apollo 13*, which tells the story of the ill-fated Apollo 13 moon mission in 1970. Tom Hanks plays the main role of James Lovell, who utters the phrase "Houston, we have a problem" immediately after an explosion is heard on their way to the moon.

Handling Commands

Handling the commands generated by the menu is the same as we've seen before, but we'll tackle each possible event individually:

```
DetailsAssistant.prototype.handleCommand = function(inEvent) {

  if (this.commandMenuModel.processEvents &&
    inEvent.type == Mojo.Event.command) {
    switch (inEvent.command) {
      case "details":
        $("details_tblDetails").show();
        $("details_map").hide();
        this.commandMenuModel.items[2].disabled = true;
        this.controller.modelChanged(this.commandMenuModel, this);
      break;
```

When the details button is clicked, the <table> where the details are needs to be shown, and the <img> where the map is needs to be hidden. Then, the zoom command menu button needs to be disabled.

Conversely, when the map button is clicked, the opposite occurs:

```
      case "map":
        $("details_tblDetails").hide();
        $("details_map").show();
        $("details_map").style.top = "-58px";
        this.commandMenuModel.items[2].disabled = false;
        this.controller.modelChanged(this.commandMenuModel, this);
      break;
```

There's one additional bit of work. If you look at Figure 4-14, you'll see that the map extends all the way to the top of the card, behind the header.

Figure 4-14. *The area right around my hometown of Bay Shore, New York*

By default, this doesn't occur; the map winds up being right below the header. I'd say this is normally a good thing to occur with most scenes because you don't want the content to be obscured by the header by default. In this case, however, it looks quite odd. So, that's where the two lines setting the top style attribute of the <img> tag come into play. The value set there (which I came up with through trial and error, not magic!) ensures that the map is all the way up at the top of the card, so it fills the entire application area. It's a fairly small thing, but it makes it look quite a bit better, not to mention showing a little larger usable portion of the map to the user.

The Add To Favorites button handling is next. Note that the command we are about to handle is generated by tapping an item in the pop-up menu attached to the functions button of the scene's command menu. Yes, the same handleCommand() method is called to handle all the commands from all the menus used in this scene.

```
case "addToFavorites":
  if (!localBusinessSearch.favorites) {
    localBusinessSearch.favorites = { };
  }
  localBusinessSearch.favorites[
    "f_" + localBusinessSearch.currentBusiness.id] =
    localBusinessSearch.currentBusiness;
  localBusinessSearch.depot.simpleAdd("favorites",
    localBusinessSearch.favorites, function() {
      Mojo.Controller.getAppController().showBanner({
        messageText : "Favorite saved", soundClass : "alerts"
      }, { }, "");
    },
    function(inTransaction, inResult) {
      Mojo.Controller.errorDialog("Failure saving favorites: " +
        inResult);
    }
  );
break;
```

Recall that if there are no favorites and if the user in fact never saved a single favorite, then the localBusinessSearch.favorites object will be null. In this case, we start by creating a new empty object. Next, we add an attribute to that object whose name is the unique ID of the object for the business. Yahoo! is nice enough to provide us with this unique ID so we don't even have to expend any effort ourselves to generate one! Once that's done, the simpleAdd() method of the localBusinessSearch.depot object is called, passing it the key "favorites" to save the object under and, of course, the localBusinessSearch.favorites object to save. Yes, every time a favorite is saved, the object is overwritten. Since the key is a dynamic value and one we aren't generating ourselves, there's really no way to store each favorite individually and still be able to recall them all later, at least not without delving into the Depot API a bit more (there is the notion of something called *buckets*, which conceptually are like database tables, but I didn't see the need to go down that road). A simple banner is shown when the favorite is saved, or an error dialog box is shown if anything goes wrong.

The next command to handle deals with launching the built-in Google Maps application:

```
case "openInGoogleMaps":
  this.controller.serviceRequest("palm://com.palm.applicationManager", {
    method : "open",
    parameters : {
      id : "com.palm.app.maps",
```

```
      params : { query :
        localBusinessSearch.currentBusiness.Title + "," +
        localBusinessSearch.currentBusiness.City + "," +
        localBusinessSearch.currentBusiness.State
      }
    }
  });
break;
```

The Application Manager's open method allows us to do this, as we saw with launching the e-mail application with the previous application. The params object contains a single query attribute. The value of this attribute is a string containing the title (read: name) of the business to search for, plus the city and state, all separated by commas. This is all Google Maps needs to do a lookup. The user then has all the capabilities available to them that Google Maps provides, most importantly in this context the ability to get directions.

The final command to handle is for the zoom button:

```
case "zoom1": case "zoom2": case "zoom3": case "zoom4": case "zoom5":
case "zoom6": case "zoom7": case "zoom8": case "zoom9": case "zoom10":
case "zoom11": case "zoom12":
  localBusinessSearch.zoomLevel = inEvent.command.substr(4);
  this.getMap();
break;
  }
}

this.commandMenuModel.processEvents = true;

};
```

As you can see in Figure 4-15, it's a simple list, implemented as a pop-up menu, which the user can choose the zoom level from.

Figure 4-15. *If you have lousy eyes like me, then the larger the zoom number, the better!*

Since each item in the pop-up menu has its own command string, but also since the code executed in response to each is the same, all those cases are handled together. That code chops off the first four characters of the incoming command, the "zoom" portion, and sets the localBusinessSearch.zoomLevel field to the remainder, which is the numeric zoom level. The getMap() method is called, which results in a new map image being requested at the new zoom level.

Getting a Map Image

The getMap() method is responsible for interacting with the Yahoo! Map Image service, and so it contains the second of our two AJAX calls. Before that part, though, a bit of setup is required:

```
DetailsAssistant.prototype.getMap = function() {

  var imgWidth = 320;
  var imgHeight = 452;
  if (localBusinessSearch.lastOrientation >= 4) {
    imgWidth = 480;
    imgHeight = 292;
  }
```

By default, we assume the map is going to be in portrait orientation, which requires a width and height of 320 452. That covers the entire application card. When the last recorded orientation has a value greater than or equal to 4, though, then we need the image in landscape dimensions of 480 292, so in that situation, the imgWidth and imgHeight variables get the appropriate values.

After that comes the actual AJAX request:

```
localBusinessSearch.checkConnectivity(this,
  function() {
    new Ajax.Request(
      localBusinessSearch.mapWebServiceURL, {
        method : "get", evalJSON : "force",
        parameters : {
          appid : localBusinessSearch.appID, output : "json",
          longitude : localBusinessSearch.currentBusiness.Longitude,
          latitude : localBusinessSearch.currentBusiness.Latitude,
          image_width : imgWidth, image_height : imgHeight,
          zoom : localBusinessSearch.zoomLevel
        },
        onSuccess : function(inTransport) {
          $("details_map").src = inTransport.responseJSON.ResultSet.Result;
        },
        onFailure : function(inTransport) {
          Mojo.Controller.errorDialog("FAILURE: " + inTransport.status +
            " - " + inTransport.responseText);
        },
        onException : function(inTransport) {
          Mojo.Controller.errorDialog("EXCEPTION");
        }
      }
    );
  }.bind(this),
```

```
    function() {
      $("details_tblDetails").show();
      $("details_map").hide();
      this.commandMenuModel.processEvents = false;
      this.commandMenuModel.items[0].toggleCmd = "details";
      this.controller.modelChanged(this.commandMenuModel, this);
    }.bind(this)
  );

};
```

This is nearly identical to the search service request, but there are indeed some differences. First, the parameters object contains some new attributes, namely, longitude, latitude, image_width, image_height, and zoom. I'd bet all of these are pretty self-explanatory! The first two come from the currentBusiness object, the third and fourth come from the variables defined right before this, and the fifth comes from the localBusinessSearch.zoomLevel (which is why it is stored there, as previously hinted at).

The same sort of error handling as we saw with the search service is done here, but the handling of Internet connectivity not being available near the end is a bit different. When this happens, we flip the user back to the Item Details view, since we know that is available locally.

There's also the small matter of that processEvents attribute sitting in the command menu's model that I haven't mentioned. This is a custom attribute that webOS doesn't know about. It's used in this application to avoid a nasty situation. What happens is that if the user tries to flip to the map but Internet connectivity isn't available, the very act of updating the command menu's model triggers an event, and handleCommand() fires again. This results in a nasty loop that causes getMap() to be called again and the AJAX request to fire again. Before too long, you find that Yahoo! shuts down your access to the Map Image service temporarily because it views this rapid succession of requests as a denial-of-service (DoS) attack. The service is then unavailable for some random period of time, and so the application isn't fully usable.

To avoid this loop, the processEvents flag is set to false when connectivity isn't available. So, the next time through, handleCommand() fires, but it doesn't do anything, save one thing: it resets processEvents to true so that subsequent true user-generated events are again handled. This effectively breaks the cycle, avoids the loop, and keeps the service answering our requests and not hanging up the phone on us immediately like so many ex-girlfriends in my past!

Handling Orientation Changes

The last method in the Item Details scene's assistant is for handling orientation changes:

```
DetailsAssistant.prototype.handleOrientation = function(inEvent) {

  if (inEvent.position > 1 &&
    inEvent.position != localBusinessSearch.lastOrientation) {
    localBusinessSearch.lastOrientation = inEvent.position;
    if (inEvent.position > 2) {
      this.getMap();
    }
  }

};
```

As with the Welcome scene, we only do something here if the new `position` value is something other than values indicating the device is laying flat on its back or face down (0 or 1) and then only if the orientation has actually changed. Assuming those conditions are met, the new orientation is recorded, and `getMap()` is called.

Favorites Scene

We have only two scenes reaming to look at, the first of which is the Favorites scene. As you can see from Figure 4-16, it looks pretty much identical to the Search Results scene, just with a different header. That's very much on purpose because ultimately the user will choose an item from this `List`, just like they would on search results, to get to the Item Details scene.

Because of the similarity, not just in look and feel but also largely in code, I'm going to save a few trees by trimming this section down to the bare minimum. I'll talk about only the two things that makes this scene much different, and those are the `activate()` method of the assistant and the deleting of favorites, which obviously isn't something available in the Search Results scene.

■ **Note** I of course suggest taking a minute or two and examining, on your own, the HTML and code for what isn't discussed here. It truly is nearly the same, so it really shouldn't take more than a few minutes. Go ahead, I'll wait.

Figure 4-16. *Not much different from Search Results really*

In fact, we'll dive right into the `activate()` method now:

```
FavoritesAssistant.prototype.activate = function() {

  this.lstFavoritesModel.items = [ ];
  this.controller.modelChanged(this.lstFavoritesModel, this);

  if (localBusinessSearch.favorites) {
```

```
        for (var f in localBusinessSearch.favorites) {
          this.lstFavoritesModel.items.push(localBusinessSearch.favorites[f]);
        }
        this.controller.modelChanged(this.lstFavoritesModel, this);
      } else {
        this.controller.showAlertDialog({
          onChoose : function(inValue) {
            this.controller.stageController.popScene();
          },
          title : "Nothing Found",
          message : "You have no saved favorites",
          choices : [
            { label : "Ok", type : "affirmative"}
          ]
        });
        return;
      }

};
```

At the end of the day, we're populating a List widget, and at this point that's second-nature for us! The only real difference is that the source of data is the localBusinessSearch.favorites object that we read in from the Depot at startup. If this field is null, then we don't have favorites, in which case the else branch executes and an alert dialog box is shown to inform the user. When this dialog box is dismissed, the scene is popped, and users will find themselves back at the Welcome scene.

Assuming there are favorites, however, we just iterate over the attributes of the object and push each into the items array of the List model. A quick call to our good friend Mr. modelChanged() later, and we're done!

Deleting favorites is done with a right-to-left swipe as we've seen previously, and that fires the uninspiringly named deleteFavorite() method:

```
FavoritesAssistant.prototype.deleteFavorite = function(inEvent) {

  delete localBusinessSearch.favorites["f_" + inEvent.item.id];
  localBusinessSearch.depot.simpleAdd("favorites",
    localBusinessSearch.favorites, function() { },
    function(inTransaction, inResult) {
      Mojo.Controller.errorDialog("Failure saving favorites: " + inResult);
    }
  );

  if (!localBusinessSearch.doesObjectHaveAttributes(
    localBusinessSearch.favorites)) {
    localBusinessSearch.favorites = null;
    this.controller.stageController.popScene();
  }

};
```

The basic JavaScript delete keyword removes the appropriate attribute from the favorites object. The name of the attribute being deleted is f_XXX, where XXX is the numeric ID of the business as given to us by Yahoo! (remember that an all-numeric name for an object attribute is invalid in JavaScript). Once that's done, we use the `simpleAdd()` method of the `depot` object again to write out the `favorites` object, just like when a favorite was added. Finally, we do a quick check of the `favorites` object using the `doesObjectHaveAttributes()` utility method that we saw earlier. If it returns `false`, then the scene is popped since there's no favorites to view—but not before setting `localBusinessSearch.favorites` to `null` so that if the user tries to come back to this scene, we can tell them they have no favorites. (Remember, if the `favorites` object doesn't have any attributes, the `List` would still be populated here, even though it would wind up being empty, because an empty object isn't the same as a `null` reference, either in general or logically within the context of this application.)

Preferences Scene

The final scene left for us to explore is the Preferences scene, where the user can choose a different background for the application. Figure 4-17 shows this scene, but what it doesn't show is that quite a few options are available, spread across three categories.

Figure 4-17. Yes, I know, an animated background is annoying…but it's cool that it works, no?

The three categories—tiled, full-screen, and animated—are the three types of images. The tiled images are smaller images that get tiled across the page. The full-screen images are just that: full-screen! The animated images are like the tiled images but are animated GIFs. The three sections are collapsible and expandable using a new UI metaphor: the collapsible divider (but, underneath, it's something familiar, as you're about to see!)

The View HTML

The view HTML is quite simple, but because the markup for the three categories is highly redundant, I'll just show the first category's markup to save some time and space:

```
<div class="palm-page-header">
  <div class="header-icon preferences"></div>
  <div class="header-text">Preferences</div>
</div>
```

```
<table class="palm-divider collapsible" x-mojo-tap-highlight="momentary">
  <tbody>
    <tr>
      <td class="left"> </td>
      <td class="label" style="color:#ffffff; ">Tiled </td>
      <td class="line" width="100%"></td>
      <td><div class="palm-arrow-closed arrow_button"
        id="preferences_btnTiled"></div></tr>
      <td class="right"> </td>
    </tr>
  </tbody>
</table>
<div id="preferences_drwTiled" x-mojo-element="Drawer"
  style="position:relative;top:-30px;">>
  <div class="palm-list">
    <div class="palm-row single">
      <div class="palm-row-wrapper textfield-group"
        x-mojo-focus-highlight="true">
        <div class="title">
          <div id="preferences_lstTiled" x-mojo-element="List"></div>
        </div>
      </div>
    </div>
  </div>
</div>
...
```

Following the usual header, we find a `<table>`. Within this table a single row is present, and there are five columns in the row. The first and last cells just have a nonbreaking HTML entity character in them, and they are to ensure the structure of this works properly when the section below is expanded (without them, that expanded section would overlap the divider).

The second cell is of course the text label, and the cell after that is the arrow that the user clicks to expand or contract the section below. This is a simple `<div>` with the `palm-arrow-closed` and `arrow_button` styles applied. This provides the graphic for the button and styles it as appropriate.

Below this table is a `<div>` that…wait a minute…looks pretty familiar! Yes, it's our friend the `Drawer` widget! You see, the divider line above—more specifically, that third cell in the table and the `<div>` that becomes the graphical button—is just like the `Buttons` above each `Drawer` in the previous application that was used to expand the `Drawer`. As stated previously, there's no technical reason a `Drawer` has to be opened and closed by a `Button`, although that's fairly typical.

Within the `Drawer` is a `<div>` that will become a `List`. The rest of the markup surrounding that `<div>` is typical of what we've seen before.

The Scene Assistant

The scene assistant for the Preferences scene starts out in the ordinary way:

```
function PreferencesAssistant() { };

PreferencesAssistant.prototype.drwTiledModel = { open : false };
PreferencesAssistant.prototype.drwFullScreenModel = { open : false };
PreferencesAssistant.prototype.drwAnimatedModel = { open : false };
```

Each Drawer has an associated model with the usual open attribute in it. All of them begin closed here, so their initial values are false.

```
PreferencesAssistant.prototype.lstTiledModel = { items : [
  { description : "Stars", filename : "background01" },
  { description : "Grey Fog", filename : "background02" },
  { description : "Splotchy", filename : "background03" },
  { description : "Bio Mesh", filename : "background04" },
  { description : "Dark Marble", filename : "background05" },
  { description : "Velvet", filename : "background06" },
  { description : "Twinklies", filename : "background07" },
  { description : "Armor", filename : "background08" }
] };
...
```

The lstTiledModel object is the model for the tiled background List. Each List gets its own model, but only this one is shown. Each has a description and a filename. Note that the filename has no extension; this is added dynamically later (it is assumed that the background images are all GIFs, which they just so happen to be!)

The setup() method comes next:

```
PreferencesAssistant.prototype.setup = function() {

  this.controller.setupWidget(Mojo.Menu.appMenu,
    localBusinessSearch.appMenuAttributes, localBusinessSearch.appMenuModel);

  this.controller.setupWidget("preferences_drwTiled", { },
    this.drwTiledModel);
  Mojo.Event.listen(this.controller.get("preferences_btnTiled"),
    Mojo.Event.tap, function() {
      this.drwTiledModel.open = !this.drwTiledModel.open;
      if (this.drwTiledModel.open) {
        $("preferences_btnTiled").className =
          "palm-arrow-expanded arrow_button";
      } else {
        $("preferences_btnTiled").className = "palm-arrow-closed arrow_button";
      }
      this.controller.modelChanged(this.drwTiledModel, this);
    }.bind(this)
  );
  this.controller.setupWidget("preferences_lstTiled", {
    itemTemplate : "preferences/list-item"
  }, this.lstTiledModel);
  this.controller.listen("preferences_lstTiled",
    Mojo.Event.listTap, this.selectBackground.bind(this));
...
};
```

After the application menu is set up, each Drawer is set up (again, only the code for the tiled category is shown; the other two categories are handled the same basic way). After the Drawer is set up, we attach a Mojo.Event.tap listener to the graphical button (really the <div>, but remember, the Palm-supplied styles give it the graphical button look). When this element it tapped, the inline function executes. This code is like the code behind the `Buttons` attached to `Drawers` in the previous application: the value of the open attribute in the `Drawer`'s model is reversed, and `modelChanged()` is called. If the `Drawer` is opened, we also change the class applied to the button `<div>` to `palm-arrow-expanded` and `arrow_button`. This changes the graphic to what you see over the animated category in the previous screenshot: the arrow points down to indicate the section is expanded.

Finally, the `List` is set up, in the normal way. The `Mojo.Event.listTap` event is listened for, and it triggers the `selectBackground()` method:

```
PreferencesAssistant.prototype.selectBackground = function(inEvent) {

  document.body.style.background = "url(images/" + inEvent.item.filename +
    ".gif) center center";

  localBusinessSearch.preferences.background = inEvent.item.filename;
  localBusinessSearch.depot.simpleAdd("preferences",
    localBusinessSearch.preferences, function() { },
    function(inTransaction, inResult) {
      Mojo.Controller.errorDialog("Failure saving preferences: " + inResult);
    }
  );

};
```

The job of this method is twofold. First, the background style attribute of the document's body element is changed to the selected image. Second, the background attribute of the `localBusinessSearch.preferences` object is updated to reflect the newly selected background, and then the object is written out to the Depot, as previously seen. Note that the user wouldn't even be able to get this far if the Depot wasn't opened at the start because, as shown earlier, the menu item wouldn't have been available to get to this scene.

Suggested Exercises

The basic functionality this application provides is, I believe, useful. However, there's certainly no shortage of things that could make it better, and I have a few suggestions to toss your way:

- One of the outright limitations I purposely left in place is the 20 maximum result limitation. Twenty is in fact a limitation placed on any single result set returned by the search service. However, a given search may result in hundreds of matches. My suggestion is to modify the code to make repeated AJAX requests to the service to get the complete list of results. You could do this all at once, which wouldn't be too tough, or you could use the callback mechanism the `List` has available to progressively load it as the user scrolls. The first suggestion shouldn't be too tough, but the latter could be rather difficult. You can judge how much pain you want! Both exercises are worth doing.

- Add the ability to e-mail the details and possibly the map for a given result.

- Google also has some web-accessible APIs available, so why not look into those and allow a direct Google search for a given business? The interaction model is nearly identical to the Yahoo! services, so that shouldn't be too tough at all, but the differences that do exist should make for an interesting exercise.

I have no doubt you can come up with your own ideas as well, but the bottom line is that this is definitely an application with some possibilities, so have fun with it!

Summary

In this chapter, we got on board with the Web 2.0 craze and built what can rightly be called a mashup that allows the user to look up businesses in an area, get details on it, map it, and store it as a favorite. In the process, we learned about making AJAX requests from a webOS application. We also learned about creating "dark theme" applications, opening up a new world of UI look-and-feel options to us. The Depot data storage mechanism was explored for storing favorites as well as preferences. We even saw how exploiting the fact that a webOS application is a web application lets us pull off some neat visual tricks, such as animated backgrounds. We also saw how to use command menus, `RadioButtons` and `Sliders`. We learned how to deal with orientation events too. The ability to create a fancier drawer metaphor with collapsible divider lines was also demonstrated. How to deal with network availability was explored, and finally, we learned how to interact with the GPS service of the device to get the users' current location and base a search on that information (including how to deal with not being able to obtain a GPS fix).

All in all, we covered quite a bit of ground in this one project!

In the next chapter, we'll switch gears a bit and build an application that will be quite a bit different from all the others in this book, namely, a game! After all, it's not all about business, like this chapter. We should be able to have some fun with our expensive smartphones too!

■ ■ ■

Time for a Break: Engineer, a webOS Game

All Work and No Play Makes Everyone Dull, So Let's Make Ourselves a Game!

Palm in general has a history as a business-oriented company. Its earlier PDAs were always top-notch at performing tasks such as making appointments, maintaining contacts, and taking notes. That focus has, largely, been extended into webOS and the Palm Pre.

However, life isn't all about slaving away at a desk, sitting in on meetings, and all that jazz. Sometimes, you just need to cut loose and play some games! A little fun is often just what you need to keep your wits about you, even more so than a good organizer.

With that in mind, in this chapter we're going to build ourselves a game! In the process, we'll learn about some of the capabilities Palm provides for such endeavors, and we'll also see how we can build a webOS application that is a little bit different and, in a way, doesn't lean quite as heavily on the Mojo framework. This may sound counter to the goal of this book as a whole, but in fact I think it's very much on point: seeing alternative ways to build applications for the platform is, in my estimation, a very valuable exercise.

The other benefit to creating a game is that game creation requires you to think differently and to tackle a lot of widely varying topics. Things such as physics, graphics, audio, AI, data compression, and UI interactions all come into play. It has often been said that game programming is one of the most challenging and yet rewarding things you can ever write, and my experience absolutely tells me that is true, so it's a great project to do in a more general sense, even putting aside learning about webOS.

Oh yeah, and in the end, we should wind up with a fun yet challenging game to play while our boss babbles away in front of a whiteboard for hours on end! Of course, *my* boss never does that, and I always listen intently to every word he has to say, but I'm saying, maybe that's not the case for you. ☺

What's This App Do Anyway?

A game is a great project because you can just let your mind roam free and come up with whatever zaniness you want...so long as you can implement it!

So, in this game entitled Engineer, you play the part of the...wait for it...*engineer* of a starship! For some odd reason, a spaceship that can break the known laws of physics and travel at faster than light speeds doesn't have a computer powerful enough to handle simple tasks, so your job is to sit around pressing buttons to divert particles released from a generator into the correct injector ports to keep the ship going. What's worse is that if you get it wrong too many times, the engine will overheat, and your starship, and all hands onboard, will meet its fiery (but yet silent because, after all, in space, no one can hear you scream![1]) doom.

So, what are some of the requirements for a game? Largely this comes down to the specifics of the rules, but there's some other stuff to go along with that too:

- The application will have two scenes, one a title scene and one the actual game scene. On the title scene we'll also show some instructions, and we'll do so with a nice little vertical scroller, just like the old C64[2] demo days!

- The game itself will be done using the HTML5 `<canvas>` tag, since this will allow us some nice graphical capability, such as enclosing the game-play area in what will attempt to look like an old video game cabinet, complete with blinking lights along the sides, a marquee up top, and the images of two hands at the bottom— one holding a joystick and another over a button. And yes, the hands will move as the player plays the game!

- The game-play area will consist of four injector points in each of the four corners of the screen, a generator in the middle with what looks sort of like electricity pulsating, and four diverters around the generator.

- Four types of particles will be generated, each with a different look and a color matching one of the injector points, and that's how the player knows where they should go. Each of the diverters will have six different types of waveguides that the player must correctly (and quickly!) choose between to keep the particles moving around the circuit path that connects the generator, diverters, and injector ports.

- If the player puts a particle in the wrong injector port, or a particle goes back into the generator, the player will lose points (they gain points when particles go into the correct ports), and the engine will heat up a little. This will be depicted by a `ProgressBar` below the play area. If this fills up all the way, the game ends. The player can tap anywhere other than the diverters to cool the engine.

- We'll use the System Sounds service to play sounds for diverter clicks, particles going into ports (different sound for correct and incorrect), the engine being cooled down, particles emerging from the generator, and the game ending.

- A high score will be stored via cookies and displayed on the `titleScreen`.

- When the game ends, we'll use a custom dialog box to indicate that the ship has blown up (and we'll try to be a bit witty about that unfortunate fact!). The player's final score will be shown, and if it's the new high score, they will be congratulated.

---

[1] "In space, no one can hear you scream" is of course the famous tagline of the great movie *Alien*. This is one of my personal favorites because it scared the living daylights out of me when I snuck to watch it at roughly age nine. I slept in my parents' room for a week after that! Recently, I decided to let my own nine-year-old son watch it, and I was extremely disappointed when he just shrugged it off and was like, "So what? That wasn't scary at all!" I'm not sure if I was just a wimpy kid or if kids today are way too desensitized to horrific imagery!
[2] C64 is short for Commodore 64. If you're old enough to have had experience with this computer, you'll likely remember that as "the good old days." If you were a little more advanced, you may have been part of the demo scene, as I was. If you never used or owned a C64, sorry, you missed out on something special!

- We want our game to be a good webOS citizen, so any time it is "cardified," we'll shut down its activity. For example, if the user minimizes the game while in the middle of playing, the game will pause (and the card will indicate the game is paused). No code will be running in this state to save the battery.

OK, that about does it. Let's get to this thing; it should be a lot of fun!

PORTING A GAME: ENGINEER AND K&G ARCADE

Engineer isn't an original game, not in this form anyway.

Engineer appeared as part of a Windows Mobile game entitled K&G Arcade. The letters *K* and *G* stand for the two antagonists in the game, wise-cracking aliens Krelmac and Gentoo (think Beavis and Butthead meet Kang and Kodos from *The Simpsons*).

K&G Arcade was an adventure game that had in it 25 mini-games that the user had to play (and attain certain scores in) to complete each level of the game and ultimately escape the clutches of Krelmac and Gentoo. Engineer was one of those games, although that version did not include the concept of the overheating engine; that was added specifically for the webOS version presented here.

This explains the marquee you see in this version: Krelmactron 5000 was an inside joke we put in K&G Arcade, obviously referring to Krelmac and referencing the sort of television name that used to be commonly seen in 50s sci-fi shows and movies.

Incidentally, all the graphics seen here (except for the Engineer title and the paused graphic) were done by an artist friend of mine named Anthony Volpe, who I have worked on a number of projects with (and he has done illustrations for most of my books as well). He also is the voice of Gentoo (I voiced Krelmac).

If K&G Arcade sounds interesting, it's actually available (for free) in a PC version too! Check it out at `http://www.etherient.com/kgarcade`.

One more note of interest to classic computer lovers: the Engineer logo uses the system font from the old Amiga computer. Award yourself several million points if you realized that before you read this!

Planning the Application

As compared to previous applications, this one has a very simple flow: there are a grand total of two scenes! And, as if that wasn't simple enough, one of them you'll see only once, when the application starts up! Still, because we have some issues here in dealing the application being minimized and because there's going to be a custom dialog box involved, it's still definitely worth whiteboarding the overall flow, and Figure 5-1 is the resulting diagram.

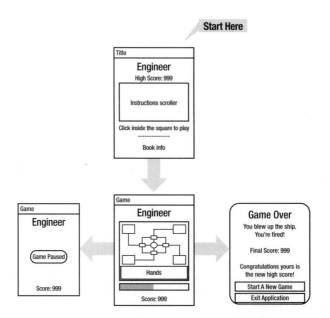

Figure 5-1. A whiteboardish sketching of the scene flow of the application

When the application starts up, the titleScreen scene is what the user sees. They'll see an Engineer title logo at the top, the current high score (if any), and a green square where instructions will scroll upward. Below that box will be some text indicating to click in the box to begin the game, and below that is some information about this book.

When they begin the game, they are tossed over to the gameScreen scene. This has the same logo graphic up top, with the game-play area in the middle. The game-play area is further subdivided into the area where the game actually takes place, and then below that is an area with two hands, one on a joystick and one hovering over a button. These hands will mimic the actions taken by the user. I think this is a little bit of fun that the player would enjoy seeing. Below the game-play area is a ProgressBar widget that shows the engine overheat status, and below that is the player's current score.

When the game ends as a result of the engine overheating, a dialog box pops up, and that's shown off to the right from the gameScreen scene. This dialog box has some text indicating the game is over, as well as the final score. If the final score is the new high score, there is some text indicating that as well. Below that are two Button controls, one to start a new game and one to exit the application entirely.

The game can be minimized at any time, and that's what the smaller window off to the left from the gameScreen scene indicates. The user will see the Engineer logo, their current score at the bottom, and a graphical "Game Paused" message in the middle. Not that not shown here is the minimized version of the application if they do so from the titleScreen scene. I didn't show this because it's just a shrunken version of that scene, with the instructions scroller frozen.

So, like I said earlier, this isn't a complicated flow at all, but it should give you an idea of the planning involved nonetheless and give you an overview of the application.

Creating the Skeleton

You would create the skeleton of the application just like any other, using the Eclipse wizard. You'll create two scenes, titleScreen and gameScreen, which will result in the directory structure shown in Figure 5-2.

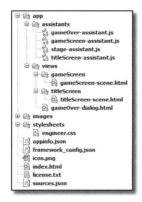

Figure 5-2. The application's directory structure and file contents

I didn't expand the `images` directory this time as I've done in other chapters because there are quite a few more images this time around and they frankly wouldn't have all fit in the figure! Table 5-1 summarizes the images you'll find in the game. Note that all of them, except for the Engineer logo and the "Game Paused" graphic, are PNGs. The other two are GIFs (not for any particular reason, other than the graphics tool I used happened to save those two as GIFs, and there was no reason I saw to convert them to PNGs).

Table 5-1. The Images Used in This Game

Image(s)	Description
`console_left`, `console_middle`, `console_right`	These are the images that make up the background of the console where the hand are.
`diverter_down_left`, `diverter_down_right`, `diverter_up_left`, `diverter_up_right`, `diverter_horizontal`, `diverter_vertical`	These are the six types of diverters that can be present in any of the four converters. The first four are the corner-type diverters, which the last two are simple horizontal and vertical line types.
`engineer`	This is the Engineer logo graphic.
`game_background`	This is the background of the play area. It contains the four injector ports, the waveguide tracks, the generator, and the placeholders for the diverters.
`left_hand_normal`, `left_hand_down`, `left_hand_left`, `left_hand_right`, `left_hand_up`	These are the images for the left hand, the one with the joystick. The `left_hand_normal` graphic is when the player hasn't tapped a diverter, so the hand is in its default, "not doing anything at the moment" position.
`mini_game_frame`	This is the frame around the game-play area.

Table 5-1. The Images Used in This Game (continued)

mini_game_frame_X	There are ten graphics, five for the left and five for the right, each with a number where you see X here from zero to four, and these are the lights around the edges of the frame.
nucleus_X	There are eight graphics, with a number from zero to seven where you see X here, and these are the frames of animation for the generator in the middle.
particleX_Y	There are a total of eight images for the four different types of particles in the game, two frames of animation each. The X here is the particle type as a number from zero to three, and Y is the animation frame, either 0 or 1.
paused	This is the "Game Paused" graphic.
progress_bar_progress	This is a graphic used to style the overheat ProgressBar.
right_hand_down, right_hand_up	These are the graphics for the right hand. The hand is either up or down (read: pressing the button).

Aside from the images, the rest of the files should hold no surprises for you at this point, save one: the gameOver-dialog.html file in the views directory (and the corresponding gameOver-assistant.js file in the assistants directory). As we'll see later, the dialog box seen when the game ends is very much like a scene, which means it has its own view HTML file and its own assistant. However, it doesn't fall into the same directory structure as all our scenes do, meaning we don't need to create a gameOver directory in the views directory for it; we can just throw it in the views directory directly. It *could* be in its own directory; the choice is ours since we'll be specifying exactly where the file is located when the dialog box is shown.

The Data Model

This application doesn't have a data model per se, although the cookie used to store the high score could definitely be considered the data model. The name of the cookie is Engineer_highScore, and it simply stores a numeric value, nothing fancy.

Application Configuration

We'll take a very quick look at the configuration files here, just to keep that pattern of exploration going in this chapter, but there's nothing new to be found here at all.

The appinfo.json File

Listing 5-1 shows the appinfo.json file, and there are no surprises here.

Listing 5-1. The `appinfo.json` *File*

```
{
  "id": "com.etherient.engineer",
  "version": "1.0.0",
  "vendor": "Etherient",
  "type": "web",
  "main": "index.html",
  "title": "Engineer",
  "icon": "icon.png"
}
```

The `icon.png` is the same logo used for K&G Arcade, and it's a headshot of Krelmac.

The sources.json File

The `sources.json` file has the usual content as well, as shown in Listing 5-2.

Listing 5-2. The `sources.json` *File*

```
[
  { "source" : "app/assistants/stage-assistant.js" },
  {
    "source" : "app/assistants/gameScreen-assistant.js", "scenes" : "gameScreen"
  },
  {
    "source" : "app/assistants/titleScreen-assistant.js",
    "scenes" : "titleScreen"
  },
  { "source" : "app/assistants/gameOver-assistant.js" }
]
```

We have the stage assistant, the assistants for the title scene and game scene, and the assistant for the custom Game Over dialog box that is seen when the engine overheats. This is perhaps a bit interesting: a custom dialog box gets its own assistant, just like a scene. In fact, it *is* a scene, just one in the guise of a dialog box. We can do anything in a dialog box like this that we can in a regular scene that we know and love; it's just presented a little differently on the screen.

The framework_config.json File

Finally, the `framework_config.json`, shown in Listing 5-3, has just the one attribute we've come to expect.

Listing 5-3. The `framework_config.json` *File*

```
{ "logLevel" : 99 }
```
As always, this file is optional, and you can adjust the `logLevel` as you see fit.

Global-Scope Code

This application actually has no global-scope code; everything is contained within one of the two scene assistants, so we can move right along to the stage at this point.

Setting the Stage

The stage in this application, like in many others, is very bare, just containing the, pardon the pun, bare essentials. You can see this for yourself in Listing 5-4.

Listing 5-4. *The Stage HTML, As Unexciting As It Is!*

```
<?xml version="1.0" encoding="UTF-8"?>
<!DOCTYPE html PUBLIC "-//W3C//DTD XHTML 1.1//EN"
  "http://www.w3.org/TR/xhtml11/DTD/xhtml11.dtd">

<html xmlns="http://www.w3.org/1999/xhtml" xml:lang="en">

  <head>
    <title>Engineer</title>
    <script src="/usr/palm/frameworks/mojo/mojo.js" type="text/javascript"
      x-mojo-version="1" />
    <link href="stylesheets/engineer.css" media="screen" rel="stylesheet"
      type="text/css" />
  </head>
  <body></body>
</html>
```

As you can see, it's nothing but the usual mojo.js import and the application's style sheet, nothing more. The stage assistant is similarly sparse, as Listing 5-5 proves.

Listing 5-5. *The Stage Assistant, Such As It Is!*

```
function StageAssistant() { };

StageAssistant.prototype.setup = function() {
  this.controller.pushScene("titleScreen");
};
```

Fortunately, being so simple means we can continue to more interesting stuff in short order. First, however, let's talk about the style sheet.

A Matter of Style

As in the past, I'll mix in discussion of the style information as needed to give it the proper context, but as usual there are some more general style sheet parts to look at, just one in this case:

```
body.palm-default {
```

```
    background-color : #000000;
}
```

As we saw in the Code Cabinet project, this sets the color of all scenes to a given color, black in this case.

There are ten other style classes in the style sheet, about half for the titleScreen scene and half for the gameScreen scene, just to foreshadow that a bit. Right now, though, let's get into the actual code, starting with the titleScreen scene.

A Scene-by-Scene Account

As previously mentioned, this application has only two scenes (three if you consider the end of game dialog box), and for the sake of this discussion, we will in fact lump it in with the other two. As we look at this code, you'll find that the vast majority of the code involved in making this game work is contained in one scene.

Before we get to that one however, we'll tackle the titleScreen scene.

titleScreen Scene

The titleScreen scene is the very first thing the player sees when the game is started. As you can see in Figure 5-3, it shows the current high score, if any; instructions for playing the game via a vertical scrolling section in the middle; and some information about this book underneath.

Figure 5-3. *The titleScreen scene*

Although the game itself is built using the HTML5 <canvas> tag, this scene uses nothing but plain old HTML, CSS, and JavaScript, even to accomplish the scrolling instructions.

The View HTML

The scene's view HTML is really just a lot of straightforward HTML, as Listing 5-6 proves.

Listing 5-6. *The Contents of gameScreen-scene.html*

```
<img src="images/engineer.gif" class="cssEngineerLogo" />

<div class="cssHighScore" id="divHighScore"></div>

<div id="divHowToPlay" class="cssHowToPlay">
  <div id="instructions" style="position:relative;top:210px;">
    <center>
      How to play Engineer
      <br><hr width="75%" />
    </center>
    Your job as the engineer of the starship Prenterprise (hehe) is to direct
    particles created by the generator in the center of the screen into the
    correct injector port at the corners based on color. You do this by tapping
    the particle diverters around the generator, or by pressing the
    keys W, A, S and Z which correspond to the top, left, right and bottom
    diverters respectively, to cycle through the diverter states. Choose the
    right one to complete the circuit and thereby keeping a particle moving.
    If a particle goes into the wrong port, or back into the generator, or hits
    a diverter with an incorrect state and cannot continue, you lose points.
    Also, when they go back into the generator, or the wrong port, the engine
    heats up a little. The bar below the play area fills up as the engine gets
    hotter. Tap the game area somewhere other than the diverters, or press P,
    or physically shake your Pre, to cool the engine down a bit.  The game ends
    if the engine overheats.
  </div>
</div>

<div class="cssClickToBeginDiv"><center>
  Click inside the green square to play<br>
  <hr width="50%" />
</center></div>

<div id="divTitleInfo" class="cssTitleInfo">
  <center>
    From the book<br>
    "Practical webOS Projects With the Palm Pre"<br>
    (Apress, 2009, ISBN-13: 978-1-4302-2674-1).<br>
    &copy;2009 Frank W. Zammetti. All rights reserved.<br>
    A product of Etherient: http://www.etherient.com
  </center>
</div>
```

Unless HTML is completely new to you, I doubt there's much here that needs explaining. The one thing worth pointing out is the positioning style information on the <div> with the ID instructions.

Generally, style information should be externalized in a separate style sheet file, just for the sake of good code structure (separation of style of structure and all that jazz). However, when dealing with animation of style properties via JavaScript, it is often necessary to have certain bits of style inline. This is because of the cascading nature of CSS. If things like the position and top style attributes are only in a style sheet, depending on how they are declared, you can easily find that they are overridden when the page renders, making them not work as expected, or at all. Therefore, for things such as positional information, putting the style settings in-line avoids these problems.

It is that <div> that allows us to show the instructions scrolling, although that wouldn't be obvious just from looking at this HTML. What may help is looking at the cssHowToPlay style class:

```
.cssHowToPlay {
  overflow : hidden;
  padding : 4px;
  font-size : 80%;
  width : 290px;
  height : 188px;
  position : absolute;
  left : 7px;
  top : 96px;
  color : #ffffff;
  border : 4px groove #00ff00;
}
```

Most important is the overflow setting of hidden. This means that any content contained with the <div> styled with this class will be truncated at the border or the <div>. Imagine what it might look like if content within this <div> that is larger than the <div> itself slowly has its top style attribute decreased through negative numbers (hint, hint!)

Aside from the instructions, the Engineer logo at the top and the high score are styled using these two classes, respectively:

```
.cssEngineerLogo {
  position : absolute;
  left : 21px;
  top : 16px;
}
.cssHighScore {
  font-size : 70%;
  width : 320px;
  height : 20px;
  position : absolute;
  left : 0px;
  top : 72px;
  color : #ffffff;
}
```

As you can see, they are positioned absolutely. Doing it this way, rather than letting them be positioned by the normal page layout, allows for a greater degree of control over where they wind up on the screen. The same is true for the text telling the player to click in the green box to start the game, as well as the information about this book:

```
.cssClickToBeginDiv {
  position : absolute;
  left : 0px;
  top : 306px;
  width : 100%;
  color : #ffffff;
```

```
}
.cssTitleInfo {
  font-size : 70%;
  position : absolute;
  left : 0px;
  top : 354px;
  width : 100%;
  color : #ffffff;
}
```

All of these, save for cssEngineerLogo, are setting a text color of white (#ffffff), which is fortunate since the default text color is black and would therefore not be visible on the black scene background. Incidentally, I used percentages to specify the font-size for all of these because it seemed to yield better results. I knew I had to make the text a little bit smaller than I'd otherwise like in order to fit it all on one nonscrolling screen, but if I specified the sizes using points or pixels, the text quality seemed to degrade. I'm not really sure if it was just a figment of my imagination or the fact that my eyes aren't what they once were, but using percentages seemed to make the text look better.

The Scene Assistant

The code for the titleScreen scene is, I think, surprisingly simple, beginning with this bit of code:

```
function TitleScreenAssistant() { };

TitleScreenAssistant.prototype.instructionsTop = 210;

TitleScreenAssistant.prototype.insInterval = null;
```

Both of the variables are involved in scrolling the instructions. The instructionsTop field holds the current top style attribute value for the instructions <div>, and insInterval holds a reference to a running interval that makes the scrolling happen (details coming soon!)

The setup() method is next:

```
TitleScreenAssistant.prototype.setup = function() {

  Mojo.Event.listen(this.controller.stageController.document,
    Mojo.Event.stageActivate,
    function() {
      this.insInterval = setInterval(this.scrollInstructions.bind(this), 50);
    }.bind(this)
  );

  Mojo.Event.listen(this.controller.stageController.document,
    Mojo.Event.stageDeactivate,
    function() {
      clearInterval(this.insInterval);
    }.bind(this)
  );

};
```

The Mojo.Event.stageActivate event is fired whenever the stage is activated, such as when the application is brought to the foreground from its cardified minimized state (which you can see in Figure 5-4). This is necessary so that the instructions scrolling can be resumed. When the Mojo.Event.stageDeactivate occurs, which is listened for here as well, a call to clearInterval() on the reference to the interval (insInterval) is made to stop the scrolling. The reason you want to do this is to save the battery: the more that is running in the background, even if a relatively minor thing such as scrolling instructions, the more battery the application is chewing through. I dare say, if someone couldn't make an emergency phone call on the side of a dark road when their car broke down because the instructions for Engineer were scrolling in the background the past four hours, someone would be a *tad* upset! So, when the stage is activated again, we call setInterval() and direct it to fire the scrollInstructions() method every 50 milliseconds to resume the scrolling.

Figure 5-4. Engineer minimized from the titleScreen scene

Upon activation of the scene, we have some work to do as well:

```
TitleScreenAssistant.prototype.activate = function() {

  var highScoreCookie = new Mojo.Model.Cookie("Engineer_highScore");
  var highScore = highScoreCookie.get();
  if (!highScore) {
    highScore = "None yet!";
  }
  $("divHighScore").innerHTML =
    "<center>High Score: " + highScore + "</center>";

  this.insInterval = setInterval(this.scrollInstructions.bind(this), 50);

  Mojo.Event.listen($("divHowToPlay"), Mojo.Event.tap,
    function() {
      Mojo.Controller.stageController.swapScene("gameScreen");
    }, true
  );

};
```

The cookie Engineer_highScore is retrieved and then its value. If no value is previously scored, then the value "None Yet!" is used. Then, the high score text is inserted into the divHighScore <div> by updating its innerHTML attribute.

Next, an interval is begun to scroll the instructions. This line of code is the same as that seen in the Mojo.Event.stageActivate event handler in setup().

■ **Note** The Mojo.Event.stageActivate even does *not* fire when the stage is first shown, only after it is restored from a minimized state, which is why the interval needs to be kicked off here. We cannot simply rely on the event handler set up in setup(), because it won't fire the first time around.

Finally, an event handler is set up to listen for the Mojo.Event.tap event on the container around the instructions (the <div> with the green border in other words). When that area is tapped, the gameScreen scene is pushed, effectively beginning a new game. Note that I could have easily allowed a tap anywhere on the screen to begin the game by hooking up the event listener to the document object, but I wanted to demonstrate to you that you can listen for events on a specific object on the screen instead (and yes, you can of course have any number of listeners on any number of objects, as required by your application).

The last bit of code in this assistant is the scrollInstructions() method that we've seen reference to before, and you may be surprised at how little there really is to doing the scrolling:

```
TitleScreenAssistant.prototype.scrollInstructions = function() {

  this.instructionsTop = this.instructionsTop - 1;
  if (this.instructionsTop < -560) {
    this.instructionsTop = 210;
  }
  $("instructions").style.top = this.instructionsTop + "px";

};
```

Yep, that's it! This method fires every 50 milliseconds, and all it does is subtract one from the instructionsTop variable. When it's less than -560, it is reset to 210, which you'll note is the initial top attribute value of the instructions <div>. Remember that the <div> that contains the instructions <div> had an overflow value of hidden. That means that if you position the instructions <div> to a negative number, which is perfectly valid, then some portion of the instructions will be cut off at the top. If you keep making the top value more negative, eventually all the instructions would be rendered "above" the containing <div>, which means they wouldn't be visible at all. They would have appeared to the user to scroll of the top of the containing <div>. The completed scroll cycle, when the text is no longer visible, occurs when the top value reaches -560, at which point the scrolling starts again at the bottom (the value 210 does the opposite: it pushes the instructions <div> so far "down" that they are cut off by the bottom of the containing <div> and are not visible). The last line of the method sets the value of the top attribute of the instructions <div>, thereby making all that <sarcasm>complicated calculus</sarcasm> before it show up on the screen (note that the top style attribute doesn't simply accept a number; you need to tell it the units too, px for pixels in this case, which is the reason for the addition of px you see there).

If this is your first time seeing scroll code like this, you may be amazed at how little there is to it. Remember, it all hinges on the overflow:hidden style attribute. Without that, scrolling wouldn't work (incidentally, horizontal scrolling, or any other sort of scrolling, works in the same way). It's a simple, but effective, trick to know.

Game Screen Scene

Now we come to the real meat of this application, the bit where all the action is, namely, the gameScreen scene. This is where the game is played, as shown in Figure 5-5.

Figure 5-5. The gameScreen scene

It contains the same Engineer title logo at the top and then what is meant to look like an old-fashioned arcade machine,[3] complete with joystick and button in the control area, flashing lights along the sides, and even a marquee up top.

The View HTML

The HTML for this scene is shown in Figure 5-7, and there isn't much more going on in it than there was in the titleScreen scene.

Listing 5-7. The Contents of gameScreen-scene.html

```
<img src="images/engineer.gif" class="cssEngineerLogo" />

<img src="images/paused.gif" id="imgPaused" class="cssGamePaused"
```

---

[3] You kids today ("Get off my lawn!") with your Xbox and PlayStation and Wii...when I was a wee lad, we actually had to go down to something called a "video game arcade." This was a building (or a large room in the local mall or other establishment) where they had large machines that you stood in front of that had a video screen in front and some controller hardware built into it such as a joystick and some buttons. You put quarters into this thing and played the game, usually not for very long because the games tended to be quite hard until you got the hang of them, and you kept doing that for hours on end until the $5 your father gave you to get you out of the house ran out! I know...sounds positively backward, doesn't it?!

```
  style="display:none;" />

<canvas id="mainCanvas" width="240" height="300" class="cssMainCanvas"></canvas>

<div x-mojo-element="ProgressBar" id="pbOverheat"
  class="cssOverheatProgress"></div>

<div id="divScoreContainer" class="cssScoreArea">
  <center>Score: <span id="divScore"> </span></center>
</div>
```

The Engineer logo is again styled with the cssEngineerLogo class, as on the title screen. Below that is the "Game Paused" graphic, which is initially hidden via display:none. The style class applied to it, cssGamePaused, is as follows:

```
.cssGamePaused {
  position : absolute;
  left : 15px;
  top : 190px;
}
```

That puts is roughly centered on the scene, taking the position of the logo and score at the bottom into account so that it looks nice when the game is minimized.

After that is the <canvas> element, where the game-play area, arcade machine border, and controller area are drawn, which has applied to it the cssMainCanvas style class:

```
.cssMainCanvas {
  position : absolute;
  left : 40px;
  top : 76px;
}
```

Note that the width and height attributes are used rather than specifying these using CSS. The reason for that is that if you use CSS, you'll find that drawing operations on the canvas don't work right: they get cut off about halfway down the canvas. This is a fairly well-known bug in the <canvas> tag's implementation in the WebKit render engine that underlies all of webOS. Fortunately, using the width and height attributes, while maybe slightly disturbing to the CSS purists out there, avoids that problem entirely.

Below the canvas is the ProgressBar that shows the heat status of our engine. This widget is styled with the cssOverheatProgress class:

```
.cssOverheatProgress {
  position : absolute;
  left : 25px;
  top : 390px;
  width : 270px;
}
```

This of course just positions the widget and sets its horizontal size. However, there is actually a bit more styling that goes into the ProgressBar, and that comes courtesy of the indirectly applied (because it overrides the default styling that the ProgressBar automatically gets) progress-pill-progress class:

```
.progress-pill-progress {
  width : 100%;
  height : 11px;
  border-width : 0px 6px 0 6px;
  -webkit-border-image : url(../images/progress_bar_progress.png) 0 6 0 6 repeat repeat;
  -webkit-box-sizing : border-box;
  position : absolute;
}
```

This is in fact overriding the default styling for a ProgressBar. (Don't let the fact that its name indicates it's for the ProgressPill; that's just an unfortunate naming choice. It in fact *does* apply to the ProgressBar widget.)

OK, here's the situation: one of the things I wanted to be able to do in this game was to programmatically change the color of the ProgressBar as it fills up, starting with green and turning red so as to give a better visual indication to the user of the engine's status. Unfortunately, there's no easy way to do this because the default blue color of the bar is the result of an image, progress_bar_progress.png specifically. Now, my first thought was to simply have a couple of different colored graphics and override the image used for the ProgressBar. This, however, is inefficient since you need to have X number of images, one for each possible color the bar can have. Instead, I turned things around a bit: what if I instead set the background color of the ProgressBar and make the image used to draw the widget a negative mask, meaning that it will let the background "shine through" where the bar graphic would usually be drawn? Since I can easily (sort of) manipulate the background color programmatically, that might do the trick.

In fact, it works very well! It requires two things: this style override (which, aside from pointing the -webkit-border-image attribute to my custom masking image, is basically the same as the original style definition) and a little bit of "black magic" in the code that we'll see later in order to manipulate the background color.

The last element in this scene is the text displaying the current score, which uses the cssScoreArea class:

```
.cssScoreArea {
  position : absolute;
  left : 0px;
  top : 412px;
  width : 100%;
  color:#ffffff;
}
```

This again is primarily for positioning and, as we saw with the title screen, for setting the text color to white to we can see it.

That is the final style class from stylesheets.css by the way, as well as wrapping up the HTML for this scene. Now it's time for the code and the implementation of the game itself!

The Scene Assistant

The GameScreenAssistant class is a rather long piece of code, so naturally we're going to break it down bit by bit. Let's begin by looking at the constants (such as they are in JavaScript!) that are defined as part of this class, summarized in Table 5-2.

Table 5-2. *The "Constants" of* GameScreenAssistant

Constant	Value	Description
PARTICLE_IRIDIUM	0	Represents one of the four types of particles that can be moving around the play area
PARTICLE_HELIUM	1	Represents one of the four types of particles that can be moving around the play area
PARTICLE_MCKAYDIUM	2	Represents one of the four types of particles that can be moving around the play area
PARTICLE_UNOBTANIUM	3	Represents one of the four types of particles that can be moving around the play area
DIRECTION_UP	0	Value for when a particle is moving up
DIRECTION_DOWN	1	Value for when a particle is moving down
DIRECTION_LEFT	2	Value for when a particle is moving left
DIRECTION_RIGHT	3	Value for when a particle is moving right
DIVERTER_UP_LEFT	0	Value for when a diverter has the waveguide with paths leading up and to the left
DIVERTER_UP_RIGHT	1	Value for when a diverter has the waveguide with paths leading up and to the right
DIVERTER_DOWN_RIGHT	2	Value for when a diverter has the waveguide with paths leading down and to the right
DIVERTER_DOWN_LEFT	3	Value for when a diverter has the waveguide with paths leading down and to the left
DIVERTER_HORIZONTAL	4	Value for when a diverter has the waveguide with a path going right to left
DIVERTER_VERTICAL	5	Value for when a diverter has the waveguide with a path going up and down
DIVERTER_TOP	0	A value to indicate a particle is in the top diverter, needed when the code decides which direction the particle should travel next as a result of being redirected by the diverter

244

Table 5-2. *The "Constants" of* GameScreenAssistant *(continued)*

DIVERTER_BOTTOM	1	A value to indicate a particle is in the bottom diverter, needed when the code decides which direction the particle should travel next as a result of being redirected by the diverter
DIVERTER_LEFT	2	A value to indicate a particle is in the left diverter, needed when the code decides which direction the particle should travel next as a result of being redirected by the diverter
DIVERTER_RIGHT	3	A value to indicate a particle is in the right diverter, needed when the code decides which direction the particle should travel next as a result of being redirected by the diverter
XADJ	20	The amount of pixels horizontally to adjust coordinates by to account for the frame around the play area
YADJ	22	The amount of pixels vertically to adjust coordinates by to account for the frame around the play area
TAP_LEEWAY	15	The amount of pixels around a diverter that will be considered within range to register a tap on the diverter

Of those constants, the two that need some immediate explanation are XADJ and YADJ. The entire game is of course drawn on the <canvas> element. This includes the frame that makes up the arcade machine cabinet. Within this frame is the real game-play area. So, let's say you wanted to paint the pixel in the upper-right corner of this game-play area red. What would the coordinates of this point be? If the frame is 20 pixels wide and 22 pixels tall on the top, that means the coordinates would be 20,22 because that's the first pixel that is within the framed area.

However, writing code with that in mind would be a pain. Instead, it would be much simpler to assume that the coordinates of that pixel are actually 0,0. To make that work, we need to add 20 to the X value and 22 to the Y value of every pixel we draw (or every image we draw), and that's precisely how XADJ and YADJ are used throughout the code, as you'll see. This also, in theory at least, means that we can adjust the frame's size, and so long as we adjust those two constant values accordingly, our game code shouldn't need to change.

After the constants, you'll find the declaration of a number of data fields that store information used throughout the game. Although some of these can't be fully understood without seeing how they are used, I think it is very worthwhile to enumerate them and give at least a brief overview of what they are so you start to get a feel for how things work.

The first of these fields, the first four fields in fact, are objects defined like so:

```
GameScreenAssistant.prototype.topDiverterBounds = {
  x1 : null, y1 : null,  x2 : null, y2 : null
};
...
```

These define the upper-left corner (x1,y1) and the lower-right corner (x2, y2) or the top diverter. There is one such object for each of the four diverters, but I've shown only one here for the sake of brevity. The actual values of the four attribute are populated in the setup() method, as you'll see shortly, because doing so relies on the values of XADJ, YADJ, and TAP_LEEWAY, which we need an instance of GameScreenAssistant to get at.

The next field is ctx:

```
GameScreenAssistant.prototype.ctx = null;
```

This is a reference to the 2D context of the <canvas> element, which is the object on which all canvas drawing operations are performed. The context object pointed to by this field exposes a number of methods for interacting with the canvas, as we'll see a bit later. Frequently, you'll see JavaScript that uses <canvas> retrieve this context for each operation performed, but this is very inefficient and can slow down the code a lot. When the scene is set up, one of the tasks will be to get the context and store the reference to it in this field, which will allow the remainder of the code to avoid this expensive lookup inside the main game loop.

Next we find the mainLoopInterval field:

```
GameScreenAssistant.prototype.mainLoopInterval = null;
```

This will hold a reference to the interval that fires 33 times a second and that is our main game loop. This is the code responsible for moving particles and such around the screen, determining when a particle enters an injector port, and everything involved in making the game work.

The next field is overheatBarModel:

```
GameScreenAssistant.prototype.overheatBarModel = { progress : 0 };
```

As the name implies, this is the model for the engine heat ProgressBar. The progress attribute is the current value of the widget and is what we'll adjust in 2/10th increments as the engine heats up during game play.

The next field, I dare say, is completely self-explanatory:

```
GameScreenAssistant.prototype.score = null;
```

Yep, it's the current store—'nough said!

The lightChangeCounter field is next:

```
GameScreenAssistant.prototype.lightChangeCounter = null;
```

The value of this field is used as part of the process of flashing the lights on the side of the cabinet to determine when it's time to change the state of each light (hint: this happens every 15 frames).

After that comes the particles field:

```
GameScreenAssistant.prototype.particles = new Array(3);
```

There can be a maximum of three particles moving around at any one time, and each of those particles is represented by an object in this array. The object will contain information about each particle such as its location and what frame of animation is currently showing. We'll see these details later, but this is the array it's all stored in.

After that we find four fields:

```
GameScreenAssistant.prototype.topDiverter = null;
GameScreenAssistant.prototype.bottomDiverter = null;
GameScreenAssistant.prototype.leftDiverter = null;
GameScreenAssistant.prototype.rightDiverter = null;
```

Each diverter is represented by a field here, and the field tells us what waveguide is currently in that diverter. The values of these fields are updated when the user taps a diverter (or used the keyboard to do so).

Similarly, the next two fields are for the hands:

```
GameScreenAssistant.prototype.leftHand = null;
GameScreenAssistant.prototype.rightHand = null;
```

The leftHand field tells us what image is currently showing for the left hand, and ditto for the rightHand field, but for the right hand of course.

When the user taps a diverter or presses a key to change waveguides in them, the hands move accordingly (the left hand moves up, down, left, or right depending on which diverter is tapped, and the right hand presses the button when the engine is being cooled down). To help make this work, the leftHandDelay and rightHandDelay fields are used:

```
GameScreenAssistant.prototype.leftHandDelay = null;
GameScreenAssistant.prototype.rightHandDelay = null;
```

These denote how long a hand has been shown in the state corresponding to the last user action, and when it reaches a certain threshold, it indicates to the main game loop that the hand should be returned to its default location.

After this, we find a rather large group of fields that are references to images used in the game. I've listed them in Table 5-3.

Table 5-3. The Image Field Members in GameScreenAssistant

Field Name	Description
imgPaused	The "Game Paused" graphic.
imgGenerator	This generator in the center of the game-play area.
imgFrame	The frame around the game-play area.
imgBackground	The background of the game-play area.
imgLightsLeft	An array of the images for each light on the left.
imgLightsRight	An array of the images for each light on the right.
imgConsoleLeftSide	The background for the left half of the control console area.
imgConsoleRightSide	The background for the right half of the control console area.
imgConsoleMiddle	A small background image that goes in between imgConsoleLeftSide and imgConsoleRightSide.
imgLeftHandNeutral	The image for the left hand in its neutral (not doing anything) position.

Table 5-3. The Image Field Members in GameScreenAssistant (continued)

`imgLeftHandUp`	The image for the left hand when the top diverter is tapped.
`imgLeftHandDown`	The image for the left hand when the bottom diverter is tapped.
`imgLeftHandLeft`	The image for the left hand when the left diverter is tapped.
`imgLeftHandRight`	The image for the left hand when the right diverter is tapped.
`imgRightHandUp`	The image for the right hand in its neutral (not doing anything) position.
`imgRightHandDown`	The image for the right hand when the engine is being cooled down.
`imgDiverters`	An array of images, one for each of the waveguide images that can appear in a diverter.
`imgParticles[4][2]`	A multidimensional array of images. The first dimension holds one of the four types of particles, and the second dimension holds two frames of animation for each particle.

All of these images are loaded as part of the `setup()` method, which is what we're going to look at right now.

Setting Up the Scene

The `setup()` method is responsible for the one-time setup required to make the game work, things like loading images, calculating bounding boxes for the diverters, and so forth. In fact, the very first chunk of it is exactly those bounding box calculations:

```
this.topDiverterBounds = {
  x1 : this.XADJ + 91 - this.TAP_LEEWAY,
  y1 : this.YADJ + 40 - this.TAP_LEEWAY,
  x2 : this.XADJ + 91 + 19 + this.TAP_LEEWAY,
  y2 : this.YADJ + 40 + 19 + this.TAP_LEEWAY
};
...
```

It's ugly to use magic numbers[4] like this, but sometimes it's the simplest way. You can begin to see how XADJ and YADJ are used here; without those, the box defines by these coordinates wouldn't be where

---

[4] Magic numbers are a code smell, that is, something that most programmers consider bad form. A magic number is a "naked" number statically present in code whose meaning and derivation isn't immediately obvious from the code. Generally, constants and/or variables are a better choice because they give the numbers some semantic meaning. For instance, I could have had two variables named `diverterX` and `diverterY` instead of the values 91 and 40 (and `diverterWidth` and `diverterHeight` instead of 19). This arguably would have made the code more readable, but also would have meant there was more code to parse, and sometimes a more concise form is preferable, even if it means using a magic number. It's a stylistic choice

the top diverter is, it would wind up being a little above and to the left of it, which would make taps not work properly since these coordinates will be used to determine when a tap on the screen falls within the bounds of a diverter. From this point on I won't mention XADJ and YADJ anymore unless there's something new about their usage that needs to be discussed; I think you get the idea at this point!

The next bit of setup is for the ProgressBar:

```
this.controller.setupWidget("pbOverheat",
  { modelProperty : "progress" }, this.overheatBarModel
);
```

Setting up widget models is of course old news by now, and there's certainly nothing new about this example, so let's move on to this:

```
this.imgFrame = new Image();
this.imgFrame.src = "images/mini_game_frame.png";
```

If you've ever written graphical rollovers in JavaScript, that is, where an image is changed to another when the user moves the mouse over it, then you'll certainly recognize this sort of code! It's creating a new Image object and then loading the frame graphic into it by setting the src attribute to point to the appropriate PNG file. Note that I haven't set the dimensions of the Image object when instantiating it as you nearly always would do when coding for rollovers. The reason you normally do that is because it makes the loading a little more efficient since the size of the image doesn't have to be dynamically determined after the graphic is loaded. This can matter a great deal on a web page because the graphics are being loaded from a server, so there is network latency to think about. However, when loading graphics locally on a Pre, this isn't a concern since it is all local content. The reason I didn't put the dimensions in is simply so that if I decided to change graphics somewhere and the size wasn't the same, I wouldn't have to touch the code as well. It's just a convenience thing, nothing more, and there's certainly no technical reason that I didn't put dimensions in.

There are a number of other images loaded in this fashion just a little further down in the code: imgBackground, imgConsoleLeftSide, imgConsoleMiddle, imgConsoleRightSide, imgLeftHandNeutral, imgLeftHandUp, imgLeftHandDown, imgLeftHandLeft, imgLeftHandRight, imgRightHandUp, imgRightHandDown, and imgPaused. I have not shown the code for those images here because that code is identical to that for imgFrame. However, let's look at the code for loading the lights around the frame, which *is* slightly different:

```
this.imgLightsLeft = [ ];

var lightsLeft0 = {
  img : new Image(), width : 20, height : 21, x : 0, y : 22
};
lightsLeft0.img.src = "images/mini_game_frame_l0.png"
this.imgLightsLeft.push(lightsLeft0);
...
```

This continues four more times and then essentially repeats five more times for the lights on the right side of the frame. Each image is loaded and then push()'d onto the imgLightsLeft array (or

here, but magic numbers really do make code harder to read most of the time, and you should therefore take this as an example of what you should, typically anyway, *not* do in your own code!

imgLightsRight for the right side of the frame). This will allow the code that manipulates the lights to be written fairly generically since it can just iterate over this array to deal with the lights (as you'll see).

Similar to this is the code for loading the eight images that make up the animation cycle for the generator:

```
this.imgGenerator = [ ];
for (var i = 0; i < 8; i++) {
  this.imgGenerator.push(new Image());
  this.imgGenerator[i].src = "images/nucleus_" + i + ".png";
}
```

Each image is one frame of animation, so as you can probably guess, drawing the generator will require an index into the imgGenerator array to draw to determine which animation frame to draw. As it happens, this index is random, but I'm getting ahead of myself a bit! First, we have to load some diverter graphics:

```
this.imgDiverters[0] = new Image();
this.imgDiverters[0].src = "images/diverter_up_left.png";
...
```

This section repeats for each of the six types of waveguides that can appear in a diverter. Recall from playing the game (you *have* played it, right?!?) that each time you tap a diverter, it cycles through the waveguides. Doing so is a simple matter of cycling through the elements of the imgDiverters array, which is why each waveguide image isn't loaded into its own variable: making them part of an array makes cycling through them easy.

The final bit of code is to load the images for the four types of particles:

```
for (var y = 0; y < 4; y++) {
  for (var x = 0; x < 2; x++) {
    this.imgParticles[y][x] = new Image();
    this.imgParticles[y][x].src =
      "images/particle" + y + "_" + x + ".png";
  }
}
```

The imgParticles array is a multidimensional array, which of course doesn't actually exist in JavaScript, at least not as an intrinsic part of the language as is the case with some other languages. At the end of the day, though, a multidimensional array is simply an array of arrays, and that's easy to do in JavaScript. So, the y for loop runs for four times, once for each type of particle. Then, the x loop runs twice, once for each frame of animation for a particle. The inner iteration creates a new Image object and then loads the appropriate particle image (named particleYX.png, where Y is the value of the y loop and X is the value of the x loop). Recall that earlier we saw that these arrays are constructed already, so there's no worry about creating them now; we simply need to load the elements into the array and we're all set.

Activating the Scene

When the scene is activated, there's a little work to be done, including setting up some listeners and actually starting the game:

```
GameScreenAssistant.prototype.activate = function() {

  this.ctx = $("mainCanvas").getContext("2d");

  Mojo.Event.listen($("mainCanvas"), Mojo.Event.tap,
    this.tapHandler.bind(this), true);

  Mojo.Event.listen(this.controller.document, Mojo.Event.keypress,
    this.keypressHandler.bind(this), true);

  Mojo.Event.listen(this.controller.stageController.document,
    Mojo.Event.stageActivate,
    function() {
      $("imgPaused").hide();
      $("mainCanvas").show();
      $("pbOverheat").show();
      $("divScoreContainer").show();
      this.mainLoopInterval = setInterval(this.mainLoop.bind(this), 33);
    }.bind(this)
  );

  Mojo.Event.listen(this.controller.stageController.document,
    Mojo.Event.stageDeactivate,
    function() {
      clearInterval(this.mainLoopInterval);
      $("imgPaused").show();
      $("mainCanvas").hide();
      $("pbOverheat").hide();
    }.bind(this)
  );

  this.controller.listen(document, "shaking", function(inEvent) {
    this.keypressHandler(
      { originalEvent : { keyCode : Mojo.Char.p } }
    );
  }.bind(this));

  // Start the game.
  this.startGame();

};
```

First, we need to cache a reference to the 2D context of the <canvas> for performance reasons, as discussed a few pages back. Next, an event handler is set up for the Mojo.Event.tap event. We'll be listening for this event on the <canvas> element, since that's where our diverters are, so there's no point in listening at a higher level, such as the document itself. We also need to listen for the Mojo.Event.keypress event, since the player can control the game via the keyboard as well. In this case, we *do* want to listen for events at a higher level than the <canvas> itself, since the <canvas> isn't the type of element that, usually, has focus and can accept user input, so by referencing this.controller.document, which holds a reference to the document object automatically, we can listen for the event at the document level and not have to worry about inadvertent focus switches breaking our game (that is, if the user tapped the score <div> for example, but we were listening for the event on the <canvas> element, the event wouldn't fire since the <div> would receive it where we aren't listening for it).

Just like for the titleScreen scene, we need to listen for the Mojo.Event.stageActivate and Mojo.Event.stageDeactivate events so that we can shut down the main game loop (read: pause the game) when the application is minimized to save battery life. It's the same sort of setInterval() and clearInterval() code as before, but here we're also hiding the mainCanvas and the pbOverheat ProgressBar and showing the imgPaused "Game Paused" graphic when the stage is deactivated and showing them again (and hiding imgPaused) when it is activated again. In Figure 5-6 you can see what the game looks like when minimized.

■ **Note**   Notice that the reference to the <canvas> element is not cached, which would seem on the surface to be a great opportunity for optimization. Indeed, it would be, except that we never need to touch the <canvas> element again directly! Therefore, there's no DOM lookup to be avoided here, at least none that matters, since activate() won't be called frequently enough for the inefficiency of redundant DOM lookups executing to be of any concern.

Figure 5-6. Engineer minimized from the gameScreen scene

After that, we set up an event listener for the shake event. At the time of this writing, there is no Mojo.Event.shaking constant, so you have to use the literal string "shaking" as the event to listen for. When this event fires, we're making a call to the as yet undiscussed keypressHandler() method. As you'll see the screen tap events, as well as the shake event, piggyback on this method so that all the code for the user interactions are in one place and everything else just makes use of that so as to avoid redundant coding. The keypressHandler() takes in an event object that contains an attribute originalEvent. This originalEvent object contains a keyCode attribute that tells us which key is being pressed, so we can pass the value Mojo.Char.p as the value of the keyCode attribute to essentially emulate the P key being pressed, which is the key the player presses to cool down the engine.

Starting a New Game

The final line of code in the `activate()` method is a call to the `startGame()` method, which, not surprisingly, starts the game!

```
GameScreenAssistant.prototype.startGame = function() {

  this.overheatBarModel.progress = 0.0;
  this.controller.modelChanged(this.overheatBarModel);
  $("palm_anon_element_0mojo-scene-gameScreenpbOverheat_progress").style.backgroundColor =
    "#00ff00";

  this.score = 0;
  $("divScore").update("0");

  this.lightChangeCounter = 99;

  this.topDiverter = this.DIVERTER_DOWN_RIGHT;
  this.bottomDiverter = this.DIVERTER_DOWN_LEFT;
  this.leftDiverter = this.DIVERTER_DOWN_RIGHT;
  this.rightDiverter = this.DIVERTER_DOWN_LEFT;

  this.particles[0] = {
    type : null, frame : null, frameDelay : null, direction : null,
    alive : false, emergeDelay : 0, x : null, y : null
  };
  ...

  this.leftHand = this.imgLeftHandNeutral;
  this.rightHand = this.imgRightHandUp;
  this.leftHandDelay = 0;
  this.rightHandDelay = 0;

  this.mainLoopInterval = setInterval(this.mainLoop.bind(this), 33);

};
```

First, the `ProgressBar` is reset to zero so that it is completely unfilled. Then, a bit of black magic happens.

Recall from earlier discussions that the color of the `ProgressBar` is dynamic and dependent on the heat level of the engine. Also recall that this works by setting its background color and then masking off other parts so that the color "shines through." How you set the background color is by setting the `backgroundColor` style attribute of the `ProgressBar`. Unfortunately, this wouldn't appear, based on the HTML for the scene, to be possible. If you tried the obvious, using the ID on the `ProgressBar` and setting the `backgroundColor` of it, you'd find that it didn't work as expected. The reason is that when Mojo converts a `<div>` that you've specified an `x-mojo-element` for into a real widget, what gets inserted into the DOM is a complex HTML structure. So, the element pointed to by the ID `pbOverheat` isn't actually the element you want to set the `backgroundColor` on; what you're really after is some child element of that element.

Unfortunately, there's no easy way to determine what element to go after, so this is where the black magic comes in. What I had to do was use the Palm Inspector.

The Palm Inspector is a tool that comes with the SDK that allows you, among other things, to examine the DOM structure of your application. It also contains a debug logging window that keeps you from having to SSH into the emulator (or a real device). To use the inspector, you need to run your application in debug mode and also flip a switch to enable inspection. In Figure 5-7 you can see how you would do so in Eclipse by altering the debug run profile accordingly.

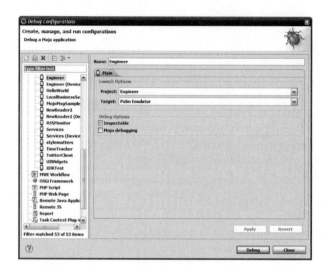

Figure 5-7. *Enabling inspection by altering the debug configuration for the project*

You simply select the Inspectable option and you're all set. When you click Run, the application launches in the emulator like normal, and you can then start the Palm Inspector application, which will appear something like Figure 5-8.

Figure 5-8. *The Palm Inspector, in all its majesty*

This screenshot actually shows up after turning on the debug pane at the bottom and digging through the DOM of the application a bit, so you won't see all of this initially. This gets us back to the discussion at hand, however.

■ **Note** Unfortunately, as you can see from Figure 5-8, the inspector actually froze up on me while doing this! It's not a perfect panacea to be sure, but even with some warts it is definitely a useful tool in the toolbox.

If you look through the DOM tree there, you'll see there is an element with an ID of `palm_anon_element_0mojo-scene-gameScreenpbOverheat_progress`. Through some trial and error (sometimes the only way to figure out what you need when working with webOS, at this point at least), I discovered that this is the element on which the `backgroundColor` needs to be set. I say this is a bit of "black magic" because it's obvious that the ID there is being generated dynamically, and my guess is it is based on how many widgets there are in the scene and the ordering of them. Assuming that's true, it means that if I were to add more widgets, especially widgets before the `ProgressBar`, this ID would probably change, and I'd have to inspect the application again to find the correct value. (I think you can reasonably guess how the ID is constructed, so maybe you could guess it and get it right the first time, but you see my point I'm sure.) Still, sometimes this is the only way to pull things off, so you work with the hand you're dealt!

The good news is that the ID doesn't change with each application invocation, so as long as the scene's HTML doesn't change, we can assume (barring changes in Mojo itself resulting from webOS updates) that the ID will always be what you see here, so in that regard at least, it should be safe.

Getting back to the startGame() method, the next thing done is to reset the score to zero, both in the variable score and what appears on the screen. After that, each of the variables topDiverter, bottomDiverter, leftDiverter, and rightDiverter, which, again, store a reference to the current waveguide image in each diverter, are reset to their starting types. These are chosen so that if the player does nothing, the game will eventually end by virtue of particles going back into the generator, but it should take a little while so that the player has time to get into the swing of things.

Next, three particles are created. Each is represented by a simple JavaScript object. The particles are actually created as part of the main game loop, which is why a lot of these attributes are null: they will be populated with values when the particle emerges from the generator. This code is really responsible for setting up the objects for the particles and ensuring they are in a state representing them being in the generator and not "in play" yet (remember, this method will be executed every time a game begins, so this effectively resets the particles if a game was just played).

The hands, like the diverters, are then reset to their initial "waiting for the player to do something" positions. In other words, the left hand is moving moved in a direction, and the right hand is hovering over the button.

Finally, the mainLoopInterval is created, which runs our main game loop. This loop runs once every 33 milliseconds, which corresponds to a frame rate of 30 frames per second (FPS) by virtue of 1000/33=~30 (1,000 milliseconds in a second, each frame taking 33 milliseconds).

Playing a Sound (and Avoiding Redundant Code!)

We're just about ready to tackle the main game loop, but before we do so, let's look at one quick and simple method that we'll see used throughout that loop:

```
GameScreenAssistant.prototype.playSound = function(inSound) {

  this.controller.serviceRequest("palm://com.palm.audio/systemsounds", {
    method : "playFeedback", parameters : {name : inSound }
  });

};
```

This method plays a specified system sound using the System Sound service. The purpose of this method is so that the serviceRequest() doesn't have to be repeated everywhere. It also allows the possibility of *not* using this service later. One of the difficulties I had in creating this game—indeed, the difficulty many game developers are having with webOS at the time I wrote this—is that audio support in Mojo is lacking. Trying to play your own sounds, which is ideally what I would have done with this game, leads to huge performance impact that makes the game unplayable.

The System Sound service, however, does not suffer from this problem. Unfortunately, this means you are limited to a predefined set of sounds. For this game, that didn't prove to be a big problem because there's a lot of abstract-type sounds needed, and that's what the System Sound service essentially provides. For more robust games, though, it would be a significant limitation.

However, by creating this playSound() method, it means that if down the road a better way to play sound is exposed to developers, this is the only code in the game that should have to be changed! The main game loop calls on this method, which can then use the System Sound service as it does now, or some alternate method, to play the sounds. The value of inSound can still be used to determine what sound to play and the "how" can be determined by this method.

So, not only does this allow the main game loop code to be a bit more concise by avoiding repeated `serviceRequest()` method calls, but it also allows for flexibility down the road, both being extremely good things in my book! And since *I'm* writing the book, that's what counts. ☺

The Main Game Loop

Now, at last, we come to the crux of turning Engineer the application into Engineer the game. In the `startGame()` method, you'll recall that an interval is kicked off to execute the `mainLoop()` method every 33 milliseconds. This method represents the main game loop (and hence the name!) and is where we find all the game logic and the code that puts everything on the screen. User input is also, somewhat indirectly, handled by this method.

Drawing the Frame and Flashing the Lights

Let's begin by looking at the first dozen or so lines of this method:

```
GameScreenAssistant.prototype.mainLoop = function() {

  this.lightChangeCounter = this.lightChangeCounter + 1;
  if (this.lightChangeCounter > 15) {
    this.lightChangeCounter = 0;
    this.ctx.drawImage(this.imgFrame, 0, 0, 240, 240);
    for (var i = 0; i < 5; i++) {
      if (Math.floor(Math.random() * 2) == 1) {
        this.ctx.drawImage(this.imgLightsLeft[i].img,
          this.imgLightsLeft[i].x, this.imgLightsLeft[i].y,
          this.imgLightsLeft[i].width, this.imgLightsLeft[i].height
        );
      }
      if (Math.floor(Math.random() * 2) == 1) {
        this.ctx.drawImage(this.imgLightsRight[i].img,
          this.imgLightsRight[i].x, this.imgLightsRight[i].y,
          this.imgLightsRight[i].width, this.imgLightsRight[i].height
        );
      }
    }
  }
}
```

The job of this bit of code is to flash the lights on the frame around the game-play area. With each execution of this method, `lightChangeCounter` is bumped up by one. When it reaches 15 (remember there's 30 frames a second being executed, so every half a second the lights are updated), then it's time to change the lights. First, the frame itself is redrawn. To do this, we use the `drawImage()` method of the 2D context (ctx) of the `<canvas>` that was cached in the `activate()` method. This method accepts a reference to the image to draw, the X and Y location to draw it, and its width and height. The frame graphic itself shows all the lights in their unlit state, so this effectively resets them all.

Next, we iterate over the five lights (five on each side of the frame). For each, we randomly pick a number, 0 or 1, and if it's a one, then we draw the light in its lit state (the corresponding Image element pointed to by the img attribute of the object in the `imgLightsLeft` or `imgLightsRight` arrays). The X, Y, width, and height attributes of the object in the array provides the other information needed by the `drawImage()` method. We do this for both the left and right sides, effectively blinking all ten of the lights randomly.

Drawing the Control Console and Hands

The next step is to draw the background of the control console at the bottom:

```
this.ctx.drawImage(this.imgConsoleLeftSide, 0, 240, 29, 60);
this.ctx.drawImage(this.imgConsoleMiddle, 108, 240, 37, 60);
this.ctx.drawImage(this.imgConsoleRightSide, 215, 240, 25, 60);
this.ctx.drawImage(this.leftHand, 29, 240, 79, 60);
this.ctx.drawImage(this.rightHand, 145, 240, 70, 60);
```

Each of these has a well-defined location and size, so all the X, Y, width, and height values are hard-coded. That's arguably not a good thing since it means touching this code if we modify these graphics in any way that alters their location or size, but I know that's not going to happen, so I can live with it in this instance.

One thing I want to point out right now, because it's especially important in game programming, is that this loop is nowhere near as efficient as possible. For example, is there really any need to redraw the background images with each invocation of this method? No, not really. We could just redraw them when the hands change (in fact, the imgConsoleMiddle image really needs only to be drawn the very first time through). In general, the main loop of a game (which is most typically how games are written by the way) should be as tight and efficient as possible. Do as little work in it as possible because the execution of this method has to take less than 33 milliseconds; otherwise, we'll start skipping frames, and the action on the screen will appear choppy. Fortunately, this code performs at that level as is on a real device, and certainly does so in the emulator too, so we're fine. In general, though, you should seek to avoid any work that isn't actually necessary and optimize the work as much as possible.

Notice that as part of drawing the background, both hands are also drawn in their default position.[5] We now have to deal with the hands because they may not actually be in their default positions:

```
if (this.leftHand != this.imgLeftHandNeutral) {
  this.leftHandDelay = this.leftHandDelay + 1;
  if (this.leftHandDelay > 2) {
    this.leftHand = this.imgLeftHandNeutral;
  }
}
if (this.rightHand != this.imgRightHandUp) {
  this.rightHandDelay = this.rightHandDelay + 1;
  if (this.rightHandDelay > 2) {
    this.rightHand = this.imgRightHandUp;
  }
}
```

When the user presses one of the keys corresponding to a diverter, or taps one on the screen, we immediately point leftHand to point to the appropriate hand image. The next iteration of mainLoop(),

---

[5] This is another big opportunity for optimization: why draw the hands in their default position when they are, potentially, going to be redrawn by this code? You probably have heard the adage about not optimizing too soon, and you've also probably learned over the years that over-optimizing code is usually a waste of time, given the hardware of today. In game programming, however, the story is quite different, and I've purposely left some of these inefficiencies in place to illustrate the point (and also, frankly, to make the code as simple as possible). Optimization in a game loop like this is something you should be thinking about from the outset. Cut out as much work (read: code) as possible at all costs!

this code executes, and the hand is drawn in the appropriate position. The hand needs to stay in that position for some period of time so the user can see the movement on the screen. To do this, the leftHandDelay (or rightHandDelay) variable is set to zero. Then, when mainLoop() executes, the value of the variable is incremented. When it reaches three, meaning the hand has been in its nondefault position for three frames (1/10th of a second), then they are returned to their default position. This period of time is short enough that a subsequent movement probably won't override this one (and even if that happens, no harm is done, the hand simply moves with the next execution of this method) but is long enough to be perceptible by the player.

Drawing the Game-Play Area

At this point, the frame, lights, control area, and hands are drawn, so now we can shift our focus to the game-play area.

```
this.ctx.drawImage(this.imgBackground, this.XADJ, this.YADJ, 200, 200);
this.ctx.drawImage(this.imgGenerator[Math.floor(Math.random()*8)],
  this.XADJ + 74, this.YADJ + 73, 53, 53);
this.ctx.drawImage(this.imgDiverters[this.topDiverter],
  this.XADJ + 91, this.YADJ + 40, 19, 19);
this.ctx.drawImage(this.imgDiverters[this.bottomDiverter],
  this.XADJ + 91, this.YADJ + 140, 19, 19);
this.ctx.drawImage(this.imgDiverters[this.leftDiverter],
  this.XADJ + 40, this.YADJ + 90, 19, 19);
this.ctx.drawImage(this.imgDiverters[this.rightDiverter],
  this.XADJ + 141, this.YADJ + 90, 19, 19);
```

The first step is to redraw the background image. This effectively clears the game-play area since anything that was there before will be overwritten by the background image. So, the next thing we do is draw the generator in the middle. Recall that there are eight frames of animation for the generator, so we select a random number from zero to seven and use that as the index into the imgGenerator array to randomly select one of the animation frames, and we draw it, once again using XADJ and YADJ, plus some hard-coded X/Y coordinates, to place it in the center.

Then, it's time to draw the four diverters. The image that is drawn is dependent on the waveguide type that is currently displayed in the diverter, as specified by the topDiverter, bottomDiverter, leftDiverter, and rightDiverter variables. These are an index value into the imgDiverters array, which illustrates why the images are put into an array, as was previously hinted at.

■ **Note**   The four injector ports are parts of the background image itself, so there's no corresponding code needed to draw them.

The Main Game Logic (As Implemented for Each Particle)

Recall that there are three particles active at any given time. A given particle may not have emerged from the generator, but there are still three particles in play. The real logic of the game is based entirely on each of those particles, so we're going to enter a loop next, an iteration of which executes for each of those three particles. The code inside this loop represents the true "logic" behind the game.

```
for (var i = 0; i < 3; i++) {

  if (this.particles[i].alive) {

    this.ctx.drawImage(
      this.imgParticles[this.particles[i].type][this.particles[i].frame],
      this.XADJ + this.particles[i].x, this.YADJ + this.particles[i].y,
      11, 11);

    this.particles[i].frameDelay = this.particles[i].frameDelay + 1;
    if (this.particles[i].frameDelay > 2) {
      this.particles[i].frameDelay = 0;
      this.particles[i].frame = this.particles[i].frame + 1;
      if (this.particles[i].frame > 1) {
        this.particles[i].frame = 0;
      }
    }
  }
```

A particle can be in one of two states: alive or dead. When it's alive, the `alive` flag of the object describing the particle (a particle descriptor object, if you will) in the `particles` array is set to true. This means it is moving around the game-play area. When it is dead (then the `alive` attribute is `false`), that means it has not yet emerged from the generator and is waiting there for a short period of time before emerging.

When the particle is alive, we enter the `if` branch. The first thing done in that case is to draw the particle at its current location as denoted by `this.particles[i].x` and `this.particles[i].y`. The image that is drawn is taken from the multidimensional `imgParticles` array. The first dimension is the type of the particle, so the index into the array is `this.particles[i].type`. Recall that each particle has two frames of animation, which is the second dimension, and that is denoted by the value of `this.particles[i].frame`.

The next step is to increment the `frameDelay` attribute of the particle descriptor object. This lets some time pass before flipping between the two frames of animation for the particle. When the value exceeds two, it's time to flip to the next frame.

With the particle now drawn at its current location, the next step is to move the particle as appropriate:

```
switch (this.particles[i].direction) {
  case this.DIRECTION_UP:
    this.particles[i].y = this.particles[i].y - 1;
  break;

  ...
```

The current direction the particle is moving in is stored in `this.particles[i].direction`. Its value is one of the four constants: `DIRECTION_UP`, `DIRECTION_DOWN`, `DIRECTION_LEFT`, or `DIRECTION_RIGHT`. There is a case in the switch statement for each of those (only the `DIRECTION_UP` case being shown here; the rest are nearly identical except for whether they manipulate the X or Y location of the particle and whether it is incremented or decremented).

The first real bit of logic follows this movement update:

```
if (this.particles[i].x == 95 && this.particles[i].y == 94) {
  this.playSound("back_01");
  this.addToScore(-50);
```

```
    this.addOverheat(0.2);
    this.particles[i].alive = false;
    this.particles[i].emergeDelay = Math.floor(Math.random() * 100);
  }
```

If the particle finds its way back into the generator, that's bad, m'kay? This situation is determined by seeing whether the particle's location is 95,94, dead-center in the generator. When this happens, we call on the playSound() method to play the system's back_01 sound, we add –50 to the player's score by calling the addToScore() method, and we also add two-tenths to the overheat state of the engine by calling the addOverheat() method, both of which we'll see later. The alive flag in the particle descriptor object is then set to false, so it won't be drawn with the next iteration of the main loop, and we also set the emergeDelay field to a random number from 0 to 100. This will determine how many frames elapse before the particle comes back to life and reemerges from the generator.

The next set of conditions that need to be dealt with are when the particle reaches the corner pieces in the track they move around. When they hit these pieces, they need to change direction:

```
if (this.particles[i].x == 95 && this.particles[i].y == 12) {
  this.particles[i].direction = this.DIRECTION_RIGHT;
}
...
if (this.particles[i].x == 44  && this.particles[i].y == 44 &&
  this.particles[i].direction == this.DIRECTION_UP) {
  this.particles[i].direction = this.DIRECTION_RIGHT;
}
if (this.particles[i].x == 44  && this.particles[i].y == 44 &&
  this.particles[i].direction == this.DIRECTION_LEFT) {
  this.particles[i].direction = this.DIRECTION_DOWN;
}
...
```

The first example, the first of 12 total, is the corner piece at the top of the game-play area, the one that leads to the red injector port. In that case, when the particle hits it, there is only one outcome: it begins to move right. So, the direction attribute of the particle descriptor object is changed accordingly.

For some of the corner pieces, such as the second example that corresponds to the upper-left corner (near the green injector port), there are two possible outcomes; if the particle is currently moving up, it will now move right, or if the particle is currently moving left, then it will now move down. That's why there's two different if statements with the same X and Y values. Note that each adds an and clause to the check, which is the current direction of movement of the particle.

Handling the four diverters is similar in nature to handling the corner pieces of the track:

```
if (this.particles[i].x == 95 && this.particles[i].y == 44) {
  this.particles[i].direction = this.changeDir(this.DIVERTER_TOP,
    this.particles[i].direction);
  if (this.particles[i].direction == -1) {
    this.playSound("discardingapp_01");
    this.particles[i].alive = false;
    this.particles[i].emergeDelay = Math.floor(Math.random() * 100);
  }
}
...
```

This is one of four `if` statements, one for each diverter. For each, we call the `changeDir()` method, passing it the constant to tell it which diverter we're dealing with. We'll look at this method shortly, but for now it's enough to know that it performs some logic and ultimately returns a new direction for the particle to move in.

It also can return –1, which denotes the case where the waveguide in the diverter doesn't allow the particle to continue on the track. In that situation, we play the `discardingapp_01` sound and "kill" the particle, again randomizing the time it will take for it to emerge from the generator again.

With the corners and the diverters out of the way, the last thing to deal with logically is when a particle enters one of the four diverters:

```
if (this.particles[i].x == 177 && this.particles[i].y == 177) {
  if (this.particles[i].type == this.PARTICLE_MCKAYDIUM) {
    this.playSound("browser_01");
    this.addToScore(75);
  } else {
    this.playSound("delete_01");
    this.addToScore(-25);
    this.addOverheat(0.2);
  }
  this.particles[i].alive = false;
  this.particles[i].emergeDelay = Math.floor(Math.random() * 100);
}
...
```

As before, only one of the `if` statements is shown here, but there are actually three more after the one shown here. The code again uses some magic numbers corresponding to the center of the injector port. When the particle reaches those coordinates, the `if` statement, which corresponds to the yellow injector port in the lower-right corner of the screen, first checks the type of the particle. If it's the expected type, `PARTICLE_MCKAYDUM`[6] in this case, then the player got the right particle to the right port! The `browser_01` sound is played, and 75 points are added to the score. However, if it wasn't the right type of particle, then the `delete_01` sound is instead player, and –25 is added to the score (which is the same as subtracting from the score of course), and the engine heats up a little. In either case, the particle is rendered dead and awaits "remergence" from the generator.

The very last thing inside the iteration over the particles is this final bit of code:

```
this.particles[i].emergeDelay = this.particles[i].emergeDelay - 1;
if (this.particles[i].emergeDelay < 0) {
  this.playSound("card_01");
  this.particles[i].x = 95;
  this.particles[i].y = 94;
  this.particles[i].alive = true;
  this.particles[i].frameDelay = 0;
  this.particles[i].frame = Math.floor(Math.random() * 2);
  this.particles[i].type = Math.floor(Math.random() * 4);
  this.particles[i].direction = Math.floor(Math.random() * 4);
```

---

[6] MCKAYDIUM is my attempt to pay homage to Dr. Rodney McKay of *Stargate Atlantis* fame, played by the fabulous David Hewlett. The show, unfortunately, was canceled after "only" five seasons (a good run for most shows, but only half as much as its predecessor, *Stargate SG-1*), and if you were a fan, you'll appreciate this constant's name, and if you never watched, then I'm sorry, you missed out! Catch the reruns!

```
    }
```

This is the code in the else branch of the if statement checking whether the particle is alive or dead. If it's dead, we have to wait some period of time before the particle emerges from the generator, and that period of time is counted down by using the emergeDelay attribute of the particle descriptor object. When it goes below zero, it's time to emerge! At that point, the card_01 sound is played, and its initial X/Y coordinates are set to the center of the generator. The alive flag is set to true, and the frameDelay value is set to zero so we can start counting down (well, counting *up* technically in this case!) to when it's time to switch the frames of animation. Which frame is initially shown is randomly decided, as is the type of the particle, and the direction it is initially moving (that is, which direction is leaves the generator from).

That concludes the main game loop! We still have a few methods to look at, some of which we saw reference to in the main game loop, and of course the ones that we know must exist, since we saw references to them during scene setup, to handle user input (and besides, since it wouldn't be much with a game with them, we can be doubly sure they exist!).

Changing a Particle's Direction

In the mainLoop() method you saw that the changeDir() method is called when a particle hits a diverter in order to determine what direction the particle should now move in. Here's that method now:

```
GameScreenAssistant.prototype.changeDir = function(inDiverter, inCurrDir) {

  var retVal = 0;
  var diverterState = 0;

  switch (inDiverter) {
    case this.DIVERTER_TOP: diverterState = this.topDiverter; break;
    case this.DIVERTER_BOTTOM: diverterState = this.bottomDiverter; break;
    case this.DIVERTER_LEFT: diverterState = this.leftDiverter; break;
    case this.DIVERTER_RIGHT: diverterState = this.rightDiverter; break;
  }

  switch (inCurrDir) {

    case this.DIRECTION_UP:
      switch (diverterState) {
        case this.DIVERTER_DOWN_RIGHT: retVal = this.DIRECTION_RIGHT; break;
        case this.DIVERTER_DOWN_LEFT: retVal = this.DIRECTION_LEFT; break;
        case this.DIVERTER_VERTICAL: retVal = this.DIRECTION_UP; break;
        default: retVal = -1; break;
      }
    break;
    ...

  }

  return retVal;

};
```

The first step that is done is to interrogate the value passed in as inDiverter, which tells us which diverter the particle hit. Based on this, the current waveguide in that diverter is retrieved, and the variable diverterState stores that information. This way, the rest of the code in this method works regardless of which diverter is being dealt with.

Next, we enter a switch statement where each case is one of the possible directions the particle may currently be moving in. Based on this, and then based on the current waveguide in the diverter, the next direction for the particle is determined. For example, if the diverter currently has the waveguide with the track going down and to the right and the particle is currently moving up, then the particle needs to start moving to the right. Note that the default case for the switch is any situation where the particle cannot continue.

In all cases, retVal has the next direction, and it is in the end the return value from the method.

Heating Up the Engine

A particle that winds up back in the generator, or in the wrong injector port, results in the engine heating up a little bit. A call to the addOverheat() method from within the main game loop accomplishes that:

```
GameScreenAssistant.prototype.addOverheat = function(inAmount) {

  var progress = this.overheatBarModel.progress;
  progress = progress + inAmount;
  if (progress < 0) {
    progress = 0;
  }

  this.overheatBarModel.progress = progress;
  this.controller.modelChanged(this.overheatBarModel);

  $("palm_anon_element_0mojo-scene-gameScreenpbOverheat_progress").style.backgroundColor =
    "#" +
    Math.round((progress * 255)).toString(16) +
    Math.round((255 - (progress * 255))).toString(16) +
    "00";
```

The current progress value of the model for the ProgressBar is retrieved, and the inAmount passed in is added to it. This method is also called when the user cools down the engine. A negative value is passed in for that case, so we need to check whether the value of progress is less than zero and override it to zero in that case since a negative value isn't a valid value for a ProgressBar.

As the ProgressBar fills up, the bar becomes more reddish in tint, as you can see in Figure 5-9. We've already discussed how the background color gets set, but the math behind it here is a new piece to that puzzle.

Figure 5-9. *The overheat ProgressBar filling up*

It works by constructing an RRGGBB value for the color. The red portion of the color is calculated by multiplying the current progress value by 255 and then converting it to hexadecimal. For the green portion, the same is done, but the result is subtracted from 255. This results in the red and green components having values between zero and 255, and the higher the value of progress, the higher the value of red and, conversely, the lower the value of green. The result is that the bar starts off green, then becomes a brownish color, then a bit yellowish, and then finally red, as the red and green components pass each other as one gets higher and one gets lower.

One last task remains for this method, and that's to determine whether the game has ended:

```
if (this.overheatBarModel.progress >= 1) {
  clearInterval(this.mainLoopInterval);
  this.playSound("focusing");
  this.gameOverDialog = this.controller.showDialog({
    template : "gameOver-dialog", assistant : new GameOverAssistant(this),
    preventCancel : true
  });
}
```

When the ProgressBar is all filled up, the very next increase makes the value of progress in the model go above one, which means the engine has overheated. When this happens, we need to stop the main game loop by clearing the interval. We then play the focusing system sound and, finally, show the Game Over dialog box.

The dialog box is like a scene in that it has an HTML document that describes its structure, as well as an assistant. This assistant needs a reference to the assistant of the scene that showed the dialog box; that's why the keyword this is seen as the argument to the GameOverAssistant constructor. We'll see how this is used very soon.

Updating the Players' Score

Updating the player's current score, whether adding to it or subtracting from it, is done by calling the addToScore() method:

```
GameScreenAssistant.prototype.addToScore = function(inScore) {
```

```
  this.score = this.score + inScore;
  if (this.score < 0) {
    this.score = 0;
  }
  $("divScore").update(this.score);

};
```

As you can see, this simply adds the inScore value to the score field of the assistant. Since inScore can be negative, we need to check whether the score is negative after the addition and make it zero if it is. Finally, the divScore <div>'s contents are updated to show the score. Note here that instead of directly setting innerHTML, the update() method that the Prototype library adds to the node, is used. There's really no reason to do one vs. the other, not in this particular case anyway, but I thought seeing something a little different might be interesting for you.

Handling Player Input

Handling player input is handled by two methods, tapHandler() and keypressHandler(). You'll recall that these are the methods referenced when the event handlers were set up in activate(). Let's begin with tapHandler():

```
GameScreenAssistant.prototype.tapHandler = function(inEvent) {

  var x = inEvent.down.x - 40;
  var y = inEvent.down.y - 66;

  if (x >= this.topDiverterBounds.x1 && x <= this.topDiverterBounds.x2 &&
      y >= this.topDiverterBounds.y1 && y <= this.topDiverterBounds.y2) {
    this.keypressHandler(
      { originalEvent : { keyCode : Mojo.Char.w } }
    );
    return;
  }
  ...
  else {
    this.keypressHandler(
      { originalEvent : { keyCode : Mojo.Char.p } }
    );
  }

}
```

When a tap event occurs, the first thing we need to do is take the location where the tap occurred, as given to us via inEvent.down.x and inEvent.down.y, and adjust them so that they are zero-based. This is similar to the usage of XADJ and YADJ. Remember that the <canvas> element is centered on the screen, so its X/Y location isn't 0,0, and even if it were, we're interested in the location inside the game-play area, so we'd need to factor the frame out of it anyway. As it turns out, subtracting 10 from the X value and 66 from the Y value results in the tap coordinates being translated so that location 0,0 is the upper-left corner of the game-play area, precisely what we want.

Once that's done, we run through a series of four if statements, one for each diverter. Only the first is shown here. This is where those bounding box calculations we did early on come into play: topDiverterBounds defines the box around the top diverter. So, we need to see whether the tap occurred inside that box. That box already includes a few pixels of leeway around it, so the tap can occur a little bit outside the diverter as well and still register, which makes playing the game a little better because a little less accuracy is needed to make a diverter change.

If the tap falls within the bounds of the box, then the keypressHandler() method is called, passing the value associated with the key corresponding to the diverter that was tapped. This allows the actual work of changing a diverter to reside only in the keypressHandler() method, and this tapHandler() method can piggyback on that.

If the tap doesn't occur within the bounds of any of the diverters, then the else branch kicks in, and we treat that as an engine cooldown request.

Now, the keypressHandler() method is as follows:

```
GameScreenAssistant.prototype.keypressHandler = function(inEvent) {

  switch (inEvent.originalEvent.keyCode) {

    case Mojo.Char.w: case Mojo.Char.w + 32:
      this.playSound("down2");
      this.topDiverter = this.topDiverter + 1;
      if (this.topDiverter > 5) { this.topDiverter = 0; }
      this.leftHand = this.imgLeftHandUp;
      this.leftHandDelay = 0;
    break;
    ...
    case Mojo.Char.p: case Mojo.Char.p + 32:
      this.playSound("launch_02");
      this.addOverheat(-0.2);
      this.rightHand = this.imgRightHandDown;
      this.rightHandDelay = 0;
    break;

  }

};
```

There are five total case statements, one for each key associated with a diverter and one for cooling the engine down. Each of these cases is really two cases because each covers both lowercase and uppercase characters, so that shift being enabled on the keyboard won't break anything. The constants, such as Mojo.Char.w here, correspond to the uppercase letters, so adding 32 to that, since the value is an ASCII value, gives us the appropriate code for the lowercase version of the same letter.

When a diverter is to be changed, we begin by playing the down2 system sound. Then, the value of the appropriate variable, topDiverter in this case, is incremented by one. This effectively cycles to the next waveguide type. However, if the value of that variable is greater than five, then we need to cycle back around to the first waveguide type. Next, we set the left image to be drawn to the image appropriate for the diverter, imgLeftHandUp here, and reset leftHandDelay so that the hand is drawn during the next mainLoop() execution.

Similar logic is in play for the cooldown key, except that we play the launch_02 sound this time and cool the engine down a little via the call to addOverheat() and passing a negative value. The right image is updated and the delay reset, just like for the left hand.

Game Over Dialog Box

When a point is reached in the game where the overheat ProgressBar fills up, that's the trigger condition for the game ending. This is in fact the only way the game can end without the user manually closing the application. When this end-of-game condition occurs, the Game Over dialog box is shown. This dialog box looks like what you see in Figure 5-10.

Figure 5-10. *That's it…game over, man, GAME OVER!*[7]

This is as the dialog box looks if the final score is not the new high score (in that case there is some added verbiage, as you'll see later).

The interesting thing about custom dialog boxes is that they are effectively scenes! They are constructed the same way, they have many of the same life-cycle methods, and you can do just about anything with a dialog box that you can with a scene, including having widgets on them. The only real differences are how a dialog box gets shown and the fact that they are modal, meaning they block user activity against the rest of the application until the dialog box is dismissed.

The View HTML

Being essentially a scene means that a custom dialog box has its own view HTML file, as Listing 5-8 shows that file's content for the Game Over dialog box.

Listing 5-8. *The Contents of gameOver-dialog.html*

```
<center>
  <h1>Game Over</h1>
  <h2>You blew up the ship.<br>You're fired!</h2>
  <h3>Final score: <span id="spanFinalScore"></span></h3>
```

---

[7] Yes, that is indeed *two* references to *Alien*! This time it's from *Aliens*, the sequel to *Alien*, specifically the scene when the marines, plus Ripley, Newt, and Burke are trapped in the control room trying to figure out what to do next. Apparently, Private Hudson, played by the great Bill Paxton, thinks the only course of action is to simply die!

```
  <h3 id="divNewHighScore" style="display:none;">
    Congratulations, yours is the new high score!
  </h3>
</center>

<div id="btnNewGame" x-mojo-element="Button"></div>
<div id="btnExit" x-mojo-element="Button"></div>
```

As you can see, it looks like many other HTML files we've look at for other scene, complete with Button controls.

Note the divNewHighScore element, which is initially hidden by setting display:none in its style attribute. This element is shown only when the final score is the new high score.

The Scene Assistant

Once again, we see that a custom dialog box has a lot in common with a scene (again, because it really *is* a scene!) in that it too has an assistant. Let's look at the code for that class, beginning with its constructor:

```
function GameOverAssistant(inAssistant) {
  this.assistant = inAssistant;
};
```

Most of the assistants we've seen to this point have had an empty constructor. However, that isn't a requirement. In this situation, since a custom dialog box is not pushed like a scene is, our code has to instantiate this assistant, as you saw in the main game code earlier. Recall that when that instantiation occurs, a reference to the gameScene's assistant is passed to the constructor. Now we can see why: the GameOverAssistant stores that reference in its assistant field since the rest of the code requires that reference to do its work.

This assistant has a setup() method as well:

```
GameOverAssistant.prototype.setup = function() {

  this.assistant.controller.setupWidget("btnNewGame", { },
    { label : "Start A New Game", buttonClass : "palm-button affirmative" }
  );
  Mojo.Event.listen(this.assistant.controller.get("btnNewGame"),
    Mojo.Event.tap, this.newGame.bind(this)
  );

  this.assistant.controller.setupWidget("btnExit", { },
    { label : "Exit Application", buttonClass : "palm-button negative" }
  );
  Mojo.Event.listen(this.assistant.controller.get("btnExit"),
    Mojo.Event.tap, this.exit.bind(this)
  );

};
```

The focus here is setting up the two Buttons. Notice that it's actually the gameScreen scene's assistant that is doing this work, which is the reason for the assistant field we just talked about.

When this dialog box is activated, its `activate()` method is executed:

```
GameOverAssistant.prototype.activate = function() {

  $("spanFinalScore").innerHTML = this.assistant.score;
  if (this.assistant.score > 0) {
    var highScoreCookie = new Mojo.Model.Cookie("Engineer_highScore");
    var highScore = highScoreCookie.get();
    if (!highScore || this.assistant.score > highScore) {
      highScoreCookie.put(this.assistant.score);
      $("divNewHighScore").show();
    }
  }

};
```

Here we're displaying the final score by setting the `innerHTML` attribute of the `spanFinalScore` `<span>` to the value stored in the `score` field of the gameScreen scene's assistant. If that score is greater than 0, then we load the high-score cookie. Assuming that cookie has a value (remember, it may not if no score was previously saved), and if the current score is greater than the current high score, then the cookie is written out with the current score as the new value, and `divNewHighScore` is shown, resulting in the dialog box shown in Figure 5-11.

Figure 5-11. *This time, a slightly more positive outcome: this ship didn't make it, but you got the high score!*

The two `Buttons` are present regardless of whether it's the new high score, and clicking the Start A New Game `Button` results in execution of the `newGame()` method:

```
GameOverAssistant.prototype.newGame = function() {
  this.assistant.startGame();
  this.assistant.gameOverDialog.mojo.close();
};
```

A call to the startGame() method of the gameScreen scene's assistant starts the game. Then we need to close the dialog box, which doesn't happen automatically. Remember that when the dialog box was shown, a reference to it was stored in the gameOverDialog field of the gameScreen scene's assistant. That object contains a method mojo.close() that closes the dialog box, so a call to that method takes care of it for us, and the new game is now running and ready to be played.

Finally, if the Exit Application Button is clicked, then the exit() method is executed:

```
GameOverAssistant.prototype.exit = function() {
  window.close();
};
```

Remember always that a webOS application is, for all intents and purposes, a web application, and therefore we can do a lot of the same sorts of things with it that we can do with any web application or web page. This includes calling window.close() to exit the application! That's all it takes, and the application is immediately exited.

Suggested Exercises

The great thing about games is that there are *always* things you can do with them to make them better; all you have to do is let your imagination run wild! However, I wouldn't be doing my job if I didn't offer some suggestions to get you started, so here goes:

- Instead of storing a single high score, store the top five scores instead, and allow the user to enter their initials. For those of you old enough to have grown up in video arcades, you know that there's nothing quite as fun as entering A-S-S as your initials!

- If you have some server-side programming experience, create a web service that you can upload scores to, and modify the game to display a list of, say, the top 100 scores. This would add a nice social aspect to the game and give people more incentive to play it and try to do better.

- Implement the notion of difficulty levels. Perhaps as the game plays now could be the medium difficulty level. Then, the easy level would have only one particle at a time, while the hard difficulty would have maybe five, and maybe they move a little faster.

- Do you remember the game Defender? Do you remember the smart bomb? If not, let me explain: it was a magical button that you could hit (assuming you had any left) that would annihilate any enemy currently on the screen. It was in a sense a "get me the heck out of this mess!" card you could play. Create something like that for this game: make it explode all particles on the screen without loss of points and, at the same time, instantly cool the engine off completely. That way, the player can avoid the situation where a couple of particles are going in the wrong place at once. Of course, you'll want to animate the explosions.

All of these suggestions would make good additions in terms of game play and features but would also challenge you to think outside the box a bit, as is the case any time you make a game.

Summary

In this chapter, we constructed a game for the webOS platform and the Palm Pre. We learned a little bit about the <canvas> tag available in HTML5 (and the WebKit rendering engine used in webOS). We saw the use of the System Sound service and learned about handling screen tap events and keyboard events. We learned how to make our applications battery-friendly by scaling back their activity when the application is not the current application, and we generally got some more experience with Mojo and even saw some different ways of constructing a webOS application.

In the next chapter, we'll build a background application whose job it will be to run in the background and alert us to keywords in RSS feeds so that we never miss a beat with regard to the topic of interest to us. It will, like this game, be a bit of a change from the first two applications presented, so it should be a lot of fun!

Join me in the next chapter when you're ready, won't you?

CHAPTER 6

■ ■ ■

Keeping an Eye on Friends: Twitter Monitor

An Application That Alerts You of Keywords in Twitter Feeds

These days, everyone wants their 15 minutes of fame, and more important, everyone can get it thanks to the Internet! Everyone has a place to spout off about anything they want, whether it's pointless drivel or thoughtful insights into the world at large. The social Web, as it has come to be known, is at once a fantastic creation and a source of annoyance since there's plenty of noise to cut through.

Of all the web sites that have contributed to this social web concept, Twitter is undoubtedly one of the more recent leaders. Twitter is a micro-blogging site: you "tweet" a small thought, limited to 140 characters in length. People "follow" you to see what you're up to, and you follow those friends you are interested in.

In this chapter, we'll build an application for monitoring the "feeds" of your friends for specific keywords. To be clear, this won't be a full-featured Twitter client at all; you won't be able to post anything with it or interact with Twitter in a dynamic way. You'll simply select the friends you want to watch and specify one or more keywords to watch for. When a keyword is found in a posting from the friend, you'll be alerted and be able to view the message. This application will run in the background but in an omnipresent way that won't interfere with your other work. It should prove to be a useful tool if you're into the Twitter thing!

What's This App Do Anyway?

In many ways, this is the simplest application you'll find in this book. In fact, it can be summarized in just a few quick bullet points:

- The user should be able to enter their username and password for their Twitter account and have it verified.

- Once verified, a list of the users' friends, those users they are following, is retrieved.

- The user can then select which of their friends they want to monitor and can enter keywords to monitor them for. This can all be changed at any time, of course.

- The application should run in the background but will always be visible via a new type of stage that we haven't seen in action before: a dashboard stage. All user interactions occur within the dashboard, save for selecting friends and entering keywords, which will live on a typical card stage (which is what we've been using thus far).

- The user should be able to cycle through the statuses of their friends that were flagged as containing the keywords entered. This should be possible from the dashboard itself without having to open a whole new card view.

Yep, that really is about it! Like I said, it's not a complex application conceptually, but we'll have to implement a number of tricks to make it all work. Before we can get to that, though, let's discuss Twitter a little bit and the web services available to us from it.

Meet the Twitter Web Services

As I mentioned in the opening of the chapter, Twitter (www.twitter.com) is what's known as a *micro-blogging* site. Users have just 140 characters to tell the world exactly what they're thinking and doing at a given moment in time. These posts are referred to as the users' *status*, and a given status is called a *tweet*.

A user of Twitter is often referred to as a *twerson* (hence, a group of twersons is collectively termed a *tweeple*). I suppose you could call them a *tweeter* too if you wanted. Yes, the terminology is a little silly, but what can you say? Welcome to the world of Web 2.0!

Twitter is a great example of a social networking site. When you find a twerson you are interested in (for whatever reason!), you can choose to follow them. This means their tweets will appear on your Twitter home page in a consolidated listing of status updates from all those you are following.

That's Twitter in a nutshell, but it doesn't tell us anything about interfacing with Twitter. As it happens, another advantage of this Web 2.0 thing is the ability to aggregate data from multiple sites using those same sorts of web services we saw in the Local Business Search project. Twitter offers its own set of APIs for getting at its data. The Twitter API is fairly large and complex, and whole books can (and have!) been written about it. For this project, however, only three specific functions are needed.

The RESTful Approach to Web Services

The Twitter API uses what's known as REST, which stands for Representational State Transfer. REST is an architectural approach to providing web services, not a specific standard. The basic idea is that a given URL represents a resource, and a client can interact with that resource using standard HTTP methods such as PUT, GET, POST, and DELETE (which correspond to the well-known CRUD methods of Create, Retrieve, Update, and Delete).

For example, let's say you want to provide access to a bank account resource. The URL might be as follows:

```
http://www.fakebank.com/accounts/checking/123456789.json
```

If you access this URL with an HTTP method of GET, you will retrieve checking account 123456789, assuming it exists, of course. The format of the response in this case would be JSON, since that's the extension used. Some RESTful web services, as many people refer to this model as, allow you to request a response be in XML, JSON, or other formats, while some don't give you the choice (in which case you might not have an extension there at all).

The response is a representation of the checking account resource, which is where the "state transfer" portion of REST comes from. Likewise, if you wanted to update an attribute of this account, you would POST back to the same URL, and the contents of the POST body would be the JSON for the account with the changes in it. To create a new account, use the HTTP PUT method and leave off the account number part of the URL; to delete the account, just use the DELETE method without sending any content (and, most likely, without the JSON extension part of the URL).

One thing to notice here is that the URL for a RESTful service refers to nouns, not verbs. For example, the URL doesn't include anything like getAccount?acctNum=123456789, like you might typically see in a normal URL. Instead, the HTTP method used is the verb, or the action to execute, and the URL includes the noun, or the object (or type of object) that is being operated on.

REST is a pretty simple model for web services but one that is gaining a lot of traction precisely because it is so simple! It's very easy to write clients in a variety of technologies, and creating RESTful service providers is no more difficult. It builds on the standards we all know and love and use every day (HTTP) and can make use of the same sorts of security mechanisms used in such environments.

So, what specific capabilities will be needed from Twitter? Let's have a look-see now at exactly what part of the Twitter REST API we're going to use here.

■ **Note** All of the functions we'll be using use the GET method, since we're not creating, updating, or deleting anything on Twitter in this application.

Verifying a User

The account/verify_credentials API allows us to validate that a given username and password is valid. To use it, we access the following URL:

http://twitter.com/account/verify_credentials.json

As previously mentioned, you could specify XML as the return type here, but we'll only be dealing with JSON in this application.

In a way, this isn't the best example of a RESTful API function because what's in the URL isn't really a noun per se, although arguably the noun would be credentials. In that case, however, verify would be the verb, so it's still not the most "pure" REST design.

That's just some theoretical musings at the end of the day! The function does what we need, so we can debate the finer points of REST implementation some other time. The other piece to use this function is of course passing in the username and password. For this particular function, that information is passed in as basic auth headers.

If you are unfamiliar with it, *basic auth* is a simple authentication mechanism frequently used on the Web. All it means is that a request header Authorization is passed. The value of this attribute is in the form Basic username:password. The username:password portion must be Base64 encoded.

That's all this particular function requires. If the supplied credentials are valid, then the JSON returned will include a host of information about the user, including their latest status, number of tweets, and so on. If the credentials are not valid, then an HTTP error code 403 will be returned to indicate the user is not authorized. This too is typical of RESTful web services: instead of returning error information as part of a "successful" response, meaning an HTTP 400 response, the HTTP protocol is further exploited by returning error codes (which can also contain other information in the form of headers and the response body itself).

Getting a List of Friends

The next thing we'll need to be able to do is to get a list of those the user is following, their friends, in other words. To do so, we use the statuses/friends function at the following URL:

http://twitter.com/statuses/friends.json

For this function, we need to pass a request parameter named id. This is the ID of the user we want to get friends for.

By default, this function returns 100 friends (that's someone more popular than me!) However, someone may be following more than 100 people. For this reason, there is a request parameter called cursor. Initially, you send a value of -1 for this parameter. Then, each response will give you an attribute next_cursor as part of the JSON response. You can then make a subsequent request, passing the value of next_cursor as the value of the cursor parameter to get the next 100 friends. You can keep doing this until you reach the end (represented by next_cursor having a value of zero).

This function actually returns a boatload of information about each friend, but as we'll see later, we're interested only in a very small subset of that information. Unfortunately, there doesn't appear to be a more lightweight function to use, so this will have to do.

Getting the Most Current Status of a Specific User

The final function we'll need is to be able to get the most current status, or tweet, of a given user. This function is the users/show function at the following URL:

http://twitter.com/users/show.json

This function just requires an id parameter, which is the ID of the user to get the status for.

You can use this, or either of the other functions, via the same Ajax.Request() function we saw in the Local Business Search application. So, it will be quite familiar to you, even though the remote service is somewhat different from what Yahoo! provided for that application.

Planning the Application

As always, we'll sketch out a basic diagram of the scenes this application contains, even though, as we'll see, the term *scenes* has a somewhat different meaning this time around! Figure 6-1 is the result of that work.

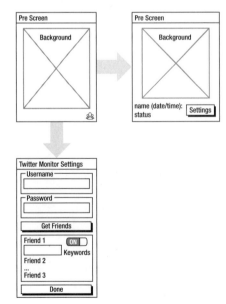

Figure 6-1. A whiteboardish sketch of the scene flow of the application

This application differs from all the others in this book in one important way: this is a "background" application. This means it doesn't have a typical card view as all our other applications have (in fact, they all have multiple card views).

When the typical kind of application that we've dealt with so far starts up, a stage is by default created on which all our view cards are displayed (one at a time of course). This default type of stage is a card stage because card views are displayed on it.

It is also possible, however, to manually create a stage, and when you do so, you have the opportunity to create other types of stages. One of these types is a dashboard stage. In Chapter 1, we looked at what the dashboard is, but to briefly recap, it's a small area at the bottom of the screen, larger than a banner notification but still only a small portion of the screen. An application can provide part of its user interface in the dashboard area. The user can continue to use other applications in the foreground while the application using the dashboard does some background processing. That's exactly what this application does.

Since with a background application there is no stage created by default, there is initially no stage assistant in which to push our first scene, like other applications throughout this book have done. For a background application, we have a new entity to deal with, and that's the application assistant, or *app assistant* for short.

This is just like a stage assistant in many ways and as such lives in the assistants directory. It has a specific name: app-assistant.js. Just like a stage assistant, the app assistant has a setup() method. This is the first method that gets called when the application starts up. You may or may not have anything to do in this method, but you almost certainly will have something to do in the other app assistant method, handleLaunch(). This is conceptually similar to the activate() method of a stage assistant, and it is called after setup() is. It is in handleLaunch() that you will most likely create a stage of some sort and push a scene onto it.

Creating a stage is a fairly simple affair:

```
this.controller.createStageWithCallback(
  { name : "dashboardStage" },
  function(inStageController) {
    inStageController.pushScene(
      { name : "main", sceneTemplate : "main/main-scene" },
      { }
    );
  }, "dashboard"
);
```

A stage is given a name so we can refer to it later, and since creating a stage is an asynchronous operation, we need to provide a callback function. This function then uses the stage controller reference passed into it to push a scene onto the stage using the familiar pushScene() method.

The type of stage is specified as the second argument to createStageWithCallback(); in this example, we're creating a dashboard stage.

We'll see this in action within the code of this application (in fact, the previous example code is taken right out of this application). The other aspect to this is that you can in fact have more than one stage in use by your application at a time. The web browser application is a good example of this: each separate browser window you have open is its own card stage. You can also have a dashboard stage and a card stage open within an application simultaneously, as you'll see in this application.

Going back to Figure 6-1 for a moment, you'll notice that there's no "Start Here" as has been the case in previous sketches for other projects. That's because although it's true that there is a scene initially shown, it's shown as the dashboard right there on the Pre's "home" screen, so to speak, and because of this, it seemed a little odd to call it a starting point, at least in the sense like other applications have had.

Still, in the diagram, the square in the upper left is what you'd see initially, which is the Pre's main screen with just an icon in the bottom right. Tapping this icon (or in fact the blank area to the left of it too) expands the dashboard and leads to the box to the right of that where you can see previously flagged tweets, if any (and the user can tap that area to cycle through the tweets), as well as an icon to the right that brings up the Settings scene when tapped. The Settings scene is shown on the bottom and consists of a TextField for entering the username and a PasswordField for entering the password for the Twitter account with a Button below, which serves to verify the account and then to get the list of friends. Below that is a List where the friends are shown. Next to each is a ToggleButton widget that determines whether the friend is being monitored or not, and below that is a TextField where the keywords to look for are entered. Finally, at the bottom is a Done Button that is responsible for saving what has been entered (saving is *not* done automatically on a back swipe or anything else; only tapping this Button saves anything).

Creating the Skeleton

If you were to create this application from scratch, you would again use the Palm-supplied application wizard to do so and then add to it two scenes. Figure 6-2 shows the directory structure at the end of that process.

Figure 6-2. The application's directory structure and file contents

Here we can see that we have the usual suspects: two scene assistants, two scenes in the views directory, and a style sheet named after the application in the stylesheets directory. The images directory contains just two files: btnMenu.png is the settings icon shown on the dashboard, and icoSettings.png is the icon on the Settings scene. We also see that there is a new assistant floating around here, an app assistant, which we'll look at shortly. Also, there is no stage assistant as we've typically seen. Since this has in the past been the place where our code really kicked in, we can surmise there's a different entry point this time around…but let's not get ahead of things!

There is also a Base64.js JavaScript file in the app directory, which provides Base64 encoding functionality and which will be dealt with in more detail in the global-scope code a few pages hence.

The Data Model

In this application, because the data storage needs are quite simplistic, we'll again use the Depot API to make things a bit easier on us. Although a straight HTML5 database would have been fine too, I thought that would really just introduce a lot of code that didn't really need to be there since Depot does the job just fine. Note that cookies wouldn't really have been a viable alternative since the user could select many friends to monitor and since that quickly could lead to a volume of data that wouldn't fit in a single cookie (and trying to manage multiple cookies can get fairly complex in a hurry too). In other words, all things considered, I think this is a perfect case for Depot, and as such, there really isn't a data model per se to discuss here (what actually gets stored we'll look at when we examine the relevant pieces of code).

Application Configuration

As far as configuration goes, we have our three good friends as usual along for the ride in this application: appinfo.json, sources.json, and framework_config.json.

The appinfo.json File

The appinfo.json file follows the same generic pattern that we've seen before, with one big difference, which you can try to spot now as you look at Listing 6-1.

Listing 6-1. The appinfo.json File

```
{
  "id": "com.etherient.twittermonitor",
  "version": "1.0.0",
  "vendor": "Etherient",
  "type": "web",
  "main": "index.html",
  "title": "Twitter Monitor",
  "icon": "icon.png",
  "noWindow": "true"
}
```

Aside from the usual id and title attributes, which differ for every application, there is the new noWindow attribute sitting there staring us in the face mockingly!

When this attribute is set to true as it is here, it indicates to the operating system that the application is intended to run in the background, and it will take responsibility for creating a stage (or multiple stages, as we'll see in this application). Instead of a stage being automatically created, the application will have to do that itself from its application assistant.

This is the first part of the equation of making a background application; we'll see the rest of that equation as we explore the rest of the application.

The sources.json File

The volume of code this project contains is a fair bit less than many of the others, and sources.json, shown in Listing 6-2, bears that out.

Listing 6-2. The sources.json File

```
[
  {
    "source" : "app/Base64.js"
  },
  {
    "source" : "app/assistants/app-assistant.js"
  },
  {
    "source" : "app/assistants/main-assistant.js", "scenes" : "main"
  },
  {
    "source" : "app/assistants/settings-assistant.js", "scenes" : "settings"
  }
]
```

We have an application assistant in this project, which is the first time we've seen that, as well as two other scenes, defined in the usual way. There's also a JavaScript file named Base64.js that is imported here, which is used when making certain AJAX calls to Twitter, as we'll see shortly.

The framework_config.json File

Finally, the framework_config.json, shown in Listing 6-3, has just the one attribute we've come to expect.

Listing 6-3. The framework_config.json File

```
{ "logLevel" : 99 }
```

As always, this file is optional, and you can adjust the logLevel attribute as you see fit.

Global-Scope Code

The only bit of global code in this application is actually code I didn't write! As discussed earlier with regard to validating the users' Twitter account, this application requires the ability to Base64 encode a string. Unfortunately, that isn't something built into Java, nor does Mojo or even Prototype provide this capability. Therefore, we need some code from somewhere else.

The Base64.js file contains just such code. This code is a Base64 class that provides both encoding and decoding capabilities, so it's just the ticket. Using it is as simple as calling Base64.encode() and passing in the string to be encoded. The encoded version is returned, and you could decode that if you wanted using the not surprisingly named Base64.decode() method.

■ **Note** This code comes from the site www.WebToolkit.info whose authors kindly provide a number of JavaScript, CSS, PHP, and other bits of code free for all to use. I couldn't find specific names to thank, so whoever you folks are, thank you very much!

Setting the Stage

The starting point of this application, like all others, is an HTML file in the root of the application, shown in Listing 6-4.

Listing 6-4. Yes, Even for a Background Application, We Still Need a Starting HTML Document

```
<?xml version="1.0" encoding="UTF-8"?>
<!DOCTYPE html PUBLIC "-//W3C//DTD XHTML 1.1//EN"
  "http://www.w3.org/TR/xhtml11/DTD/xhtml11.dtd">
<html xmlns="http://www.w3.org/1999/xhtml" xml:lang="en">
  <head>
    <title>Twitter Monitor</title>
    <script src="/usr/palm/frameworks/mojo/mojo.js" type="text/javascript"
      x-mojo-version="1" />
    <link href="stylesheets/twittermonitor.css" media="screen"
      rel="stylesheet" type="text/css" />
  </head>
  <body></body>
</html>
```

It is, like others, very bare-bones and is responsible for loading Mojo itself and our application's style sheet. The fact that this is a background application and that it has multiple stages doesn't change the need for this file. This is still a web app we're talking about, so it needs to start with an HTML page somewhere after all.

A Matter of Style

We have only a small handful of style classes to talk about in this application, beginning with this one:

```
.header-icon.settings {
    background : url(../images/icoSettings.png) no-repeat;
}
```

This is for the icon on the Settings scene, just like we've done in previous applications.

The main dashboard, as we'll see a bit later, is constructed using a table, and because a dashboard is a well-defined size, we need to have some styles to make sure everything fits, and that's where the next class comes into play:

```
.cssMainDiv {
  font-size : 52%;
  padding-left : 4px;
  line-height : 11px;
}
```

Although the font size here is quite a bit smaller than Palm's UI guidelines say is good, which I generally agree with, in this case I think breaking the rules is OK because there's a limited amount of space to work with. Fortunately, however, since we know there's a hard 140-character limit to any particular tweet, I discovered that 52% ensures the entire tweet fits, including timestamp information, so long as the line-height is 11 pixels.

The cssMainStatus class styles the area where tweets are displayed:

```
.cssMainStatus {
  height : 50px;
}
```

Making sure it's 50 pixels ensures it fits nicely on the dashboard and also ensures that vertical centering within the table cells (as you'll see later) really does center things properly.

When the List of friends is shown as part of the Settings scene, a couple of style classes are used:

```
.cssSettingsFriend {
  height : 120px;
}
```

The cssSettingsFriend style wraps a given row in the List and makes it big enough so that the username, ToggleButton, and TextField all fit nicely.

Finally, there is this:

```
.cssSettingsKeywords {
  color : #babaff;
}
```

This styles the "Keywords" label next to the TextField in the List.

A New Kind of Helper: The Application Assistant

As previously discussed, the application assistant is the starting point for a background application and is defined just like any other assistant:

```
function AppAssistant() { }
```

You could of course do any sort of setup in this constructor you need to, but as with most of the assistants in this book, it's common to just have an empty constructor.

A Couple of Data Fields

The app assistant contains a number of data fields that provide a shared set of data for the rest of the application. In other applications in this book, we created a class for this purpose, as well as for providing common functions used throughout the application. An app assistant effectively serves the same purpose, though, so I saw no need to introduce a second JavaScript source file for this. Table 6-1 summarizes the data fields.

Table 6-1. The Data Fields of the App Assistant

Field	Description
pauseUpdates	This is a flag that gets set to true when the settings view is shown. The background processing that monitors Twitter feeds will not do anything when this flag is set to true so as to avoid trying to use the list of friends that might be in the process of changing.

depot	The Mojo Depot object used to store data.
friends	This is a list of objects that contains information about friends associated with the specified Twitter account. This object contains information such as the username, the ID of the last tweet (or status) that was examined, and whether the friend is being monitored by this application.
tempFriend	This is a temporary array of friend objects, just like is stored in the friends field, that is used during retrieval of the friends list from Twitter. This is necessary, as you'll see, to deal with the way Twitter chunks large result sets back to the client.
accountInfo	This is an object that contains two fields, called username and password, which are the credentials of the user's Twitter account.
tempAccountInfo	This is a temporary version of accountInfo when the user is modifying settings. It helps ensure that no changes are saved until the user explicitly saves them.

Well that's not too much, is it? Now we can move into examining the actual code, starting with the handleLaunch() method.

Handling Launch

The handleLaunch() method of the app assistant is called when the application starts up and is also called when the application is relaunched. This situation arises when a keyword is found in a Twitter status of a user being monitored and the user taps the banner notification displayed for this. So, we have to deal with both situations in this method, and doing so is the job of this first chunk of code:

```
var sa = this.controller.getStageController("dashboardStage")
if (sa) {
this.controller.removeAllBanners();
sa.activate();
return;
}
```

The getStageController() method returns to us a reference to a named stage. Remember in the earlier example that a stage gets a specific name—now you know why! If we get anything other than null, then the application is already running. In this case, we remove all banner notifications by calling removeAllBanners() because otherwise the notification will have precedence over the dashboard and will obscure it when the next step is done, which is an activate() call on the returned stage assistant, resulting in the dashboard being shown again so the user can see the new tweet.

If no stage assistant is located, then the application must be starting up for the first time, so the previous code doesn't come into play. The first step to starting the application up is to deal with the Depot:

```
this.depot = new Mojo.Depot(
  { name : "TwitterMonitor", version : 1, replace : false },
  function() {
    this.depot.simpleGet("accountInfo",
```

```
      function(inObject) {
        if (inObject) {
          this.accountInfo = inObject;
        }
      }.bind(this),
      function(inTransaction, inResult) {
        Mojo.Controller.errorDialog(
          "Failure reading accountInfo from depot: " + inResult);
      }.bind(this)
    );
    this.depot.simpleGet("friends",
      function(inObject) {
        if (inObject) {
          this.friends = inObject;
        }
      }.bind(this),
      function(inTransaction, inResult) {
        Mojo.Controller.errorDialog("Failure reading friends from depot: " +
          inResult);
      }.bind(this)
    );
  }.bind(this),
  function(inTransaction, inResult) {
    Mojo.Controller.errorDialog("Failure opening depot: " + inResult);
    this.depot = null;
  }.bind(this)
);
```

There's not much new here from when we saw the Depot API in the Local Business Search. There are two objects that need to be retrieved: accountInfo and friends. The accountInfo object is the one that contains the username and password, and friends is the array of friends associated with the Twitter account. If neither is found, which is the case the first time the application is run, the app assistant fields remain null, and we'll deal with them later.

The only other method you'll find in the app assistant is the checkConnectivity() method that was introduced as part of the Local Business Search. As such, there's no need to go into it here, but I wanted to make you aware that it was here because you'll see it called before the AJAX requests that will be performed later.

A Scene-by-Scene Account

There are effectively only two scenes in this application, and one of them is our dashboard view of things. Still, what you see in the dashboard actually is a scene, complete with scene assistant and all that good stuff, so we'll explore it along with the other more traditional scene, the Settings scene.

Main Scene

The Main scene, aside from being what is seen on the dashboard stage, also contains the code that contacts Twitter to monitor the specified friends. Like any other scene, the dashboard-based scene can be minimized or maximized, but the terms have slightly different meanings in this context, as Figure 6-3 begins to show.

Figure 6-3. *I realize it's not much to look at, but there it is at the bottom!*

This is what the Main scene looks like when it is "minimized." Figure 6-4, a few pages hence, shows its "maximized" look. As you can see, it's not the same as maximizing and minimizing a card-based scene.

The View HTML

The view HTML for this scene is, to say the least, minimal. In fact, you may have a hard time believing at first that Listing 6-5 is the complete HTML document, but I swear, it is!

Listing 6-5. *Really, That's It, I Swear, That's All There Is to This Scene's View HTML!*

```
<div class="cssMainDiv">
  <table width="100%" cellpadding="0" cellspacing="0" border="0"><tr>
    <td id="tdStatus" valign="top" class="cssMainStatus"> </td>
    <td width="56" align="center" valign="middle">
      <img src="images/btnMenu.png" id="btnMenu" />
    </td>
  </tr></table>
</div>
```

Not only is it very spartan, but it's also extremely simple! The outer `<div>` with `cssMainDiv` applied gives us a container for the content and specifies a height that nicely fits it onto the dashboard stage. Some padding is also added to the left because without that I found that the content bumped right up against the edge of the screen and didn't look that great.

The table within the `<div>` gives us the left/right structure we need to show the tweets right next to the settings icon. Since both the area where the tweets appear and the icon are manipulated later—the status area obviously to insert the text and the icon to hook up a tap event handler to it—they both have IDs.

The Scene Assistant

The scene assistant for the Main scene begins with the usual constructor function:

```
function MainAssistant() { }
```

After that we find two fields added:

```
MainAssistant.prototype.statuses = [ ];
```

The statuses field stores all the statuses (tweets) for the friends being monitored that have been flagged thus far. This data is cleared when the application shuts down.

To go along with that, we have the statusesIndex field:

```
MainAssistant.prototype.statusesIndex = -1;
```

This field is used to allow the user to cycle through the statuses. Each time the user taps the status text area of the dashboard, this field is incremented and is then used as the index value into the statuses array. When the value of this field equals the length of the statuses array, it is reset to zero (it starts at –1 so that the first tap displays the first element in the array, if there is any).

Setting Up the Scene

The next step is to set up the scene, and there's little work to do here:

```
Mojo.Event.listen($("tdStatus"), Mojo.Event.tap,
  function() {
    if (this.statusesIndex > -1) {
      this.statusesIndex = this.statusesIndex + 1;
      if (this.statusesIndex >= this.statuses.length) {
        this.statusesIndex = 0;
      }
      $("tdStatus").innerHTML = "<b>" +
        this.statuses[this.statusesIndex].screen_name + " (" +
        this.statuses[this.statusesIndex].created_at + "): </b>" +
        this.statuses[this.statusesIndex].text;
    }
  }.bind(this)
);
```

The first task performed by this chunk of the setup() method's code is to attach a Mojo.Event.tap handler to the status text area of the dashboard (the table cell to the left if you think back to the scene's view markup). This is what allows the user to cycle through any statuses flagged thus far. As you can see, the statusesIndex field is manipulated as previously described and then used to get the appropriate element of the statuses array, if any. The innerHTML of the table cell is updated to display the information including the username (screen_name) of the friend, when the status was entered by them (created_at), and the text of the tweet itself (text).

Figure 6-4 shows what it looks like when a status is being viewed. This of course would only be seen if the user has tapped the dashboard area to "maximize" the scene.

Figure 6-4. *A status message being displayed in the dashboard*

Similar to that is the next bit of code, which attaches a tap handled to the settings icon to the right:

```
Mojo.Event.listen($("btnMenu"), Mojo.Event.tap,
  function() {
    if (Mojo.Controller.getAppController().getStageController(
      "settingsStage")) {
      return;
    }
    Mojo.Controller.getAppController().createStageWithCallback(
      { name : "settingsStage" },
      function(inStageController) {
        inStageController.pushScene(
          { name : "settings", sceneTemplate : "settings/settings-scene" },
          { }
        );
      }, "card"
    );
  }
);
```

When this icon is tapped, the first thing we do is ask the app controller for a reference to the stage controller for the stage named settingsStage. This would only return a non-null value if the Settings scene is already up, but since the user can maximize the dashboard and tap the icon even in this case, we wouldn't want to try to re-create the stage (that actually results in an error, so it's definitely something to avoid!).

Assuming this check is passed, then the task is to create that settingsStage and push the Settings scene onto it. This is just like the stage creation code we saw to start the application, but this time the stage type is card, so this will look and work like any other scene we've ever seen, even though we're creating the stage for it manually.

Activating the Scene

With the stage set up, we now move on to activating the scene, with the usual `activate()` method. In fact, there are only two lines of code in this method, but they are, as the saying goes, all-important:

```
setInterval(this.checkFeeds.bind(this), (1000 * 60 * 5));
setTimeout(this.checkFeeds.bind(this), (1000 * 5));
```

To do something in a background application in a useful way, there are really two avenues you can go. One is to use the Alarm service to periodically wake your application up and do some processing. This can be a good choice if the interval you want to do something at is fairly long, measured in many minutes. The nice thing about this approach is that the device isn't incurring any sort of overhead from your background processing (even if you minimize the amount of work actually being done, as is the case in this application). The downside is that your application actually closes after each wake-up and processing iteration. That means you will incur overhead as the application starts up, and the coding could possibly be more complex to deal with the constant shutdowns and startup, depending on how you choose to write your application.

The other approach is to use the intrinsic JavaScript methods `setInterval()` and `setTimeout()`. In fact, `setInterval()` is really the one you want because it continually executes your code at a set interval until you explicitly stop it. The `setTimeout()` method executes some code just once after a specific period of time.

■ **Note** Initially, I had designed the application so that the interval would be set as part of the app assistant, which to me makes more sense logically. However, since both `setInterval()` and `setTimeout()` are methods of the `window` object and since there *is* no `window` object when the app assistant executes, this wouldn't work. It doesn't hurt my head to have to put this code in this scene, however, since it has to be visible for the application to be running, but I wanted to make you aware of this situation.

I've used both here because initially I want the application to check on the feeds it is monitoring five seconds after the application starts up. This gives all the initialization plenty of time to complete but gives the user a more or less immediate response in terms of whether any of their friends have posted statuses with specific keywords. The `setInterval()` call waits five minutes between executions by contrast. Both `setInterval()` and `setTimeout()` here execute the same thing, but if `setTimeout()` wasn't used, then the first update would be five minutes after the application started up, and I'm a basically impatient person, so I'd hate to wait that long!

It is important to realize that webOS will shut down your application very soon after the last stage is no longer visible. Therefore, *some* part of your application must be visible at all times; otherwise, whatever code initially calls `setInterval()` will shut down at that point, and you will no longer have any background processing going on. That's why the dashboard stage is used in this application. Without that, feeds wouldn't be monitored as soon as there was no stage visible (and in fact, once you swipe away the dashboard, Twitter is no longer being monitored). If this limitation, so to speak, is a problem in terms of your application design, then using the Alarm service is probably the way you will need to go, but for this application, it's not needed.

■ **Note** As always, when you have a background application or one that is minimized, you should seek to reduce processing as much as possible to conserve device resources (battery, network bandwidth, and so on). In this case, since the polling interval is a fairly long five minutes and is in fact not adjustable by the user by design, there's not a whole lot less reduction that could be achieved anyway.

Getting to the Heart of the Matter: Monitoring Feeds

Only one more method remains in the Main scene's assistant, and that's the `checkFeeds()` method that we saw being called by the `setInterval()` and `setTimeout()` calls in the `activate()` method. We'll walk through this little by little, starting with this single line at the top:

```
var appAssistant = Mojo.Controller.getAppController().assistant;
```

You'll recall from earlier when we looked at the app assistant that there is some shared data there that, as it happens, is needed in this method. Therefore, we need a reference to the app assistant, and to save some typing, this line of code gets that reference and sets the appAssistant variable to point to it:

```
if (appAssistant.pauseUpdates) {
  return;
}
```

When the Settings scene is showing, we don't want monitoring to occur because the list of friends, keywords, or even the Twitter account itself could be in the process of changing. To avoid concurrency issues that might arise, the appAssistant.pauseUpdates field will be set to true in that case, which causes this method to immediately return, so the current iteration of the interval will be skipped.

Next, we begin the actual processing:

```
for (var f in appAssistant.friends) {
  if (appAssistant.friends[f].monitoring) {
```

The `appAssistant.friends` field contains objects for each friend associated with the Twitter account of the user. We iterate over this list, which as a result of being stored by the Depot service is actually an object with members whose names are the IDs of a given friend. So, we can't iterate over this as an array because it in fact is *not* an array; we instead have to iterate the members of the object using the for(var in) loop variant.

For each, we check the monitoring field to see whether its value is true. This is the case if the user has selected to monitor the friend by tapping the ToggleButton on the Settings scene's List of friends. If this friend is being monitored, we have to make an AJAX request:

```
new Ajax.Request("http://twitter.com/users/show.json", {
  method : "get", evalJSON : "force",
  parameters : { id : appAssistant.friends[f].id,
    f : appAssistant.friends[f], fAttr : f },
```

This is the same kind of AJAX request we saw in the Local Business Search application, but there is one interesting thing to note here. In the callback function, we're going to need a reference to the correct friend object in the appAssistant.friends object (read that again—it actually makes sense!), but how can you get at the object later? If you simply try to access appAssistant.friends[f] in the callback, as your first inclination might be, you'll find that it doesn't work because by the time the code executes, the value of f has changed, and so you'll be messing with the wrong friend object! So, what I've done is that I've included a reference to the appropriate element in appAssistant.friends, as well as the current value of f, as parameters to the AJAX call. The Twitter API doesn't know or care about these parameters, so they are simply ignored. However, Prototype is kind enough to store this information and provide it as an attribute on the transport object passed in to the callback. This is a fairly nice, clean way to pass that information in an indirect sort of way.

■ **Note** A closure could have been used here as well, but I tend to want to avoid closures whenever possible because it's fairly easy to run into odd problems with them. I'm not *against* closures at all, just to be clear; I use them frequently. I just try to minimize their usage as much as I can, and since I had another choice in this case, I went with it.

The callback then needs to determine whether one of the specified keywords appears in the latest status (which would cause the dashboard notification as shown in Figure 6-5) using the following code.

Figure 6-5. Alert! Alert! Pay attention to me NOW!

```
onSuccess : function(inTransport) {
  var friend = inTransport.request.parameters.f;
  if (inTransport.responseJSON.status.id == friend.lastStatusID) {
    return;
  }
  friend.lastStatusID = inTransport.responseJSON.status.id;
  appAssistant.friends[inTransport.request.parameters.fAttr] = friend;
  var keywords = friend.keywords;
  if (keywords) {
    keywords = keywords.split(",");
```

```
        for (var i = 0; i < keywords.length; i++) {
          var keyword = (keywords[i].strip()).toLowerCase();
          var status = inTransport.responseJSON.status.text.toLowerCase();
          if (status.indexOf(keyword) != -1) {
            Mojo.Controller.getAppController().showBanner({
              messageText : "Alert: Tweets Flagged", soundClass : "alerts"
            }, { }, "");
            $("tdStatus").innerHTML = "<b>" +
              inTransport.responseJSON.screen_name + " (" +
              inTransport.responseJSON.status.created_at + "): </b>" +
              inTransport.responseJSON.status.text;
            this.statuses.push({
              screen_name : inTransport.responseJSON.screen_name,
              created_at : inTransport.responseJSON.status.created_at,
              text : inTransport.responseJSON.status.text
            });
            this.statusesIndex = this.statusesIndex + 1;
            break;
          }
        }
      }
    }
  }.bind(this),
```

One check needs to be performed even before keywords are scanned for, and that's to see whether this status has already been checked. If the ID of the status retrieved is the same as the lastStatusID field of the friend object, then the callback is aborted.

Assuming it's a new status, however, we then update the friend object to record this as the last status checked. Next, the keywords specified for the friend is retrieved. There may not be any, of course, so that condition is checked for, and nothing is done if there are no keywords.

If there are some, though, since the user entered a (potentially anyway) comma-separated list of keywords, we use the String's split() method to get an array of keywords. Each keyword is trimmed and converted to lowercase so we can do a case-insensitive search. For each keyword, we use the indexOf() String method to see whether it is present in the status. If it is, we use the showBanner() method to display a generic message indicating a keyword was found, as shown in Figure 6-5. Note that this banner may be overwritten by subsequent notifications if other users' statuses also contain one or more keywords (the loop is broken here, however, so this user won't be checked for further keyword matches at least).

In addition to the banner, the status is also inserted into the tdStatus cell in the Main scene. Just like with the banner, this means that if ten users are flagged during this iteration of the interval, then only the last one flagged will be displayed. However, that's where being able to tap the status test area and cycle through them comes in.

```
        onFailure : function() { }
        onException : function() { }
```

Because this is a background application, I didn't think there was a whole lot of point in trying to handle failures or exceptions; I prefer in this case that there simply is no update. I of course wouldn't object if you wanted to update the application (hint, hint!) to deal with errors some other way, at a minimum alerting the user that an error occurred via banner notification (arguably it should be this way now, but hey, I've gotta leave some room for you, dear reader, to improve things!).

Settings Scene

The Settings scene is all that remains for us to examine, and I use the term "all" here lightly because this scene by far contains the largest volume of code. We'll walk through it bit by bit, though, so I don't think it'll be too bad. ☺ First, though, feast your eyes lovingly on Figure 6-6 that shows the scene in (the first half) of its glory.

Figure 6-6. *A shot of the settings scene, part of it anyway*

The List of friends here can of course be a lot longer than what is shown in this screenshot, so the scene scrolls, and below that is a Done Button that the user taps to save all their changes.

The View HTML

The view HTML for this scene is really fairly short, as you can see in Listing 6-6. Markup-wise, this is far from a complex scene.

Listing 6-6. The Setting Scene's View HTML

```
<div class="palm-page-header">
  <div class="header-icon settings"></div>
  <div class="header-text">Twitter Monitor Settings</div>
</div>

<div class="palm-group">
  <div class="palm-group-title">Username</div>
  <div class="palm-list">
    <div class="palm-row single">
      <div class="palm-row-wrapper textfield-group"
        x-mojo-focus-highlight="true">
        <div class="title">
```

```
            <div id="settings_txtUsername" x-mojo-element="TextField"></div>
          </div>
        </div>
      </div>
    </div>
  </div>

  <div class="palm-group">
    <div class="palm-group-title">Password</div>
    <div class="palm-list">
      <div class="palm-row single">
        <div class="palm-row-wrapper textfield-group"
          x-mojo-focus-highlight="true">
          <div class="title">
            <div id="settings_txtPassword" x-mojo-element="PasswordField"></div>
          </div>
        </div>
      </div>
    </div>
  </div>

  <div x-mojo-element="Button" id="settings_btnGetFriends"></div>

  <div class="palm-group">
    <div class="palm-group-title">
      Friends
    </div>
    <div class="palm-list">
      <div id="settings_lstFriends" x-mojo-element="List"></div>
    </div>
  </div>

  <div x-mojo-element="Button" id="settings_btnDone"></div>
```

The usual header element is present, using the `palm-page-header` style class to give us the iconic settings page-type header, as opposed to the more typical general-type scene "pill" header.

After that we find the two `TextField`s, using the same sort of markup as was used in previous applications. I said two `TextField`s there, but in fact the second one is actually a `PasswordField`. This is the first time this widget has been used. For all intents and purposes, it's a `TextField`; the difference is that a `PasswordField` masks the users' input as they type. As far as defining it in the HTML, though, it's identical.

The Get Friends `Button` is below that, and this is in every way just a plain old `Button`. If you've played with the application, however, you'll know that when tapped, a `Spinner` appears on it. Interestingly, there's no mention of a `Spinner` anywhere in this markup, in contrast to where a `Spinner` was used in other applications to mask off the entire screen. In those cases, the `Spinner` appears in the markup. We'll see how it winds up on the `Button` when we look at the assistant code because, as I'm sure you've figured out by now, it's done in a programmatic way in this case.

The friends `List` is next, and once again it is using familiar markup in terms of structure and style classes.

Finally, we have the Done `Button` at the bottom, completing our examination of the scene's view HTML. All in all, it's typical and what you by now should come to expect to see in a scene of this nature.

The Scene Assistant

We begin the Settings scene's assistant with a line of code that is something new for us:

```
var appAssistant = Mojo.Controller.getAppController().assistant;
```

Recall that the app assistant has some shared code and some data fields, and those fields (and a method) are needed by this assistant as well. Rather than having to type the previous code numerous times, the reference is grabbed in placed in global scope here so that appAssistant can be referenced throughout.

■ **Note** Each stage, of any type, represents its own window, and a window corresponds to global scope. This means that global-scoped variables, such as appAssistant here, defined in code that will be executed as part of a scene on one stage, will not be accessible from code running as part of scenes on other stages. For example, if I had created a TwitterMonitor class, similar to previous applications, it would not be possible to create an instance of that class that was accessible from both the Main scene assistant and the Settings scene assistant…unless it was a member of the app assistant, which is why the shared data is on the app assistant here (and creating a TwitterMonitor class just to make it a member of the app assistant seemed superfluous to me in this case in light of that).

The first thing we find defined in the assistant is this object:

```
SettingsAssistant.prototype.models = {
  txtUsername : { value : null },
  txtPassword : { value : null },
  btnGetFriends : { label : null, disabled : null },
  lstFriends : { items : null }
};
```

This single object contains the models for the username TextField, the password PasswordField, the Get Friends Button, and the friends List. Note that the Done Button doesn't have a model here because the code will not need to manipulate it, and so the model will be inline with the call to setupWidget() later.

Setting Up the Scene

Setting up the scene in the setup() method is where we come to next, and it opens with a simple line of code:

```
appAssistant.pauseUpdates = true;
```

From earlier, you'll recall that setting this flag to true causes the periodic background processing to check for keywords in feeds to not occur. After that is the following:

```
this.controller.setupWidget(Mojo.Menu.appMenu, { },
  { items : [
    { label : "About...", command : "about-TAP" }
```

```
    ] }
);
```

An About item is added to the application menu so as to give me a chance to be vain! Following that is some setup code:

```
this.models.btnGetFriends.label = "Get Friends";
this.models.btnGetFriends.disabled = false;
```

As you'll see in a bit, there's a trick that needs to be played to make this scene work, and that trick results in this scene being shown again. However, the assistant is instantiated only once, which means that if we by chance modify the label and disabled status of the Get Friends Button (hint: that's exactly what happens!), then we need a way to reset the values; otherwise, the model values will persist the next time the scene is shown. Note that the model isn't explicitly updated here via a call to modelChanged() because the Button is effectively set up again, which negates the need to explicitly update the model here. The model is just a plain old JavaScript object until it is attached to a widget after all, so we can change values all we like before attaching it to a widget (at which point, calling modelChanged() would be necessary to get the changes up on the screen).

The next task is conceptually similar to what was just discussed:

```
if (appAssistant.tempAccountInfo) {
  this.models.txtUsername.value = appAssistant.tempAccountInfo.username;
  this.models.txtPassword.value = appAssistant.tempAccountInfo.password;
} else {
  if (appAssistant.accountInfo) {
    this.models.txtUsername.value = appAssistant.accountInfo.username;
    this.models.txtPassword.value = appAssistant.accountInfo.password;
  }
}
appAssistant.tempAccountInfo = null;
```

If the user has previously set up an account, it'd be nice if the application displayed the username, password, and friends list that they set up. However, there's an oddity here that I alluded to earlier that we can get into now.

When the user taps the Get Friends Button, assuming there are no failures, then their list of friends is retrieved, and the List would need to be updated to show them. However, the List contains some widgets, namely, a ToggleButton and a TextField for each friend. The problem we face is that setupWidget() can be called from nowhere other than the setup() method, owing to the initialization flow that webOS goes through when setting up a scene. It's a basic although frustrating limitation. So, somehow, we need to have that list of friends available when the scene is being built, which is when setup() is normally executed.

The way this is accomplished, as you'll see a bit later, is to use the swapScene() method of the stage controller. This method is essentially a combination of the popScene() and pushScene() methods. You specify a scene, the current scene is popped, and the new scene is pushed (so, you're swapping one scene for another, which is why it's named that). In this case, the Settings scene is effectively swapped for…*itself!* This results in the scene being constructed again, which means setup() is called again, which in turn means that if we've done things right, we have the list of friends to use the second time around.

The same is true of the username and password. I didn't want any changes by the user to be saved in any way until they explicitly want to by tapping the Done Button. So, the username and password are saved in the appAssistant.tempAccountInfo object. That's the reason for the branching code here: if this scene is launched and that field is null, then the scene is being shown for the first time, that is, *not* as a result of the user having tapped the Get Friend Button, in which case we take whatever values were previously saved in the appAssistant.accountInfo, if any. If appAssistant.tempAccountInfo is *not* null, though, then this is the second time this scene is shown, so we populate the TextField and PasswordField with the values just entered (but not yet persisted) by the user. At the end of that, the appAssistant.tempAccountInfo field is set to null so that the next time through, whether as part of loading friends from the Twitter account or not, things work as expected.

The same sort of logic is then applied for the friends List:

```
this.models.lstFriends.items = [ ];
if (appAssistant.tempFriends) {
  for (var i = 0; i < appAssistant.tempFriends.length; i++) {
    this.models.lstFriends.items.push(appAssistant.tempFriends[i]);
  }
} else {
  if (appAssistant.friends) {
    if (Object.isArray(appAssistant.friends)) {
      for (var i = 0; i < appAssistant.friends.length; i++) {
        this.models.lstFriends.items.push(appAssistant.friends[i]);
      }
    } else {
      for (var f in appAssistant.friends) {
        this.models.lstFriends.items.push(appAssistant.friends[f]);
      }
    }
  }
}
appAssistant.tempFriends = null;
```

The data in the appAssistant.tempFriends array will be present only when the user is in the process of changing settings, and in that case we just transfer that data into the model for the List; otherwise, the data is taken from the appAssistant.friends object, which contains the previously saved friend data.

Note that at the point where we're using the temporary friends list, it is a normal array, but the permanent list on the app controller is an object. This is a result of the way the Depot stores the information. This only really matters because it changes the method used to iterate over the friends; otherwise, the two are conceptually identical. There is, however, one other related issue to deal with, and that's the fact that the Prototype library will have added some members to the intrinsic JavaScript Array object, and as a result, the second time the user loads this scene, iterating over the members of the object will result in these new members as well. What winds up happening is that the List is rendered with some extra blank elements at the end, one for each of the members Prototype adds. To avoid this, a check is done using the isArray() method that Prototype[1] adds to the Object prototype. If this function returns true, then we iterate over the array like a normal array, which avoids accessing the Prototype-added members; otherwise, the for...in construct is used to iterate over the members of the object. It's a bit of an ugly situation, but it's a simple enough fix (and credit for it goes to my astute technical reviewer who noted this problem!).

With all of that taken care of, we can now move on to setting up the widgets:

---

[1] The irony is not lost on me that I'm solving a "problem" caused by Prototype mucking about with intrinsic JavaScript objects by using a function that Prototype adds to an intrinsic JavaScript object!

```
this.controller.setupWidget("settings_txtUsername",
  { focusMode : Mojo.Widget.focusSelectMode,
    textCase : Mojo.Widget.steModeLowerCase }, this.models.txtUsername
);

this.controller.setupWidget("settings_txtPassword",
  { focusMode : Mojo.Widget.focusSelectMode,
    textCase : Mojo.Widget.steModeLowerCase }, this.models.txtPassword
);
```

This is the same sort of setup code we've seen numerous times before, and the same is true of both of the Buttons:

```
this.controller.setupWidget("settings_btnGetFriends",
  { type : Mojo.Widget.activityButton }, this.models.btnGetFriends
);
Mojo.Event.listen(this.controller.get("settings_btnGetFriends"),
  Mojo.Event.tap, this.getFriendsTap.bind(this)
);

this.controller.setupWidget("settings_btnDone",
  { }, { label : "Done" }
);
Mojo.Event.listen(this.controller.get("settings_btnDone"), Mojo.Event.tap,
  this.doneTap.bind(this)
);
```

As mentioned earlier, the Done Button is not manipulated in any way, because the Get Friends Button is, as you'll see, so the model can be inline in that case.

The List now needs to be set up:

```
this.controller.setupWidget("settings_lstFriends", {
  itemTemplate : "settings/list-item" }, this.models.lstFriends);
for (var i = 0; i < this.models.lstFriends.items.length; i++) {
  this.controller.setupWidget(
    "tglFriends_" + this.models.lstFriends.items[i].username,
    { modelProperty : "monitoring" }, this.models.lstFriends.items[i]
  );
  this.controller.setupWidget(
    "txtKeywords_" + this.models.lstFriends.items[i].username,
    { focusMode : Mojo.Widget.focusSelectMode, modelProperty : "keywords",
      textCase : Mojo.Widget.steModeLowerCase },
    this.models.lstFriends.items[i]
  );
}
```

Here we have something new! The List itself is set up by that first line of code and is completely typical of the List setups we've seen in the past. What's new is what comes after that. Earlier I said that the List contains widgets, a ToggleButton and a TextField for each friend. Being widgets, and widgets we need to get data from, they need to have models attached to them, as well as a configuration attributes object. So, we iterate over the items array in the model for the List, and for each element we make two setupWidget() calls: the first to set up the ToggleButton and the second to set up the TextField. Each of these is given an ID in the form tglFriends_xxx and txtKeywords_xxx, where xxx is the username of the friend. This ensures each widget has a unique ID, which allows the setupWidget() method to be used on each one.

The actual setup is all pretty ordinary, except that the modelProperty configuration attribute is used for both. Recall that by default most widgets get the values from a value attribute in the model. The modelProperty configuration option allows us to specify a different model attribute to get the value from. This is necessary because, if you look carefully, you'll notice that both the ToggleButton and the TextField use the same model. This works perfectly well save for the fact that both would by default use the value attribute, which would obviously be bad! By specifying different attribute names for each widget, sharing the model object can be made to work.

■ **Note** Why share the model objects at all? I hear you ask. Simply put, it makes the code simpler. The objects in the items array of the List are objects that contain all the information about a given friend, and they are what are saved to the Depot. In other words, they contain all the information we need when constructing the List, so it makes sense to use them in the model. The alternative would have been moving data around between various objects just to avoid this sharing, in other words, one version of the object that gets stored in the Depot, then another with just a subset of the data for the List, then another two—one for each of the models for the ToggleButton and TextField, not to mention all the extra code to move data around between them! No, sharing the objects I think is a far more elegant approach, once you get past the conflicting default attribute name issue.

The List Template

As you well know by now, a List, like that shown in Figure 6-7, requires a template to render each item in it.

Figure 6-7. Friends: we all need 'em!

Listing 6-7 shows that template.

Listing 6-7. The `list-item.html` *Template File for the* `List`

```
<div class="palm-row" class="cssSettingsFriend">
  <div class="palm-row-wrapper">
    <div class="title">
      <table border="0" cellpadding="0" cellspacing="0" width="100%">
        <tr>
          <td>#{username}</td>
          <td><div x-mojo-element="ToggleButton"
            id="tglFriends_#{username}"></div></td>
        </tr>
        <tr>
          <td colspan="2">
            <div class="textfield-group" x-mojo-focus-highlight="true">
              <div class="title">
                <div class="label" class="cssSettingsKeywords">Keywords</div>
                <div id="settings_txtKeywords_#{username}"
                  x-mojo-element="TextField"></div>
              </div>
            </div>
          </td>
        </tr>
      </table>
    </div>
  </div>
</div>
```

The usual markup with the usual styling wraps the actual content, with one exception: the `cssSettingsFriend` class applied to the outer `<div>`. This class defines the height of a given row and is set such that all of the content fits nicely.

The content itself is a bit more complex this time out because a table is used to make the layout work. Still, at the end of the day, it's just plain old HTML, so no big deal, I dare say! You can see how the IDs of the `ToggleButton` and `TextFields` are set here such that they can be addressed as we saw in the `setup()` method a few pages ago.

Cleaning Up After Ourselves

Recall that when the scene was set up, the background monitoring work was paused by setting `appAssistant.pauseUpdates` to true. Well:

```
SettingsAssistant.prototype.cleanup = function() {
  appAssistant.pauseUpdates = false;
};
```

The `cleanup()` method of a scene assistant fires when the scene is popped and gives the application a chance to do any sort of cleanup work that is required. This makes it an ideal place to resume that background processing since this will execute regardless of how the scene goes away, be it automatically when the Done `Button` is tapped or when the user flicks it away.

Getting Friends List from Twitter, Part I

The next thing we'll discuss is the first part of getting the list of friends from the Twitter account, and this occurs when the Get Friends Button is clicked. This is handled in the getFriendsTap() method that was attached to the Button as the Mojo.Event.tap handler:

```
SettingsAssistant.prototype.getFriendsTap = function() {

  this.models.btnGetFriends.label = "Working, Please Wait...";
  this.models.btnGetFriends.disabled = true;
  this.controller.modelChanged(this.models.btnGetFriends);
  this.controller.get("settings_btnGetFriends").mojo.activate();

  appAssistant.checkConnectivity(this,
    this.verifyAccount.bind(this),
    function() {
      this.resetButton();
      Mojo.Controller.errorDialog("Internet connectivity not available");
    }.bind(this)
  );

};
```

First we need to deal with that Get Friends Button. If you've played with the app, you already know that when clicked, the Button gets disabled (to keep the user from triggering the AJAX call twice), and it also gets a Spinner on it. Changing the label and disabling it is a simple matter of updating its model, but the Spinner is something new. As it happens, all it takes is a call to the mojo.activate() method of the Button, which we obtain a reference to by using the scene controller's get() method. You see, *all* Buttons intrinsically have the ability to show a Spinner like this, and all it takes is that call to mojo.activate() to start it and then mojo.deactivate() later to stop it. Pretty cool, eh?

Once the Button is modified, we use the checkConnectivity() method exposed on the app assistant to make sure Internet connectivity is available. The callback function is the verifyAccount() method of this same scene assistant. If connectivity isn't available, then two things need to happen. First, the Get Friends Button needs to be restored to its initial state, and the handy resetButton() method does that:

```
SettingsAssistant.prototype.resetButton = function() {

  this.models.btnGetFriends.label = "Get Friends";
  this.models.btnGetFriends.disabled = false;
  this.controller.modelChanged(this.models.btnGetFriends);
  this.controller.get("settings_btnGetFriends").mojo.deactivate();

};
```

As you can see, it's literally just reversing what was done to start the getFriendsTap() method in terms of the label, the disabled state, and the Spinner being turned off. Finally, after the Button is restored, a standard error dialog box is shown to inform the user that they're boned because the Internet isn't there...<HomerSimpsonVoice>Oh my, wherever did it go?!?</HomerSimpsonVoice>.

Verifying the Twitter Account

After Internet connectivity is confirmed, we begin a two-step process consisting of first verifying the Twitter account is valid and then getting the list of fiends. The verifyAccount() method is the first part of that equation:

```
SettingsAssistant.prototype.verifyAccount = function() {

  new Ajax.Request(
    "http://twitter.com/account/verify_credentials.json",
    {
      method : "get", evalJSON : "force",
      requestHeaders : {
        Authorization : "Basic " + Base64.encode(
          this.models.txtUsername.value + ':' + this.models.txtPassword.value
        )
      },

      onSuccess : function(inTransport) {
        appAssistant.tempAccountInfo = {
          username : this.models.txtUsername.value,
          password : this.models.txtPassword.value
        };
        appAssistant.tempFriends = [ ];
        this.getFriends(-1);
      }.bind(this),

      onFailure : function(inTransport) {
        this.resetButton();
        Mojo.Controller.errorDialog("Unable to verify account.  " +
          "Please check entered credentials and try again."
        );
      }.bind(this),

      onException : function(inTransport, inException) {
        Mojo.Controller.errorDialog("EXCEPTION: " + inException);
      }.bind(this)

    }
  );

};
```

The verify_credentials Twitter API method that was described earlier is used for this purpose. The requestHeaders object contains the basic auth Authorization header. To construct the value of this attribute properly, we grab the username and password that the user has entered and concatenate that together, separated by a colon, with the string BASIC before it. The username and password are Base64-encoded using the Base64 class's encode() method.

The onFailure and onException callbacks are pretty basic and I suspect don't need much in the way of explanation, but the onSuccess callback is where the action is. In this callback, the username and password values are set in the tempAccountInfo object so that when this scene is reshown (which is coming up shortly!), the username and password fields will be populated from this object. Also, the tempFriends array is cleared, and then the getFriends() method is called. Note that this method is passed a value of –1. We'll come back to that soon.

Actually, we'll come back to that now.

Getting Friends List from Twitter Part II: The Sequel!

The getFriends() method will wind up, potentially at least, being called multiple times recursively. The code for this method is as follows:

```
SettingsAssistant.prototype.getFriends = function(inCursor) {

  new Ajax.Request(
    "http://twitter.com/statuses/friends.json",
    {
      method : "get", evalJSON : "force",
      parameters : { id : this.models.txtUsername.value, cursor : inCursor },

      onSuccess : function(inTransport) {
        for (var i = 0; i < inTransport.responseJSON.users.length; i++) {
          appAssistant.tempFriends.push({
            id : inTransport.responseJSON.users[i].id,
            username : inTransport.responseJSON.users[i].screen_name,
            keywords : "", lastStatusID : null, monitoring : false
          });
        }
        if (inTransport.responseJSON.next_cursor != 0) {
          this.getFriends(inTransport.responseJSON.next_cursor);
        } else {
          Mojo.Controller.stageController.swapScene("settings");
        }
      }.bind(this),

      onFailure : function(inTransport) {
        this.resetButton();
        Mojo.Controller.errorDialog("Unable to get friends list: " +
          inTranspot.responseText);
      }.bind(this),

      onException : function(inTransport, inException) {
        Mojo.Controller.errorDialog("EXCEPTION: " + inException);
      }.bind(this)

    }
  );

};
```

The Twitter API's friends method is what we use here, and as you'll recall from earlier, this method by default returns 100 friends. However, there could be quite a bit more, which is where the inCursor parameter comes into play. A value of –1 tells the API to return the first 100 friends, if there even are that many. The method looks for a cursor parameter with this value, as well as an id value that is the username we want friends for, so it's what the user entered here, of course.

The onSuccess callback then takes the list of users that was returned and for each constructs a simple object containing the id, username (corresponding to the returned screen_name field), keywords (initially none), lastStatusID (null initially to indicate none has yet been retrieved), and a flag monitoring to determine whether the friend is being monitored.

Once that's done, the next_cursor attribute of the response object is examined. If this field has a value of anything other than zero, that means there are more friends to retrieved, in which case getFriends() is called again, passing the value of next_cursor into it. The whole cycle repeats until no more friends are left to retrieve.

When that end condition occurs, that's where that trick I talked about earlier comes into play: the stage controller's swapScene() method is used to swap this scene out for itself. This effectively reloads the scene, meaning setup() executes again too. At this point, the tempAccountInfo and tempFriends fields have data in them, so setup() will update the models of the widgets from that data instead of the persisted versions hanging off the app controller, so to the user, it just looks like the scene has refreshed with the friends list (they will see a very quick transition, which actually could be done away with if you wanted, but I saw no real need…it kinda looked cool to me the way it is).

Saving Changes

The next method we find in the scene assistant is the tap handler for the Done Button:

```
SettingsAssistant.prototype.doneTap = function(inReshow) {

  appAssistant.accountInfo = {
    username : this.models.txtUsername.value,
    password : this.models.txtPassword.value
  };
  appAssistant.depot.simpleAdd("accountInfo",
    appAssistant.accountInfo, function() { },
    function(inTransaction, inResult) { }
  );

  appAssistant.friends = [ ];
  for (var i = 0; i < this.models.lstFriends.items.length; i++) {
    appAssistant.friends.push(this.models.lstFriends.items[i]);
  }
  appAssistant.depot.simpleAdd("friends",
    appAssistant.friends, function() {
      Mojo.Controller.getAppController().closeStage("settingsStage");
    },
    function(inTransaction, inResult) { }
  );

};
```

There's not really much to this: first, the persistent version of the tempAccountInfo object that hangs off the app controller is updated with the data from the temporary version on this scene assistant. Next, this object is stored in the Depot using the familiar simpleAdd() method. Next, the same thing is done for the list of friends: the data is copied from the model of the List to the friends array on the app controller. Finally, in the callback for the second simpleAdd() call, the stage is closed by calling the closeStage() method of the app controller. This method requires the name of the stage to close since there can (and in this application, there is) more than one open at a time.

Handling Application Menu Commands

The last thing to look at in this application is the code that handles application menu taps. The only thing available is the About dialog box, as shown in Figure 6-8.

Figure 6-8. *The boring old About box alert*

To handle this, we have the typical handleCommand() method floating around:

```
SettingsAssistant.prototype.handleCommand = function(inEvent) {

  switch (inEvent.type) {
    case Mojo.Event.command:
      switch (inEvent.command) {
        case "about-TAP":
          this.controller.showAlertDialog({
            onChoose : function(inValue) {},
            title : "Twitter Monitor v1.0",
            message : "From the book " +
              "'Practical webOS Projects With the Palm Pre' " +
              "(Apress, 2009, ISBN-13: 978-1-4302-2674-1). " +
              "Copyright 2009 Frank W. Zammetti. All rights reserved. " +
              "A product of Etherient: http://www.etherient.com",
            choices : [
              { label : "Ok", value : "" }
            ]
          });
        break;
      }
```

```
    break;
  }

};
```

The code here is pretty much identical to what we've had in other applications, so I won't go into any lengthy explanation.

Suggested Exercises

Since this application wasn't intended to be a full-fledged Twitter client, there perhaps aren't as many suggested exercises as there might otherwise be. However, as usual, I have a few for you to consider:

- You may have noticed that each time you shut down the application, the list of statuses that were flagged is blown away. Although this makes the code simpler and *sort of* makes sense to the extent that Twitter by its nature is meant to be transient (in other words, a friends' status is expected to change frequently), that's probably not ideal. What would probably be better is if statuses flagged were stored in the database and the user had a way to clear them. So, how about doing that? Push each status update onto an array, and save that array to the depot. Then, perhaps on the Settings scene, provide a button to clear the status "log," as you might call it at that point. That way, the user can cycle through all flagged statuses until they explicitly clear the log.

- Add code to highlight the keywords that caused a status to be flagged. I suggest just changing the color, perhaps to red, when displayed. That way, you won't run into any size issues (for example, if you made the text bold, it could conceivably be too large and get truncated at the bottom).

- Allow for multiple Twitter accounts. Although I suspect most people only have one, there could be some use cases where someone wants to be able to work with more than one.

You could, if you really wanted to, add the ability to post a status update yourself. That would move this application toward being a full-fledged Twitter client, and if that's a direction you wanted to go, then this would probably be the logical first step to take.

Summary

In this chapter, we learned how to build background applications by creating a dashboard stage so our application could run unobtrusively while we do other work. In the process we saw how to explicitly create stages and deal with multiple stages in a single application. We saw the ToggleButton widget in action, and we played a bit with putting a Spinner on a Button, a variation on the theme we've seen in previous applications. We worked a little more with web services, this time provided by Twitter, so the idea of working in the cloud was expanded a bit from the previous chapter.

In the next chapter, we'll build what will be the most complex application so far: a tool for managing and tracking projects. We'll see some server-side coding as well and learn how to effectively interact with it from the Pre. It will prove to be a nice culmination of everything you've learned about to this point, so get ready for an exciting ride!

■ ■ ■

CHAPTER 7

Project Management for All: Time Tracker

A Multiuser Project Management/Time-Tracking Application on the Go

I don't like to mince words, so here goes: I hate project management! To me, it's a rather dull endeavor. It's a lot of time spent bugging people on the phone asking them what they've accomplished since the last time I bugged them (Scrum[1] methodologies excepted, which I can say from experience make it all a fair bit easier to swallow). It is, generally speaking, a lot of time spent writing status reports for stakeholders and explaining why this is late or why that is taking longer than anticipated, and so on.

Given all that, project management is an absolutely necessary evil, and I respect those who do the job. It isn't easy and requires great skill to do well (and you pretty well always know when it's *not* done well!). Although project management, for me at least, isn't the most exciting job imaginable, I see no reason not to make the chore as fun as possible when you've got to do it!

So, the goal of this chapter is to create a basic project management and time-tracking application. In the process we'll deal with some interesting new problems related to remote data services, concurrency, and connectivity concerns. We'll play with a few new bits of Mojo and webOS, and in the end, you'll wind up with a useful tool (albeit not quite on par with Microsoft Project) for tracking the status of a project in at least a rudimentary way.

What's This App Do Anyway?

Microsoft Project is one of the top tools in use today for project management. This feature-rich program tracks projects, tasks that are part of that project, resources assigned to the project, and much more. It provides numerous views of the project, including Gantt[2] charts. It allows you to perform resource leveling[3] and create critical path schedules[4] as well as critical chain[5] and event chain methodology[6] (by way of add-ons).

---

[1] Scrum is an iterative project methodology that is considered an Agile methodology for running a project. Scrum utilizes the concepts of *sprints*, that is, short (two- to four-week) mini-development cycles. Product owners prioritize the stories, which roughly equate to features, that they want implemented in each sprint. After each sprint, useful functionality should be delivered, even if it is only a small piece of the whole set of requirements.

[2] A Gantt chart is a specialized type of bar chart that graphically describes a project's schedule. It provides an at-a-glance summary of a project's status in a visual way (for those who can make sense of them!).

[3] *Resource leveling* is a project management task focused on resolving conflicts that arise from tasks running in parallel that may contend for resources, resources that are over-allocated, or other sorts of resource allocation imbalances that can occur during project planning.

If all this is foreign to you, count your blessings! Project management is actually an expansive area and a study that requires lots of, well, *study*, to master. I am in no way, shape, or form an accomplished project manager (PM for short), although I know the basics, and what little bit you've read here certainly doesn't qualify you to be a PM of a project, but it *is* enough to give a context for the application.

Fortunately, for the purposes of this book, these sorts of basics are all we need to worry about, and in fact we'll only be dealing with the most basic of basics! Managing a project boils down to three essential things: the project itself (obviously), the tasks that make up the project, and the resources (people, usually) assigned to the tasks. With these basics in mind, we can begin to outline what this application needs to do:

- The user should be able to create any number of projects. For each we should be able to specify a name, a starting date, a target ending date, and the PM for the project.

- We should be able to create tasks and allocate them to projects. To make things simple to implement, any given task can be associated with only a single project. (In real life, you might have tasks that are associated with multiple projects, but as far as using this application goes, it's not such a burden to have to create two copies of the same underlying task to manage, even if that strategy isn't quite ideal.) For each task, we should be able to specify a name, a starting date, a target ending date, the number of hours allocated to the task, and the resource assigned to work on it.

- We should be able to create resources and assign them to tasks. Let's make another simplifying assumption here: a task can be worked on by a single resource only. This again isn't ideal or necessarily reflective of the real world, although I'd point out that some PMs believe this should in fact be the way it's done! For a resource, we can specify a name and designate the resource as a PM (so they can be the PM of projects being tracked).

- We should be able to delete projects, resources, and tasks as needed.

- We should be able to modify projects, tasks, and resources as well. Pretty much everything can be modified except for the name, which we'll be using as a key for all three items.

- We should be able to book time against a task for a given resource.

- For projects, tasks, and resources, there will be a summary view that gives us the most pertinent information about each entity at a glance.

---

[4] The *critical path* is a mathematical algorithm used to schedule a set of tasks within a project. More often than not, though, you hear people talk about the critical path of a project in the context of the linear set of tasks that must be completed for a project to reach a successful conclusion.

[5] The *critical chain approach* puts more of an emphasis on resources than on tasks and rigid schedules, as is the case with the critical path approach.

[6] The *event chain methodology* focuses more on the events that occur during the lifetime of a project more so than on tasks and resources. This approach allows for a less rigid schedule that provides more flexibility to deal with uncertainty and the inevitable changes that occur as a project progresses.

- This application will use a remote service to store its data. We'll code this server-side component ourselves and will host it on Google App Engine, a cloud-based hosting environment provided by Google.

- Being a cloud-based application, we'll allow for multiple users. That way, PMs can track the time resources booked against tasks. However, we'll put some constraints on who can do what in order to handle concurrency concerns as a result of the underlying design of the application.

- However, since the remote service could be down at any point in time, the application should be at least somewhat fail-safe, so we'll utilize a local HTML5-based database to warehouse data updates on a given device when the remote service isn't available, and we'll synchronize those changes with the remote data store in the background when it's available again.

As you can see, the basics are covered fairly well, and you can actually track work with this application, although it admittedly doesn't hold a candle to Microsoft Project.

Before we can really start tearing into the code for this application, we have to discuss this Google App Engine thing I mentioned earlier, and in fact, the server-side code will be the first thing we look at.

■ **Note** The server-side portion of this application is written in Java. If you aren't familiar with Java, don't fret, because I've tried to make the code as gentle and easy to follow as possible, even if you've never seen Java before. At the end of the day, you're here to learn about webOS, not Java and server-side coding, so although I'll walk through a representative portion of the Java code, enough for you to get a good picture of what it's all about, I won't go into it in exquisite detail.

Google App Engine: Life in the Cloud(s) Is Good!

So far in this book, all the applications have fallen into two categories—two *paradigms*, if you will: either an application runs on the Pre all by itself without connection to the outside world with just local data stores or it uses some web services provided to the public at large by outside vendors to get (and maybe even store) data. Although you can build some really cool stuff using one of these two paradigms, being able to use a server-side component that you design and code gives you a lot more power and flexibility. You can offload processing to the server as needed, you can store data in any way you see fit on the server, and you can provide a remote API that your webOS-based application can make use of to interact with those processing and data storage facilities.

However, not everyone has a server infrastructure on which to host the application, in other words, a place for that server-side code to run and be accessible to the webOS application. Application hosting like this typically costs money, requires management capabilities by you, and in most organizations represents a whole class of employees who are dedicated to such issues.

Your friendly neighborhood search giant, Google, saw these problems and decided that something needed to be done about it. That's where the Google App Engine, heretofore abbreviated as GAE, comes from. GAE is an application-hosting environment that lets you worry about your application and your code, not the infrastructure it runs on. What's better, using GAE is free—at least to some degree!

GAE provides to you a full dynamic web serving environment using common web technologies such as Python and Java-based code. It provides a persistent data storage mechanism including features such as sorting, queries, and transactions. GAE also gives you e-mail sending capabilities as well as a security infrastructure to authenticate and authorize users as you see fit. For the most part, there are few limitations placed on what your application can or can't do, but there are a few. Most notably, you cannot spawn background threads, you cannot write to the local file system, and there are requirements for how fast any given request is serviced. For example, if a response to an incoming request isn't provided by your code within 30 seconds, GAE will step in and stop the processing. This ensures no runaway processes chew up server resources because of bad code.

YOUR FIRST FORAY INTO "CLOUD COMPUTING"

For many, including me frankly, this application will represent your first development exposure to cloud computing in a somewhat substantial way.

Simply stated, the term *cloud computing* refers to a new model for application deployment where the underlying technical infrastructure that hosts your application code is abstracted away from you and where resources that make up that infrastructure are virtualized and scalable without direct interaction by you or your application. In other words, it's a "resources on demand" kind of model.

You can look at this as being akin to the utility model you enjoy from your electricity or water supplier: the more stuff you plug in at your house, the more electricity is pulled in off the grid for your usage (although you'll have to pay for the extra usage later), and you don't care how the extra electricity gets to you or from where. There's a shared pool of resources that applications can draw from, and because the underlying implementation of the infrastructure (vis-a-vis servers, storage, and networks) is abstracted away from you, it's a completely separate concern.

Cloud computing also refers to remote data and function providers that a locally running application can interact with. Your data no longer lives on an individual device but lives out "in the cloud" and is accessible from anywhere, any device. The application in this chapter has characteristics of both of these components of cloud computing.

The infrastructure supports load balancing so that your app isn't bogged down when the load increases. Speaking of load, GAE also supports scaling. So, let's say you create the next uber-hit Facebook game and host it in the GAE. At first, a few people play. Then a few more play. Then word of mouth really gets your game in the public consciousness, and all of a sudden you have millions of people playing. Guess what? GAE will automatically scale your application in terms of running it across more servers and load-balancing across them so that your application will be able to handle this sudden increase in demand. Yes, you'll pay for that increase to be sure, but it's nice that you don't have to worry about it yourself; it'll just happen!

Speaking of paying, I said early on that using GAE was free, and that is true to an extent. You can sign up for GAE and run applications in it (up to ten) without paying a dime! Google gives you a fairly generous allotment of CPU usage, storage, bandwidth, and other considerations at no cost. Once you pass some thresholds, you'll have to start paying, of course, but it's very nice that you can start hosting an application and build it up, including the traffic to it, without having to make a financial investment up front.

■ **Note** For the purposes of this book, the free hosting that GAE provides is far more than enough for our purposes: 1GB of data storage, 1GB of bandwidth per day, and a decent helping of CPU time. In fact, during the entire development cycle, the logs showed that the application had used zero CPU time, zero storage, and zero bandwidth because the actual amount used was so low it got rounded down to zero! However, if the usage were to somehow jump astronomically, the application would shut off when it hit the free quota limits and would become available again at a later time when the quota time period elapsed. So, there's no fear of suddenly getting a $40,000 bill in the mail from Google!

As mentioned, GAE allows you to run Python or Java-based applications, and the choice is just a personal preference kind of thing. I've chosen to go with Java because it's what I work in all day long, so I know it best. Have no fear, though, if you're not a Java guru; the code we're going to write here is fairly simple, and I've tried to write it in such a way that even people with no Java experience can follow it. That means I haven't always done things in the most efficient way possible; I was more concerned with simplicity and readability. So, if you're an expert in Java, don't go too nuts if you notice things that you might not have done the way I have; there's probably some things that even I wouldn't have done the way I did for real! That being said, the server side of this application really isn't all that involved anyway, and it all begins with defining the remote API that the webOS application on the Pre will interact with.

Getting Started with GAE

To work with GAE, you need two things. The first is the GAE SDK, and the second is a GAE account.

You can download the SDK here: `http://code.google.com/appengine`. The SDK gives you the command-line tools you need to develop GAE applications and run them in a full-featured local version of GAE. That way, you can develop your application, test it, and get it working just how you want before you even upload it to the real GAE.

When you go to the download page, you'll have a choice of downloads for multiple platforms (Windows, Mac, and Linux), and you'll also be able to choose between Python and Java support.

Before you rush off and start downloading anything, though, I need to tell you that there is also a GAE plug-in for Eclipse available, and that is in fact what you should go and download. Since we've been doing all our webOS development in Eclipse thus far, it makes sense to do the same for our GAE-based code too. You'll find a link to the plug-in's download location at the same URL as the other SDK downloads, and you install the plug-in like any other: point Eclipse to the appropriate URL, and use the Install New Software function in Eclipse.

From this point on, I'm going to assume that you've installed the plug-in. In that case, the next step is to sign up for a GAE account. You can do this at the previously mentioned URL as well. If you already have an account with Google, say for Gmail, you'll simply link that account to GAE, and you're good to go. If you need to create a new account, that's very simple too; all the information you need is at the mentioned location. As with the plug-in, I'll from here on out assume you have an account set up and ready to go.

The first thing you'll probably want to do is to create a simple application and try it. To do so, select the New option in the File menu in Eclipse and then select Other. With the plug-in installed, you should see a Google group there that you can expand and in which you'll find an option Web Application Project. Select that, and you'll see the dialog box shown in Figure 7-1.

Figure 7-1. *The GAE new project wizard*

Give the project any name you'd like, and enter a package. If you are new to Java, a *package* is just a way to group *classes*, which are the units of code that make up your application. This package is typically in the form com.xxx.yyy, a reverse form of an Internet domain, such as com.etherient.wostimetracker, for example. This isn't a requirement though; you can put anything you like here (it's probably easiest to just make it the same thing as the title of the application).

Be sure the option to create a new project in the workspace is selected, and then deselect the Use Google Web Toolkit option. Google Web Toolkit is an application framework that is 100 percent optional when developing a GAE application, and in the case of this application, it's completely unnecessary. However, ensure that the option User Google App Engine is selected, and also ensure the Use default SDK option is selected.

Once that's all done, click Finish, and a basic, yet completely working web application will be created. To see it in action, right-click the project in the Navigator or Project Explorer pane, whichever you happen to have open; select Run As; and then select Web Application. If you have the Console pane open, you should see a message indicating that the server is running. Assuming you do, pop open your favorite web browser and load up the URL http://127.0.0.1:8080/. You should see a page that looks like Figure 7-2.

Figure 7-2. *The new project's start page*

Click the name of the project you created, GAETest in my case, and you'll see a new page that just says "Hello, world." This proves that the application is fully functional and running on your local server.

■ **Note**   The URL that is shown in the Console pane doesn't seem to be correct; at least, it doesn't work on my machine. I played around with host file setting, and nothing I did seemed to work, except for using the local loopback IP address (127.0.0.1) as the URL. Your mileage may vary, but at least the URL I show here should work regardless.

The next step is to put that application out in the GAE and see it work there. This too is a simple process. First, right-click the project again and look for the Google menu item. Select it and then select Deploy to App Engine. This should result in the dialog box in Figure 7-3.

Figure 7-3. *Getting ready to deploy to the GAE*

As you can see, there's a problem to be resolved. Any application you deploy the GAE needs to have an ID assigned to it. To do so, click the link as directed by the dialog box text, and you'll find a text field where you can enter an ID. When you're done doing that, the dialog box will reappear, sans the error message, and you'll be able to deploy the application. You'll need to enter your password each time, but once you do, the deployment itself shouldn't take more than a few seconds. Once it indicates the deployment has succeeded, you'll be able to access your application out on the Internet. The address you use will be in the form `http://xxx.appspot.com/xxx` where xxx is the ID you assigned to the application.

Once that's done, you can access the GAE administration console, which you can find a link for at the previously mentioned URL. There you can manage your applications, as you can see in Figure 7-4.

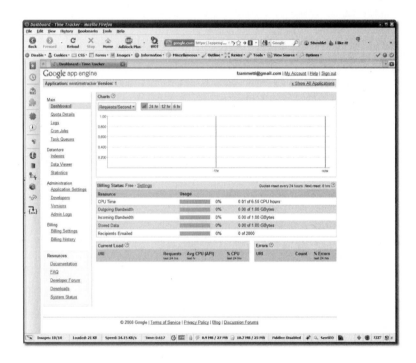

Figure 7-4. *The GAE administration console*

Note that you are limited to ten applications at a time, so you may want to delete this little test application once you're done playing with it.

At this point, you have all the tools you need to develop applications bound for the GAE, including the server side of the Time Tracker application. Speaking of which, let's start thinking a bit about what that code is going to look like, beginning with the API that will be exposed to the webOS-based client portion of the application.

▓ **Note**   As you can tell from these screenshots, I have the server side of Time Tracker running in the GAE engine already, so barring any unforeseen problems, you can in fact just run the application right "out of the box" without having to deploy anything yourself. I'm using the free hosting, though, so if this book sells well…and of course it will because I have two children who need to go to college someday…you may find that the application has blown past its free allotments and isn't available. But, at least in that case you now know how to deploy it yourself!

Defining the API: Let's Take a REST

In the previous chapter, the topic of RESTful web services was introduced as we interacted with the services supplied by Twitter. Since REST is all the rage these days, I figure this project should use that same paradigm. As a reminder, a remote API, which is what we're talking about creating here, can be done in any number of ways; there's no right or wrong answer to it. However, when you're talking about a JavaScript-based client, which is what a webOS application is, after all, there are some good arguments to be made that a REST-based interface coupled with JSON is a natural fit.

Using an existing RESTful API is one thing, but designing our own is another. One of the beauties of REST, however, is that the API is, by and large, defined for us: if you follow the typical pattern, there is little guesswork.

So, we begin to define the interface by defining the entities we're going to deal with since, for the most part, a REST API works on entities. In this project, there are three obvious entities: projects, tasks, and resources. A project is broken up into tasks, and a task is worked on by a resource,[7] a person in other words. If we stick with the usual mapping used in REST, then we come up with a series of URL mappings and HTTP methods, as shown in Table 7-1.

Table 7-1. *The REST API Mappings for a Project*

URL	HTTP Method	Operation
*/project	POST	Creates a new project
*/project/xxx	PUT	Updates an existing project identified by xxx
*/project/xxx	GET	Gets a project identified by xxx (xxx can be all, which gets us all projects)
*/project/xxx	DELETE	Deletes a project identified by xxx

In the table I've only shown the mappings for projects, but simply replace project in the URL with task or resource, and you have the operations for those entities as well. The portion of the URL before

___

[7] Resources in project management circles don't *have* to be people, but usually that's what *resource* means. Some argue that consultants aren't, or at least shouldn't be considered, people. I've known a few consultants who I wouldn't consider people, more like wastes of protoplasm and air…that certainly doesn't apply to *all* consultants, so I leave determining the truth of this conjecture to you!

the type of entity being dealt with is the same for all operations as is dependent on where and how the API is hosted. We'll see this URL "base" in the code to come.

Now, it should be obvious that for the project creation and update operations there will be more data to be transmitted. For all the rest, the only data necessary is in the URL, but for those two, it isn't. How this data is transmitted is up to the designer of the API. Some choose to send JSON, and that's perfectly valid. I've chosen instead to use plain old request parameters. The reason is that even though dealing with JSON on the server isn't difficult, it does require some effort. Since I can't assume that you know Java well, I decided to try to make the code as simple as possible, which means basic request parameters, since that's *very* simple to work with. Since the create method uses the POST HTTP method and update uses the PUT[8] method, we have to use the POST (or PUT) body to pass the parameters rather than as part of a query string on the URL.

Now that we understand the API we're going to build, let's jump into the server-side code that implements it.

■ **Note**   This isn't 100 percent perfect REST because getting all entities of a type should really just be `/project/` using a GET, but I've used the `all` string after that for this purpose. I've done this because it eliminates a little bit of code on the server side, just to make life a little easier.

The Server-Side Code

Again, my goal here is to present the code generally, assuming you aren't really familiar with Java. That being said, I will necessarily gloss over some details to try to keep you focused on the important details. I unfortunately can't teach you Java from the ground up, but I've written the code in such a way that even if you don't understand every last statement, you can still follow the overall flow, which is the important bit to grok.[9]

One DTO As an Example: Project

In Java, programs are constructed by building classes. A class is just a unit of code, in simplest terms. The first such class we're going to be looking at is what is known as a *data transfer object* (DTO). It's a simple class that contains some data fields and setter and getter methods, which are functions that are used to manipulate the data fields.

```
package com.etherient.timetracker;
```

Every class in Java gets put into a package as previously described. Next, any other classes that this class needs to use are *imported*, or made available to the code:

```
import java.util.Date;
```

---

[8] Well, it *should* use PUT, but it doesn't, for a good reason as we'll see. None of this discussion is invalidated by this fact, however, but it's good to know nonetheless.

[9] Because I'm under the misguided impression that women can be impressed by the books you've read, I'm of course here referring to Robert A. Heinlein's coining of the term *grok* in his 1961 book *Stranger in a Strange Land*. I am *not* referring to the popular geek usage of this term. No, absolutely not, why would I? I'm cool, not at all a geek! Now please, can I have your phone number, pretty please??

```
import javax.jdo.annotations.IdentityType;
import javax.jdo.annotations.PersistenceCapable;
import javax.jdo.annotations.Persistent;
import javax.jdo.annotations.PrimaryKey;
```

The Date object in the java.util package comes with the Java JDK and represents a date. The rest of the imports are classes from the javax.jdo.annotations package and will be discussed shortly, but take note of the jdo portion of the package name.

JDO, which stands for *Java data objects*, is a method for accessing data in a database that lets you treat that data like Java objects (instances of classes). It keeps you from having to manually create the database and its structure. You simply say, "I want to store this object that represents a bank account," and JDO figures out how to construct the database to store that data.

Annotations are a way in Java to add information to your class that isn't strictly speaking code. You can annotate parts of your code using annotations, and the Java compiler and runtime knows what those annotations mean and how to react to them. It's similar in concept to wrapping text in a <b> tag in HTML. The browser knows to make that text bold because you've annotated it as such.

So, when we combine the notion of JDO with annotations, we can begin to do things like this:

```
@PersistenceCapable(identityType = IdentityType.APPLICATION)
public class Project {
```

Annotations begin with an at sign and are then followed with the name of the annotations (notice that PersistenceCapable is one of the classes we imported…as it happens, annotations in Java are just a special kind of class). The annotation is in most cases placed above some line of code that it is meant to annotate. Here, the annotation is saying that this class can be persisted, that is, stored in the database using JDO. The extra information in the parentheses tells JDO something about the class; in this case, it tells it what kind of identity, or *key*, to use. The IdentityType.APPLICATION tells JDO that our application code will determine the key for any object stored in the database (you can also let JDO do this for you automatically).

Next, we define a couple of data fields, akin to the data fields we define all the time in JavaScript classes:

```
@Persistent
@PrimaryKey
private String name;

@Persistent
private Date startDate;

@Persistent
private Date targetDate;

@Persistent
private String projectManager;
```

Each of these fields has a @Persistent annotation on it, which tells JDO that they are to be stored with the object in the database (not having this annotation means the field can have data while in memory, but it will not be saved to the database). The first field, name, is also annotated with a @PrimaryKey annotation (multiple annotations are perfectly fine). This tells JDO that the name field will be the unique key for any object stored.

Each field here is given a visibility, all private, which means that those fields can be accessed only from code within this class. They also all have a type defined, with two Strings and two Dates. (Note that

Date here is java.util.Date. Once you import a class in Java, you can refer to it by its name alone; otherwise, you have to type java.util.Date everywhere.)

So, how would code outside this class gain access to these fields? This is where those getter and setter[10] methods I mentioned earlier come from. Let's look at those methods for the name field:

```java
public void setName(final String inName) {
  this.name = inName;
}
public String getName() {
  return this.name;
}
```

These methods are public, which means any other class can call them. The first, the setter, is what sets a value into the name field. It takes in as an argument a String called inName. It then sets the value of the name field to the value of inName. There is no return value from this method, which is what the void keyword means before the method name. Also note that the inName argument is declared as final, which means that its value cannot be altered within the method. This is a good programming practice to help avoid hard-to-diagnose problems.

The getter method returns a String and takes no arguments. It simply returns the current value of the name field.

Each of the three types of entities we're dealing with—projects, tasks, and resources—has a corresponding DTP. We'll skip looking at the Task and Resource DTOs because they only differ in the fields they contain, and we'll get to know those fields pretty well as we progress through the code.

■ **Note** There is also a toString() method in each of these DTOs. In Java, any time you try to display the value of a class, its toString() method is called. In many cases, what you get is pretty much useless information internal to the virtual machine the code is running in. You can, however, implement your own more meaningful version of toString(). The version in all three DTOs displays the value of all the fields, which is very handy for debugging. If you're a Java programmer, you might be interested to know that my toString() implementation uses reflection and has no intrinsic knowledge of the class, which means you can rip[11] it out and drop it into any other class to get the same "prettfied" toString() output.

Defining Responses: OkResponse and ErrorResponse

There are two other DTOs that we need to code, and they represent the responses that can come back from our REST API. The OkResponse class is the first (Listing 7-1).

---

[10] The logic behind getters and setters is that you can do validation and/or manipulation of the incoming value before setting it onto the private field. In most cases, however, a DTO is written exactly as you see here with none of that, which some people argue makes it completely pointless: why not just make the fields public and not have to bother with the getter and setter methods? It's a valid point in my opinion, but I tend to still write code this way just in case I need to add some validation or manipulation later; this way, the public interface that my DTO presents stays the same, and no calling code needs to be touched.

[11] The consulting bill will be in your mailbox sometime next week.

Listing 7-1. *The OkResponse Class's Source*

```
public class OkResponse {

  private String name;

  public OkResponse(final String inName) {
    this.name = inName;
  }
    public String getName() {
    return this.name;
  }

}
```

As you can see, it's a very simple DTO with a single field, name. An instance of this class will be returned (after it's converted to JSON technically, but we'll get to that when we examine the servlets a bit later) for create, update, and delete operations. The name will be the name of the entity that was created, updated, or deleted.

Similarly, the ErrorResponse will be returned when certain error conditions occur, such as if the caller tries to delete a nonexistent entity. In that case, the DTO contains an error field that is an error message to be displayed on the client. We'll skip looking at that class since the only difference between it and the OkResponse is that instead of name, there is an error field.

Some Utilities to Make Life Easier
The next class to look at is named Utils, and it's just to make the rest of the code a little simpler (Listing 7-2).

Listing 7-2. *The Utils Class's Source*

```
package com.etherient.timetracker;

import javax.jdo.JDOHelper;
import javax.jdo.PersistenceManager;
import javax.jdo.PersistenceManagerFactory;

public final class Utils {

  private static final PersistenceManagerFactory persistenceManagerFactory =
    JDOHelper.getPersistenceManagerFactory("transactions-optional");

  private Utils() { }

  public static PersistenceManager getPersistenceManager() {
    return persistenceManagerFactory.getPersistenceManager();
  }

}
```

When you work with JDO, you perform all your operations by working with a `PersistenceManager`. This is the object that is responsible for interacting with the database on your behalf. You need to get an instance of this thing every time you want to do something, which means a lot of repeated code. Instead, I've wrapped up that code into this class. The `getPersistenceManager()` method returns that `PersistenceManager` instance we need. Note the `static`[12] keyword before the method name. This indicates that you don't need to have an instance of the `Utils` class in order to call the method. You can instead write `Utils.getPersistenceManager()` any time you like, and that's all you need to do.

Handling Requests: ProjectServlet

The next bit of Java code to look at is far and away the most important, but before we dive into it, let's talk about what a servlet is.

A *servlet* is simply a special Java class (special in that it has certain methods and other characteristics) that handles incoming HTTP requests.

Because it is just a class in essence, it begins by being packaged, and any classes it needs are imported:

```
package com.etherient.timetracker;

import flexjson.JSONSerializer;
import java.io.IOException;
import java.text.ParseException;
import java.text.SimpleDateFormat;
import java.util.Collection;
import java.util.Date;
import java.util.logging.Logger;
import javax.jdo.JDOObjectNotFoundException;
import javax.jdo.PersistenceManager;
import javax.jdo.Query;
import javax.servlet.http.HttpServlet;
import javax.servlet.http.HttpServletRequest;
import javax.servlet.http.HttpServletResponse;
```

Without going into too much detail, here's what these classes are and what they're for:

- `JSONSerializer`: This is used to generate a string of JSON from a Java object.

- `IOException`: Java uses the exception model of error handling that you're already familiar with in JavaScript, although it's more robust in at least one way; there are many, many types of exceptions that can be thrown, and most are represented by their own class, of which `IOException` is one.

- `ParseException`: This is another type of exception that can occur when converting data from one form to another.

- `SimpleDateFormat`: This is used to format dates in various ways.

---

[12] Static is, roughly, how you implement global code in Java because it allows you to call on some bit of code without needing an instance of a class created first.

- Collection: Quite literally, this is a container for objects.

- Date: This is the most common type of date object in Java.

- Logger: This is used to spit out log messages in a configurable, controllable way.

- JDOObjectNotFoundException: Yet another type of exception, this one can occur if an object is requested via JDO and can't be found in the database.

- PersistenceManager: This is our gateway into the wonderful[13] world of JDO.

- Query: This is a class needed to look for objects in a JDO-based database.

- HttpServlet: This is a base class that our own servlet extends from.

- HttpServletRequest: This is a class representing data about the incoming request.

- HttpServletResponse: This is a class used to form the response sent back to the caller.

- Following the imports is the beginning of the class itself:

```
@SuppressWarnings("serial")
public class ProjectServlet extends HttpServlet {
```

The @SuppressWarnings annotation tells the compiler not to complain about certain conversion operations that it warns us could be unsafe but that I know actually are. We won't worry about this too much. ☺

The class extends the HttpServlet, which means it inherits all the behaviors and fields found in that class. I'm going to assume[14] you know about object-oriented programming in general and inheritance in particular.

Next we define a Logger:

```
private static final Logger log =
   Logger.getLogger(ProjectServlet.class.getName());
```

A Logger allows us to write messages out to log files (or other locations). We're here getting an instance of a Logger by calling the static getLogger() method of the Logger class. (I know, that seems really bizarre if you've never seen this before…just go with it!) The getLogger() method expects a String that names the Logger, and here we're using the ProjectServlet.class.getName() method that every class in Java has to return the name of the class dynamically.

---

[13] JDO is a form of ORM, or object-relational mapping. Some people love it, some people hate it. I've historically not been a huge fan because I'm a control freak and I can't stand not knowing what my database really looks like underneath. I'll admit, however, that JDO made this project quite pleasant to develop, so I may have to reevaluate my hatred at a later date!

[14] If you don't, might I suggest that interviewing for a job with me might prove to be the most agonizing experience of your life, and if you're into that sort of stuff (no, I won't be any more specific!) , then you might actually enjoy it.

Creating and/or Updating a Project

Now, an HttpServlet has a couple of methods that are important to us, and they revolve around the HTTP methods. For example, the doPost() method is what gets called when a POST request comes in:

```
public void doPost(final HttpServletRequest inRequest,
  final HttpServletResponse inResponse) throws IOException {

  String logPrefix = "Project doPost(): ";
  log.info(logPrefix + "Entry");
```

As you can see, it accepts an incoming request object and a response object. Both of these are built by the server the servlet is running in, and you are expected to use them in your code. The throws clause indicates that this method might throw an IOException, and the server can handle this appropriately (normally this will mean rendering some sort of error page and returning it to the caller in place of a real response).

We also output a log message using the info() method of the log Logger instance. The logPrefix string will be used throughout the code to give a prefix to any log message that is output.

The first real work we need to do is to determine what HTTP method was requested:

```
String _method = (String)inRequest.getParameter("_method");
if ( _method != null && _method.equalsIgnoreCase("delete")) {
  log.info("Redirecting to doDelete()");
  doDelete(inRequest, inResponse);
}
```

"Wait!" I hear you exclaim…didn't you just say the doPost() method is called to service an HTTP POST request? I did indeed, you astute reader, you! The problem is something I alluded to earlier, which is that a web browser (of which webOS fundamentally is, remember) can only send POST and GET requests directly; it can't use other methods. So, when an AJAX request is made using Prototype, an operation that would normally use the PUT or even DELETE methods in a RESTful API can't really be done. What happens is a bit of trickery: Prototype will allow you to specify one of those methods just fine, but in the background it automatically added a special parameter to the request named _method. This will contain the name of the requested HTTP method, but the request itself will use a POST.

Therefore, in our doPost() method, we grab the _method parameter and see whether its value is delete. If it is, then we call over to the doDelete() method of the servlet.

■ **Note** The typical PUT operation in a RESTful interface is handled by POST here as well, as is discussed elsewhere in this chapter. There's no branching required for that, although arguably the code would be more readable if it was. However, it would also require more code because there would be a doPut() method that would frankly duplicate a great deal of what's in this method, so I chose to do it this way to spare you that redundancy.

Now, assuming we haven't jumped over to the doDelete() method, the doPost() method continues:

```
JSONSerializer js = new JSONSerializer().exclude("*.class");
```

```
inResponse.setContentType("application/json");
```

We create a new instance of the JSONSerializer class, which we'll need later, so let's come back to that. Next, we need to get a PersistenceManager to work with:

```
PersistenceManager persistenceManager = null;
```

This line of code simply declares a variable of type PersistenceManager; we're going to get an instance of it next:

```
try {
```

The call to Utils.getPersistenceManager() can result in an exception being thrown, so we wrap that (and the rest of this code) in a try…catch block so we can deal with that.

Then, the instance is *finally* gotten:

```
persistenceManager = Utils.getPersistenceManager();
```

That sets us up for some work, so the next step is to determine the name of the entity being updated (if any):

```
String requestURI = inRequest.getRequestURI();
String nameString = requestURI.substring(requestURI.lastIndexOf("/") + 1);
nameString = java.net.URLDecoder.decode(nameString, "UTF-8");
log.info(logPrefix + "nameString = " + nameString);
```

The getRequestURI() method of the HttpServletRequest object gets us the URL that was requested by the client. Then, we use the substring() method to find the index of the last forward slash and then push one character beyond that, which results in the variable nameString having the part of the URL at the end, namely, the name. This will be blank if an entity is being created, but that's not a problem.

Next, we use the java.net.URLDecoder() class to decode the nameString value. This is necessary because if the name of the entity is, say, Burt Lancaster, it will be sent from the client, URL-encoded as Burt%20Lancaster, which means when we look it up in the database, it won't be found. The decode() method turns the %20 back into a space.

Next, we determine whether we're doing a create or an update:

```
Project project = null;
if (nameString != null && !nameString.equalsIgnoreCase("") &&
    !nameString.equalsIgnoreCase("project")) {
  project = persistenceManager.getObjectById(Project.class, nameString);
  log.info(logPrefix + "project(1) = " + project);
  if (project == null) {
    inResponse.getWriter().print(
      js.serialize(new ErrorResponse(
        logPrefix + "No Project with name " + nameString + " found")
      )
    );
  }
}
```

If nameString has a value, then we use the PersistenceManager instance gotten earlier, via its getObjectById() method, to retrieve the Project object from the database. If the project isn't found, then we need to return an ErrorResponse. So, one is constructed with the appropriate error message and is then passed to the serialize() method of the JSONSerializer we saw constructed earlier. This results in a String of JSON representing the ErrorResponse object. This string is then written to the response, which sends it back to the client.

Next, all the incoming parameters are grabbed from the request object, and the projectManager parameter is decided like the nameString we saw earlier:

```
String name = (String)inRequest.getParameter("name");
name = java.net.URLDecoder.decode(name, "UTF-8");
String pStartDate = (String)inRequest.getParameter("startDate");
String pTargetDate = (String)inRequest.getParameter("targetDate");
String projectManager = (String)inRequest.getParameter("projectManager");
projectManager = java.net.URLDecoder.decode(projectManager, "UTF-8");
log.info(logPrefix + "name = " + name);
log.info(logPrefix + "pStartDate = " + pStartDate);
log.info(logPrefix + "pTargetDate = " + pTargetDate);
log.info(logPrefix + "projectManager = " + projectManager);
```

With parameters in hand, we can do some validations, beginning with ensuring we got a name:

```
if (name == null || name.equalsIgnoreCase("")) {
  inResponse.getWriter().print(
    js.serialize(new ErrorResponse(
      logPrefix + "name must be specified"))
  );
  return;
}
```

For the dates, we would have received Strings, but we need true Date objects:

```
Date startDate = null;
if (pStartDate == null) {
  pStartDate = "none";
}
try {
  startDate = new SimpleDateFormat("MM/dd/yyyy").parse(pStartDate);
} catch (ParseException pe) {
  pe.printStackTrace();
  inResponse.getWriter().print(
    js.serialize(new ErrorResponse(
      logPrefix + "startDate must be in the form MM/dd/yyyy")
    )
  );
  return;
}
```

The SimpleDateFormat class is used to parse the incoming pStartDate String, and this returns a Date object set to the appropriate date. However, if the pStartDate value wasn't in a valid MM/dd/yyyy format, then a ParseException is thrown, which means we need to send back an ErrorResponse as before.

The pTargetDate parameter is handled the same way, and then the projectManager parameter is handled like the name parameter was, so we'll skip that little bit of code and jump ahead to this:

```
if (project == null) {
  log.info(logPrefix + "New Project");
  project = new Project();
}
```

```
project.setName(name);
project.setStartDate(startDate);
project.setTargetDate(targetDate);
project.setProjectManager(projectManager);
log.info(logPrefix + "project(2) = " + project);
```

If no Project object was retrieved from the database, then that means this request is to create a new project. In that case, a new Project object is constructed. Whether that happens or whether we use the Project object retrieved from the database, we then use its setter methods to set all the data into it.

Once that's done, we can store, or persist, the Project object:

```
persistenceManager.makePersistent(project);
```

JDO makes it very easy to do: the makePersistent() method of the PersistenceManager instance accepts an object that it then saves to the database. How that black magic works, I don't know, but that's kind of the point of JDO!

At the end of this process, we need to return an OkResponse that includes the name of the project created (or updated):

```
inResponse.getWriter().print(js.serialize(new OkResponse(name)));
```

With that, the happy path[15] is complete. What's left is handling any exceptions that might have been thrown:

```
} catch (Exception e) {
  e.printStackTrace();
  inResponse.getWriter().print(
    js.serialize(new ErrorResponse(
      logPrefix + "Unexpected Exception: " + e)
    )
  );
  return;
} finally {
  if (persistenceManager != null) {
    persistenceManager.close();
  }
}
```

Although it's bad form to catch a generic Exception (you usually want to be as specific as possible here), in this case I thought it was acceptable so as to not complicate things more than necessary. The e.printStackTrace() line dumps the stack trace, that is, a large block of text that helps you debug the problem, to the stdout on the server, and an ErrorResponse is returned.

Also, there is a finally block. In Java, the code in the finally clause of a try…catch block executes no matter what and is usually used to clean up resources that were allocated in the previous code. Here, we need to close the PersistenceManager to avoid leaking any database-related resources.

---

[15] "Happy path" does *not* refer to a row of opium dens in certain European countries! Of course, if it did, you probably wouldn't know at this point.

Retrieving Project(s)

The doGet() method executes when a request comes in to retrieve one or more projects. It begins in the same fashion as doPost():

```java
@SuppressWarnings("unchecked")
public void doGet(final HttpServletRequest inRequest,
  final HttpServletResponse inResponse) throws IOException {

  String logPrefix = "Project doGet(): ";
  log.info(logPrefix + "Entry");
  JSONSerializer js = new JSONSerializer().exclude("*.class");
  inResponse.setContentType("application/json");
  PersistenceManager persistenceManager = null;
```

One new thing here is the call to the setContentType() of the response. This tells the browser what kind of content was returned, in this case, JSON. Next, the same sort of code to get the name requested is done:

```java
try {

  String requestURI = inRequest.getRequestURI();
  String nameString = requestURI.substring(requestURI.lastIndexOf("/") + 1);
  nameString = java.net.URLDecoder.decode(nameString, "UTF-8");
  log.info(logPrefix + "nameString = " + nameString);
```

And, once again, a PersistenceManager instance is gotten:

```java
  persistenceManager = Utils.getPersistenceManager();
```

Next, we determine whether we're retrieving all projects or a specific one:

```java
  if (nameString.equalsIgnoreCase("all")) {

    Query query = persistenceManager.newQuery(Project.class);
    Collection projects = (Collection)query.execute();
    log.info(logPrefix + "projects = " + projects);
    inResponse.getWriter().print(js.serialize(projects));
```

If we're retrieving them all, then a new Query object is created by calling the newQuery() method of the PersistenceManager. To that method we pass Project.class, which lets the PersistenceManager know we are looking for Project objects.

Next, we call query.execute() to get back our list in the form of a Collection. Finally, the Collection is converted to JSON and written out the response.

If a single project is being requested, then the else branch executes:

```java
  } else {

    try {
      Project project =
        persistenceManager.getObjectById(Project.class, nameString);
      log.info(logPrefix + "project = " + project);
      inResponse.getWriter().print(js.serialize(project));
    } catch (JDOObjectNotFoundException jonfe) {
```

```
      jonfe.printStackTrace();
      inResponse.getWriter().print(
        js.serialize(new ErrorResponse(
          logPrefix + "No Project with name " + nameString + " found")
        )
      );
    }

  }
```

This is the same sort of code, using persistenceManager.getObjectById(), as we saw earlier in doPost(). It's also the same sort of error handling and output generation we saw there, so we don't dwell, boys and girls.[16]

Exceptions are handled in the same way as in doPost(), and the PersistenceManager is cleaned up the same way too, so we'll end our discussion of doGet() here and move on to doDelete() instead.

Deleting a Project

The doDelete() method opens just like doPost() and doGet() did: some initial logging, a JSONSerializer created, a PersistenceManager gotten, and nameString figured out.

The next thing that is done is the delete itself, which is accomplished in two steps:

```
    try {
      Project project =
        persistenceManager.getObjectById(Project.class, nameString);
      log.info(logPrefix + "project = " + project);
      persistenceManager.deletePersistent(project);
      inResponse.getWriter().print(js.serialize(new OkResponse(nameString)));
    } catch (JDOObjectNotFoundException jonfe) {
      jonfe.printStackTrace();
      inResponse.getWriter().print(
        js.serialize(new ErrorResponse(
          logPrefix + "No Project with name " + nameString +
            " found for delete")
        )
      );
    }
```

First, we try to retrieve the specified project. If it's not found, an exception is thrown, and an ErrorResponse is returned to the client. Assuming it's found, though, we have only to call the deletePersistence() method of the PersistenceManager, passing to it the Project object to delete, and we're golden.

The rest of the code in this method is…wait for it…just like the doPost() and doGet() methods, so no need rehashing the past I figure.

---

[16] You may be one or the other, or both. I'm not judging. If you are neither, though, I'd be intrigued to meet you.

Tasks and Resources

We're not going to explore the code of the TaskServlet and ResourceServlet at all here because the ProjectServlet more than gives you the flavor for how they work. In fact, when I wrote this code, I simply copied the ProjectServlet when I had it all working and changed all the instances of project to task and resource to create the other two servlets, so they are *truly* the same! Besides, we're here to talk about webOS, so we don't want to spend *too* much time in Java land I'd say!

A Little Bit of Configuration

The last step that we need to take in terms of the server side isn't really coding at all but is a matter of simple XML configuration. A Java-based web application uses a special file named web.xml[17] to define attributes of the web application it is in. This, most important for us, includes mapping URLs to servlets that will service them. Listing 7-3 shows the web.xml file for our Time Tracker application.

Listing 7-3. The web.xml Configuration File

```xml
<?xml version="1.0" encoding="utf-8"?>

<web-app xmlns:xsi="http://www.w3.org/2001/XMLSchema-instance"
  xmlns="http://java.sun.com/xml/ns/javaee"
  xmlns:web="http://java.sun.com/xml/ns/javaee/web-app_2_5.xsd"
  xsi:schemaLocation="http://java.sun.com/xml/ns/javaee
  http://java.sun.com/xml/ns/javaee/web-app_2_5.xsd" version="2.5">

  <servlet>
    <servlet-name>ProjectServlet</servlet-name>
    <servlet-class>com.etherient.timetracker.ProjectServlet</servlet-class>
  </servlet>
  <servlet>
    <servlet-name>TaskServlet</servlet-name>
    <servlet-class>com.etherient.timetracker.TaskServlet</servlet-class>
  </servlet>
  <servlet>
    <servlet-name>ResourceServlet</servlet-name>
    <servlet-class>com.etherient.timetracker.ResourceServlet</servlet-class>
  </servlet>

  <servlet-mapping>
    <servlet-name>ProjectServlet</servlet-name>
    <url-pattern>/wostimetracker/project/*</url-pattern>
  </servlet-mapping>
  <servlet-mapping>
    <servlet-name>TaskServlet</servlet-name>
    <url-pattern>/wostimetracker/task/*</url-pattern>
  </servlet-mapping>
  <servlet-mapping>
```

---

[17] This file must appear in a directory named WEB-INF in the root of the web app's directory structure.

```
    <servlet-name>ResourceServlet</servlet-name>
    <url-pattern>/wostimetracker/resource/*</url-pattern>
  </servlet-mapping>

</web-app>
```

A lot of this is just boilerplate, and we're really interested in only two bits: the `<servlet>` elements and the `<servlet-mapping>` elements. The `<servlet>` elements, of which there are three, describe to the server hosting this application the servlets that the web app contains. We have three, one for each entity type, and we need to give each a name via the `<servlet-name>` element and also specify the class that implements the servlet in the `<servlet-class>` element. The value of that element is the full-qualified class name, meaning the name of the class itself preceded by the package it's in.

For each `<servlet>` element, there is a corresponding `<servlet-mapping>` element.[18] This tells the server what servlet will handle what URLs. For example, we're telling the server that any requests to a URL ending with `/wostimetracker/project`, regardless of what comes after that portion of the URL (as denoted by the asterisk at the end), are to be handled by the `ProjectServlet`, which you'll note is the name given to that servlet earlier.

That's all there is to it in this particular application
. There's a lot more stuff you can cram into a `web.xml` file, but for our purposes we don't need any of it, so we're done! The application can now be deployed to GAE and run, ready to service requests from the webOS-based portion of Time Tracker, which is precisely what we're now ready to dive into!

Planning the Application

Time Tracker has more scenes in it than any of the previous applications in this book, as the diagram in Figure 7-5 shows.

---

[18] You can in fact map multiple URLs to a single servlet, but here it's a direct one-to-one mapping.

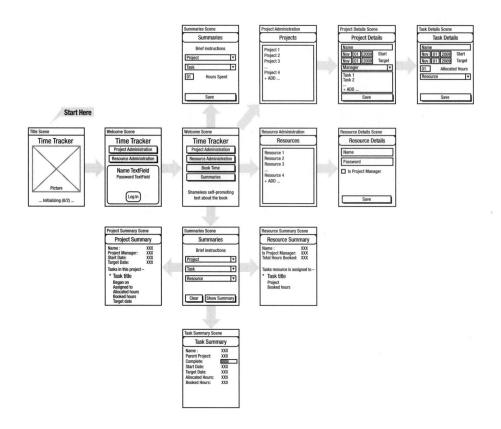

Figure 7-5. *A whiteboardish sketch of the scene flow of the application*

The flow through it, however, is fairly straightforward. First we have the Title scene. This appears at startup and stays on the screen until initialization is complete. After that, the Welcome scene is pushed, and immediately a pop-up dialog is shown for the user to authenticate with. They enter their name and password and click the Log In Button, and, assuming the credentials are valid, they wind up on the Welcome scene with all four of the Buttons on it enabled.

The user can then click the Project Administration Button, assuming they are a project administrator. This brings them to the Project Administration scene where they see a List of projects. Tapping a project causes the Project Details scene to be pushed. This scene includes a List of tasks under the project. The user can tap a task to edit it or add a new one, both of which results in the Task Details scene appearing.

The user could also click the Resource Administration Button, again assuming they are a project administrator. Similar to the Project Administration scene is the Resource Administration scene where the user again is presented with a list of resources. Tapping one gets the Resource Details scene pushed onto the screen.

The user can also click the Book Time Button, and they will then wind up on the Book Time scene. There is no further navigation from this point.

Finally, the Summaries Button leads to the Summaries scene where the user can select to see a summary for a project, task, or resource, each of which leads to its own corresponding scene.

Creating the Skeleton

The directory structure for this application follows the same model as all the previous applications have, as shown in Figure 7-6. Because there was no way to show everything expanded in one image, I've instead shown everything side-by-side so that you can see all the constituent directories.

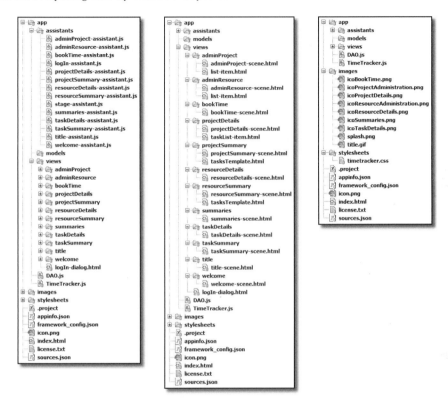

Figure 7-6. *The application's directory structure and file contents*

We have the usual assortment of assistants and views as well as some images, style sheets, and all the configuration files.

The Data Model

Time Tracker stores its data on the server as previously discussed, but it also has another neat trick up its sleeve: if the server is unavailable, a local "warehouse" is used. In this way, the user can continue to work on things locally, and their changes will be synchronized with the server later.

To facilitate this, we need to create a database that roughly mimics the database on the server. Since JPA was used there, we don't truly know the database structure, so we have some latitude in designing the local database. It's a fairly obvious structure, though: three tables, one each for projects, tasks, and resources. Figure 7-7 shows the first of these, the projects table.

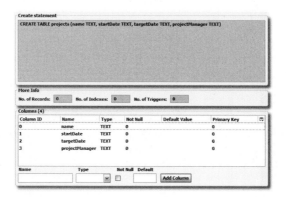

Figure 7-7. The structure of the projects table

I decided to store everything as text here since that's the way the data is transmitted from the server and also the way it is retrieved from the server, so obviously there will need to be conversions done in the client code for things such as numbers and dates; making the database mimic what you get from the server will make the code less complex.

The columns in this table are probably all pretty obvious, but I'll point out that the name column of this table, and in fact the other two, is the key column. So, when a project is linked to a project manager (a resource), the projectManager column is a foreign key to the name column of the resources table.

Figure 7-8 shows the structure of the tasks table. You can see the SQL statement that created this and the projects table, and just like the projects table, it's likely pretty obvious. Once again, we have the project column acting as a foreign key to the name column of the projects table.

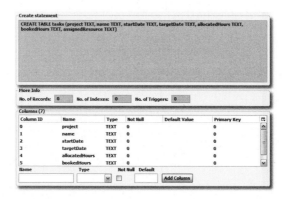

Figure 7-8. The structure of the tasks table

The resources table in Figure 7-9 is the last table to see.

Figure 7-9. The structure of the resources table

It is a little simpler than the other two, as you can see, with only three fields in it and no foreign keys in this case since there is no linkage from this table (the other tables link to records in the resources table, though).

Application Configuration

The configuration for the application is, as usual, pretty minimal. In fact, because this chapter is naturally as long as it is, I've decided not to show the usual files here, namely, the appinfo.json, sources.json, and framework_config.json files. Their content is basically what we've seen before, so there's probably no real reason to show them at this point. However, please take a quick look on your own just to be sure they make sense to you. That is in fact a good test: if you know what's going on in them without an explanation, then you've definitely gotten things down!

Global-Scope Code

For this application, we have two bits of global-scope code—two classes that are shared by all the scenes, namely, the TimerTracker class and the DAO class, which is what we'll look at first.

The DAO.js File

We'll look at the DAO class first since it's the one that most of the application depends on. The DAO class begins with two fields, db and databaseName, and these have the same meaning as in previous DAO classes. db is a reference to the opened local HTML5 database, and databaseName is, literally, the name of said database.

After that, we find a series of string variables that contain the SQL statements used throughout the DAO. These are grouped into the statements that deal with projects, tasks, and resources. In Table 7-2 you can see those that apply to projects.

Table 7-2. *The SQL Statements to Deal with Projects*

Field	SQL Statement
sqlCreateTable_projects	CREATE TABLE IF NOT EXISTS projects (name TEXT, startDate TEXT, targetDate TEXT, projectManager TEXT); GO;
sqlCreate_project	INSERT INTO projects (name, startDate, targetDate, projectManager) VALUES (?, ?, ?, ?); GO;
sqlRetrieve_project	SELECT * FROM projects WHERE name=?; GO;
sqlRetrieve_projects	SELECT * FROM projects; GO;
sqlUpdate_project	UPDATE projects SET name=?, startDate=?, targetDate=?, projectManager=? WHERE name=?; GO;
sqlDelete_project	DELETE FROM projects WHERE name=?; GO;

They are relatively simple statements, and I trust you'll have no problem understanding them without digging into the details. The statements dealing with tasks are next, shown in Table 7-3.

Table 7-3. *The SQL Statements to Deal with Tasks*

Field	SQL Statement
sqlCreateTable_tasks	CREATE TABLE IF NOT EXISTS tasks (project TEXT, name TEXT, startDate TEXT, targetDate TEXT, allocatedHours TEXT, bookedHours TEXT, assignedResource TEXT); GO;
sqlCreate_task	INSERT INTO tasks (project, name, startDate, targetDate, allocatedHours, bookedHours, assignedResource) VALUES (?, ?, ?, ?, ?, ?, ?); GO;
sqlRetrieve_task	SELECT * FROM tasks WHERE name=?; GO;
sqlRetrieve_tasks	SELECT * FROM tasks; GO;
sqlUpdate_task	UPDATE tasks SET project=?, name=?, startDate=?, targetDate=?, allocatedHours=?, bookedHours=?, assignedResource WHERE name=?; GO;
sqlDelete_task	DELETE FROM tasks WHERE name=?; GO;
sqlDeleteForProject_task	DELETE FROM tasks WHERE project=?; GO;

There are a few more of them because deleting a project also means deleting all the tasks underneath it, so there is the one extra statement for that at the bottom.

Finally, Table 7-4 lists the statements for working with resources.

Table 7-4. *The SQL Statements to Deal with Resources*

Field	SQL Statement
sqlCreateTable_resources	CREATE TABLE IF NOT EXISTS resources (name TEXT, isProjectManager TEXT, password TEXT); GO;
sqlCreate_resource	INSERT INTO resources (name, isProjectManager, password) VALUES (?, ?, ?); GO;
sqlUpdate_resource	UPDATE resources SET name=?, isProjectManager=?, password=? WHERE name=?; GO;
sqlRetrieve_resource	SELECT * FROM resources WHERE name=?; GO;
sqlRetrieve_resources	SELECT * FROM resources; GO;
sqlDelete_resource	DELETE FROM resources WHERE name=?; GO;

With all that out of the way, we can move on to the code, beginning with the init() method that is called on startup of the application to initialize the DAO.

Initializing the DAO

Initializing the DAO is done in a similar fashion to the other DAOs we've looked at; basically, the database is opened, and the tables are created, if necessary:

```
dao.db = openDatabase(dao.databaseName, "", dao.databaseName, 65536);
dao.db.transaction((function (inTransaction) {
  inTransaction.executeSql(dao.sqlCreateTable_projects, [],
    function() {
      Mojo.Log.error("#### PROJECTS TABLE CREATED (OR LEFT ALONE)");
    },
    function() {
      Mojo.Log.error("#### COULD NOT CREATE PROJECTS TABLE");
    }
  );
  inTransaction.executeSql(dao.sqlCreateTable_tasks, [],
    function() {
      Mojo.Log.error("#### TASKS TABLE CREATED (OR LEFT ALONE)");
    },
    function() {
      Mojo.Log.error("#### COULD NOT CREATE TASKS TABLE");
    }
```

```
      );
      inTransaction.executeSql(dao.sqlCreateTable_resources, [],
        function() {
          Mojo.Log.error("#### RESOURCES TABLE CREATED (OR LEFT ALONE)");
        },
        function() {
          Mojo.Log.error("#### COULD NOT CREATE RESOURCES TABLE");
        }
      );
    }));
```

I've left the log messages in for this code so you as a developer can see what's going on if you choose to watch the messages fly by in the emulator.

Creating an Entity

In previous DAOs, there has been a separate create, retrieve, update, and delete method for each entity type that was dealt with. To make the code in this DAO more concise, however, there is only a single create(), retrieve(), update(), and deleteEntity() method, and each of them works on all three types of entities (projects, tasks, and resources).

■ **Note**   The reason there is no delete() method (it is named deleteEntity() instead) is that delete is a reserved keyword in JavaScript, and trying to name a method delete() causes an error.

The first of these that we'll look at is the create() method:

```
this.create = function(inType, inEntity, inCallback, inSaveToWarehouse) {

  if (inSaveToWarehouse) {

    var sqlParams = [ ];
    if (inType == "project") {
      sqlParams.push(inEntity.name);
      sqlParams.push(inEntity.startDate);
      sqlParams.push(inEntity.targetDate);
      sqlParams.push(inEntity.projectManager);
    }
    if (inType == "task") {
      sqlParams.push(inEntity.project);
      sqlParams.push(inEntity.name);
      sqlParams.push(inEntity.startDate);
      sqlParams.push(inEntity.targetDate);
      sqlParams.push(inEntity.allocatedHours);
      sqlParams.push(inEntity.assignedResource);
    }
    if (inType == "resource") {
      sqlParams.push(inEntity.name);
      sqlParams.push(inEntity.isProjectManager);
```

```
      sqlParams.push(inEntity.password);
  }
```

The first thing to notice is that we begin by branching on the incoming inSaveToWarehouse argument. If this is true, then this create() method was in fact called by itself! You see, the rest of the Time Tracker code calls create() and passes just the type of entity, the entity itself, and the callback function as arguments and does *not* pass anything for inSaveToWarehouse. So, the else clause of the if statement here will in fact execute first and, as you'll see, will attempt the AJAX call to the server. It's only if that call fails that create() will be called again in reentrant fashion, this time passing true as the value for inSaveToWarehouse, causing the code in the if branch to execute.

As you can see, the first argument to this method is the type of entity we're dealing with. Based on that, the array of parameters is constructed, specific to the SQL statement for the requested entity type. The data for the parameters is taken from the second argument, which is an object describing the entity to be created.

Once that is done, the database transaction is begun:

```
dao.db.transaction((function (inTransaction) {
    inTransaction.executeSql(dao["sqlCreate_" + inType], sqlParams,
```

Note how the appropriate SQL statement to execute is dynamically formed based on the value of inType, and the appropriate field of the DAO is referenced using bracket notation. The array of parameters to the SQL statement that was constructed previously is passed as the second argument.

Next, handling a successful response is done:

```
        function() {
          inCallback({
            responseJSON : {
              msg : "The " + inType + " was saved to the local warehouse " +
                "because the remote operation failed.  " +
                "Synchronization will be attempted in the background."
            }
          });
        },
```

Since this would occur only on a reentrant call, we know that we're warehousing a failed server create function at this point, so we can return a message that is displayed to the user, as shown in Figure 7-10.

Figure 7-10. When a remote operation fails

The other possibility of course is that the database transaction itself fails, which, although pretty unlikely, has to be handled nonetheless:

```
function(inTransaction, inError) {
  Mojo.Log.error("DAO ERROR - create:(" + inError.code + ") : " +
    inError.message);
  inCallback({
    responseJSON : {
      error : "An error occurred while saving the " + inType + " " +
        "to the local warehouse after a failure occurred during " +
        "the remote operation.  This is typically an " +
        "unrecoverable error, although you can try the operation " +
        "again if you wish, you might get lucky!"
    }
  });
}
);
}));
```

Note that both this and the success callback return an object that mimics what the server call would return, and this object is passed to the callback method provided in the original call to create(). In this way, the caller of the create() method doesn't really care what happened; all it knows is that if an object comes back with an error attribute in it, then something went wrong, and it needs to display the message.

As mentioned previously, we've effectively looked at this code out of order because it's actually the else clause of the outer if statement that executes first:

```
} else {

  new Ajax.Request(timeTracker.apiURL + inType + "/", {
    method : "post", evalJSON : "force",
    parameters : inEntity,
    onSuccess : inCallback,
    onFailure : function(inTransport) {
      dao.create(inType, inEntity, inCallback, true);
    }
  });

}

};
```

This is the AJAX call that, if it fails, results in calling dao.create() again, as you can see in the onFailure handler. If the call is successful, then the specified callback is called. Note how the URL is dynamically constructed, making this work generically for all three types of entities (which means I didn't have to duplicate all the error-handling code all over the place).

Retrieving Entities

Retrieving entities is next, and that is contained in the retrieve() method:

```
this.retrieve = function(inType, inCallback, inName, inPassword) {

  if (inName == null) { inName = "all"; }
```

There are two possibilities to cover here: either a specific entity is being retrieved or we want a list of all of them. The inName argument names a specific entity, so if it is null, then we assume the caller wants all of them. We'll see how the value of inName being set to all here matters shortly.

The next possibility is that this method is called in order to authenticate a user with the server, which occurs at startup. In that case:

```
var params = { };
if (inPassword) {
  params.password = inPassword;
}
```

The inPassword argument will only have a value in this situation, and it winds up being the only parameter passed to the server. This is true because of what goes into the URL:

```
new Ajax.Request(timeTracker.apiURL + inType + "/" + inName, {
  method : "get", evalJSON : "force",
  parameters : params,
```

There's that inName argument again! As we saw when we talked about the design of the REST API on the server side, passing a name all as the name of the entity to retrieve via a GET operation results in all the entities being returned. Otherwise, it's a specific name of a specific entity to retrieve.

If the call is successful, then the following code executes:

```
onSuccess : function(inTransport) {
  if (params.password) {
    if (inTransport.responseJSON.error) {
      inCallback();
      return;
    } else {
      inCallback(inTransport.responseJSON);
    }
  }
  var results = [ ];
  for (var i = 0; i < inTransport.responseJSON.length; i++) {
    results.push(inTransport.responseJSON[i]);
  }
```

There are two situations to deal with here. The first is when an authentication request was made, in which case we will get back an ErrorResponse with an appropriate error message. So, if the params object associated with the request has a password attribute, then we know it's an authentication request. If an error attribute is present in the responseJSON, the callback method is called, and the fact that it gets a null as its argument indicates the authentication request failed. In any other situation, the responseJSON itself is returned, and the callback knows the user was authenticated (a user object gets returned in this case).

If this *wasn't* an authentication request, then we take the array of returned object and push them onto a results array for later use. This is because not only do we need to retrieve the data from the server, but we also need to retrieve any data that might be sitting in the local warehouse database and combine those two data sets, and *that* is what ultimately will be passed to the callback function.

Next we do a data retrieval from the database:

```
dao.db.transaction((function (inTransaction) {
  var plurality = "";
  var sqlParams = [ ];
  if (inName == "all") {
    plurality = "s";
  } else {
    sqlParams.push(inName);
  }
  inTransaction.executeSql(dao["sqlRetrieve_" + inType + plurality],
    sqlParams,
    function(inTransaction, inResultSet) {
      if (inResultSet.rows) {
        for (var i = 0; i < inResultSet.rows.length; i++) {
          results.push(inResultSet.rows.item(i));
        }
      }
      inCallback(results);
    },
```

The determination about whether a single entity is being retrieved or whether we want all of them is made, and this determines which SQL statement to execute. For a single entity, the inName passed to this method is pushed onto the array of parameters for the SQL statement; otherwise, in the case of all, the array remains empty because that SQL statement doesn't have any parameters.

The SQL statement is then executed, and the successful response is handled by adding all the returned objects to the results array. This array is then passed to the callback, which now has in its possession a complete collection of entities of the requested type, both those on the server and those in the local warehouse database.

In the case of an error, a simple response is sent to the callback:

```
function(inTransaction, inError) {
  Mojo.Log.error("DAO ERROR - retrieve:(" + inError.code + ") : " +
    inError.message);
  inCallback({ responseJSON : {
    error : "Error retrieving data from warehouse: " +
      inError.code + " - " + inError.message
  }});
}
);
}));
},
```

This again mimics what the server would send back in the case of an error, so as long as the callback knows how to handle this properly,[19] the user will be informed.

The final bit of code is the handling of failures of the AJAX call itself:

```
onFailure : function(inTransport) {
```

---

[19] Hint: they do. Or at least, they'd better, or my minions will exact my revenge upon them!

```
      if (inTransport.responseJSON) {
        inCallback(inTransprt);
      } else {
        inCallback({ responseJSON : {
          error : "Unknown AJAX failure: " + inTransport.status + " (" +
            inTransport.request.url + ")"
        }});
      }
    }
  });

};
```

The handling is done in the same fashion, which is exactly what we'd want to happen in these sorts of situations!

Updating an Entity

The update() method is about 99 percent the same as the create() method, which makes a lot of sense when you think about it! An update is really just a create where you specify an existing record to write to. All the data for the entity being updated is passed to the server, even those attributes that aren't changing, which makes it even *more* like a create. In fact, the only real difference is that for an update you need to pass the name of the entity being updated as part of the URL (the last part in fact) as dictated by the RESTful design of the API.

In light of all of this, we'll skip an in-depth look at the update() method and move on to the deleteEntity() method, which is a bit different. Take a look at update() on the side, though, and you'll see the similarities to create() are more than skin deep![20]

Deleting an Entity

The deleteEntity() method is next and is in fact a lot simpler than all the rest:

```
  this.deleteEntity = function(inType, inName) {

    dao.db.transaction((function (inTransaction) {
      inTransaction.executeSql(dao["sqlDelete_" + inType], [ inName ],
        function() { },
        function(inTransaction, inError) {
          Mojo.Controller.errorDialog("Delete from the local database failed");
        }
      );
    }));
```

It begins by deleting the entity from the local warehouse database and then doing the delete on the server:

---

[20] Not that I have any problem with skin deep. After all, I like supermodels as much as the next guy, and as a heterosexual man, I can at least appreciate what women see in Brad Pitt and Hugh Jackman.

```
    new Ajax.Request(timeTracker.apiURL + inType + "/" + inName, {
      method : "delete", evalJSON : "force",
      parameters : { },
      onSuccess : function () { },
      onFailure : function(inTransport) {
        Mojo.Controller.errorDialog("Delete from the remote database failed");
      }
    });

};
```

There's no logic involved and no branching; it's just "Delete this darned thing from everywhere!" This works because even if the entity exists in only one place (perhaps a previous create failed against the server), it won't result in an error; there's simply nothing to delete. Likewise, we want a delete to *always* occur both on the server side and locally, so again, there's no need to decide anything; just fire off a delete operation to the local database as well as the server side, and all is right with the world.[21]

The TimeTracker.js File

The TimerTracker class begins with a couple of fields for sharing data between scenes:

```
this.user = null;
this.projects = [ ];
this.resources = [ ];
this.tasks = [ ];
this.apiURL = "http://wostimetracker.appspot.com/wostimetracker/";
this.retryInterval = null;
```

When the application is started up, the user must authenticate with the server in order to be able to do anything. When this occurs, the user field will contain an object with the information about the user returned by the authentication request that we'll see later. The projects, resources, and tasks fields each store an array of objects for each project, resource, and task that was retrieved from the server *as well as* from the local warehouse database. The apiURL field is the base of the URL that all AJAX requests to the server go to. The portion of the URL that follows, for at least some types of requests, is added on dynamically. That too is something we'll see later. The retryInterval field is a reference to an interval that is kicked off to perform background synchronization with the server when a connection could not be made, either because the phone does not currently have an Internet connection or because the server side of the application isn't responding.

The next thing we have is a simple utility function for formatting a JavaScript Date object into a string:

```
this.formatDate = function(inDate) {

  var month = "" + (inDate.getMonth() + 1);
  if (month.length == 1) {
    month = "0" + month;
  }
```

---

[21] All has in fact not been right with the world for quite some time, but I suspect you know that already!

```
var day = "" + inDate.getDate();
if (day.length == 1) {
  day = "0" + day;
}
var year = "" + inDate.getFullYear();
return (month + "/" + day + "/" + year);

};
```

This is needed because when we send a date to the server, it has to be a string in the form mm/dd/yyy, but what we have from the DatePicker is a true JavaScript Date object. If we pass that Date object to this method, we'll get back a string in the appropriate format.

■ **Note**   You may wonder why I didn't use the Mojo.Format.formatDate() method; that was my first thought—I wanted to use it, but it simply doesn't have the capability to convert to the format I needed. It doesn't let you specify the format to return specifically enough.

The next method we encounter is the synchronize() method:

```
this.synchronize = function() {
  timeTracker.syncOp("project");
  timeTracker.syncOp("task");
  timeTracker.syncOp("resource");
};
```

You'll discover in the stage assistant later that an interval is started that calls this method every five minutes. Its job is to send any records sitting in the local warehouse database to the server. To duplicate as little code as possible, the syncOp() method is called three times, one for each type of entity to be sent. That method is as follows (broken up for easy digestion):

```
this.syncOp = function(inType) {

  dao.db.transaction((function (inTransaction) {
    inTransaction.executeSql(dao["sqlRetrieve_" + inType + "s"], [ ],
      function(inTransaction, inResultSet) {
        if (inResultSet && inResultSet.rows && inResultSet.rows.length > 0) {
          for (var i = 0; i < inResultSet.rows.length; i++) {
            var entity = inResultSet.rows.item(i);
            Mojo.Log.error("### synchronize->syncOp: Sending " + inType +
              " " + entity.name);
```

So, the first step is to retrieve all the records from the database of the type passed in as inType and using the SQL statements that are members of the DAO class (the name of the DAO field is dynamically constructed here and referenced via bracket notation). Once we get the results and after we check to ensure there actually are some records to synchronize, the next step is to iterate over the returned records. For each we'll make an AJAX request to send it to the server:

```
new Ajax.Request(
  timeTracker.apiURL + inType + "/", {
  method : "post", evalJSON : "force",
  parameters : entity,
  onSuccess : function() {
    dao.db.transaction((function (inTransaction) {
      inTransaction.executeSql(dao["sqlDelete_" + inType],
        [ entity.name ],
        function() {
          Mojo.Log.error("### synchronize->syncOp: Successful " +
            inType + " resend, name=" + entity.name);
        },
        function() { }
      );
    }));
  },
```

This is the same sort of AJAX request we've previously seen. The URL to send to is dynamically constructed here and follows the REST pattern previously discussed. Assuming the operation is successful, the record is deleted from the database since it is now synchronized with the server.

If a failure occurs, here's the code:

```
onFailure : function(inTransport) {
  Mojo.Log.error("### synchronize->syncOp: " +
    inTransport.status + " - " +
    inTransport.request.url + " - ");
},
```

If you have shelled into your device or emulator, then you'll see these log messages there. Since this is meant to be a background operation, the user isn't informed in any way.

The same thing is done for exceptions:

```
onException : function(inone, inException) {
  Mojo.Log.error("### synchronize->syncOp: EXCEPTION: " +
    inException);
  }
});
}
```

Only one more piece of the puzzle remains, and that's if there were no records of the specified type to synchronize:

```
} else {
  Mojo.Log.error("### synchronize->syncOp: No " + inType + "s");
  }
},
function() { }
);
}));

};
```

Once again, we just write out a log message for the developer who might be checking out the application; otherwise, the user is none the wiser, as should be the case in this, err, case!

Setting the Stage

The index.html file for this application holds absolutely no surprises and is no different from all the others we've seen, so I've opted to not show it here. The stage assistant, however, has a little bit of interesting code in its setup() method:

```
dao.init();
this.controller.pushScene("title");
timeTracker.retryInterval =
  setInterval(timeTracker.synchronize, 1000 * 60 * 60);
```

The init() method of the DAO instance (dao) is called to set up our local database access, and the Title scene is pushed. Finally, that interval I mentioned earlier is kicked off and set for a five-minute interval. Note that this will execute regardless of what else is going on with the application; however, it will do a minimum amount of work if there is nothing to synchronize.

A Matter of Style

The style sheet for this application is fairly minimal and quite simplistic, but we'll have a go at it nonetheless:

```
.cssTitleBackground {
  position : absolute;
  left : 0px;
  top : 0px;
}
.cssTitleText {
  position : absolute;
  left : 0px;
  top : 440px;
  width : 100%;
  z-index : 10;
  text-align : center;
}
```

These two style classes are used on the Title scene to show the background image (the nice picture of the friendly, happy, hardworking team of people seemingly trying to decide which way the nearest coffee shop is, and the Time Tracker logo above it) and ensure it takes up the entire scene. This scene is set to display full-screen, so this image is a full 320~TMS480, which is the size of the Pre screen in portrait mode. The cssTitleText class is applied to the text below that tells the user that the application is initializing and what the progress of that process is.

The next two styles are used on the Welcome scene that comes after the Title scene:

```
.cssWelcomeTitle {
  padding-top : 30px;
  padding-bottom : 15px;
}
```

```
.cssWelcomeMessage {
  font-size : 75%;
  padding-top : 15px;
  padding-left : 6px;
  padding-right : 6px;
}
```

The `cssWelcomeTitle` class is used to put some space around the Time Tracker 3D logo up top, and `cssWelcomeMessage` is applied to the shamelessly self-promoting text at the bottom.

After that is a serious of classes, all of which are very similar, so I'll just show one, and you can take it as a representative sample:

```
.header-icon.projectAdministration {
  background : url(../images/icoProjectAdministration.png) no-repeat;
}
```

These classes are for each of the scenes that have a title section up top with an icon next to it. I opted to use the styling for these headers that Palm recommends for preference-type scenes rather than the typical "pill" header that I've used in most of the applications, for no other reason than I thought it added a little bit of visual pizzazz to the scenes!

The final group of four classes are used by the three summary scenes:

```
.cssSummaryLabel {
  font-size : 75%;
  font-weight : bold;
}
.cssSummaryData {
  font-size : 75%;
}
.cssSummaryLineItemTitle {
  font-weight : bold;
  padding-bottom : 4px;
}
.cssSummaryLineItem {
  font-size : 75%;
  line-height : 10px;
  padding-bottom : 8px;
}
```

The project, task, and resource summary scenes make use of these styles. The `cssSummaryLabel` and `cssSummaryDate` classes are used to show the table of information about an entity where the title of a given piece of information is in bold. For example, on the Project Summary scene, there is a line that shows the name of the project. In that case, the information is shown like this:

Name: Project1

Note that the word *Name* is in bold, whereas the name of the project (*Project1*) is not. Style class `cssSummaryLabel` is applied to *Name:*, and `cssSummaryData` is applied to *Project1*.

The `cssSummaryLineItemTitle` and `cssSummaryLineItem` classes are applied to the lists on these summary scenes, where needed. For example, the Project Summary scene shows a list (using a plain `<ul>` element) of tasks in the project. The name of the task gets the `cssSummaryLineItemTitle` class applied to it so that it stands out, and then all the data below it is styled with `cssSummaryLineItem`.

A Scene-by-Scene Account

This project by far has the largest number of scenes of any project in this book, but by and large they are no more complex than most of the others we've seen. We'll examine them in roughly the logical order a user is likely to encounter them, beginning with the Title scene.

Title Scene

The Title scene serves as a "splash page," as seen on many web sites and as part of many applications. It's a title screen that pops up initially and typically, as is the case here, and gives the user something (presumably) pretty to look at while the application does some initialization that the user has to wait for. Figure 7-11 shows this Title scene.

Figure 7-11. The Title scene

A simple title graphic is shown, and some text is written below it that tells the user how far along the initialization is. In this case, there are two steps to that initialization, so a simple "X of Y" message is sufficient. I could have used a `ProgressBar` here too, but that would have been a little bit of overkill in my mind, and because the initialization generally is pretty quick, the user likely wouldn't see much of it anyway, so a simple text message is what I went with.

The View HTML

The markup for this scene couldn't be simpler, as you can see in Listing 7-4.

Listing 7-4. Scene View HTML for the Title Scene

```
<img src="images/splash.png" class="cssTitleBackground"></img>
<div id="divInitProgress" class="cssTitleText">
  ... Initializing (0/2) ...
</div>
```

Yep, that's it! You'll recall that the `cssTitleBackground` class positions the graphic absolutely and "pins" it, so to speak, to the upper-left corner of the screen, so it fills the entire screen because the graphic itself is 320~TMS480 pixels in size. Similarly, the status text at the bottom is also positioned absolutely, and the text is centered by virtue of the cssTitleText class giving the <div> a width of 100 percent and setting the text-align attribute to center.

The Scene Assistant

The scene assistant for the Title scene is also quite simple, although since we have that initialization to perform, there's a little bit more to it than you might think. We'll begin with a couple of data fields:

```
TitleAssistant.prototype.projectsLoaded = false;
TitleAssistant.prototype.resourcesLoaded = false;
```

The two steps of initialization to be performed are to load all the projects and resources from the server and combine them with any data stored in the local warehouse database. Since this will involve some AJAX calls and since they are asynchronous, we need a way to track when each of those things has loaded, and that's what these flags are for.

After that comes the setup() method:

```
this.controller.enableFullScreenMode(true);
```

Yep, that's it! Most of this application, with one exception that we'll see in a bit, runs in full-screen mode, meaning the omnipresent status bar at the top of the Pre screen will go away and give our application a few more pixels to work with. Every scene has to be switched into full-screen mode; it's not a global setting that you do once. The enableFullScreenMode() method of the scene controller is how we do that switch (and yes, you can switch between full-screen mode and regular mode, which is accomplished by passing false instead of true, any time you like during the lifetime of a scene).

Next up is the activate() method:

```
dao.retrieve("project", this.processProjectResults.bind(this));
dao.retrieve("resource", this.processResourceResults.bind(this));
```

Yes, that too is all there is to it! The retrieve() method of the DAO is called to retrieve projects and resources. Note that each type of entity is retrieved with its own call, which means these two retrieval operations will occur asynchronously.

So, what happens when the projects are retrieved? The answer is that the processProjectResults() method fires:

```
if (Object.isArray(inResults)) {
  timeTracker.projects = inResults;
}
this.projectsLoaded = true;
if (this.projectsLoaded && this.resourcesLoaded) {
  Mojo.Controller.stageController.swapScene({
    transition : Mojo.Transition.crossFade, name : "welcome"
  });
} else {
  $("divInitProgress").innerHTML =
    $("divInitProgress").innerHTML = "... Initializing (1/2) ...";
}

};
```

Assuming an array is returned, which we determine by using the handy isArray() method that the Prototype library adds to the Object base class, we first copy that array into the projects field of the TimeTracker class instance, saving the projects for later. The projectLoaded flag is then flipped to true. Next we check to see whether both projects and resources have been loaded. Since this is happening asynchronously and since there is a corresponding processResourceResults() for the resource retrieval, we don't know in what order these callback methods will fire in, so the initialization could be completed in either; therefore, as you can guess, this same check will be performed in processResourceResults() as well. If both projects and resources have completed loading, then we use the swapScene() method to show the Welcome scene. A crossFade transition is used since the Title scene and the Welcome scene are effectively at the same level in the scene hierarchy and we wouldn't want the user to be able to gesture back to the Title scene. If both steps of the initialization haven't completed, then the status text at the bottom is updated to indicate that one of the two steps has completed.

As mentioned, there is a processResourceResults() method as well, and it looks nearly identical to processProjectResults(), so I've elected to not list it here.

■ **Note** Tasks are not loaded because tasks are tied to a project and are retrieved when a project is selected (or the user is booking time), so there's no need to load them here, although they could be too without any harm…but also arguably with no real benefit; that's the reason I didn't load them too. It's better to get the application up and running as quickly as possible I think!

Welcome Scene

The Welcome scene, shown in Figure 7-12, is what appears after the Title scene. This is basically a main menu screen where all use operations branch out from.

Figure 7-12. The Welcome scene

The four Buttons give the user access to the four main areas of functionality, assuming they have rights to them. If the user is not a project manager, then the Project Administration and Resource Administration Buttons would be disabled.

The View HTML

The view markup is just some straightforward HTML, as Listing 7-5 decisively demonstrates.

Listing 7-5. Scene View HTML for the Welcome Scene

```
<center>
  <img class="cssWelcomeTitle" src="images/title.gif" />
  <div id="welcome_btnProjectAdministration" x-mojo-element="Button"></div>
  <div id="welcome_btnResourceAdministration" x-mojo-element="Button"></div>
  <div id="welcome_btnBookTime" x-mojo-element="Button"></div>
  <div id="welcome_btnSummaries" x-mojo-element="Button"></div>
  <div class="cssWelcomeMessage">
    From the book<br>
    "Practical webOS Projects With the Palm Pre"<br>
    (Apress, 2009, ISBN-13: 978-1-4302-2674-1).<br>
    &copy;2009 Frank W. Zammetti. All rights reserved.<br>
    A product of <a href="http://www.etherient.com">Etherient</a>
  </div>
</center>
```

There isn't much in the way of CSS even, aside from the one cssWelcomeMessage class applied to the text at the bottom. Otherwise, it's plain-vanilla[22] markup.

The Scene Assistant

The scene assistant is similarly not too complex, and there's nothing that we haven't seen before frankly.

```
WelcomeAssistant.prototype.buttonModels = {
  projectAdministration : {
    label : "Project Administration", disabled : true
  },
  resourceAdministration : {
    label : "Resource Administration", disabled : true
  },
  bookTime : { label : "Book Time", disabled : true },
  summaries : { label : "Summaries", disabled : true }
};
```

Since the Buttons can be disabled depending on whether the user is a project manager, we need to have models that we can manipulate. Even though the Book Time and Summaries Buttons don't get disabled in the same way, I provided models for them here just in case I wanted to change the design

---

[22] I happen to like vanilla the best of any iced cream flavor, and so do a lot of people, so if that phrase brought offense to you, you're not alone because I offended myself just writing it!

later. In fact, as a bit of advice, I suggest always having the models separate like this, as opposed to making them inline in the setupWidget() call, as you've seen me do in other projects. Although I think inlining them makes the code a little more readable because you don't have to jump around to follow the code, it ultimately makes it easier to change the application to not do that because you'll have access to the model if you need to change it programmatically later. It also is more memory efficient because when you inline an object, you create a new object with each execution of the statement, using more memory (and also incurring a greater garbage collection hit later, which can be a big problem in some applications, such as games). This is avoided if you create the object external to the setupWidget() call in the fashion shown here, so all in all, this is the model you probably should follow.

The setup() method is next:

```
this.controller.enableFullScreenMode(false);

this.controller.setupWidget("welcome_btnProjectAdministration", { },
  this.buttonModels.projectAdministration
);
Mojo.Event.listen(this.controller.get("welcome_btnProjectAdministration"),
  Mojo.Event.tap, this.btnProjectAdministrationTap.bind(this)
);
```

Full-screen mode this time is turned off, and the reason for that will be clear when we look at the login assistance a bit later. Then, each of the Buttons is set up in the usual way. To save some space, I've shown only one here, but the rest are basically the same.

With the scene set up, activation can now be handled via the activate() method:

```
if (!timeTracker.user) {
  this.logInDialog = this.controller.showDialog({
    template : "logIn-dialog", assistant : new LogInAssistant(this),
    preventCancel : true
  });
}
```

As mentioned earlier, the user needs to authenticate with the server to be able to do any work. So, if the timeTracker.user field is null, then the user has not yet authenticated, and we need to allow them to do so. This is accomplished via a pop-up dialog box, which we'll look at next. Note that the user must complete that step in order to continue, so preventCancel is set to true. Either they can authenticate or they can close the application via an up-swipe gesture, but that's all they can do until they authenticate.

Finally, each of the Buttons has an associated tap event handler. Each of them does the same thing, so we'll just look at one:

```
Mojo.Controller.stageController.pushScene("adminProject");
```
The appropriate scene is pushed, and that's that!

Log In Dialog Scene
Once the Title scene is shown, the first thing it does is shows a pop-up dialog box where the user enters their credentials in order to authenticate with the remote server. This dialog box is what you see in Figure 7-13.

Figure 7-13. *The Log In pop-up dialog box scene*

The user can't go any further until they log in (that is, authenticate).

The View HTML

The markup behind the dialog box, contained in the `logIn-dialog.html` file, begins as follows:

```
Please enter credentials and tap Log In to authenticate
<br><br>
```

A little bit of instruction is always a good thing, even if what they need to do should be abundantly[23] obvious!

```
<div class="palm-row">
  <div class="palm-row-wrapper">
    <div class="textfield-group" x-mojo-focus-highlight="true">
      <div class="title">
        <div id="login_txtName" x-mojo-element="TextField"></div>
      </div>
    </div>
  </div>
</div>
```

The user has to enter their name and their password, and the first part of this is a simple `TextField`, defined in the usual way. For the password, we use a `PasswordField`:

```
<div class="palm-row">
  <div class="palm-row-wrapper">
    <div class="textfield-group" x-mojo-focus-highlight="true">
```

---

[23] Never count on anything when it comes to users except that their brains are switched off. Remember, I'm not only a developer, but I'm also a user, and I know that my brain tends to switch off at the most inopportune times and without any sort of advanced warn…

```
        <div class="title">
          <div id="login_pwdPassword" x-mojo-element="PasswordField"></div>
        </div>
      </div>
    </div>
</div>
```

This field too is wrapped in the same sort of markup we've seen previously. Both of these fields are styled to show a "flat" sort of look; that is, there's no border and title around them as you saw in the Code Cabinet project, for example. It's simply a matter of taste how you want these fields to look, but in this application, I decided to make all of them have this flat kind of appearance.

Finally, we have a Button:

```
<div id="login_btnLogIn" x-mojo-element="Button"></div>
```

Tapping this Button calls the server to try to authenticate the user, as we'll see in the assistant code that we're now going to look at.

The Scene Assistant

The assistant begins, as they all do, with a constructor:

```
function LogInAssistant(inAssistant) {
    this.assistant = inAssistant;
};

LogInAssistant.prototype.models = {
  txtName : { value : null },
  pwdPassword : { value : null },
  btnLogIn : {
    label : "Log In", buttonClass : "affirmative", disabled : false
  }
};
```

This constructor is a little different, however, in that it is passed a reference to the parent scenes' assistant. This will be necessary in the rest of the code, and so we'll hold on to this reference by storing it in the assistant field.

We also have a models object that contains the models for the three widgets, namely, the name TextField, the password PasswordField, and the Login Button. The Button needs to have a model like this because we'll be turning on the Spinner that is part of the Button when the call to the server is happening.

The setup() method is next, as usual:

```
this.assistant.controller.setupWidget("login_txtName",
  { hintText : "Name", focusMode : Mojo.Widget.focusSelectMode },
  this.models.txtName
);

this.assistant.controller.setupWidget("login_pwdPassword",
  { hintText : "Password" }, this.models.pwdPassword
);

this.assistant.controller.setupWidget("login_btnLogIn",
```

```
{ type : Mojo.Widget.activityButton }, this.models.btnLogIn
);
Mojo.Event.listen(this.assistant.controller.get("login_btnLogIn"),
  Mojo.Event.tap, this.btnLogInTap.bind(this)
);
```

No surprises[24] there I hope! The TextField, PasswordField, and Button are all set up in the usual ways, with the Button's Mojo.Event.tap event being handled by the btnLoginTap() method. Note that the Button is a type Mojo.Widget.activityButton, so it has the built-in activity Spinner available to us.

Speaking of which…

```
if (this.models.txtName.value == null || this.models.txtName.value.blank()) {
  Mojo.Controller.getAppController().showBanner({
    messageText : "A name must be entered", soundClass : "alerts"
  }, { }, "");
  return;
}
if (this.models.pwdPassword.value == null ||
  this.models.pwdPassword.value.blank()) {
  Mojo.Controller.getAppController().showBanner({
    messageText : "A password must be entered", soundClass : "alerts"
  }, { }, "");
}
```

The first thing done is to confirm that the user entered something in both fields; otherwise, there's not really anything to do. Interestingly, I used a banner notification to inform them of their foul-up because showing a dialog box using Mojo.controller.errorDialog() causes the pop-up dialog box to be dismissed, which means I'd had to have built in some code in the Title scene's assistant to show the dialog box again. Since this dialog box is already showing, I saw no sense in that extra effort, so a banner notification works better. However, you can't show a banner notification when in full-screen mode, which is the reason we saw earlier that full-screen mode is turned off when the Title scene is set up (recall that the Welcome scene is full-screen).

The next thing we need to do is deal with a backdoor:[25]

```
if (this.models.txtName.value.toLowerCase() == "admin" &&
  this.models.pwdPassword.value.toLowerCase() == "admin") {
  this.processResults({
    name : "admin", password : "admin", isProjectManager : true
  });
  return;
}
```

The server-side database initially has no users (resources) defined, so there would initially be no way for any user to log in. One option would have been to create a user when the server code starts up if

---

[24] I thought about asking my publisher to include the technology, as seen in some greeting cards, to play an MP3 when you got to this page so that Chris Daughtry's song *No Surprise* would play here. Then I thought of the royalty issue, which seemed like a lot of work, so you'll have to just hum the tune in your head. (Just don't let the RIAA hear you; they may sue you under the DMCA for that!)
[25] As evidenced by the movie *WarGames*, backdoors are generally a Really Bad Thing™ in terms of security, but here we don't have too many options.

none is found in the database, but that would have meant more Java code to discuss here. Although there are other options too, the simplest I figured was just having a backdoor in, meaning a predefined "virtual user." If the user enters *admin* and *admin* for both the name and password, they'll get "logged in" automatically. This login is virtual in the sense that the server is not consulted. Instead, the callback function that would normally be called when the server response is retrieved, the processResults() method, is manually called and passed an object mimicking what the server sends back for a successful authentication.

Next, assuming they haven't used the backdoor, we begin the process of authenticating with the server:

```
this.models.btnLogIn.label = "Working, Please Wait...";
this.models.btnLogIn.disabled = true;
this.assistant.controller.modelChanged(this.models.btnLogIn);
this.assistant.controller.get("login_btnLogIn").mojo.activate();

dao.retrieve("resource", this.processResults.bind(this),
  this.models.txtName.value, this.models.pwdPassword.value);
```

First, the label of the Button is changed to reflect that we're trying to authenticate them, and the Button is also disabled to avoid a double-submit. The Button is then activated so that the built-in Spinner shows.

The processResults() method is called when the server response comes back:

```
this.models.btnLogIn.label = "Log In";
this.models.btnLogIn.disabled = false;
this.assistant.controller.modelChanged(this.models.btnLogIn);
this.assistant.controller.get("login_btnLogIn").mojo.deactivate();
```

The Button is first reset to its initial state. Next, the response is interrogated:

```
if (inResults && inResults.name) {

  timeTracker.user = inResults;
  if (inResults.isProjectManager) {
    this.assistant.buttonModels.projectAdministration.disabled = false;
    this.assistant.buttonModels.resourceAdministration.disabled = false;
  }
  if (inResults.name != "admin") {
    this.assistant.buttonModels.bookTime.disabled = false;
    this.assistant.buttonModels.summaries.disabled = false;
  }
  this.assistant.controller.modelChanged(
    this.assistant.buttonModels.projectAdministration, this.assistant);
  this.assistant.controller.modelChanged(
    this.assistant.buttonModels.resourceAdministration, this.assistant);
  this.assistant.controller.modelChanged(
    this.assistant.buttonModels.bookTime, this.assistant);
  this.assistant.controller.modelChanged(
    this.assistant.buttonModels.summaries, this.assistant);

  this.assistant.controller.enableFullScreenMode(true);
```

```
this.assistant.logInDialog.mojo.close();
```

If the response JSON includes a name attribute, then the user was successfully authenticated. In that case, we record the returned object in the TimeTracker.user field. Next, if the user is a project manager, as dictated by the value of the isProjectManager field, then we enable the Project Administration and Resource Administration Buttons on the Title scene. Note that the scene assistant for that scene, as stored in the assistant field of this class, is used to get to the models for those fields. Assuming the name entered by the user wasn't the special *admin* value, then the Book Time and Summaries Buttons are enabled (the admin account can only create projects and resources, and you could argue it should only be able to create resources). We then switch the Title scene to full-screen mode since we no longer have to show banned notifications, and the dialog box is closed.

Now, assuming the authentication attempt fails, the else branch of the if statement in the processResults() method executes:

```
} else {
  Mojo.Controller.getAppController().showBanner({
    messageText : "Authentication failed. Try again!", soundClass : "alerts"
  }, { }, "");
}
```

This is the code responsible for showing the banner notification shown in Figure 7-14.

Figure 7-14. *A failed login attempt*

Note that the pop-up dialog box is now in a state ready for the user to try again, and their entries are still present for them to edit if they want.

Project Administration Scene

The Project Administration scene, as shown in Figure 7-15, is a simple enough scene: a single List is present, and that's it!

Figure 7-15. The Project Administration scene

This scene is the entry point into creating, deleting, and updating projects, and the markup and code behind it reflect that.

The View HTML

First up is the markup, as shown in its entirety in Listing 7-6.

Listing 7-6. Scene View HTML for the Project Administration Scene

```
<div class="palm-page-header">
  <div class="header-icon projectAdministration"></div>
  <div class="header-text">Project Administration</div>
</div>

<div class="palm-scrim" id="adminProject_divScrim" style="display:none;">
  <div id="adminProject_divSpinner" x-mojo-element="Spinner"></div>
</div>

<div id="adminProject_lstProjects" x-mojo-element="List"></div>
```

We have a page header, using the palm-page-header style, which means it's the style usually used for preference-type scenes. Each scene that we'll see from here on out has an icon in the header, using the styles we looked at earlier. Below the header is our *scrim*, with a Spinner inside. Finally, the List is below that, ready to be set up in the assistant.

The Scene Assistant

Since we have a List, we have a model, and that's the first thing in the assistant:

```
AdminProjectAssistant.prototype.lstProjectsModel = { items : [ ] };
```

Next is the setup() method, which is fairly short:

```
this.controller.enableFullScreenMode(true);

this.controller.setupWidget("adminProject_divSpinner",
  { spinnerSize : "large" }, { spinning : true }
);

this.controller.setupWidget("adminProject_lstProjects", {
  addItemLabel : "Add...", swipeToDelete : true,
  itemTemplate : "adminProject/list-item"
}, this.lstProjectsModel);
this.controller.listen("adminProject_lstProjects", Mojo.Event.listTap,
  this.selectProject.bind(this));
this.controller.listen("adminProject_lstProjects", Mojo.Event.listAdd,
  this.addProject.bind(this));
this.controller.listen("adminProject_lstProjects", Mojo.Event.listDelete,
  this.deleteProject.bind(this));
```

Once again, we have to set the application into full-screen mode in each scene, so that's the first thing done. Then the List is set up, and it is defined as using the list-item.html template in the adminProject view directory. The Mojo.Event.listTap, Mojo.Event.listAdd, and Mojo.Event.listDelete events are all handled and tied to methods to deal with them.

Listing 7-7 shows the template for the List.

Listing 7-7. *Template Markup for the Projects in the List of Projects*

```
<div class="palm-row" x-mojo-tap-highlight="momentary">
  <div class="palm-row-wrapper textfield-group">
    <div class="truncating-text">#{name}</div>
  </div>
</div>
```

As you can see, it's quite simplistic, just displaying the name attribute of a given project object. The activate() method is next:

```
this.lstProjectsModel.items = [ ];
this.controller.modelChanged(this.lstProjectsModel);
$("adminProject_divScrim").show();
dao.retrieve("project", this.processResults.bind(this));
```

First, the model for the List is cleared, just for aesthetics, and then the scrim is shown. Finally, the retrieve() method of the DAO is called to get the list of projects from the remote service as well as the database. The processResults() method is the callback from this asynchronous operation, and the code for that method is as follows:

```
if (Object.isArray(inResults)) {
  timeTracker.projects = [ ];
  for (var i = 0; i < inResults.length; i++) {
    if (inResults[i].projectManager == timeTracker.user.name) {
      timeTracker.projects.push(inResults[i]);
    }
  }
```

```
  this.lstProjectsModel.items = timeTracker.projects;
  this.controller.modelChanged(this.lstProjectsModel);
} else {
  Mojo.Controller.errorDialog(inResults.responseJSON.error);
}

$("adminProject_divScrim").hide();
```

Assuming an array was returned by the DAO's retrieve() method, we iterate over that array and push each project object into the array of projects stored on the TimeTracker instance. However, this is done only if the project manager for the project is the current user because only a project manager can modify a project. If anything but an array was returned, then some sort of error occurred, so an error dialog box is shown, and the error attribute of the returned object is the message displayed for the user.

The three event handler methods for the List are next. The selectProject() method, called when a project is tapped to edit it, and the addProject() method, called when the Add item in the List is clicked, simply push the projectDetails scene, and in the case of selectProject(), the project object is passed as the second argument (by way of the item attribute of the incoming event object). As we'll see, the projectDetails scene knows that if no project object is passed in, then it must be the add operation; otherwise, the project object is used to populate the entry fields on the scene…but I'm getting ahead of things just a little!

The deleteProject() method simply calls the deleteEntity() method of the DAO, passing it the name of the project to delete (which is gotten by referencing the name attribute of the object pointed to by the item attribute of the incoming event object).

Project Details Scene

When the user selects a project to edit or selects the Add item from the List on the Project Administration scene, the Project Details scene appears looking like what you see in Figure 7-16.

Figure 7-16. *The Project Details scene*

The list of tasks for this project, if any, is retrieved at this time and is displayed here as well; that's why there is no task administration scene: you only see a List of tasks in relation to a project.

The View HTML

To start with, I'd like to point out that most of the scenes to come have a header and a scrim; however, I've removed them from the markup listings just to save a little space. They are just like what we saw in the previous scenes, however, so we're not missing anything!

```
<div class="palm-row">
  <div class="palm-row-wrapper">
    <div class="textfield-group" x-mojo-focus-highlight="true">
      <div class="title">
        <div id="projectDetails_txtName" x-mojo-element="TextField"></div>
      </div>
    </div>
  </div>
</div>
```

The name field is a TextField where the name of the project is entered. Below that are two DataPicker widgets, one for start date and one for target date:

```
<div class="palm-row">
  <div class="palm-row-wrapper">
    <div class="textfield-group" x-mojo-focus-highlight="true">
      <div class="title">
        <div class="label">Start</div>
        <div id="projectDetails_dtpStartDate" x-mojo-element="DatePicker"></div>
      </div>
    </div>
  </div>
</div>
```

I've showed only one, the start date, since the target date DatePicker is defined just like this. The DatePicker is a widget we haven't seen in action before. It provides the user with a simple way to enter dates that isn't as prone to errors as manually[26] entering the date is. It splits up the day, month, and year into three separate LisSelectors essentially.

```
<div class="palm-row">
  <div x-mojo-element="ListSelector"
    id="projectDetails_lssProjectManager"></div>
</div>
```

The ListSelector after the two DatePickers is where the project manager of the project is selected. Only resources that have the isProjectManager flag set to true will appear in this list.

Next is the area where the List of tasks under the project will appear:

```
<div class="palm-group" id="projectDetails_divTasks">
  <div class="palm-group-title">Task</div>
  <div class="palm-list">
```

---

[26] To some people, it's also less convenient. I've done a lot of web development of back-office type of applications where data-entry speed is a primary concern, and in those cases a simple text box that does some validation is often best. In a small form factor like the Pre, though, a DatePicker is arguably better.

```
        <div id="projectDetails_lstTasks" x-mojo-element="List"></div>
    </div>
</div>
```

Since this section should stand out a bit from the rest of the scene, I wrapped it in a `<div>` with the palm-group style class applied to it. A title is given to this section as well, so it's clear this is grouping should be thought of a little differently, even though it's clearly part of a project definition by virtue of being in the scene.

Finally, we have a Button for saving the changes:

```
<div id="projectDetails_btnSave" x-mojo-element="Button"></div>
```

■ **Note**   One thing worth noting is something I've frankly done "wrong" throughout this book, and that's having Buttons for saving entries. Palm recommends that instead of explicit Buttons like this, you do an implicit save when the back gesture is performed. To be blunt about it, I don't necessarily agree with this recommendation, and that's why I haven't followed it throughout. I wanted to point it out, though, here in the last project, and let you know that I've purposely flaunted[27] the rules a bit in this one case throughout. ☺

The Scene Assistant

Now it's time to look as the assistant for this scene. I've left out the constructor here, but you need to be aware that, like the constructor for the login scene, this one too takes in an object, a project object in this case, and stores a reference to it in the projects field of this class. If none is passed in, then this scene knows the user wants to add a new project rather than edit an existing one.

```
ProjectDetailsAssistant.prototype.projectBeingEdited = null;

ProjectDetailsAssistant.prototype.models = {
  txtName : { value : null, disabled : false },
  dtpStartDate : { value : null },
  dtpTargetDate : { value : null },
  lssProjectManager : {
    label : "Manager", choices : null, value : null
  },
  lstTasksModel : { items : [ ] }
};
```

When a project is being edited, the aptly named projectBeingEdited field holds a reference to the passed-in project object. This, you'll see next, determines whether the list of tasks is shown. You can see the models for all the fields the user can edit here, and note that the name field has the disabled attribute set to false. This will be flipped to true when editing a project since the name is the key of the project records in the database, so we can't let the user modify that.

The setup() method is the first method we find:

---

[27] Wow, I'm such a rebel…whether I am without a cause or without a clue is up for debate.

```
this.models.lssProjectManager.choices = [ ];
if (this.projectBeingEdited) {
  $("projectDetails_divTasks").show();
  this.models.txtName.disabled = true;
  this.models.txtName.value = this.projectBeingEdited.name;
  this.models.dtpStartDate.value =
    new Date(this.projectBeingEdited.startDate);
  this.models.dtpTargetDate.value =
    new Date(this.projectBeingEdited.targetDate);
  this.models.lssProjectManager.value =
    this.projectBeingEdited.projectManager;
} else {
  $("projectDetails_divTasks").hide();
  this.models.txtName.disabled = false;
  this.models.txtName.value = null;
  this.models.dtpStartDate.value = new Date();
  this.models.dtpTargetDate.value = new Date();
  this.models.lssProjectManager.value = null;
}
```

You can see here branching done based on the value of that projectBeingEdited field. When not null, the list of tasks is shown, and the name TextField is disabled. The values of all the fields are set from the passed-in project object. Note that the DatePicker requires a Date object to set its value, but all we have is a string representation of a date stored in the project object. So, we construct a new Date and pass into its constructor that string, and the Date class dutifully constructs[28] a Date object from it.

If no project is being edited, then the list of tasks is hidden, and all the data-entry fields are cleared out.

Next, the scene is switched into full-screen mode:

```
this.controller.enableFullScreenMode(true);
```

After that we set up all the widgets:

```
this.controller.setupWidget("projectDetails_divSpinner",
  { spinnerSize : "large" }, { spinning : true }
);

this.controller.setupWidget("projectDetails_txtName",
  { hintText : "Project Name", focusMode : Mojo.Widget.focusSelectMode },
  this.models.txtName
);

this.controller.setupWidget("projectDetails_dtpStartDate",
  { label : " ", modelProperty : "value" },
  this.models.dtpStartDate
);

this.controller.setupWidget("projectDetails_dtpTargetDate",
  { label : " ", modelProperty : "value" },
```

---

[28] Assuming, of course, that the string is in the appropriate format, which it just so happens to be.

```
  this.models.dtpTargetDate
);
```

Most of this is not new,[29] but setting up the DatePicker is. Fortunately, it follows the same model as all widget setups do. We specify the modelProperty explicitly here just so that the attribute that carries the widgets' value is the same (value) as all the others, just as a matter of consistency.

Did you notice how the label attribute in the configuration object for these widgets is a single blank space? This deals with some problems I encountered when labeling these widgets. Most widgets have a label attribute that can be used to provide a label for them. Unfortunately, it doesn't always do what you want. Some widgets show their labels on the left and some show them on the right, and although there are settings you can change to alter this, the settings unfortunately don't currently work in all cases! To deal with this, for some widgets, I use the label attributes, and in other cases, like these DatePickers, I manually place the label on them in the view markup. However, the label attribute, if not specified, results in a default label being displayed, so to override that, you need to specify something, a blank space being the right choice. These labeling tricks you'll see in other scenes as well, and I won't discuss them at those points since these comments would apply to them as well.

The next step is to populate the list of project managers:

```
for (var i = 0; i < timeTracker.resources.length; i++) {
  if (timeTracker.resources[i].isProjectManager) {
    this.models.lssProjectManager.choices.push({
      label : timeTracker.resources[i].name,
      value : timeTracker.resources[i].name
    });
  }
}
this.controller.setupWidget("projectDetails_lssProjectManager",
  this.models.lssProjectManager, this.models.lssProjectManager
);
```

Since the timeTracker.resources field is an array of resources that was previously populated, all we need to do is iterate over this array and look for any resource whose isProjectManager field is set to true. For any we find, we push the object onto the array that is the value of the choices attribute in the model for the ListSelector. Each item in that array is an object with a label attribute and a value attribute, and in this case those two attribute happen to have the same value, but that's in no way a requirement.

Also note that the configuration object passed to setupWidget() is actually the model for the widget. Although this may be a little unusual, there's no reason you can't do this. I just thought it saved needing to have two objects floating around. The setupWidget() method doesn't care, so long as the objects passed in have the attributes it expected and so long as they don't conflict with one another, then this will work just fine.

The next bit of setup to do is with the tasks List:

```
this.controller.setupWidget("projectDetails_lstTasks", {
  addItemLabel : "Add...", swipeToDelete : true,
  itemTemplate : "projectDetails/taskList-item"
```

---

[29] However, the hintText is something we haven't seen much of. This is simply some text, like a label essentially, that is placed in a TextField before the user enters anything, and it clears out automatically when the user starts typing It's in a sense like a transient label, but it saves space since it's right in the widget, not on the side of it, as is the case with many of the others.

```
}, this.models.lstTasksModel);
this.controller.listen("projectDetails_lstTasks", Mojo.Event.listTap,
  this.selectTask.bind(this));
this.controller.listen("projectDetails_lstTasks", Mojo.Event.listAdd,
  this.addTask.bind(this));
this.controller.listen("projectDetails_lstTasks", Mojo.Event.listDelete,
  this.deleteTask.bind(this));
```

That's just a typical List setup, and since we want the user to be able to add, edit, and delete tasks, we hook up event listeners for all three corresponding events. Listing 7-8 shows the template used to render the list.

Listing 7-8. Template Markup for the Tasks Under the Project

```
<div class="palm-row" x-mojo-tap-highlight="momentary">
  <div class="palm-row-wrapper textfield-group">
    <div class="truncating-text">#{name}</div>
  </div>
</div>
```

This is, like was the case for the project administration List, just a simple display of names, nothing more.

Finally, we have the Save Button to set up:

```
this.controller.setupWidget("projectDetails_btnSave", { },
  { buttonClass : "affirmative", label : "Save" }
);
Mojo.Event.listen(this.controller.get("projectDetails_btnSave"),
  Mojo.Event.tap, this.btnSaveTap.bind(this)
);
```

Once again, that's nothing but typical Button setup code, so there's no need to dwell[30] on it I think! The activate() method is what we stumble upon next, and this is the entire thing:

```
this.models.lstTasksModel.items = [ ];
this.controller.modelChanged(this.models.lstTasksModel);
if (this.projectBeingEdited) {
  $("projectDetails_divScrim").show();
  dao.retrieve("task", this.processResults.bind(this));
}
```

The tasks List is populated when the scene is shown as a result of calling on the DAO to get the tasks (which in turn results in an AJAX call). Before that DAO is called on, though, we clear the model for the List and show the scrim. That way, the List is empty as it is being loaded, which looks better than seeing "stale" data that then vanishes (more precisely, is replaced by what is returned by the DAO).

The call to the DAO's retrieve() method results in the processResults() callback being executed, which is this code:

---

[30] My therapist says I dwell on things too much as it is anyway.

```
if (Object.isArray(inResults)) {
  timeTracker.tasks = inResults;
  for (var i = 0; i < inResults.length; i++) {
    if (inResults[i].project == this.projectBeingEdited.name) {
      this.models.lstTasksModel.items.push(inResults[i]);
    }
  }
  this.controller.modelChanged(this.models.lstTasksModel);
} else {
  Mojo.Controller.errorDialog(inResults.responseJSON.error);
}

$("projectDetails_divScrim").hide();
```

We take the returned array (after checking to ensure it was an array that was returned) and check each element to see whether it is a task that belongs to this project. If so, then the task object is pushed onto the array that is the model for the List, and then the modelChanged() method is called when all is said and done. If the response wasn't an array, then we show an error dialog box with the returned error message displayed, and in either case the scrim is then hidden.

The next three methods in this class—selectTask(), addTask(), and deleteTask()—are basically the same as what you saw in the Project Administration scene before, so they aren't shown here. The first two just push the taskDetails scene, and the third just calls the dao.deleteEntity() method.

When the Save Button is clicked, however, the btnSaveTap() method fires, and that code is as follows:

```
if (this.models.txtName.value == null || this.models.txtName.value.blank()) {
  Mojo.Controller.errorDialog("A name must be entered");
  return;
}
if (this.models.lssProjectManager.value == null) {
  Mojo.Controller.errorDialog("A project manager must be selected");
  return;
}
```

First things first: did our friendly neighborhood user actually enter anything for the name field, and did they select a project manager? If not, they will be virtually slapped with the message shown in Figure 7-17.

Figure 7-17. *Failing validation*

Since the two `DatePicker` widgets always have a value, there's no such validation to be done there. The dates may not be correct, of course, in terms of what they should be for the project, but that's the user's problem, not ours. ☺

Once that's out of the way, the scrim is shown, and we get ready to call on the DAO:

```
var operation = "create";
if (this.projectBeingEdited) {
  operation = "update";
}
dao[operation]("project",
  {
    name : this.models.txtName.value,
    startDate : timeTracker.formatDate(this.models.dtpStartDate.value),
    targetDate : timeTracker.formatDate(this.models.dtpTargetDate.value),
    projectManager : this.models.lssProjectManager.value
  },
```

Which method of the DAO gets called is determined by the value of the `projectBeingEdited` field. If it's not `null`, then we need to call the `update()` method; in the other case, it's the `create()` method. Using bracket notation to call the method allows us to determine this dynamically.

The call to the DAO accepts what type of entity is being dealt with, `project` here, and then an object that is to be saved where the values for the attributes in it come from the models of the widgets in the scene. The `startDate` and `endDate` values come from the `DatePickers`, and what we get from them is a `Date` object. However, we want to save a string, so we use the `formatDate()` method of the `TimeTracker` class we saw earlier. This returns to us a string in the form `mm/dd/yyyy`, which is exactly what we want.

When the response comes back from the DAO, the inline callback function is executed:

```
function(inTransport, inException) {
  $("projectDetails_divScrim").hide();
  if (inTransport && inTransport.responseJSON) {
    if (inTransport.responseJSON.name) {
      Mojo.Controller.stageController.popScene();
    } else if (inTransport.responseJSON.msg) {
```

```
          this.controller.showAlertDialog({
            onChoose : function(inValue) {
              Mojo.Controller.stageController.popScene();
            },
            title : "Project warehoused",
            message : inTransport.responseJSON.msg,
            choices : [
              { label : "Ok", value : "Ok", type : "affirmative"}
            ]
          });
        } else if (inTransport.responseJSON.error) {
          Mojo.Controller.errorDialog(inTransport.responseJSON.error);
        }
      }
    }.bind(this)
  );
```

The scrim is first hidden, and then we deal with the two possible outcomes. The first outcome is that an object is returned by the server that contains a name attribute. This indicates the object was saved to the remote database successfully. In this case, we just pop the scene, and we're done.

If, however, we find that the response object contains a msg attribute, then that means some sort of error occurred. This is the convention adopted for the DAO's public API. In this case, we show an alert[31] dialog box and pop the scene only once it's dismissed.

Task Details Scene

The Task Details scene, shown in all its majesty in Figure 7-18, is where the user winds up when they select a task for editing on the Project Details scene or when they want to add a new task to the project.

Figure 7-18. The Task Details scene

---

[31] Why not an error dialog box? you ask. Well, simply because this isn't an error situation per se. Since a remote operation that fails gets stored in the local warehouse database for later synchronization, it's more an informational-type message rather than an error.

It has a fair bit in common with the Project Details scene, and owing to this, I'm going to describe it fairly superficially. Take a moment to examine the full source code on your own, however, just to ensure you're not missing anything.

The View HTML

The view markup especially is similar to the Project Details scene. There's a header and scrim, a name TextField, and two DatePickers for start date and target date. After that, there's an IntegerPicker for selecting how many hours are allocated to this task, and the markup for that widget is this:

```
<div class="palm-row">
  <div class="palm-row-wrapper">
    <div class="textfield-group" x-mojo-focus-highlight="true">
      <div class="title">
        <div class="label">Allocated Hours</div>
        <div x-mojo-element="IntegerPicker"
          id="taskDetails_inpAllocatedHours"></div>
      </div>
    </div>
  </div>
</div>
```

An IntegerPicker allows the user to choose from a list, just like a ListSelector, a number in a defined range. This provides built-in range validation (because they can't choose a value outside the defined range) and also keeps them from having to slide open the keyboard to type a number.

Below the IntegerPicker is a ListSelector containing a list of resources that can be assigned to work on the task and of course a Save Button at the end.

The Scene Assistant

The scene assistant too is very much similar to the project details assistant, beginning with its constructor. However, the constructor in fact *is* a little different, so let's take a look at it now:

```
function TaskDetailsAssistant(inTask, inProjectName) {
  this.taskBeingEdited = inTask;
  this.projectName = inProjectName;
};
```

This constructor takes in a task object to be edited (or it can be null when creating a new task), which is like the project details constructor. However, this constructor takes in a second argument as well: the name of the project to which the task belongs. This is needed when the task is saved since the task is tied to a project.

There is a taskBeingEdited field that holds a referenced to the passed-in task object (if any), just like the projectBeingEdited field in the Project Details scene, and the models for the widgets hold no surprises.

The setup() method too is nothing special. It opens with an if statement that branches on whether taskBeingEdited is null. If it isn't null, then the values of the widgets' models are set from it; otherwise, they are all cleared.

```
this.models.lssAssignedResource.choices = [ ];
if (this.taskBeingEdited) {
```

```
    this.models.txtName.disabled = true;
    this.models.txtName.value = this.taskBeingEdited.name;
    this.models.dtpStartDate.value = new Date(this.taskBeingEdited.startDate);
    this.models.dtpTargetDate.value = new Date(this.taskBeingEdited.targetDate);
    this.models.inpAllocatedHours.value = this.taskBeingEdited.allocatedHours;
    this.models.lssAssignedResource.value =
      this.taskBeingEdited.assignedResource;
  } else {
    this.models.txtName.disabled = false;
    this.models.txtName.value = null;
    this.models.dtpStartDate.value = new Date();
    this.models.dtpTargetDate.value = new Date();
    this.models.inpAllocatedHours.value = 0;
    this.models.lssAssignedResource.value = null;
  }
```

The scene is switched into full-screen mode, and all the widgets are set up. The IntegerPicker for
the allocated hours is set up like so:

```
this.controller.setupWidget("taskDetails_inpAllocatedHours",
  { min : 1, max : 100, label : " ", modelProperty : "value" },
  this.models.inpAllocatedHours
);
```

As you can see, the valid range of values is defined in the configuration object passed to the
setupWidget() method.

The list of resources is then populated, but unlike the same code in the project details assistant, *all*
resources are shown here, not just project managers. Finally, the Save Button is set up, and its
Mojo.Event.tap event is bound to the btnSaveTap() method. Before we get to that, though, take a longing
gander at Figure 7-19, which shows this scene in action, with the list of resources expanded.

Figure 7-19. *Listing resources that can be assigned to this task*

The btnSaveTap() method is, once again, very much similar to its sibling method in the Project
Details scene. It opens with two checks to ensure a name was entered and that a resource was selected.
Then, the scrim is shown, and the name of the DAO method to call is dynamically determined in the same

fashion as we saw earlier. The DAO method is then called, passing in an object describing the task based on the data the user entered. If an OkResponse is returned by the servlet, then the scene is popped; otherwise, the msg attribute of the ErrorResponse is displayed in an alert dialog box, and *then* the scene is popped.

Resource Administration Scene

Now we've come to a point where we have a scene, Resource Administration, that, for all intents and purposes,[32] is identical to the Project Administration scene, both in form and function, as well as in code. In terms of form and function, Figure 7-20 bares this out.

Figure 7-20. *The Resource Administration scene*

In terms of code, all you need do is look back at the view markup and the scene assistant for the Project Administration scene, and anywhere you see the word *project*, change it to *resource*, and you've got it! Therefore, we'll save the lives of a few trees here and cut out a bunch of pages by not printing all that code here. As always, jump over to the downloaded source code bundle, and have a peek later if you'd like.

Resource Details Scene

Following the theme of "one of these things is just like the other,"[33] the Resource Details scene follows very closely in the footsteps of the Project Details and Task Details scenes, as you can see in Figure 7-21.

---

[32] Or, as my children used to say when they were learning how to talk: "infentts and porposes." Interestingly, my wife still says it this way when she's had a few too many to drink.

[33] That's right, *I* invented that nursery rhyme. You may have heard it as "one of these things is *not* like the other," but that's because when it was plagiarized, the pessimistic nature of the thief took over and it was bastardized to the form you've likely heard before. Have no fear, though; the law suit is pending because, after all, I live in America, and if there's two things we know, it's law suits and baseless bombing campaigns!

Figure 7-21. *The Resource Details scene*

The same is true of the code, which has a TextField for name and a PasswordField for the password. It also has a new widget, the CheckBox:

```
<div class="palm-row">
  <div class="palm-row-wrapper">
    <div class="textfield-group" x-mojo-focus-highlight="true">
      <div class="title">
        <div class="label">Is Project Manager</div>
        <div id="resourceDetails_chkProjectManager"
          x-mojo-element="CheckBox"></div>
      </div>
    </div>
  </div>
</div>
```

The markup is nothing fancy obviously, but it gives us a nice-looking CheckBox, as Figure 7-22 shows (the CheckBox being checked this time, as opposed to Figure 7-21 where it's not).

Figure 7-22. *The CheckBox widget, now checked*

The assistant, like the other two before it, accepts an object into its constructor, a resource this time, which is stored in the `resourceBeingEdited` field. The `setup()` method performs the same sort of branching based on whether that field is `null` so that the `TextField`, `PasswordField`, and `CheckBox` are populated with the values from the resource object if there was one. The `value` attribute for the `CheckBox` is a simple `boolean`, so `true` is checked and `false` is unchecked.

Setting up the `CheckBox` is like setting up any other widget, but since it's the first time we've encountered this widget, I'll show that code anyway:

```
this.controller.setupWidget("resourceDetails_chkProjectManager",
  { }, this.models.chkProjectManager
);
```

The Save `Button` is bound to the `btnSaveTap()` method to handle the tap event, and it begins by checking to be sure a name and password were entered and showing an error dialog box if not. Assuming they were, then the DAO is called upon, either the `create()` or `update()` method as appropriate, as with the previous two assistants. The rest of the code in this method follows the same pattern as those other two assistants as well, so we can in fact move on to a scene that *isn't* just more of the same, the Book Time scene.

Book Time Scene

The Book Time scene, appearing for a brief time in Figure 7-23, is where a user goes to…wait for it…*book time*!

Figure 7-23. The Book Time scene

All it takes is selecting a project, a task under that project, and a number of hours to book, and through the magic of the Internet, thy will is done!

The View HTML

The markup for this scene is rather simple:

```
<div class="palm-row">
  <div x-mojo-element="ListSelector" id="bookTime_lssProject"></div>
```

```
</div>

<div class="palm-row">
  <div x-mojo-element="ListSelector" id="bookTime_lssTask"></div>
</div>

<div class="palm-row">
  <div class="label">Hours Spent</div>
  <div x-mojo-element="IntegerPicker" id="bookTime_inpTime"></div>
</div>

<div id="bookTime_btnSave" x-mojo-element="Button"></div>
```

Take one header and scrim (not shown), two ListSelectors, an IntegerPicker, and a Button; mix well; and when the buzzer on the oven beeps, you've got yourself one fully baked[34] Book Time scene!

The Scene Assistant

The assistant has a few interesting bits, but first we have some more mundane bits to look at:

```
BookTimeAssistant.prototype.models = {
  lssProject : { label : "Project", choices : null, value : null },
  lssTask : { label : "Task", choices : null, value : null },
  inpTime : { value : null }
};
```

The models for the widgets are contained in the usual models object. The setup() method comes next and begins by clearing these models:

```
  this.models.lssProject.choices = [ ];
  this.models.lssTask.choices = [ ];
  this.models.inpTime.value = 0;

  this.controller.enableFullScreenMode(true);
```

Full-screen is again in the offing, so we turn that on as in other scenes. The widgets are all then set up:

```
  this.controller.setupWidget("bookTime_divSpinner",
    { spinnerSize : "large" }, { spinning : true }
  );

  this.controller.setupWidget("bookTime_lssProject",
    this.models.lssProject, this.models.lssProject
  );
  Mojo.Event.listen(this.controller.get("bookTime_lssProject"),
    Mojo.Event.propertyChange, this.projectSelected.bind(this)
  );
```

---

[34] I've been meaning to try out for *Iron Chef*, but something tells me I don't quite have the skills to win.

```
this.controller.setupWidget("bookTime_lssTask",
  this.models.lssTask, this.models.lssTask
);

this.controller.setupWidget("bookTime_inpTime",
  { label : " ", modelProperty : "value", min : 1, max : 100 },
  this.models.inpTime
);

this.controller.setupWidget("bookTime_btnSave", { },
  { buttonClass : "affirmative", label : "Save" }
);
Mojo.Event.listen(this.controller.get("bookTime_btnSave"),
  Mojo.Event.tap, this.btnSaveTap.bind(this)
);
```

The two ListSelectors again are using the same object for the configuration as well as their model. The choices attribute is what would appear in a separate configuration object. Since they configured the widget, they aren't actually part of its model (I personally find this a little odd, but be that as it may).

Activating the scene is the next thing handled as part of the activate() method:

```
this.models.lssProject.choices = [ ];
this.models.lssTask.choices = [ ];
this.controller.modelChanged(this.models.lssProject);
this.controller.modelChanged(this.models.lssTask);
$("bookTime_divScrim").show();
dao.retrieve("project", this.processProjectResults.bind(this));
```

Here we're loading the list of projects. One thing you should probably have noticed by now, but which I haven't explained to this point, is that in all of these scenes that we've been discussing, the collections of projects, tasks, and resources are constantly being updated from the server and stored locally in the fields of the instance of the TimeTracker class. The basic logic here is that as long as network connectivity is available and as long as the server side of the application is available, then everything should be done there in terms of data storage and retrieval. The local warehouse database should come into play only when the server can't be reached. This admittedly leads to a slight decrease in performance across the application because the server is constantly consulted when the local in-memory copy of the data would oftentimes be sufficient. I think this is a fair trade-off to make in order to keep the authoritative data store on the server in fact authoritative. The design of the application is such that concurrency issues are reduced to a bare minimum. Only a single project manager could be modifying a project at any given time, and only a single resource could be booking time to a task. There *are* some concurrency issues that can result, such as someone viewing a task summary as someone else is booking time or modifying the allocated hours, which is another reason to continually hit the server. The alternative is a lot more complex code to ensure the local cache is always in sync with the server, which I thought just wasn't necessary[35] (and would have added another 20 pages to an already very lengthy chapter!).

The processProjectResults() method is next, once the list of projects is returned by the DAO:

---

[35] It's perfectly fair for you to judge if my design decisions were good or not. After all, you can learn just as much (and oftentimes more!) from poor choices on my part! My goal is to give you the thought process behind the decisions, the why's and what-for's, and you can decide whether I should be drawn and quartered or given a parade!

```
if (Object.isArray(inResults)) {
  timeTracker.projects = inResults;
  for (var i = 0; i < timeTracker.projects.length; i++) {
    this.models.lssProject.choices.push({
      label : timeTracker.projects[i].name,
      value : timeTracker.projects[i].name
    });
  }
  this.controller.modelChanged(this.models.lssProject);
} else {
  Mojo.Controller.errorDialog(inResults.responseJSON.error);
}

$("bookTime_divScrim").hide();
```

This is of course the same kind of code we've seen a couple of times before, so I suspect you don't need it explained once more.

When a project is selected from the first ListSelector, it is then time to get the list of tasks under that project. The projectSelected() method is called in this case, and you should quickly realize that the code in it, and in the callback function it references, looks very much like what we just saw for dealing with projects:

```
this.models.lssTask.choices = [ ];
this.controller.modelChanged(this.models.lssTask);
$("bookTime_divScrim").show();
dao.retrieve("task", this.processTaskResults.bind(this));
```

The processTaskResults() method is the callback for the task retrieval:

```
if (Object.isArray(inResults)) {
  timeTracker.tasks = inResults;
  for (var i = 0; i < timeTracker.tasks.length; i++) {
    if (timeTracker.tasks[i].project == this.models.lssProject.value &&
      timeTracker.tasks[i].assignedResource == timeTracker.user.name) {
      this.models.lssTask.choices.push({
        label : timeTracker.tasks[i].name,
        value : timeTracker.tasks[i].name
      });
    }
  }
  this.controller.modelChanged(this.models.lssTask);
} else {
  Mojo.Controller.errorDialog(inResults.responseJSON.error);
}

$("bookTime_divScrim").hide();
```

Since time can only be booked to a task that a resource has been assigned to, we filter the list of tasks to only show what the current user has access to.

Finally, there is the handling of the Save Button tap in the btnSaveTap() method, which begins with this code:

```
if (this.models.lssProject.value == null) {
  Mojo.Controller.errorDialog("A project must be selected");
  return;
}
if (this.models.lssTask.value == null) {
  Mojo.Controller.errorDialog("A task must be selected");
  return;
}

$("bookTime_divScrim").show();
```

As usual, some simple validations need to be done to start and the method aborted if those validations don't pass. Assuming they do, though, the next task is to get a reference to the object for the selected task:

```
var task = null;
for (var i = 0; i < timeTracker.tasks.length; i++) {
  if (timeTracker.tasks[i].name == this.models.lssTask.value &&
    timeTracker.tasks[i].project == this.models.lssProject.value) {
    task = timeTracker.tasks[i];
  }
}
```

As it happens, booking time is done against a given task, which means that what we're really doing when we book time is updating a task. The number of hours booked against a task is one of the fields in the task object (bookedHours), so that's what is really being updated. Therefore, we need to get the task object from the timeTracker.tasks array, which means iterating over it to find the one whose name and project matches.

Once found, we call the dao.update() method, passing in the entered data:

```
dao.update("task",
  {
    project : task.project,
    name : task.name,
    startDate : timeTracker.formatDate(new Date(task.startDate)),
    targetDate : timeTracker.formatDate(new Date(task.targetDate)),
    allocatedHours : task.allocatedHours,
    bookedHours : this.models.inpTime.value,
    assignedResource : task.assignedResource
  },
  function(inTransport, inException) {
    $("bookTime_divScrim").hide();
    if (inTransport && inTransport.responseJSON) {
      if (inTransport.responseJSON.name) {
        Mojo.Controller.stageController.popScene();
      } else if (inTransport.responseJSON.msg) {
        this.controller.showAlertDialog({
          onChoose : function(inValue) {
            Mojo.Controller.stageController.popScene();
          },
          title : "Task warehoused",
          message : inTransport.responseJSON.msg,
```

```
        choices : [
          { label : "Ok", value : "Ok", type : "affirmative"}
        ]
      });
    } else if (inTransport.responseJSON.error) {
      Mojo.Controller.errorDialog(inTransport.responseJSON.error);
    }
  }
}.bind(this)
);
```

As has been the case in the past for the code like this in other scenes, the scene is popped once a successful result is returned; otherwise, an alert dialog box is shown with the message returned by the DAO. This covers the case where the write didn't reach the server, which means it was warehoused in the local database for later background synchronization. If any errors occur, then we use the `Mojo.Controller.errorDialog()` method instead to show an error message to the user.

Summaries Scene

The next scene to examine is the Summaries scene, where a user can view one of three types of summary "reports": project summary, task summary, or resource summary. This scene is shown in Figure 7-24, with one of the three `ListSelectors`, the one for selecting a task, selected.

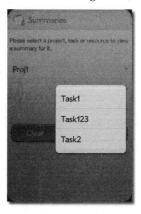

Figure 7-24. The Summaries scene

It's a simple enough scene, and we should be able to get through it pretty quickly.

The View HTML

Starting with the markup, we have what I suspect is exactly what you already have in your mind's eye:

```
<div class="cssWelcomeMessage">
  Please select a project, task or resource to view a summary for it.
  <br><br>
</div>
```

Some plain text gives the user some guidance on what to do, followed by the three `ListSelectors` that allows them to choose the type of summary report they want to see:

```
<div class="palm-row">
  <div x-mojo-element="ListSelector" id="summaries_lssProject"></div>
</div>

<div class="palm-row">
  <div x-mojo-element="ListSelector" id="summaries_lssTask"></div>
</div>

<div class="palm-row">
  <div x-mojo-element="ListSelector" id="summaries_lssResource"></div>
</div>
```

Finally, here are the two `Buttons`, placed side-by-side:

```
<table width="100%">
  <tr>
    <td width="50%"><div id="summaries_btnClear"
      x-mojo-element="Button"></div></td>
    <td width="50%"><div id="summaries_btnShowSummary"
      x-mojo-element="Button"></div></td>
  </tr>
</table>
```

Using a table, although not the only way to accomplish this layout, is perhaps the simplest, and I like simple![36]

The Scene Assistant

The assistant for this scene really amounts to pushing the appropriate scene based on what choices the user makes, but it's made a little more complicated by the need to retrieve the list of projects, tasks, and resources to display in the `ListSelectors`. Before we get to any of that though, we have these three fields:

```
this.projectsRetrieved = false;
this.tasksRetrieved = false;
this.resourcesRetrieved = false;

SummariesAssistant.prototype.models = {
  lss_projects : { label : "Project", choices : null, value : null },
  lss_tasks : { label : "Task", choices : null, value : null },
  lss_resources : { label : "Resource", choices : null, value : null }
};
```

To foreshadow just a bit, the three types of entities are going to be retrieved via calls to the DAO, and as we well know by now, those calls are asynchronous. Since their callbacks could fire in any order, we

---

[36] Simple is my middle name and is in fact my first, last, and confirmation name too, which, now that I think about it, isn't all that simple. Eh, I digress.

need to be able to tell when all three entity types have been retrieved from any of the callbacks. That's where these flags come into play. The models for the ListSelectors are also present, defined as usual.

The setup() method is next:

```
this.models.lss_projects.choices = [ ];
this.models.lss_tasks.choices = [ ];
this.models.lss_resources.choices = [ ];

this.projectsRetrieved = false;
this.tasksRetrieved = false;
this.resourcesRetrieved = false;

this.controller.enableFullScreenMode(true);
```

The models for the ListSelectors are all cleared, and the three flags are reset to false to indicate the data has not yet been retrieved.

After that, the widgets are set up:

```
this.controller.setupWidget("summaries_divSpinner",
  { spinnerSize : "large" }, { spinning : true }
);

this.controller.setupWidget("summaries_lssProject",
  this.models.lssProject, this.models.lss_projects
);

this.controller.setupWidget("summaries_lssTask",
  this.models.lssTask, this.models.lss_tasks
);

this.controller.setupWidget("summaries_lssResource",
  this.models.lssResource, this.models.lss_resources
);

this.controller.setupWidget("summaries_btnClear", { },
  { buttonClass : "negative buttonfloat", label : "Clear" }
);
Mojo.Event.listen(this.controller.get("summaries_btnClear"),
  Mojo.Event.tap, this.btnClearTap.bind(this)
);

this.controller.setupWidget("summaries_btnShowSummary", { },
  { buttonClass : "affirmative buttonfloat", label : "Show Summary" }
);
Mojo.Event.listen(this.controller.get("summaries_btnShowSummary"),
  Mojo.Event.tap, this.btnShowSummaryTap.bind(this)
);
```

As we saw in the Code Cabinet project where we had some Buttons side-by-side, the buttonfloat class is applied to the Buttons to make everything look just right.

With the scene having been set up now, the activate() method can do its thing:

```
this.models.lss_projects.choices = [ ];
this.models.lss_tasks.choices = [ ];
this.models.lss_resources.choices = [ ];
this.controller.modelChanged(this.models.lss_projects);
this.controller.modelChanged(this.models.lss_tasks);
this.controller.modelChanged(this.models.lss_resources);

$("summaries_divScrim").show();
```

Somewhat redundantly, the models are cleared, and the scrim is shown; then there's this:

```
dao.retrieve("project", function(inResults) {
  this.processResults(inResults, "projects").bind(this);
}.bind(this));
dao.retrieve("task", function(inResults) {
  this.processResults(inResults, "tasks").bind(this);
}.bind(this));
dao.retrieve("resource", function(inResults) {
  this.processResults(inResults, "resources").bind(this);
}.bind(this));
```

Yep, as we would have supposed, three dao.retrieve() calls are made, one for each entity type. Notice that each of them references the same callback method, processResults(), and that the second argument passed to it specifies the type of entity that was retrieved.

Now we can look at that very method:

```
this[inType + "Retrieved"] = true;
if (Object.isArray(inResults)) {
  timeTracker[inType] = inResults;
  for (var i = 0; i < timeTracker[inType].length; i++) {
    this.models["lss_" + inType].choices.push({
      label : timeTracker[inType][i].name,
      value : timeTracker[inType][i].name
    });
  }
  this.controller.modelChanged(this.models["lss_" + inType]);
} else {
  Mojo.Controller.errorDialog(inResults.responseJSON.error);
}

if (this.projectsRetrieved && this.tasksRetrieved & this.resourcesRetrieved) {
  $("summaries_divScrim").hide();
}
```

First, the flag for the type that was retrieved is set to true. Bracket notation is used here, and that second argument passed in allows us to dynamically name the field to set to true. Next, the returned array is iterated over, and for each we push the object into the appropriate array, again using bracket notation to access the appropriate field of the timeTracker instance. Finally, a call to modelChanged() updates the corresponding ListSelector, or an error dialog box is shown if anything went wrong.

Now, the last thing done is to check the value of all three of those flag fields mentioned earlier. If they are all true, then that means all the projects, tasks, and resources have been retrieved, in which case the scrim can be hidden, and the user can begin using the scene.

Since we have two Buttons in this scene, there are also two event handler methods, beginning with the btnClearTap() method that handles taps on the Clear Button:

```
this.models.lss_projects.value = null;
this.models.lss_tasks.value = null;
this.models.lss_resources.value = null;
this.controller.modelChanged(this.models.lss_projects);
this.controller.modelChanged(this.models.lss_tasks);
this.controller.modelChanged(this.models.lss_resources);
```

Well, that couldn't be much easier![37] Set the value attribute of the model for each of the three ListSelectors to null, call modelChanged() for each, and we're good to go, all cleared out!

Handling taps on the other Button, the Show Summary Button, is next and is handled by the btnShowSummaryTap() method:

```
if (this.models.lss_projects.value != null &&
    this.models.lss_tasks.value == null &&
    this.models.lss_resources.value == null) {
  for (var i = 0; i < timeTracker.projects.length; i++) {
    if (timeTracker.projects[i].name == this.models.lss_projects.value) {
      Mojo.Controller.stageController.pushScene("projectSummary",
        timeTracker.projects[i]);
      return;
    }
  }
}
return;
}
```

We check to see what the user selected. They will select either a project, task, or resource, and based on that, we iterate over the corresponding array field of the timeTracker instance and find the appropriate object. That object is then passed to the appropriate summary scene, which is pushed, and that's that. There is an identical section of code to this for tasks and for resources, but they aren't shown since they're virtually the same as this.

Now, if none of these three if statements is hit, then the code falls through to this chunk:[38]

```
this.models.lss_projects.value = null;
this.models.lss_tasks.value = null;
this.models.lss_resources.value = null;
this.controller.modelChanged(this.models.lss_projects);
this.controller.modelChanged(this.models.lss_tasks);
this.controller.modelChanged(this.models.lss_resources);

Mojo.Controller.errorDialog("Please select a project by itself, or a task " +
  "by itself, or a resource by itself.");
```

---

[37] It *could* be simpler, but it involves a race of genetically modified super-mice in floating brain enhancers placed strategically around the globe to form a constellation of mind-controlling satellites not at all unlike the GPS network of satellites but with much more evil intent. I am working on that right after this book is completed.
[38] I considered making a joke here about "hurling chunks," but I guess even I have my limits!

The selections are cleared, just like in the btnClearTap() method, and an error dialog box is popped up to tell them to try again.

Project Summary Scene

Once the user taps the Button indicating they want to see the summary for a report, they are treated to the screen shown in Figure 7-25.

Figure 7-25. *The Project Summary scene*

Some details about the selected project are up top, followed by a listing of the tasks associated with the project. It should be noted that nothing on the scene is actually a widget; it's all just plain HTML.

The View HTML

Speaking of plain HTML, here it is:

```
<center>
  <table border="0" cellpadding="0" cellspacing="0" width="100%"
    style="padding:10px;">
    <tr>
      <td width="1" valign="middle"
        class="cssSummaryLabel">Name:  </td>
      <td class="cssSummaryData" id="projectSummary_name"></td>
    </tr>
    <tr>
      <td valign="middle"
        class="cssSummaryLabel">Project Manager:  </td>
      <td class="cssSummaryData" id="projectSummary_projectManager"></td>
    </tr>
    <tr>
      <td valign="middle"
        class="cssSummaryLabel">Start Date:  </td>
      <td class="cssSummaryData" id="projectSummary_startDate"></td>
    </tr>
```

```
    <tr>
      <td valign="middle"
        class="cssSummaryLabel">Target Date:  </td>
      <td class="cssSummaryData" id="projectSummary_targetDate"></td>
    </tr>
  </table>
</center>
```

A simple table structure frames the project details up top, and each cell in the second column has an ID assigned to it so we can easily populate them with data from the project object.

```
<table class="palm-divider labeled">
  <tr>
    <td class="left"></td>
    <td class="label">Tasks in this project</td>
    <td class="right"></td>
  </tr>
</table>
<ul id="projectSummary_tasks" style="position:relative;top:-16px;"></ul>
```

Another table follows that, the first using the palm-divider and labeled classes to give us that divider-line-with-a-label look. Just below the table is an unordered list element, and you'll notice it has no content but *does* have an ID assigned. If you're guessing the tasks will be shown by adding <li> elements to the <ul>, give yourself a cigar![39]

The Scene Assistant

The scene assistant for the Project Summary scene begins with a constructor that slurps up a project object:

```
function ProjectSummaryAssistant(inProject) {
  this.project = inProject;
};

ProjectSummaryAssistant.prototype.project = null;
```

A reference to that object is held in the project field of the assistant, and then it's on to setting up the scene via the setup() method:

```
  this.controller.enableFullScreenMode(true);
```

Do not adjust your television screens; there is nothing missing here! Switching the scene to full-screen mode is in fact all there is to setup().

However, activate() has a bit more meat on its virtual bones:

```
$("projectSummary_name").innerHTML = this.project.name;
$("projectSummary_projectManager").innerHTML = this.project.projectManager;
$("projectSummary_startDate").innerHTML =
```

---

[39] Neither I nor Apress will be held responsible for your impending bout with cancer if you in fact do give yourself a cigar. Hey, we're all adults here. Smoke if you got 'em—just don't sue me for the consequences!

```
      timeTracker.formatDate(new Date(this.project.startDate));
    $("projectSummary_targetDate").innerHTML =
      timeTracker.formatDate(new Date(this.project.targetDate));

    var tasks = [ ];
    for (var i = 0; i < timeTracker.tasks.length; i++) {
      if (timeTracker.tasks[i].project == this.project.name) {
        var task = Object.clone(timeTracker.tasks[i]);
        task.targetDate = timeTracker.formatDate(new Date(task.targetDate));
        task.startDate = timeTracker.formatDate(new Date(task.startDate));
        tasks.push(task);
      }
    }
    var content = Mojo.View.render({
      collection : tasks, template: "projectSummary/tasksTemplate"
    })
    $("projectSummary_tasks").innerHTML = content;
```

First, the basic project details at the top are populated. The Prototype library's $() method gets a reference to the cells, and then it's just a simple matter of inserting the content via innerHTML.

Now, for the tasks, we begin by iterating over the list of tasks in the tasks field of the timeTracker instance. For each one that we find is a member of the project that the user selected, we clone the object. This is necessary because each task object will be passed to a template (more on this shortly), just like is done when populating a List widget, and part of what is displayed are the targetDate and startDate fields in the object. However, these are true Date objects, and if we just insert them into markup, they wind up being displayed in the localized date format, which in most cases is something very long and including a time. Instead, they should be displayed as mm/dd/yyyy like they are everywhere else. So, the value of those fields in the task object is replaced by the return value from a call to the formatDate() method that we looked at earlier. Since we don't want to actually mess with the task object that is stored as part of the tasks array on the timeTracker instance, cloning the object first allows us to muck with it however we want without persisting the changes.

■ **Note** The clone method is added to the Object prototype by the Prototype library. That is the prototypical thing for the Prototype library to do to the Object prototype. It should also be noted that writing the word *prototype* one more time here could cause time and space to collapse unto itself in a singularity, so I'll quit while I'm ahead (and still existing in this universe).

Once the array of task objects is completely populated, a new function is used, namely, Mojo.View.render(). This is a very handy function that generates HTML for you based on a template and, usually, some data that the template processes. I can't say for sure if the List widget uses this function internally to render its contents, but I wouldn't be even remotely surprised to find that's the case. You feed this function the name of a collection of objects, tasks in this case, and the name of a template HTML file to use, and it spits back at you the resultant HTML, which you can then do whatever you want with, such as insert it into the DOM, for example, as is done here.

The template itself is just the HTML you see in Listing 7-9.

Listing 7-9. Template Markup for the List of Tasks Under the Project

```
<li>
  <div class="cssSummaryLineItemTitle">#{name}</div>
  <div class="cssSummaryLineItem">Began on #{startDate}</div>
  <div class="cssSummaryLineItem">Assigned to #{assignedResource}</div>
  <div
    class="cssSummaryLineItem">Task is allocated #{allocatedHours} hours</div>
  <div class="cssSummaryLineItem">#{bookedHours} hours have been booked</div>
  <div class="cssSummaryLineItem">Expected to be finished on #{targetDate}</div>
</li>
```

As you can plainly see, it's the same basic structure as any of the templates used to render the contents for a List. The Mojo.View.render() method is pretty handy indeed!

Task Summary and Resource Summary Scenes

The Task Summary scene, as shown in Figure 7-26, shares a great deal in common with the Project Summary scene.

Figure 7-26. The Task Summary scene

It looks quite similar, really just missing the list underneath the basic details, and of course there's a ProgressBar widget used to show the percent of the task that has been completed. We looked at this widget in the Engineer project in some detail, and there's nothing new about its usage here.

Similarly, the Resource Summary scene is an even more obvious cousin of the Project Summary scene, as shown in Figure 7-27.

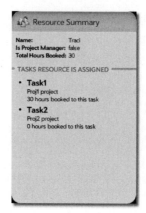

Figure 7-27. *The Resource Summary scene*

I hope you don't mind, but since we're right near the end of exploring this project and since the code is highly redundant, we won't review these two scenes here; you effectively already have by looking at the Project Summary scene. Take a look at the code yourself if you must, but I promise, you'll be disappointed[40] if you're looking for anything new and exciting!

Suggested Exercises

Time Tracker is a pretty useful little application. However, as I said in the beginning, it's certainly not on par with Microsoft Project, or any number of other project management tools. You could implement plenty of features that would make it even better. I will list some of those for you as suggested exercises:

- Did you notice that the project doesn't have a percent complete indicator? That would be a nice addition. You should be able to determine an overall percentage based on the percentages of all the constituent tasks.

- Here's a relatively quick and (probably) easy one: add a validation on start and end dates throughout the application to ensure the end date is after the start date. As it stands now, the application would allow that rather illogical situation (barring time-traveling visitors from Gallifrey[41] anyway!).

---

[40] Of course, if that's the biggest disappointment you face today, then you're having a really good day!
[41] Gallifrey is the home world of the Doctor from the long-running British sci-fi show *Dr. Who*, a member of the now-extinct Time Lord race. If you don't know the show or couldn't guess from the name of his race, the Doctor is a time traveler!

- One key concept in project management is the idea of dependencies—that is, task B can't begin until task A has been completed. Time Tracker doesn't have any notion of dependencies at all, so it might be a good idea to add that! It might be as simple as being able to specify what task(s) a new task depends on, not allowing a start date that is before the end date of any of those tasks, and not allowing time to be booked against a task that cannot have started yet. You also probably want to make the start date not required for a task that is dependent on another.

- You may have noticed that there is one (if I'm lucky!) significant flaw in this application: if you have no connectivity at all, the application isn't much good. As long as you have connectivity when you start up, then you can use the application, at least partially. If you lose that connectivity, since much of the data is pulled down at startup from the remote server, then at least partial functionality is available to the user. It would be much better if it was a truly and fully "offline-capable" application. To do this, I suggest having a separate copy of each local database table and at startup read in all the data (included tasks) from the remote server and update those tables. Obviously, don't touch them if connectivity isn't available at startup. You'll have to modify the DAO to get data from those tables rather than the remote service going forward (until connectivity is restored). In other words, cache all the data locally, not just the changes made by the mobile user. That should provide a truly untethered experience for the user, and it really shouldn't take much change outside the DAO (that was very much the design intent).

That's plenty to keep you busy I'm sure, but I think there are some fun-to-implement suggestions in there, so go for it!

Summary

In this chapter, we took a task that many people, including myself, find it hard to get too excited about, and we created an application that makes it just a little more fun than usual, and we have Palm and webOS (and Google!) to thank for that! We saw some new Mojo APIs in action, including the Mojo.View.render() method and some new widgets including the CheckBox, and we saw a lot of our old friends in terms of widgets and APIs used more. We even got to play on the server side of the world a little bit and saw how we can design and implement our own RESTful API for webOS applications (or applications on other HTTP-capable platforms) to use.

Index

■M

You Need the Companion eBook

Your purchase of this book entitles you to buy the companion PDF-version eBook for only $10. Take the weightless companion with you anywhere.

We believe this Apress title will prove so indispensable that you'll want to carry it with you everywhere, which is why we are offering the companion eBook (in PDF format) for $10 to customers who purchase this book now. Convenient and fully searchable, the PDF version of any content-rich, page-heavy Apress book makes a valuable addition to your programming library. You can easily find and copy code—or perform examples by quickly toggling between instructions and the application. Even simultaneously tackling a donut, diet soda, and complex code becomes simplified with hands-free eBooks!

Once you purchase your book, getting the $10 companion eBook is simple:

❶ Visit **www.apress.com/promo/tendollars/**.

❷ Complete a basic registration form to receive a randomly generated question about this title.

❸ Answer the question correctly in 60 seconds, and you will receive a promotional code to redeem for the $10.00 eBook.

233 Spring Street, New York, NY 10013

Offer valid through 4/10.